# FREEDOM'S LAST STAND

### A Common Sense Guide to Understanding the Tyranny of Collectivist Ideology and How We the People Can Recover Our Stolen Constitutional Rights

## CLIFFORD N. RIBNER

emerge
publishing

TULSA, OKLAHOMA

20 19  18  17  16    10 9 8 7 6 5 4 3 2 1

FREEDOM'S LAST STAND – A Common Sense Guide to Understanding the Tyranny of Collectivist Ideology and How We the People Can Recover Our Stolen Constitutional Rights

©2016 Clifford N. Ribner

TULSA, OKLAHOMA

*Published by:*

Emerge Publishing, LLC
9521B Riverside Parkway, Suite 243
Tulsa, Oklahoma 74137
Phone: 888.407.4447
www.EmergePublishing.com

Library of Congress Cataloging-in-Publication Data

BISAC Category:
POL035000 POLITICAL SCIENCE / Political Freedom
POL042020 POLITICAL SCIENCE / Political Ideologies / Conservatism & Liberalism
POL010000 POLITICAL SCIENCE / History & Theory

Other Formats: Kindle / Nook / iBook
Paperback ISBN: 978-1-943127-39-9
E-book ISBN:  978-1-943127-40-5

Printed in the United States of America

# Freedom's Last Stand

By

Clifford N. Ribner

Published by
Emerge Publishing
Tulsa, Oklahoma

# TABLE OF CONTENTS

# BOOK PART ONE:

## WHERE WE ARE NOW AND WHERE WE NEED TO GO

# CHAPTER 1

## Overview of This Book

Things have been <u>forced</u> apart, in this the best of all nations; they have not simply fallen. It has become the worst of times.

For years, no less than 68% of us have been telling pollsters that America is "on the wrong track," with that number approaching 75% most recently. You probably agree.

The tiny minority who disagree, and think we are on the right track, either actively desire the destruction of our prosperity and/or our liberty (yes, such scum exist – some in very high offices), or are just blissfully unaware that this is precisely what is and has been happening – and for a very long time.

Many among us have succumbed to doublethink. As Orwell taught us decades before 1984 actually arrived, doublethink is the greatest moral and ontological catastrophe, and self-betrayal – more so even than its near cousin, doublespeak: in doublespeak, one outwardly pretends, in a "politically correct" (i.e., dictatori-ally-compelled) act, that a fraud/lie is true; in doublethink, one <u>actually believes</u> the fraud/lie, while simultaneously knowing its falsity. As Orwell also taught us, tyranny always both demands doublethink, and makes thought-crime the only truly unforgivable sin. What do you think "political correctness" – and frequent, baseless accusations of "racism," "sexism" etc.— are all about?

How could we possibly have gotten to this point, here in this amazing nation?

Consider: Socialism occurs whenever the state forcibly (the only way it can be done) takes for itself, away from private hands, any right, duty or activity of any kind. Things so taken can include the management or control, or any other property right, over any business, or any other property. Less obviously, social-ism's targets can also include any citizen's erstwhile <u>duty</u> to provide anything for himself or his family: stripping a free citizen of his duty insults him no less than stripping him of his property — or of his work.

One of the biggest targets for such socialist taking-over by the state is the unique combination of both right and duty known as providing charity to others.

Welfare in all its forms, after all, is nothing but the socialization of charity. Like charity, the source of every cent it distributes is the property of private citizens; except that, unlike real charity, the state takes that property from them by force; and it is bestowed to others, without the consent of its true owners, others who have done nothing to earn it.

Also unlike real charity, the invariable, real-life consequence of state welfare is that, because of its inherent injustice, it corrupts and destroys everything in society it touches, including the lives of its recipients, the rule of law itself – and, incidentally, all national debates concerning immigration: welfare poisons those debates because of existing citizens' legitimate concern that new immigrants may be coming not for the liberty and opportunity for personal success we offer, but simply to consume our welfare's free stuff – all taken from citizens who have earned it.

Long before we had Welfare, America attracted millions of Europeans and Asians escaping here for freedom and the opportunity to create their own prosperity. Twice in the 20th century America alone liberated and/or protected every single country in Europe – supposedly home to the brilliant, sophisticated and wise, especially compared to us American rubes – from their wars, madness, mass death, cruelty and tyranny – those horrors being what Continental Europe always (yes, always) has produced, along with perpetually anemic economic growth (always half, or less, of ours), with such consistent regularity. And both those times, America asked Europe for absolutely nothing in return.

Yes, I'm talking about the America which, since even before its founding as a nation, has been known around the world as the sole haven for those seeking prosperity and, above all, individual liberty from oppressive governments – that is, monstrous, parasitic, lawless governments, like those which all but a tiny handful of people have lived under since the Stone Age.

Ever since the 1840s – when the incredible energy, inventiveness and wealth-creation our unique laws and Constitutionally-guaranteed individual liberty produced turned us into a major world power overnight — sworn enemies, both here and abroad, of that very idea of individual liberty have constantly slandered us as a supposedly predatory, racist, imperialist tyranny.

Yet somehow, undeterred by those slanders, people from everywhere else would do anything to escape their native tyrannies, come here and become one of us. Becoming fully-assimilated Americans was their goal. Because all those anti-American slanderous lies and smears always collapsed in the face of our reality.

But how can we fix all this now — and get back to being safe and rich and powerful and, above all, free, and again have boundless opportunities for all of us?

Consider this: Every servant has a master. When his being a servant is involuntary, and he is forced to serve that master, the servant is, at best, a serf. When that master has existential power over him, and the state permits him to deploy that power in his sole discretion, there is only one name for that servant: he is that master's slave.

Beginning in 1887 – nearly 100 years after the Constitution's ratification – American politicians have been legislating radically-new (for America) federal law based on legal principles which had for centuries been typical of all the other (tyrannical) nations in the world – particularly European nations – legal principles utterly alien to America, and forbidden – as the very politicians enacting them well knew – by America's Constitution.

That initial, 1887 unconstitutional, embrace of those European-type, absolutist legal principles has, beginning in 1906, been multiplied many times over, which has had the following effects:

(1) it has dramatically, and progressively, reduced Americans' liberty and freedom of choice,

(2) demonstrably caused cataclysmic economic problems (e.g. the Great Depression, and every financial panic or crisis since the 1880's), and has destroyed innovation and value in every sector of the economy which the federal government has effectively taken over,

(3) has dramatically slowed the rate of growth of the American economy below what it could have been: from 1869 through 1889, the U.S. economy never grew at an annual rate less than 3.8%, with real wages enormously increasing steadily and GDP doubling during the 1880s, rates of improvement which have never been equaled since then. This decline in the rate of growth has itself accelerated, along with the continued growth of the federal government, and its relentless, and completely unconstitutional, subjugation of more and more entire market segments, since the mid-1960's, leaving us with a median income today of roughly $54,000 – less than half of the over $125,000 it would be had even the post-War GDP growth rate up to 1972 simply continued – and less than it was in 2007! And

(4) it has had the effect, by the beginning of the 21st century, of turning virtually every business in the nation – and, necessarily, its owners and managers – into virtual slaves (this is no exaggeration) of the state. This is because the state has made itself their complete master, with it and its politicians and bureaucrats seizing discretionary, existential power over all those businesses, their owners and managers and, far from incidentally, over all the rest of us indirectly through that control over those businesses and the goods and services and employment they provide us.

Because it is from those now-enslaved businesses alone that we citizens acquire all goods and services that we actually want and need; and it is those now-enslaved businesses which we mostly depend on to provide productive and rewarding employment for us to earn a living.

The federal government — and its functionaries — now possess an existential legal stranglehold over all those businesses it now "regulates:" it and its bureaucrats have the discretionary power to destroy, without regard to law or decency, any business they so "regulate." And all that massive power in no way benefits anyone, other than a tiny, corrupt few, and has reduced the rest of us all to serfs by forcing us all to live under the unelected bureaucrats' mandates dictatorially-governing the tiniest details of the goods and services we wish to purchase or sell, the markets we wish to engage in, and the employment opportunities available, all of which are dramatically constricted as a result of that "regulatory" control.

That last point – the invariable destructiveness to the choices and value, and so to the freedom and prosperity, available to everyone who uses any of those (now virtually all) "regulated" businesses for any purpose, including as their customers – is not rationally debatable.

For example, typical of these "regulatory" agencies was America's first one – the Interstate Commerce Commission, created to "regulate" the railroad industry in 1887: even the federal government itself finally admitted, nearly 100 years later, that, notwithstanding countless legislative and other efforts to "fix" it, it had never achieved anything of value whatsoever, and had massively damaged the American railroad industry, producing none of the benefits promised to enact it – and incalculable harm. And it and its enabling legislation have been the models – no, I am not exaggerating – for every single major federal "regulatory" agency ever since.

Each and every one of these federal "regulatory" agencies, all modeled on similar agencies long-strangling businesses in continental Europe, have been enacted based on multiple frauds. One such fraud requires particular exposure here: it is the fraud that without such "regulatory" agencies and the laws which create them, and the laws which they create themselves, businesses now subject to them would be subject to <u>no</u> law whatsoever – what proponents of those laws invariably claim would be a "wild West," completely-lawless, law-of-the-jungle.

Interestingly, in continental Europe, where such laws began, that claim would actually have some merit; in America and, indeed, in all English-speaking nations, it is nonsense, as any attentive first-year law student would learn.

The reason for this truly-stark difference between English-speaking nations – including those, like the United States and India, whose departure from the British Empire was actively opposed by the British – can be simply stated: we have long had the Common Law (much of which has now been statutorily codified) in every American state – and the rest of the world has nothing like it.

The Common Law was developed over many centuries by English courts determining just resolutions of legal disputes by applying the 10 Commandments to real-life situations. The Common Law is, as our founders well knew, the only citizen-policing laws necessary or desirable for a free nation, and uniquely provides for the security of all citizens from all genuine misconduct by other citizens – while preventing tyranny by the state which enforces it through its courts.

As explained in this book, below, the Common Law is Good Law, which both protects and liberates the citizenry, doing so by operating in a completely different manner from "regulatory" Bad Law, which is the only type of law which continental Europe has ever known, and which the Counterrevolution has been imposing on us, bit by bit, since 1887.

This book is about where we are today, in 2016, how we got here, the theft (there is no kinder word for it) of our freedom and prosperity by politicians from all political parties, and in all branches of the federal government (yes, including the politicians who sit on benches as judges, masquerading as the objective administrators of equal justice for all which they swear oaths to be) – and how we can fix all this, with tools and, yes, weapons, which God and our founders have provided us.

Yes, I am talking about incredibly powerful – and unique in all human history – tools and weapons we have had all along, tools and weapons whose use simply requires us to wake up, open our eyes, and see all that is before us, including our own power to wield them, to employ.

<u>You Know What's Wrong; Here's A Partial List:</u>

** Our liberty is disappearing: can you do, and/or purchase, whatever you want (do you even know what you have been secretly forbidden to buy?) – without having to seek permission? Can you speak your mind with complete freedom on any subject – without risking harm to yourself or your family? Does the government force you to pay for things you don't want, including funding others' misconduct – and threaten you with harm if you object? Is your income or property even really yours – or does the government tell you what you can do with it, and how much of it it will even let you keep? Does the government let you spend as much on the things you actually want as you pay in taxes?

** The federal government soaks up endless information about us – and yet doesn't stop terrorist attacks like the San Bernardino mass shooting and the Boston Marathon bombing – even when, as in that latter case, the particular terrorists involved <u>had previously been exposed</u> by foreign intelligence services to our incompetent, but endlessly-intrusive, federal agencies; arrogant federal employees insultingly herd honest citizens like cattle at airports, refusing, in slavish service to "political correctness," to apply basic common sense to focus investigative efforts on those few who might pose any actual risk of terrorism – those few who common sense exposes, while endless, intrusive data mining of decent citizens never does;

** The federal government owns 28% of all the Republic's lands, forbidding most of us any entry to most such land, for the purpose, supposedly, of protecting all that land from the catastrophic destruction which private ownership of it supposedly would produce (as if American citizens are too stupid to know how to preserve the value, including its scenic value, of their own property!) – and every summer, millions of acres of federally-owned forests catastrophically burn, killing brave firefighters, and destroying homes. And yet, have you ever heard of a <u>single</u>, similar fire occurring on any of the millions of acres of <u>privately</u>-owned-and-managed forests? Neither have I;

** Throughout the 19th century, with no Federal Reserve (yes, we lived and prospered mightily without it for over 100 years), and <u>no other financial "regulation" whatsoever</u>, our economy grew and prospered at a rate, with <u>no</u> inflation, which it never has achieved since then. Our post-1913 real growth rate has been well below that 19th-century growth rate notwithstanding the subsequent, amazing, labor-saving – <u>American-invented all</u> – technological advances (e.g.,electricity, indoor plumbing, air-conditioning, automobiles, airplanes, telephones, agricultural equipment and technology, the Internet, computers).

The Federal Reserve nationalized the currency (thereby imitating every continental European tyranny – France, Germany and Austria-Hungary – in so doing) for the supposed purposes of preventing financial panics and preserving the value of the dollar. But actions by the Federal Reserve – together with the other financial "regulators" – since it was created in 1913 have caused <u>every single</u>, subsequent financial collapse/panic (all of which were far worse than any which occurred in 19th century America) – including the Great Depression. And the dollar today is worth <u>less than 1/23</u> of its value in 1913.

After every single financial panic/crisis since then, federal officials, whose policies, including terrifying threats to businesses, alone caused it, seeking to project their own blame onto private bankers who had been completely under their "regulatory" control, always claimed its cause was those "evil, greedy" financial services businesses and <u>insufficient</u> federal regulatory power over them. But it is a fact that those very businesses the "regulators" have blamed have been <u>the most heavily-regulated</u> businesses in the nation, forced to answer for their every action to multiple federal "regulators." And each of those numerous Federal regulators have had complete, discretionary power to destroy those businesses had they ever failed to follow "regulators'" orders.

After over 100 years of proven failure, when will it be time to admit the utter worthlessness of that entire federal financial-regulatory experiment – and yes, that's all it has ever been – strangling all those businesses which, as the nation's financiers, provide the lifeblood of our economy and, accordingly, of all our lives and fortunes? In real life, when you fail, you go under; when the federal government fails, it accuses and blames and demands more power over everyone – and the more catastrophically it fails, the more power it demands.

And the more harmful to us citizens in real life its next certain-to-occur failure is guaranteed to be.

** Automobiles all look the same today, and cost 10-20 times (in constant dollars) what they did 40 years ago – all because car companies spend all their time and money complying with endless, dictatorial federal regulations, instead of designing and building cars which we actually would want;

** All of the Constitution's Fourth Amendment guarantees against "unreasonable searches", and its Fifth Amendment right to "due process", disappear completely whenever any of us has to deal with any federal agency – such as the IRS or, if we simply want to exercise the free political speech rights we are Constitutionally guaranteed, the FEC: they can demand anything they want from us, cost us a fortune in lawyers and useless compliance costs, and send us to jail if we refuse any of their demands. And all those powers they hold over us destroy our free-speech rights: what right to speak your mind do you have when a bully is holding a gun to your head? Do you dare speak out about the bully?

** "Political correctness" Nazis dictate what words, and even what beliefs, are allowed (in what used to be "the land of the free");

** The economy is terrible – and has been for years, with median family income in 2015 thousands of dollars less than it was in 2007, no real growth, and nearly 95 million American adults not working – with most of them wishing they were – and over 50 million Americans on food stamps;

** An entire generation of college graduates has been unable to start real careers – with 30% of them living in their parents' basements, and with all of them crushed under student loan debt;

** Our public schools are both fabulously expensive and terrible – exactly like all state-controlled monopolies (thank you USSR and East Germany for revealing the model) – and the unions the teachers are forced into are nothing but corrupt, publicly-funded, self-serving, hyper-politicized lobbying organizations, contemptuous of the children, and the parents who are forced to pay for it all – parents who are also forced (want to hurt little Johnny's grades?) to shut up if they object to any part of the controlling stranglehold of unions and politicians funded by union dues;

** Our military is not allowed to fight to win, hamstrung by "rules of engagement" that make our wars endless and victory impossible. Political correctness, nonsensically pretending war can be prettified, forbids using force, violence and horror against the enemy sufficient to destroy its will – as victory requires – while our enemies have no such constraints. Politicians in both political parties have systematically eviscerated our armed forces — unilaterally disarming in the face of multiple, foreign threats, and endangering our fighting men's lives by making them jump through legalistic hoops that simply empower the enemy;

**\*\*** We are more deeply in debt – by many trillions of dollars – than we have ever been, even after World War II – and this debt was not even incurred to fund some national emergency such as war: it simply provides money which politicians use to pay for worthless, corrupt federal programs, using our money to pay off their cronies and buy votes;

**\*\*** Washington and its politicians, and charlatans claiming to be "experts," dominate everything, the federal government lords over the citizenry, treating us like serfs, demanding we treat all its officeholders (elected or appointed) like some kind of nobility or royalty, entitled both to demand our obedience, and to own their offices for life – demands absolutely forbidden in our Constitution, which requires the government to be our servant, and not vice versa, and forbids <u>any</u> nobility or other special privileges for any citizen. Senators and congressman become millionaires somehow while in office and, when they leave, are guaranteed huge salaries at law/lobbying firms living off of the need of those citizens who can afford it to buy access to federal power simply to survive — with none of those firms, or anything else in Washington, contributing anything of real value;

**\*\*** 50 years after LBJ launched his "War on Poverty," for which the nation has <u>spent $22 trillion</u> – more than on all foreign wars since then <u>combined</u> – 14.5% of Americans are classified by the government as "poor" – virtually the same percentage as was true in 1967, three years after the War on Poverty started, with the welfare system destroying entire communities – particularly black communities – by <u>actively discouraging work,</u> encouraging single-mother births, and penalizing marriage: in 1965, 7% of American children were born outside marriage; today the number is 41%, and it is a fact that the collapse of marriage is today, and has always been, <u>the main cause of child poverty. All</u> improvements in the standard of living of the poor – as for every American – have been due exclusively to the revolutionary technological and engineering advances produced exclusively by American individuals and businesses (remember how much long distance calls and air travel cost in the 1960s, e.g.?).

**\*\*** Our economy has lost all its energy and innovation, becoming static and corrupt, like those of the nations of continental Europe, which our ancestors fled here to escape – endless, crushing, top-down dictating regulations and red tape, on all businesses (i.e., those who produce <u>everything we actually want and need</u>, and who are also the nation's only real, market-funded employers and places of useful work), no growth, no opportunity for advancement for anyone without political connections, national debt the only thing growing anymore – and it is growing exponentially, with nothing of value to us to show for it.

And those are just some of the most glaring and obvious problems – with vastly more hidden behind the complexity, opacity and secrecy federal officials use ever-increasingly <u>to hide what they are doing</u> from us – and the vast corruption and, yes, thuggish lawlessness, which we know they are fomenting.

10

## We The Americans Are Not The Problem

Let's begin here with the most basic fact: the problem lies not in us, the American people, nor in anything actually permitted by our Constitution. Instead, the primary source of the destruction of our freedom and prosperity lies in all the (hundreds of) so-called "administrative" agencies which federal officials have created and empowered over us and/or our fellow citizens beginning, for the very first time, in 1887, and which the Supreme Court has failed (wrongly, as it has well-known all along) to rule unconstitutional.

Virtually all of those agencies constantly violate multiple provisions of the Constitution, including (1) the absolute requirements that federal powers (executive, legislative and judicial) never be combined in a single person or government body, (2) the requirements that no private property ever be taken except for fair and just compensation, and only after due process of law, (3) the absolute prohibition, in the very first words of Article I of the Constitution, on anyone other than Congress alone, acting exclusively through its duly-elected members, possessing any legislation-making power (what difference is there between a law and a "regulation?" Ask any of the thousands who have been ruinously fined and/or jailed for violating a "regulation"), and (4) the absolute prohibition on any state impairing any citizen's "freedom of contract" (with the federal government given no Constitutional power whatsoever which could ever effect any such impairment).

As monstrous and (justifiably) feared as it is, the IRS is the only one of all those federal administrative agencies whose existence is actually Constitutional – because of the Constitution's 16th Amendment.

## The Structure Of Politics, Law And Society– An Overview

I have concluded that there are two, profoundly-different types of each of the most important things affecting politics, law and society: specifically, I can clearly identify two, completely different types of each of the following:

(1)  of power (market power, and the power of violence),

(2)  of citizen-policing laws (good laws, which define civil and criminal misconduct and compel compensation to victims and/or punish it only after it is fairly adjudicated to have been committed, and bad laws, which restrain conduct in advance and implicitly forbid everything until government permission is granted),

(3)  of revolution ((1) those promoting collectivism/socialism or fascism, and inevitably ending in tyranny, and (2) those – our American Revolution alone – promoting individual liberty),

(4)  of nations (happy and miserable), and

(5)  of politicians (ones willing to use the "big lie", and those who will not do so).

11

This book explains all of that structural analysis — and what it means to us today. As mentioned above, the source of all of our unhappiness is the bad laws which have created all of the federal agencies, which create their own bad laws (called "regulations") which are crushing our freedom and prosperity.

But who is the <u>true author</u> of all those truly bad laws? Understanding that – those laws' true, historical origin, structure, effects and authorship – explains everything anyone needs to know about them – and their malignant, un-American nature.

And how clear it is that all those malignant federal laws are forbidden by our Constitution. All Americans, including all our politicians, knew that fact to a moral certainty throughout the 19th century – and into the 20th century even. That clear knowledge is proven <u>both</u> by their own, Indisputable actions for 100 years, and with crystal, verbal clarity in writings I will show you below by Alexander Hamilton, Presidents Madison and Monroe, and Chief Justice John Marshall – brilliant and important Founders one and all.

And how utterly corrupt and lawless the Supreme Court and the entire American legal profession have been since the 1930s in knowingly subverting the Constitution and turning it on its head, pretending that it permits such laws – while knowing perfectly well that it does not. Their fraudulent – there is no other word for it – anti-Constitutional actions in that regard – cynically lawless actions motivated purely by political ambitions and contempt for our Constitution and the intelligence and liberties of the citizenry – have, in turn, created an utterly cynical attitude among many American judges and lawyers, politicizing judicial decisions and corrupting the entire judicial process – and undermining the true rule of law.

All this is explained and proven to be the case here.

<u>Our Bad Laws' True Authors</u>

As for who the true author of those laws is: you can take your pick – Louis XIV, Louis XVI, Napoleon, Russia's czars beginning in the 17th century, the German Kaisers (including the one whose murderous tyranny we fought against in World War I): which of those authoritarian continental European tyrants is your favorite? Would we Americans want to live under the thumb of any of those tyrants? We spent massive blood and treasure in World War I precisely to prevent that.

Yet it is a fact that <u>every one of those tyrants</u> enacted, or continued, monstrous, tyrannical laws just like those which our own federal officials have been enacting here beginning in 1887 (our officials didn't dare do so before then), laws specifically designed for the central government to exercise absolute control over their countries, subjugating all like a defeated people – treating them like serfs.

Those monstrous, unconstitutional laws, and all of the "administrative" agencies they create and empower, are the sole cause of the destruction of our freedom and prosperity. Our economy, liberty and prosperity, and our nation's security, which depends on all those for the financial strength it needs, and our people's courage, patriotism and resolve which are our greatest strengths, will all improve exponentially virtually overnight <u>the instant every single one of those laws and those agencies are all repealed</u> – as will the real rule of law in the nation, which has been insulted under the thuggish, corrupt lawlessness virtually required by those malignant laws and agencies, and which has permitted them to exist.

No one other than politicians, and corrupted incumbent businesses (whose monopoly/oligopoly power results from "regulations" which serve to bar competition), federal bureaucrat functionaries, and union officials who extract rents and bullying power from them, and assorted Washington parasites in the legal and other professions, whose expensive services as intermediaries will no longer be required, will miss any of those laws or agencies, or their supposed "benefits," for a minute. The 80%+ of the population who are positively harmed by all those bad laws and agencies will experience virtually overnight the benefits of being rid of those abominations.

And, in case you're wondering: it is impossible to "reform" any of those laws or agencies: they have themselves made doing so impossible; their overwhelming complexity and sheer endlessness, and the endless, corrupt, "entitled" constituencies they create of incumbent businesses who <u>benefit</u> from the market barriers to new competitors those laws and agencies erect, make each of them, and all of them together, a modern day Gordian knot that can only be unraveled and humanized <u>by being cut through and through, and done away with by total, categorical repeal completely.</u>

Nor do any of them actually do a single thing of value worthy of preserving. Anything incidental of actual value they do — drug testing-and reporting, e.g. – can be better done by private companies possessing no monopoly, and no ability to preclude citizens' choices under threat of jail — as do all administrative agency "services" and federally-regulated-and-controlled businesses.

Like all cancers, if they are removed surgically – the only way in this case – <u>every bit must be removed</u>, or else it will all grow back. And only by removing every single one of those agencies, and the bad laws which enable them, wholesale will it be possible to prevent the rent-seeking constituencies which support each of them from demanding reparation for the loss of the special privileges they derive, and falsely believe themselves "entitled" to, all at the expense of all the rest of us.

<u>These Bad Laws Were Forbidden Here 150 Years Before Our Revolution</u>

Our founders were well-aware of tyrannical, top-down, bureaucratic, permission-requiring laws of that type, which were crushing continental Europe at the time of our Revolution. Many of them, including Adams, Jefferson, Franklin and many others, spent considerable time in Bourbon France and witnessed and experienced first-hand those laws and their devastating impact on the people directly. In our Constitution, they did everything they could to prohibit and prevent such laws. Even our most-venal and ambitious federal politicians yielded to those well-known prohibitions for our first 100 years.

And notwithstanding the huge violations of those prohibitions by our politicians since 1887, politicians who broke their oaths of office to curse us with those bad laws and the agencies they create, thanks to our founders, our Constitution still provides us with all of the tools we need to completely undo all of those violations overnight – if we simply have the clarity of vision to see the need to do so, and the will.

In short, our Constitution provides us with the tools <u>to completely undo all the damage</u> caused by over a century of those "agencies" and their enabling laws, and to do so with the speed of a revolution – all without the need for shedding a single drop of American blood!

When the English King Charles I tried to pass laws like these 150 years before our Revolution, our predecessors, the English people of that time, rose up against him and he lost his throne and his head. His son, Charles II, was not allowed to ascend to the English throne until, after decades, he renounced his right to impose discretionary, arbitrary tyranny of that nature on the English people. When Charles II's successor, James II, reneged on some of those promises, he was removed from the throne, relatively bloodlessly, in the Glorious Revolution of 1688, and replaced by William and Mary, monarchs who swore their belief in the liberties of free Englishmen.

That was the nature of the English monarchy our founders determined remained an intolerable tyranny, which they risked everything they had to fight against and found our nation. Our founders' explicit purpose was to establish a nation guaranteeing more individual liberty from state tyranny than any that had ever existed, with a written, and easy-to-understand Constitution legally preserving that individual liberty of all citizens by constricting and restricting the powers over them of the federal government – and of the states as well.

Our founders were deeply-educated in history, law and political philosophy and understood with crystal clarity that, between the individual and the state, power is always a zero-sum proposition: every bit of police power exercised by the state over the citizenry is taken solely by reducing the power/liberty of the citizens in an equal or greater amount. When Jefferson said "That government is best which governs least," he was deadly serious, and spoke for all of our founders.

The federal laws and "administrative" agencies which today are crushing our freedom and prosperity are far worse than anything our founders fought against in the British monarchy of their day: indeed, preventing Star Chamber kangaroo courts (which is precisely what all of those "administrative" agencies are), and such malignant, permission-requiring laws' existence were precisely the great victories for individual liberty secured in the English Revolution/Civil War of 1640-1660 – victories which our own, later Revolution was very consciously intended by our founders to <u>build on</u> and preserve.

In short, we suffer today under laws and federal government intrusions freedom from which was won by our English forebears hundreds of years ago – 150 years before our own Revolutionary victory.

Consider also: Huge percentages of our income are taken from us in income taxes – with us treated like recalcitrant, garnisheed judgment debtors, and with all American employers forced to act like unpaid tax collectors, garnisheeing those taxes from our paychecks – with the income-taxing government literally owning a major percentage of all our earnings – more than most of us spend on everything important to us! As if we were serfs.

And no matter how much we pay in taxes, our politicians always spend <u>even more</u>. if they had less to spend, that would force them to spend less, and the less they spend, the better it would be for all of us, as was the case for over 100 years after our Republic's founding – the hundred years in which our growth, inventiveness and relative prosperity were most pronounced and extraordinary – as was our liberty (except for the tiny minority who were black slaves, who were also freed during that same time, offered the option of being shipped to Africa, and <u>chose to stay here – wisely</u>).

Our founders, who revolted against the English taxation of their day, were subject to <u>no</u> income tax. (The first income tax ever imposed on the English people was a purely temporary measure a few decades after our Revolution, to pay for the emergency spending required to prosecute the war against Napoleon who threatened invasion – and it was repealed as soon as the danger of invasion was passed because Napoleon was defeated.)

When do-gooder "progressives" wanted an income tax and alcohol prohibition imposed on us in the early 20th century, they needed formally to enact amendments to the Constitution, under its Article V, to do so. Does anyone think our pompous, conceited federal rulers today would feel the need even to bother with obtaining a Constitutional amendment for those or any other imposition on our freedom? Their present-day contempt for their oaths of office and Constitutional obligations tells you everything you need to know about what they – and the parasites who alone benefit from the malignant laws they have imposed on us – think of us.

## The Counterrevolution We Have Been Facing–With No Resistance At All

Our suffering today under those laws results from our acquiescence in – our virtual sleepwalking while being assaulted by – a collectivist Counterrevolution which has been going on, in various forms, since early in the 19th century, a Counterrevolution which has never had genuine, popular support, but which has benefited from never facing any real opposition preventing its advance. Until now.

That Counterrevolution and its history and origins are described and deconstructed in this book.

It is a Counterrevolution which has never actually had more than minority support – like the 28% who today think we're "on the right track," perhaps – in the nation, at odds with all of our founding documents, antithetical to the nature of the American Republic itself – a Collectivist Counterrevolution against the cause of individual liberty itself. To regain our freedom and prosperity we must see to it that that Counterrevolution is completely defeated and undone. Thanks to the foresight of our founders, we can achieve that with far less difficulty than they faced in defeating Britain, the greatest superpower of their day, in our Revolution.

The nature of deeply-entrenched, tyrannical regimes is that they always seem absolutely ubiquitous, overwhelming, impregnable and permanent – until they are defeated by a determined people with a clear strategy and policy – as did our founders. As heirs to our American founders we owe it to them, and to our own heirs, to wake up and smell the coffee, agree on a strategy to undo the Counterrevolution, and actively and deliberately defeat it and reclaim the victory for individual liberty won with such hardship in our own unique Revolution — and for which so many brave Americans have given their lives since then.

All of this is explained here below. That is what this book is about. None of this requires footnotes, nor anyone claiming to be an "expert." And neither footnotes nor anyone claiming to be an "expert" is to be found in these pages. All information assembled in this book can easily be confirmed – or shown to be false, if that is the case.

What you will not find here is fraud, nor any insult to your intelligence and dignity – in other words, you will not find here precisely what is to be found in everyone claiming to be an "expert" who, by virtue of making that claim, demands that you shut up and do what he says. And to do so no matter how many times he, along with all the other self-proclaimed "experts," is proven wrong. As but a few examples out of thousands: Remember when "experts" proclaimed butter, coffee, beef, saccharine and countless other perfectly-safe foods to be virtual toxins? Never mind: now they admit that was all nonsense.

When it comes to you, your life and anything and everything that affects you, <u>you alone</u> are the closest thing to an expert there is. Anyone else claiming to be an "expert" – supposedly possessing comprehensive and authoritative knowledge or skill – is a fraud, and either a fool or a thief to boot.

<u>There Are No Experts</u>

Everywhere you look – and even where you don't – self-proclaimed "Experts" can't wait to impose their opinions on you, claiming that they and their ubiquitous "studies" have authoritatively determined every detail of how you should live your life, and for you to simply shut up if you disagree with them about anything.

The government is filled with them, as are all the print and broadcast media. Regardless what they claim, they are not there as your friends. Their sole purpose is to steal your power, for themselves, or for the government – and to get paid for doing so, ultimately by you, as the final insult to your intelligence.

This is no small matter. It is one thing if you seek out someone voluntarily to get his advice, based on your belief that he may have more information than you on a particular subject. That's how people choose their lawyer or doctor, or whatever. If you choose to call that person who you alone select an "expert" or "authority" as your reason for consulting him, that is up to you – and, most importantly, it is you who is making the choice to seek out his opinion.

But that is not how people who want to impose their dictatorial will, and take your power away, use the word "Expert."

Read on, and I will prove all this to you by simply reminding you of simple facts you already know.

First of all, the Oxford English Dictionary, which most people consider genuinely authoritative regarding the history of English language words and their definitions, defines the term "expert," when used as a noun, as "a person who has a <u>comprehensive and authoritative</u> knowledge or skill in a particular area [emphases added]."

It also states that the term "expert" was unknown – that is, the word <u>did not exist </u>in English – prior to the early 19th century, when it was first used in a statute in England providing for Government price-fixing of certain commodities, with the task of setting the prices which the government wanted imposed on sales of those commodities to be assigned to, in the statute's language, an "expert."

The reason those who wish to take away your power love claiming that individuals whose opinions they want you to subscribe to are "experts" is simple: they want to force the opinions of those so-called "Experts" on you – and for you to shut up if you have any objection. This is literally an insult to you and your intelligence — and your wallet.

When they trot out those "experts" to tell you supposed "facts," that is always a lie in and of itself: the "facts" they announce are actually no more than theories at best, and often are proven completely false not long after being announced. What is even more reprehensible is when "experts" state what even they admit are mere opinions – and expect you to accept even those as facts. Those opinions have even less substance then the theories those "experts" fraudulently pretend to be facts.

Although there are people who have indeed acquired relatively more information about a variety of subjects than others, their theories and <u>opinions</u> even on those subjects they supposedly have more information about, are no better than yours

– and when it comes to matters that affect you, they're positively worse – and an insult to you to boot if they expect you to subscribe to them.

The basic problem with anyone claiming to have actual expertise or, as the Oxford English Dictionary defines that, "comprehensive and authoritative knowledge" about anything, is that that claim really is the claim that that person is as smart as God: who else but God can have genuinely comprehensive knowledge about anything?

However much information someone may have, when it comes to his <u>opinions</u>, or even what he may think are facts, a mere one single item of <u>additional</u> information could transform the entire nature of everything he imagines he knows about that subject. Our own language proves this proposition. Consider the following sentence:

"Jack is good at typing."

The addition of a single word – "not" — before the word "good " completely changes the meaning of that sentence – to its <u>opposite</u>.

That is precisely what any new fact can do to what a so-called "learned scholar" may know – or rather, <u>think</u> he knows – about something – which may well turn out to be sheer nonsense.

Since no one knows <u>all</u> the facts about everything – Including what unknown facts would completely transform what he thinks he knows about any particular subject – no one in real life <u>ever</u> has the "comprehensive and authoritative knowledge" necessary, by definition, to be an expert <u>about anything</u>.

So when anyone claims to be an expert and wants to tell you how to live your life, and for you to shut up in obedience to his brilliance, recognize the insult to your intelligence, and the fraud he, and all those trying to force you to accept his supposed "expertise" to demand your obedience, are practicing on you.

Fundamental to the entire Counterrevolution — and the regulatory bureaucratic administrative state it has been imposing on America since 1887 — is this very demonstrably-false notion that bona fide "Experts" do indeed exist – and in multiple areas of study – and that when the government claims to rely on them to tell you what to do – under threat of destroying you, your business, your fellow citizens, or your life if you disobey – it is "progressing" the virtues of government and improving the lives of everyone. Rest assured: you are not who is benefitting from that at all.

Because, as I have just demonstrated, there is no such thing as a genuine "Expert", that fundamental claim of the Counterrevolution, on which it bases all its claims for the virtue of amassing total power in the state over the citizenry, to force the rule of such "experts" on them, is a big lie and a complete insult to you and to all free men.

<u>The Counterrevolution Can Be Completely Undone, And Our True
Revolution Reinstated, Whenever We Want – Bloodlessly!</u>

Our Founders left no stone unturned in their quest to secure and preserve individual liberty for us who have followed them as stewards of this blessed Republic America, by providing for all of the following in our Constitution – which, by its own terms, remains the only genuine, supreme law of the land:

(1)  Article I section 8 of the Constitution specifies the exclusive subjects Congress is authorized to legislate about and, in the absence of legislation authorizing federal action, the federal government can do nothing. The plain text of the Constitution, authoritative interpretations of applicable portions of it in the 19th century by its two most highly respected analysts – Pres. James Madison, himself well-known as its principal author and Chief Justice of the Supreme Court John Marshall – and the actual history of the nation for 100 years after the Constitution's enactment, leave no doubt that all of the liberty-destroying actions of our federal government since 1887 have been utterly unconstitutional – and thus reversible at any time. I will prove this to you below in this book.

(2)  All elected officials in both Congress and the White House hold their offices for specific terms which have specific beginning and ending dates; and no elected official, and no branch of government containing previously-elected officials, have <u>any power whatsoever</u> over laws and executive actions any time after their term, and they themselves, and those who succeed them, are free to repudiate and repeal any actions by previous Congresses, and any which they have taken during their own terms. To the extent that any Congress permits the actions of any previous Congress to remain in force, it is solely because <u>it effectively reenacts</u> all such actions, even if it does so only implicitly, by failing to repeal them and start anew.

(3)  Article V of our Constitution provides specific procedures which must be followed in order to amend it, and nothing in Articles I, II and III, which specify the powers granted to the only branches of the federal government authorized by the Constitution – the Legislative, Executive and Judicial branches – nor in article V, grants any of those branches, <u>not even all three of them acting together</u>, the power to amend the Constitution. That Article provides procedures for the states and citizens to undo Constitutional misconduct by the federal government when its own officers refuse to do so.

(4)  Our Constitution, itself designed and drafted by American revolutionaries, ingeniously contains unambiguous provisions expressly permitting enormous, rapid, arguably revolutionary, contractions in the size and scope of the federal government and/or its expenditures on any and all matters, <u>with no need for the shedding of a single drop of blood</u> – in other words, revolution without all its normal horrors and unpleasantness. Multiple Constitutional provisions have this potentially-revolutionary effect – the provisions

19

permitting impeachment of officials, including elected officials such as the president and vice president and judges — and, also in Article I, the power of the purse specified in section 9 thereof, which <u>explicitly exists completely apart from Congress' legislative power</u>, and forbids the expenditure of any Treasury funds for any purpose except pursuant to specific appropriations "made by Law."

That power of the purse gives a single house of Congress, or the President, acting alone the complete power, without the need to pass or repeal any laws at all, instantaneously to undo and eliminate any previous federal action of any kind, including abolishing any and all federal agencies, at any time. This is part of the Constitution's built-in "downward-ratchet" bias against federal expansion: passing legislation enabling federal actions is time-consuming and very difficult, requiring approval by both congressional chambers and, normally, the president also. <u>Undoing</u> any such action, on the other hand, can be accomplished easily and instantaneously by <u>either</u> congressional chamber at any time by simply demanding that undoing – whenever money needs to be appropriated to fund such.

And it is unconstitutional for any federal funds to be spent without such lawful appropriation.

These revolutionary provisions, permitting government-contracting revolution, when approved by the president alone, or a mere majority of either chamber of the legislative branch, without the need for actual warfare, were included in the Constitution by men who were only too well aware that, in the England they had broken with, achieving similar ends had always previously required military revolution – in the English Civil War of the 1640s, with such bloodshed minimized only fortuitously in the so-called Glorious Revolution of 1688 in which James II was removed from the throne by act of Parliament for selectively refusing to enforce duly-enacted parliamentary laws, and in our bloody, dangerous, and enormously-difficult American Revolution itself.

# CHAPTER 2

## The Complete Moral Bankruptcy of All Forms of Collectivism

Disbelief in God and, when they are candid, outright <u>repudiation</u> of all religion – especially Judaism and the various Christian churches of the West – have always been central, defining features of Collectivism since its birth as a political movement in 18th Century Revolutionary France. This is all discussed at length below.

However odd it may strike God-believers, that fact – the utter loathing of religion at the heart of Collectivism in all its forms – has never prevented Collectivists of all varieties from insisting that they personally, and all political positions they advocate, are morally superior to all alternatives. Indeed, they invariably view all opposition to them, and all of their opponents personally, as morally and existentially reprehensible.

Those among Collectivists who are forthright Marxists insist that the supposed quasi-divine force of History (yes, Marx actually insisted on this notion) compels absolute, unquestioning, *ipso facto* obedience to everything they advocate. Those Collectivists self-aware enough to recognize the religion-without-God nature of their ideology often insist, hubristically, that their self-characterized "reasoned and scientific" quasi-eschatological analysis permits them, objectively, to "advance" or" progress" beyond the Stone Age or Iron Age superstitious foolishness – that being how they invariably characterize all Western religions.

Recently, the most rigidly-anti-American Marxists (including people in very high political offices who invariably disdain the Marxist label, while undeniably propagandizing for the very ideas championed by Marx himself, as plainly shown in Chapter 6 below) have spouted new, faux-moral, and even faux-patriotic, claims in angrily demanding that Americans acquiesce in manifestly self-destructive Obama policies which are obviously so purposeless and catastrophic that it is inconceivable that any previous American politician, however dedicated to the Counterrevolution he may have been in his heart, would ever have promoted them. These policies so promoted constitute clear, direct assaults on the very safety, security and integrity of the nation itself.

Specifically, these policies have consisted of (1) providing massive financial assistance (over $150 billion) to a self-identified mortal enemy of America – Iran – which has been officially designated a terrorist state for decades, and has the blood of hundreds, if not thousands, of American soldiers and allies' lives on its hands and has sworn to annihilate both America and Israel, (2) in that same agreement with Iran, guaranteeing its unopposed development of nuclear weapons and sophisticated ballistic missiles to deliver them, (3) insisting on America accepting tens of thousands of military-age Muslim men as "refugees" without the slightest ability to determine how many of them are actually terrorist plants – while simultaneously refusing to accept genocidally-threatened Christians from throughout the Middle East, including Iraq, Syria and elsewhere as genuine refugee immigrants into America, and (4) unilaterally reducing all of our offensive nuclear capabilities, and terminating all development of our previously-advanced defensive (anti-ballistic) ones.

No plausible pragmatic argument whatsoever in favor of any of these policies has been advanced by the Obama administration. Instead, the nonsense-"moral"-and "pseudo-patriotic" language used in support of these monstrous policies has been baseless claims that "this is who we are" or "America has always done this" or words to that effect. That these are "moral" arguments is undeniable. That they have no basis in any known moral authority or facts is equally apparent.

The fact that Collectivists' arguments in favor of their positions are accurately described as moral, instead of, or in addition to, any utilitarian or pragmatic ones they may advance, is revealed by the particular language they use – or abuse – in making them: they typically claim their positions will produce greater "fairness," or what they call "social justice"– which supposedly is morally-superior to ordinary justice; or they morally-shame opposition to them by claiming it is racist, or bigoted, or regressive, or xenophobic (always pretending themselves to be innocent of such allegations), or unecological, or simply beyond the pale for allegedly-civilized nations (claiming, for example, that "all other nations" have adopted their position) or, again, "that is who we are," or something similar.

They might even invoke the supposed authority of religious leaders who they claim, often correctly unfortunately, agree with them – Including bishops, rabbis, churches, and even Popes.

But they can point to absolutely nothing in the 10 Commandments, nor any other undeniably-morally-authoritative text in support of their supposed-moral claims.

The following biblical discussion/analysis proves the patently-frivolous nature of all Collectivist's supposed moral claims, and the overwhelmingly-powerful argument, derived from the 10 Commandments themselves, that socialism and the welfare/administrative state they invariably promote are inherently immoral and directly contrary to all relevant directives in both the Old and New Testament:

The Old Testament's Political And Legal Wisdom: God's Mandatory Demands, And the Bible's Teachings regarding "Experts"

America remains a nation which has always believed, and still in the 21st century, overwhelmingly (by no less than 70%+ according to polling data) believes, in the God of the Old Testament and the divinity of Jesus Christ and, accordingly, the divine scriptural authority of both the Old and New Testaments. This is true even for those Christians and Jews who do not, like fundamentalists, believe every event described in the Bible must be accepted as literally and historically true.

And there is no denying the central importance the Old and New Testament ascribe to the 10 Commandments: of all God's many commandments throughout the entire Bible, the 10 Commandments <u>alone</u> were written <u>in stone</u>, and not simply spoken even to Moses himself: They alone were written in stone by God Himself <u>by His own hand</u>.

In just a handful of pages, Exodus provides divine (literally, to believers) wisdom regarding each and all of the following:

(1) the 10 Commandments themselves – a comprehensive, and <u>necessarily-exclusive</u>, description of <u>all</u> behavior-policing laws which are mandatory – according to God Himself – for a free people to remain free,

(2) by implication, everything a free people who want to remain free must demand of the policing features of their government, as the necessary enforcement vehicle for the 10 Commandments, and

(3) how all peoples should view all priests and other priesthoods (i.e. self-proclaimed "experts") claiming for themselves any special authority or insights regarding any subject, including the 10 Commandments themselves and morality.

All this information is contained in the few pages consisting of Exodus chapter 20 through Exodus chapter 32 (the importance of the 10 Commandments is further revealed both by its complete repetition in Deuteronomy chapter 5, and the multiple miracles attributed to the physical tablets on which God wrote them, elsewhere in the Bible).

Perhaps this important information is so condensed out of necessity since, as God says many times in the Old Testament, the people He is providing all this to are "thick-necked," and so require everything to be spelled out as simply and concisely as possible. And it is unlikely that He thought Jews different from other humans and uniquely dense in that regard.

First, Exodus' wisdom regarding the third of its three, above-enumerated divine teachings:

Exodus' and the Gospels' Divine Lessons Regarding Priests, Priesthoods
And Any Other Supposed "Experts" – i.e. Any Human Claiming
To Be As Smart As, Or Smarter Than, God About Anything

Exodus chapter 28 explicitly describes Moses' brother Aaron as, uniquely (with his sons) he who should have the role of God's priest. Chapter 31 verse 18, states explicitly that God gave Moses the 10 Commandments physically, as well as through verbal commands: "two tables of testimony, tables of stone, written with the finger of God."

Although Exodus chapters 28 through 30 describe in great detail the rituals the priest is to preside over, and the tabernacle in which he is to do so, nowhere does it suggest that he would have any particular insight regarding the contents of the Commandments – nor, indeed, any ability or duty whatsoever to comment on them or provide "expertise," or preach to the people, on that subject – nor anything else.

Among the first few Commandments is one which forbids making any graven image – especially of any other God.

Nevertheless, in the very next chapter – Exodus chapter 32, verse 2 et seq.— Aaron not only violates that Commandment by making a golden calf as an object of worship, but also corrupts others to participate in that clear violation by leading the effort to do so: "And Aaron said unto them, break off the golden earrings, which *are* in the ears of your wives, of your sons, and of your daughters, and bring them unto me….And he [Aaron] received them in their hand, and fashioned it with a graving tool, after he had made it a molten calf…"

Thus, the "priest/expert's" own actions prove his utter moral and intellectual lack of trustworthiness even with respect to his supposed area of unique, specialized, God-ordained expertise: instead of supervising the worship of God, he supervises the compound insult to God of violating that explicit Commandment and directing the creation and worship of the God-forbidden golden idol.

Thus, that biblical story of Aaron and the golden calf teaches that anyone – such as Aaron – pretending to have specialized knowledge regarding the 10 Commandments – particularly if he attempts too-cleverly to modify or change any of them – must be recognized as an evil scoundrel who, though God may forgive him, must not be followed or trusted in any manner.

Exodus' lesson regarding the invariable, false pretensions of priests and other "experts" claiming special wisdom is repeated in multiple ways, and even mirrored, in the New Testament Gospels.

Jesus explicitly declaims against the pretensions and misleading directives of all the different rabbis (i.e. priests), denouncing them both for claiming to sit in Moses' chair, and for issuing commandments for the people which are, at best, distractions from what He explicitly describes as the only two real commandments – which accurately condense and summarize both the 10 Commandments – "love your neighbor as yourself…" and "love… God," thereby condensing the verbal commandment which follows them – "Hear O Israel… Thou shalt love the Lord thy God with all thy heart, with all thy soul and with all thy might…"

Additionally, Peter, who Jesus explicitly names personally as the foundation of His church, exactly as Aaron was appointed by God as his priest, betrays Jesus three times in a single night, and is explicitly called "Satan" by Jesus Himself.

<u>The 10 Commandments' Directives And Their Purpose</u>

Regarding the 10 Commandments' requirements themselves and their importance to us as Americans: even liberal Democrat President Harry Truman observed in 1950 that,"*The fundamental basis of this nation's laws was given to Moses on the Mount.*"

And such was the power of the stone tablets which the Commandments were written on that later, when the ancient Jews, guided by Joshua, simply marched around the walls of Jericho carrying them, <u>that alone</u> was sufficient to bring those walls crumbling down.

The first few Commandments make explicit the authority, love for His people and liberating desires for them of He Who is the source all the 10 Commandments – God himself – His purpose in providing them to people who He explicitly designated as His chosen people, and directives regarding how such people were to interact with Him (i.e., completely accept His exclusive divinity, eschew graven images, not take his name in vain and honor His Sabbath).

God's <u>expressly-stated,</u> in the first Commandment, purpose in providing the 10 Commandments arises directly out of His then-recent <u>liberation of the Jews from slavery</u>. In them He provides simple, comprehensive, unambiguous rules of conduct for moral, free people to show appropriate respect both for Him and to each other – rules, in short, intended both to prevent them from ending up as slaves again, and to enable them to live decent, moral, God-obedient lives.

The Commandments are necessarily the <u>exclusive</u> laws to govern the peoples' behavior for that purpose: any <u>additional</u> rules imposed on them – necessarily by men alone and not God – policing their interpersonal behavior would necessarily <u>overly</u>-constrain them, and so reduce, if not completely eliminate, their freedom from the slavery God had recently rescued them from. And the idea that God would forget or overlook any necessary Commandment is literally an insult to Him and His intelligence – an insolent, immoral and hubristic claim by anyone asserting such of being superior to God!

In other words, in the interest of promoting and securing the liberty of the people, the 10 Commandments spell out <u>all</u> behavior which is forbidden – with all <u>other</u> behavior necessarily <u>permitted</u> for the now-free people. Obviously, forbidding any behavior not expressly forbidden in the 10 Commandments necessarily can only reduce, or even destroy, the peoples' liberty.

Again, the first few Commandments make plain that they have nothing to do with how people are to interact among themselves, nor with the state, and are almost exclusively concerned with the recently-liberated people's interactions with God alone, and restate (for the "thick-necked") who He is (the God who rescued the people from slavery). I say "almost" in that regard because one of those Commandments provides the enforcement method to ensure the integrity of the word, or promise of any person – including anyone assuming public office: "Thou shalt not take the name of the Lord thy God in vain."

That Commandment alone is what makes any oath in the Lord's name so powerful and reliable among God-believers: that Commandment makes such an oath a sacred commitment, so that breaking such an oath means damnation from violating that Commandment.

In one of His few statements with even arguable political implications (His life and teachings manifestly were devoted to providing the means and path to individual salvation for all human souls, and not to worldly matters) Jesus made plain that man's interactions with God and religious matters are, quite simply, none of the state's business, when he stated, "Render unto Caesar what is Caesar's, and unto God what is God's."

As important as those words by Jesus are in themselves, of equal importance is the fact that they clearly contain, implicitly, a command to Caesar: do not intrude in any manner on God's business.

I submit that the first few of the Commandments, similarly to that "hands-off" directive to Caesar from Jesus regarding the (lack of any) role the state should take in religious matters, implicitly demand that moral people and their state be tolerant of all religions so long as their followers obey the 10 Commandments, as is required of all Christians and Jews. As undeniable proof of the divine wisdom of such tolerance: think of all the religious strife and warfare that could have been avoided if Europeans (claiming all along to be good Christians) had obeyed and understood those clear directives from God and Jesus.

And note that we the Americans were the first ever legally to require such religious tolerance – in our Constitution's First Amendment, which both expressly forbids any establishment of religion by the federal government, and mandates the free exercise of all religions in America. And the English Common Law behavior-policing laws of every American state, which the founders and our Constitution legally prescribed would be the only citizen-policing laws (as proven in a later chapter below) in the nation, were, as the founders well knew, all based exclusively on the 10 Commandments, thereby legally-requiring conformity to the Commandments by all citizens regardless of their religion.

The next Commandment similarly involves matters which are none of the state's business and relates solely to how each person should interact with his parents: "honor your father and your mother."

All the rest of the Commandments contain very simple, unambiguous moral directives on how we all are to interact with our fellow citizens – again, if the people are to remain free and not find themselves enslaved once again. The plain implication from those Commandments is that the state is indeed required to perform the role of policing and enforcing at least some of them (see below); and, in so doing, the state itself must follow those commandments as well, and never become a vehicle for violating them – or else it would be a completely immoral state due to its participation in such Commandment violations.

Jesus' only other political statement in the New Testament consists of His (clearly-approving) succinct summary of all these Commandments: "Love your neighbor as yourself." In other words: respect the individual dignity of the life, liberty and property of your neighbor – just as you would want him to respect yours. Are your neighbors' property rights as important as any other of his rights? How would you feel about having your property forcibly taken from you? According to Jesus, that answers the question.

## The Commandments, Churches and Religious Leaders, And the Welfare State

Although these Commandments are, by divine design, simple and easy to understand, it is manifest from the actions of religious institutions and religious leaders over the past few centuries that their true import is rarely fully-appreciated, even by supposedly religious people and institutions, and their supposedly-learned and godly leaders.

Specifically, virtually all organized Christian and Jewish sects have, since the 1870s, with varying degrees of official formality, publicly embraced the supposed morality and virtue of the welfare state, which was first created in its modern form at that time under the absolute rule of the German Kaisers and their minister Bismarck. Its purpose in 19th-century totalitarian Germany, as always, was to completely subjugate and ensnare the people under the absolute control of the Kaiser and his centralized regime.

Under the welfare state, there and always, property is taken by the state from some citizens and redistributed to others who have not earned it themselves, regardless of the desires of its original owners, with the (windfall) recipients made to feel entitled to, and dependent on, what they so receive from the state, no gratitude required or expected – except to the Kaiser.

That last point – the gratitude to the Kaiser alone structurally-compelled by state welfare – itself leaves no doubt concerning state welfare's utter immorality and injustice under the moral dictates of the Bible. Specifically, the Bible teaches that each individual has his own immortal soul, which must be rewarded and punished on earth exclusively for his own actions – and neither be punished for the actions of others (which would be unjust), nor steal rewards rightfully due another ("thou shall not steal.").

Under state welfare, the only action of the Kaiser consists of stealing – for his own political advantage – property rightfully owned by some citizens, and then unjustly and gratuitously bestowing it upon others to whom it does not belong. Charity it is not. And the fraudulent pretense that welfare amounts to charity – God's work – violates Jesus' mandate to Caesar not to intrude on God's Kingdom.

Gratitude by welfare's recipients to the Kaiser is <u>additionally</u> immoral in precluding legitimately-earned gratitude to the property's true owners, who thereby suffer a double injury of having their property stolen and the loss of gratitude from its recipients. And even the welfare recipients suffer injury by their misdirected gratitude to a Kaiser who has not earned it and was simply serving his own interests through the welfare. And that is not even mentioning the numerous other poisonous effects welfare has on its recipients, including the fact that funding it harms the real economy, thereby reducing their opportunities to support themselves.

Religious leaders and institutions – notably, the Catholic Church – who have so embraced the welfare state have usually stated their reason for doing so is based on the supposed benefits of it to the poor, and their claim that welfare's wealth redistribution is akin to charity, with charity being a frequently-praised activity throughout the Bible. Somehow, the fact that the welfare state reduces the opportunities, and incentives, for the poor to improve their lives Invariably goes unmentioned by its apologists.

But, as I have already shown, for multiple reasons, welfare is not charity. Real charity is inherently a <u>private</u> transaction between the voluntary giver and the donee. Welfare is, in fact, the state-enforced <u>socialisation</u> of charity and, as shown below, because socialism invariably relies on multiple violations of the 10 Commandments, to advocate it is to advocate for their violation.

In fact, Welfare is charity's <u>opposite</u>. Unlike genuine charity, which is virtuous and involves no violation of the 10 Commandments, there is nothing voluntary about welfare. Even its recipients are effectively forced to abandon their dignity and accept it since, as mentioned above, the crushing taxes imposed by the state to finance it, and the state control over the economy that invariably accompanies it, eliminate genuine economic opportunities for those recipients to earn their own money to finance their own needs.

And welfare's necessary forcible taking of property from its true owners to finance it is indistinguishable from the theft which is explicitly forbidden in the 10 Commandments. For that reason, it makes the state itself immoral.

Moreover, welfare is inherently unjust, both because of that involuntary theft, and because the recipients of the property have done nothing whatsoever to earn it – and it may even constitute a reward for (immoral) sloth.

And, unlike charity, those from whom the property is taken – its rightful owners – play no role whatsoever in its distribution. Moreover, the <u>entitlement</u> nature of the redistribution renders it morally poisonous to its recipients since, unlike real charity, it provides no moral incentive to them to take the initiative to try to reclaim their dignity and improve their own lives: they are entitled, so why bother?

## The One Commandment-Forbidden Emotion

Returning to the 10 Commandments: they unambiguously forbid one and only one emotion – envy. They notably do not forbid hatred or anger.

They recognize that envy is unique among the emotions both in the fact that we each have the power to magnify or suppress it to a greater extent than any other emotion, and that it is uniquely toxic and capable of overwhelming the minds of those who succumb to it – rendering them susceptible to manipulation by demagogues whose true purpose always is to use the envy they incite to <u>enslave</u> them – the precise result the 10 Commandments are intended by God to prevent.

Envy is the poisonous emotion that drives people to want to <u>harm</u> their neighbors – In direct violation of Jesus' commandment to "love" them – precisely because those neighbors have achieved or acquired more than those who envy them. It is the emotion that every demagogue seeks to incite among the people to turn them into angry enemies of their more-successful neighbors – and into self-loathing, immoral victims.

It is precisely the poisonous emotion which demagogues, who want personally and unjustly to profit from the gratitude of the recipients of welfare's property redistribution, incite to demand redistribution of wealth to the envious from its rightful owners.

In short, envy is the vehicle always at hand for Caesar — or some supposed "experts" — fraudulently to masquerade as God.

In forbidding that emotion, the 10 Commandments announce that those who experience that emotion and fail to suppress it literally enslave themselves – regardless whether they succeed in also harming their neighbors as their envy compels them to do.

## The Remaining Commandments

The next Commandment — "thou shall not bear false witness" — is far more than a directive simply not to commit perjury – as a "witness" – in trials. It is a sweeping directive forbidding fraud in all interpersonal circumstances. Again, nothing is more common among demagogues seeking to turn the people against each other for the demagogue's empowerment than to commit fraud in all their communications.

The remainder of the 10 Commandments are unambiguous directives mandating respect for the life and <u>all the property</u> of all fellow citizens. Murder is forbidden, as is all theft of another's property – equally with murder itself.

## State Enforcement of the Commandments – How Much?

The 10 Commandments are silent concerning the manner and extent to which the state should be involved in their enforcement. Except for their undeniable implication: no state can claim to be moral if it outlaws any conduct not expressly-forbidden in the 10 Commandments.

I believe it is clear that some of the Commandments involve conduct exclusively between citizens and God (the first four). Because of the ecumenical directive I have inferred from them – that the state should honor and permit all religions that demand obedience to the 10 Commandments – implicit in that directive is a prohibition on the state intervening to enforce the first three. The fourth commandment – to "remember the Sabbath day" – similarly, among the rest of those, should not be enforced by state action both because different religions which respect the 10 Commandments have selected different days for their Sabbath, and because the command to "remember" does not provide any particular guidance on any particular, observable behavior required to do so, beyond the purely-internal experience of the memory itself.

Similarly, the commandment to "honor your father and your mother" says nothing about <u>how</u> one should do so, and involves purely intra-familial actions – ones that should not be intruded on by the state's monopoly on violence, particularly in the absence of any directive regarding the behavior required from children to so honor their parents when they are old enough to defy its self-enforcement by the child's own parents.

Of the remaining Commandments, it is clear that state involvement should be required to enforce the prohibitions on murder, theft and bearing false witness (i.e. fraud inflicting harm on others). Those Commandments all forbid various forms of clearly-violent misconduct <u>against others</u>, for which the state's monopoly of violence is clearly required – and to prevent the vigilantism which otherwise would become their only enforcement mechanism.

With respect to the prohibition on envy, state enforcement of such against individuals who simply experience that emotion internally, but do not otherwise act on it, would seem to be an unnecessarily-intrusive thought-crime type of state policing, for no public purpose, since the only one genuinely harmed by it would necessarily be the person experiencing the forbidden emotion himself. State policing of the Commandment forbidding envy would seem appropriate, if at all, only against persons attempting to <u>incite</u> that emotion in others, since only then is there a clearly-observable forbidden action by someone with a direct, harmful consequence to others.

The only sexual activity forbidden in the Commandments is adultery – that is, consensual sex in which at least one of the participants is married to someone else who does not condone it. Note that the Commandments have no such prohibition against any other sexual behavior – including homosexual or premarital sex, nor any act between non-adulterous heterosexuals.

Because of the married state of at least one of the participants, adultery always presents uniquely explosive problems for children, entire families, and the community – and for the injured, non-condoning, nonparticipating spouse – well beyond any other sexual acts, particularly in a very old-fashioned, patriarchal or tribal society, like that of the Mosaic Jews.

Even today, in our world blessed with effective birth control, the potential intra-familial destructiveness of adultery cannot be doubted. Should the state be involved in enforcing that particular Commandment? I believe it is ambiguous and unclear. Since marriage is a public, as well as a private institution, state involvement in enforcing that Commandment at least in the context of divorce seems perfectly permissible, if not required. I believe personally the criminal law should not be involved in enforcing this Commandment, as it often has in the past; but I honestly do not know what the Commandment requires in that respect.

A Few Words About Property Rights And Theft:

Translated from legalese into plain English, citizens possess what are known as "property rights" to the extent that they possess any or all lawful power(s) with respect to whatever is the tangible or intangible subject of those rights – i.e. the asset which comprises the property itself – including specifically the powers to control, enjoy, and/or direct its use.

Of all of these various possible powers with respect to property, by far the most significant is the power to control it and its use, since whoever controls that also controls its enjoyment and management – and its continued existence and utility. Businesses constitute the property and, indeed, the very work or industry, of their owners.

A central feature of the administrative, regulatory state, which invariably is wedded to a welfare state, is the legalized seizure by the state of all control of businesses from their owners – euphemistically called "regulation" – invariably without the payment of any compensation to them for that seizure. Once a "regulator" has control over any business, the regulator's ability to destroy the business in his discretion renders that control absolute.

In America, our Constitution unambiguously requires payment of compensation by the state whenever it takes any citizens' property. Our welfare administrative state, with the full approval of the politicians on the federal courts, has refused to pay business owners any compensation whatsoever when it imposes regulatory control over their businesses – based on the nonsensical claim that their ouster from actual control of their property is too minor a deprivation to be considered the "taking" of any of their property. In fact, the enormity of the value of that political taking is proven by the very eagerness of the politicians who effect it to do so.

Furthermore, lest there be any confusion regarding the fact that "mere" control of any asset indeed constitutes valuable property, consider: is there any doubt that stripping a common-stock owner of his voting rights would constitute a clear taking of his property? And, except in a one-man corporation, mere stockholders have nowhere near the controlling authority over a business which the state takes when it "regulates" it, necessarily armed with the power to destroy it and any of its agents who fail to comply with all its directives.

Thus, it is no exaggeration to state that when any business is "regulated" by administrative agencies, the most significant property right of all, which its owners formerly possessed, is stolen from them – in violation of the Commandment – and our Constitutional provision – forbidding theft.

Nothing in any of the Commandments suggests that, if one or more citizens are able to take sufficient control of the state to be able to use its power over their fellow citizens in a manner which would be forbidden to each of them individually to do in the 10 Commandments, such would be morally acceptable. Again, that is precisely what happens in the welfare/administrative state – property (Including control of the operations of businesses) is forcibly taken/stolen by the state from citizens who are its rightful owners, and given to others (including the politicians and bureaucrats who thereafter control it completely) who have not earned it, and have no moral right to it.

Clearly, a moral state must enforce the 10 Commandments, not use its power to inflict violence to violate them for the supposed benefit of some citizens to the detriment of others. Thus, a state that steals from one group of citizens for the purpose of bestowing what is so stolen on other citizens is no better than a thief – or a murderer.

### Charity, State Power, Socialism And the Welfare/Administrative State

Genuine charity is a blessed, voluntary giving by citizens of their own property to assist others experiencing difficulty; using state threat of violence to force them to make such transfers violates justice – and the 10 Commandments itself. Again, it is nothing like actual charity; it is immoral, enslaving injustice and theft.

Indeed, since all of the final group of Commandments clearly require political/ state power to facilitate their enforcement, it is clear they require the state's role to be limited to that of their enforcer – and never to itself become their violator.

This fact alone proves the utter immorality of socialism and the welfare/administrative state, and their direct conflict with the 10 Commandments: they both require the state to have the power to take – that is, to steal – and then gratuitously to bestow, whatever it chooses from its citizens, in complete disregard for all property rights and, indeed, destroying all property rights: When one citizen's property rights are extinguished by the state itself, no citizens' property rights are safe,

And all citizens' rights depend on the strength of their property rights as their underlying foundation: a serf or slave is, by definition, a man with no property rights. That is why the 10 Commandments absolutely forbid harming or taking another's property.

Moreover, socialism is the politics of envy itself. Without envy to drive it, invariably promoted by demagogues' fraudulent promises of the benefits which stealing from one group of citizens will provide the other, socialism rapidly implodes. So too the welfare/administrative state.

The 10 Commandments leave no doubt: morality and God demand that the state and all its citizens respect – and never envy – the property rights of all other citizens. Quite simply, socialism and the welfare/administrative state, on the one hand, and private property rights and obeying the 10 Commandments, on the other hand, are inherently mutually exclusive.

And it is a fact that advocates of socialism and the welfare/administrative state invariably rely on multiple violations of multiple Commandments: they lie about the supposed morality, justice and benefits of what they advocate – and so "bear false witness" – and do everything in their power to incite envy among the people.

There is not a single example in history in which either socialism or welfare/administrative states have produced anything other than destruction of citizens' freedom and prosperity. But that is a mere practical fact, in addition to the moral facts considered in this chapter.

Moreover, in the 10 Commandments, it is clear that God implicitly mandates that the power of the state never be greater than the absolute minimum necessary to enforce those Commandments: since that minimal state power is all that is necessary to preserve the freedom of the people, any additional state power over its people beyond that amount would necessarily reduce pro tanto the people's liberty.

It is as if God stipulated, together with Thomas Jefferson, that "that government is best which governs least" – as long as it enforces the 10 Commandments, and so preserves the life, liberty and property of all the people.

Thus, in our unprecedented-in-human-history founding documents – the Declaration of Independence and our Constitution – America became the first nation in history legally and institutionally dedicated to achieving the goal God Himself provided, millennia earlier, the 10 Commandments to achieve – setting up a national government dedicated to preserving the life, liberty, property, security and individual dignity of all its citizens in every single respect, to the maximum extent possible under law, explicitly preserving all power to police individual behavior in the states alone (since the federal government is given <u>no</u> enumerated police power whatsoever in the Constitution, except with respect to treason, Counterfeiting, piracy and insurrection), pursuant to the English/American common law which itself consisted of the legal application of the 10 Commandments to specific, real-life situations.

# CHAPTER 3

## The Federal Administrative Agencies – An Introduction

Unlike every single American until 1887, none of us alive today has ever lived in an America in which there were no federal administrative agencies at all.

You know what they are: they are all those alphabet agencies like the FCC, the FDA, the SEC, and even actual formal Executive branch cabinet departments such as HUD, the EPA, the Departments of Education, Energy, HHS, Agriculture, Justice, and God knows how many other similar official government bodies with countless employees (at Least 2,663,000 In 2014, according to the Federal Government) that, together, issue literally thousands of pages of what are called "regulations" <u>every year</u> – the total number now is over 178,000 pages – and this has been growing year after year, president after president, regardless of party. and violation of virtually every directive in those pages is a crime, punishable by often massive fines and jail time, even though not a single page of all that was passed in a manner required by Article I of the Constitution – and that is not even their most serious Constitutional violation, as I prove in later chapters.

Not a single one of those agencies existed before 1887, when the first one of them was created, and the second was not created until 1906. And we had liberty and economic growth, and innovation, and rapid improvements to everyone's lives, before then as we never have since. Every single one of those agencies has been created by our elected politicians. And not a single one of them is permitted under the Constitution (except, ironically, the IRS).

Most Americans have been propagandized endlessly, in all their education and virtually everything they read or hear, and so genuinely believe that without some or all of these agencies, our nation would suffer some grievous injury or loss – or even that without them there would be <u>no law at all</u> governing some of our fellow citizens, including the most powerful, and that, without those agencies and their regulations, terrible "predatory capitalists" would run amok lawlessly amongst us, ruthlessly taking advantage of the weakest among us and generally wreaking havoc.

In fact, that is all literally nothing but Marxist nonsense, and nothing could be further from the truth.

There is and, since even before the birth of the Republic, always has been, other, excellent, genuinely-order-and-freedom preserving law, governing all actions of all Americans, including all businesses, law whose administration and effect is utterly free from the corruption and cronyism which invariably accompany all those federal agencies, law that is infinitely superior to anything any of those agencies administer or enact — Good Law, which preserves liberty and justice, and is inevitably undermined and marginalized by the Bad Law which creates, and results from, all those agencies.

All these matters, including the nature, origin and content of Good Law and Bad Law, are discussed in a later chapter.

There is not a single one of those agencies that does anything whatsoever of value, including any "service" any of them pretend to provide, with any such nominal "service" performable far better by private citizens and/or companies, with no state involvement at all.

And, unlike all those government agencies, private citizens would not have, in performing any such services, the power to threaten anyone they deal with with punishment and/or personal and financial ruin – as every single one of those agencies has and routinely does.

Regarding any such "services," It's simple: would you prefer to buy a product from a private company that has to actually please you to make a sale? Or would you actually prefer to be forced to buy a drastically inferior version of that same product at a hyper-inflated, monopoly price from a thug who is armed to the teeth and can destroy your life if you disagree with him at all, including if you want to buy something he's unilaterally decided to prevent you from buying? The second of those two alternatives is exactly what happens when any government agency performs any "service."

And, indeed, many of those government agencies do absolutely nothing of any even-arguable value whatsoever for citizens, and do nothing but parasitically prey on the businesses comprising entire segments of the economy, exclusively benefiting politicians, bureaucrats and lawyers and other parasites whose services become essential as intermediaries for those preyed-upon businesses simply to survive in the face of those agencies' oppression, and "helping" the incumbent businesses they "regulate" by turning them into corrupted cronies/ virtual monopolies or oligopolies, by effectively precluding competition from new businesses.

Those incumbent businesses have no choice but to agree to that corrupt involvement of the government in their business and market once they are threatened by politicians with being federally-"regulated" – or else simply go out of business altogether. The government literally makes them an offer they can't refuse regarding that "regulation" – indistinguishable from mafia thugs, though dressed up by politically-passed laws.

Oh, and the presence of those agencies in those segments – which, in 2016, is virtually every single American market segment – of the economy guarantees that the products or services involved in those regulated areas will never improve, their customers' choices will be drastically limited, and will cost their customers many times what they would have if the government agency did not exist. This is no exaggeration.

Using the example of just a few of these agencies, as I do below, and comparing the promises made by politicians in creating them, with the dismal reality they have without exception produced, leaves no doubt of their utter, lawless, practical worthlessness – and their profound destructiveness to our freedom and prosperity —In utilitarian/pragmatic terms. In the chapter preceding this one, I showed how every single one of those agencies – which steal completely, without compensation, the power of actual control over every business they "regulate" – is utterly immoral under unambiguous Judeo-Christian directives. Their manifest unconstitutionality is proven in later chapters below.

Among the many, politically-driven, nonsensical legal claims the courts have sustained with respect to these agencies, and the laws which create them, is the judge-invented "legal" fiction that government-confiscation of legal and actual control over a business in the form of "regulation" of every aspect of it – including all its products and/or services, its pricing, its contractual relations with others, including its employees, its hiring and firing policies and compensation to employees, etc. – somehow, magically, simply does not constitute a "taking" of any property interest of the owner by the government; if it did, the government would be required to pay the full value for that taking under the Constitution's Fifth Amendment.

This distinction between "regulation" and confiscation of what is in fact the most important property interest – control – of any business, a distinction concocted by lawyers and judges completely out of thin air, is logically, factually and intellectually frivolous and, accordingly, legally, as well as morally, groundless.

And it is far from true that any of those agencies are, as they all invariably claim, an essential, or even decent, part of America. As mentioned above, and as amazing as it may seem today, not a single one of them existed prior to 1887 (I will tell you about its creation and history), and the second one, one of the four discussed in this chapter below, was not created until 1906.

And I have not selected the four agencies briefly described below based on their particular monstrousness: all the others – every single one of them – is equally monstrous, each in its own particular way; I selected the ones described below as mere representative examples. Even with respect to those four, I have limited my description to what space here permits. A complete description of all the horrors of every single one of these agencies would be at least as long as the tens of thousands of pages of "regulations" – unconstitutional "laws," that is – which they have produced, every single page of which reduces the freedom and prosperity of all — yes, all — Americans.

Each of these agencies was created by Congress, or in some cases simply by the president acting unilaterally and imperially, deciding to impose federal control over a designated portion of the economy – and all businesses/property and individuals affected thereby – by passing legislation outlining the type of control it wanted and creating the agency it appointed as the "regulator" to take such control, which legislation the president signed and, if and when its constitutionality was judicially challenged, the federal courts came up with arguments they manufactured (yes that is exactly how they do it – out of thin air) purportedly showing how the legislation and the agency were indeed Constitutional, and so could lawfully have been created any time prior thereto in the Republic's history since 1789.

There are hundreds (the exact number is unclear) of federal "regulatory" agencies, each of which arose as the supposed "solution" to something which some politically-potent group consisting of some combination of activist citizens, government employees, journalists, professors, politicians, or some or all of those, managed to lobby Congress to create, with each proponent of its creation pushing it for its own, particular reasons – the good of the Republic be damned.

Each of these agencies was created, in contempt of the requirements of the Constitution, by our elected officials based on their (purported utilitarian) claims that these agencies would effect genuine improvements, which would benefit the citizenry, in existing markets, each of which market was sufficiently important that it commanded the attention of politicians who coveted control over it.

In the chapters which follow this one, I prove that this claim of government capability of "improving" markets — markets which all were already subject to the discipline of the market itself and to Common-Law rules — is inherently fraudulent and impossible, for immutable, structural reasons, and that the laws creating and empowering the agencies all constitute Bad Law, and are identical to laws created previously by the worst tyrannies in history for the sole purpose of turning the people subject to them into serfs.

Each of these agencies — and its bureaucrats — has virtually unlimited power, as a practical, if not always as a strictly legal matter, to impose its will on citizens identified as its target jurisdiction, plus all others who it chooses to include within its jurisdiction as it seeks to expand it – which process of constant, practically-limitless jurisdictional expansion is one of the most constant features of all these administrative agencies.

The only limiting principles any of them recognize are the threat of damage by politicians (an extremely rare occurrence in real life), who supposedly supervise them, or, more importantly, orders by federal courts precluding them from acting in a particular manner – also exceedingly rare, for the reasons described above (the Supreme Court has cavalierly given all such agencies extraordinary discretionary powers – each one of them a miniature Court of Star Chamber, with combined legislative, executive and judicial power sufficient to destroy anyone and any business under its jurisdiction).

To illustrate the utter worthlessness – and genuine evil – apart from their utter unconstitutionality, which I prove in a later chapter below, I thought it worthwhile to describe briefly the origins and actions of four such agencies, each of which is truly monstrous in its own way, inflicting grave harm on citizens in multiple ways, for no genuine purpose whatsoever other than maintaining its power over citizens, providing a vehicle for rent-seeking by politicians, and providing employment to endless numbers of lawyers and bureaucrats without any value to the actual economy – and, indeed, inflicting grave harm on it.

### My Position With Respect to All Federal Agencies And Cabinet Departments Created since 1887

I want to be absolutely crystal clear, without the slightest possibility of confusion or ambiguity, about what precisely I prove (and that is the precise, non-hyperbolic word applicable) in this book, which I summarize as follows:

Each and every one of the federal alphabet agencies – and multiple cabinet-level executive branch departments that have been added, primarily during the 20th century – is:

(1)  created by "laws" which themselves are historically and substantively based on, and derived from, substantively-identical laws enacted by the most-tyrannical rulers of continental European nations, tyrants who devised and unilaterally (their absolute rule made popular approval and/or legislative branch enactment unnecessary) decreed such laws for the deliberate purpose of exercising absolute control over their populations, reducing their subjects' legal status to that of serfs or virtual serfs;

(2)  each of these agencies (other than the IRS), all the "laws" creating them, and all "regulations" and directives they themselves issue, are utterly unconstitutional for multiple reasons, without even a colorable claim to Constitutional legitimacy, with some such agencies even more-egregiously unconstitutional than others by virtue of their particular multiple violations of additional prohibitions in the Constitution, i.e., the FCC, the FEC and the SEC were <u>specifically formed</u> to infringe on freedoms of speech and assembly of all kinds, and the FDA routinely does the same, in addition to constituting unlawful Courts of Star Chamber, each recognizing no limits to its jurisdiction, and constantly striving to expand its power;

(3)  each of these agencies, the "laws" they are based on, and all of their actions, including their constant enacting of "regulations," are utterly immoral and plainly violate God's unambiguous directives in the 10 Commandments – including His implicit directive that those Commandments are <u>comprehensive and exclusive</u> in their scope, and implicitly declare freedom-destroying, enslaving and absolutely immoral all laws forbidding conduct which the Commandments themselves do not expressly forbid;

(4) each of these agencies, and all the "laws" creating them, impose tyrannies on the American people far worse than those imposed by the British government our founders fought our Revolution against, and freedom from precisely such tyrannical, permission-requiring, Star Chamber-creating laws and agencies had already been won by their and our forebears in the English revolutions of the 17th century, revolutions whose victories for citizens' freedom our founders specifically and deliberately intended to continue and build on in our Revolution and Constitution;

(5) not a single one of these agencies provide any actual, practical value whatsoever to the general welfare of the nation (although they each corruptly provide immediate benefits to some citizens – always at the expense of others – creating corrupt constituencies politically-supporting their continued existence); they each impose monstrous tyrannies on the lives and property of those citizens and businesses they target, diminishing the wealth and freedom of the entire nation enormously, with any "services" they pretend to perform for the public invariably performed at exorbitant, absurd cost and incompetently, in precisely the manner one would expect from a truly-tyrannical, violence-threatening, monopoly provider (which is what every one of them is), with all such services capable of being performed vastly better by private businesses forced to answer for their actions to market forces and the Common Law.

(6) each of these agencies was formed based on fraudulent claims in support of their supposed value and, in promoting its own bureaucratic interests, constantly make fraudulent pronouncements to the public, with the result that their very presence is utterly corrupt and destructive to the actual rule of law in the nation, and they invariably make themselves impervious to reform; and various "laws" enacted by Congress prescribing procedures they are to follow, together with multiple rulings of the federal courts, have had the effect of shielding all actions by these agencies from any actual political, legal, or other limits.

For example, the federal courts follow a rule under which <u>no</u> action by these agencies can be challenged <u>in advance</u> by any citizen, and the agencies themselves are free to prescribe civil penalties for violations of their directives, so that citizens are forced to wait until they have <u>actually violated</u> an agency "regulation" or other action before they can even seek the extremely-limited judicial review the courts permit – thereby exposing themselves to truly-staggering fines as a precondition to seeking even that limited review.

The abolition of any one of these agencies, let alone all of them as I am advocating in this book, would instantly increase the growth rate of the economy, with no harm to anyone other than the parasites who feast on its presence, by no less than half a percentage point per year. Freedom and justice for all of the nation would improve dramatically as a result of eliminating each, let alone all, of these agency abominations.

The particular, purely-exemplary, agencies I will be discussing here are the FDA, the SEC, the FCC, the and the FEC. And there are untold hundreds more, each one just as fraudulently-initiated and as monstrously destructive of individual liberty and our nation's prosperity as these, each in its own way.

The FDA.

The FDA was born with legislation proposed by Theodore Roosevelt, passed by Congress and signed into law in 1906, deliberately-vaguely forbidding the transportation of "adulterated" food or drugs across state lines (the interstate commerce aspect of the federal statute was a fig leaf pretending to comply with the requirements of the Commerce clause which, as clearly shown below, in chapter 11, provided no authority whatsoever for such legislation).

The deliberate vagueness of that term "adulterated," and the imposition, with no Constitutional support whatsoever, of criminal penalties for violation of that ambiguous prohibition, effectively imposed a requirement on all interstate businesses involved in any part of the producing of drugs or food of any kind to first obtain permission from the federal government for its sale, in order simply not to be in peril of having inadvertently violated the increasingly-draconian law. The legislation was modeled on similar legislation in absolutist, tyrannical Imperial Germany, which Roosevelt greatly admired.

And that permission-requiring feature of the legislation was exactly what was intended: the statute was a classic wolf in sheep's clothing, pretending that the federal government could "guarantee" "safe" food and drugs, in a way that no private businesses were capable of – notwithstanding the fact that the federal government has no competence whatsoever at performing any service other than those specified in the Constitution, none of which include guaranteeing the safety of food and drugs – or anything else.

The railroad business was the only American business which had previously been so "regulated." But the railroad business at least had obtained all its initial financing from the federal government, as discussed below, creating extraordinary windfalls for its owners. All the vast number of businesses whose effective control was taken over in 1906 had developed and grown exclusively through the efforts and success solely of their owners and managers, with no federal assistance whatsoever.

Public safety and "necessity" were, of course, the claimed purposes for this truly radical legislation – as always – with a virtual built-in guarantee that it would never be able to deliver on its promises. Like all government guarantees of that nature, also guaranteed was that any harm to anyone by any food or drug product that managed to make it through the government inspection process – and yes, that was guaranteed to happen incident to the legislation – and harmed anyone, would always be blamed on the private business or businesses involved in its production, with the government always exonerated – and invariably demanding more and more power to pretend to overcome all of its manifest, and inevitable, failures.

No human is perfect – particularly the government. The only difference is that the government always is rewarded — always at the expense of the citizenry, whether they know it or not — for its failures, instead of being put out of business, as always happens to private citizens and businesses who, unlike the government, are subject to the discipline of the market and the Common Law. The government is exempt from all that discipline, and it and its functionaries actually profit from its failures.

Self-identified "Progressives" in and out of the government, including various power-seeking bureaucrats in the federal Agriculture Department, which had been earlier established (also with no Constitutional basis), Prohibition movement supporters, self-identified Communists, and other anti-constitutionalists, had been lobbying for such a law for decades. And, there was, in fact, perfectly-adequate law in each of the states empowering them to impose civil and criminal liability for genuine misconduct – the policing function reserved exclusively for them under the Constitution. As shown in Chapter 11, the deliberate misreading of the Commerce clause, as the pretended Constitutional basis purportedly to permit the massive federal takeover involved in the FDA -creating legislation was fraudulent — and, in 1906, not even supported by a single judicial decision.

To fully understand how monstrous this frontal assault on food and drug businesses was: In the last half of the 19th century, truly revolutionary developments had been occurring in the various businesses involved in growing and raising different types of foods, and facilitating their packaging and delivery throughout the nation, particularly to city dwellers living far from the farms where the food originated. Similarly revolutionary developments were taking place in the inventing and manufacturing of what we would call drugs of all kinds. All these developments were as revolutionary as they were beneficial – literally transforming medicine and people's diets, with transformative benefits to Americans' health and lifestyles far beyond what the practice of medicine itself was capable of at that time.

Together with extraordinary technological developments of all kinds, including the invention of new kinds of farming equipment, these developments made it possible for the nation to become a nation primarily of city-dwellers, rather than rural farmers, permitting the even more rapid development of manufacturing businesses than had been occurring throughout the 19th century.

As always with such transformative benefits, all of which were, of course, available to Americans of all income levels, and were produced by American businesses and American businessmen, the various communities who hate everything businessmen do, who I have described above as the lobbyists for this particular monstrous law, had been doing so, as I said, for decades. The federal government alone was capable of suppressing all this growth in all these areas of the economy

– with nothing in the Constitution, nor in reason, permitting such – and it spent the entire 20th century doing so, benefitting no one but parasites in and out of the government — and harming everyone else.

And the industries those activists detested and wanted to "regulate" had continued to innovate and serve the public (who were happy to buy their products, whose prices got better and better through competition, as always happens in a free market) – until two things occurred making the new legislation politically possible: (1)President Theodore Roosevelt decided, as part of his manic activism and socialist and pure-snobbish loathing of all businesses, to back the legislation, and (2) a manifestly-fraudulent novel, The Jungle, appeared (yes, this made a huge difference amazingly enough) by the self-identified radical socialist Upton Sinclair which purported to describe the genuinely remarkable meat-packing business as an utterly corrupt, monstrous enterprise dedicated to crushing its own employees and poisoning its customers.

Theodore Roosevelt, who was very popular at the time, for his own reasons deliberately hyped Sinclair's book and the claims it made about that remarkable industry, knowing perfectly well that all such claims were utterly fraudulent and based on no evidence whatsoever, in his support of the legislation he apparently had wanted all along, in what is perhaps the first instance in American history of "The Big Lie."

Hitler is notorious today for admitting to using that same technique, and openly described in writing I quote in a later chapter what "The Big Lie" technique is and why it works better than telling small lies, when deployed by a sociopath – no one else would use it – against decent people.

Roosevelt's cynical and, indeed, revolutionary assault on Americans and our Constitution by using such a technique literally made him an entirely new kind of president – an anti-George Washington president – transforming the whole nature of the presidency into what he unabashedly called the "bully pulpit," meaning the extra-constitutional stage from which the president could extra-legally browbeat and harm decent, American people and businesses, and/or trick them into tolerating his Constitutionally-forbidden government actions destructive of their freedom and, ultimately of their prosperity.

Note that at the same time Roosevelt took these monstrous, cynical steps to facilitate the enactment of that radical legislation, proponents of alcohol prohibition were well aware that they needed a constitutional amendment to achieve their end – and were actively pushing for such. Roosevelt's even more radical "regulatory" legislation (considering the enormous, multiple portions of the economy taken over by it) was promoted and adopted without even bothering with the Constitution. He and Congress just went ahead and did it on their own, gratuitously.

As indicated above, they pretended to base the legislation on the Commerce clause. But if the Commerce clause supported regulation of every aspect of the food and drug businesses, why wouldn't it similarly permit "regulation" of the far-more-limited alcohol business? The question answers itself.

And the fact that alcohol prohibitionists knew they needed a constitutional amendment to institute alcohol prohibition proves that they, and Roosevelt, who did not advocate for or against prohibition itself, were similarly well aware of the utter unconstitutionality of the food and drug legislation of 1906 – which metastasized over the years and became ever more radical in its control over those two businesses – radically controlling the choices available to those businesses' customers, and drastically increasing the prices — by many orders of magnitude — we Americans have paid for the products we have even been allowed to purchase..

A few more words about the FDA's founding: Theodore Roosevelt admitted he agreed with Karl Marx on all substantive matters, other than his anti-Americanism and the permissible method for imposing his ideas on America: he was opposed to any military revolution for such. He is discussed in greater detail below, but it is worth considering how it is that this particular agency came to begin during the beginning of his second term in office, the first one in which he was actually elected as president, in 1904.

Although the agency with its full-blown powers to dictate with absolute authority what drugs and medical devices citizens are allowed to purchase, and businesses are allowed to sell them, was only in its beginning stages at the time of its creation in 1906, the knowingly-unconstitutional radicalism involved in that creation needs to be appreciated – and the utterly fraudulent reasons for its creation show the utter corruption of the entire process.

The FDA's fraudulent, Marxist origins and nature — promising everything, destroying freedom of choice and all markets it touched, killing multitudes by preventing even the sickest from trying possible cures, unable to do anything of value, and always blaming regulated businesses for any later perceived failure — have remained integral parts of its culture ever since. Its true monstrousness, and ongoing devastating harm to American citizens, both in depriving them of their own choices in purchases, and vastly increasing the expense of everything made that can go in our mouths to feed or to heal us, cannot be fully catalogued without an entire book to do so – or many.

in fact, numerous books have been written showing the FDA's utter incompetence both for supposedly "under-regulating"— because it can never achieve perfection — and "over-regulating" — by imposing impediments to new products, and creating testing regimens that are literally monstrous and reminiscent of Nazi-type human experimentation, as mandatory prerequisites for every drug to go through before the public is allowed to exercise its choice to buy it.

For example, after the FDA determines a drug is "safe" – that is, that it will harm no one if taken – the drug still is not allowed to be purchased by, or sold to, anyone until it then goes through the <u>really expensive</u> testing process whose sole purpose is the Marxist one of making it difficult for drug companies to get profits. There is no conceivable alternative explanation for the bureaucratic requirement that drug companies prove their drugs are "effective" to the satisfaction of the FDA's self-proclaimed "experts" who, in fact, notwithstanding the academic degrees they may be festooned with, know far less than the companies which actually invent, manufacture, and produce the drugs – companies which are more than capable, under the discipline of the market and the Common Law, of deciding if they want to sell them, particularly after the drugs' safety <u>has already been proven</u>.

Specifically, the manufacturer must prove to the satisfaction of the FDA "experts" that the drug, in a one-size-fits-all formulation, all by itself, is "effective" on a pure-ly-statistical basis supposedly for everyone, regardless of their genome (which, of course, is ascertainable now). If it is enormously effective when combined with some other drug, that is deemed insufficient, so that suffering patients who could benefit from it in that circumstance are prevented from buying it. Similarly, if the drug is fantastically effective for certain people with identifiable genomes, but not for others, they too are not permitted to buy it. This is horrifically-cruel, murderous Marxist madness. And utterly unconstitutional to boot, as I prove in Chapter 11.

The testing the FDA requires is what it calls "double-blind" testing – what it erro-neously and incompetently claims is the only scientific way of proving a drug's effectiveness. That testing is enormously expensive because it presumes that to be "effective" a drug must be so for virtually anyone who might take it, without regard to their personal characteristics, so a large, statistically-significant group of guinea pigs – sick humans desperate for the drug in fact – must be assembled to take it – with half of them, murderously, thinking they are getting the real drug, and hoping to God they are, but are in fact receiving a placebo instead!

As just one of thousands of glaring, monstrous instances of how evil what the FDA is doing in all respects, consider the fact that 40% of cancer patients are so desperate for help that they are eager to enter these double-blind drug studies for experimental drugs merely to have a 50% chance of even getting the drug (with the other 50% getting a placebo), standing in line and begging doctors, FDA officials etc. to do so, and only 3% of all cancer patients (less than 10% of that 40%) are able to do so, with thousands dying every year with no chance even to have that 50% chance. Congress has forced the FDA to behave in this manner through its legislation, and the FDA bureaucrats cheerfully oblige – presiding over the deaths of thousands of our fellow citizens. And all this in the name of safety and security!

At any rate, as always, there has always been state law more than sufficient to police the drug and food companies in their sales of goods which the people want to buy, and the federal government has never had any constitutional power permitting it – and unlike prohibition, the FDA was created with no Constitu-tional amendment to support it.

If the antitrust laws were amended – or, better yet, repealed – the businesses involved in producing food and drugs could more-easily and competently promote independent businesses to audit the safety and effectiveness of their products – as the accounting business does for the finances of businesses – which would be vastly more competent and even more-vastly less oppressive, less expensive, and destructive of life, liberty and justice than the FDA.

As it is, the drug companies who must comply with the onerous requirements of the FDA have been corrupted in all their own processes, as has the the entire process of science research in the nation, by the FDA and other federal agencies responsible for supervising and funding scientific research. Only the very largest companies, particularly ones who ingratiate themselves politically – as is always necessary with any government agency – have a chance of surviving with the FDA present, guaranteeing that new companies who attempt to compete are at an enormous disadvantage because of the difficulty of complying with the FDA's endless regulations.

It is impossible to know what drugs have never been produced that would have been beneficial, even if only to small populations for rare diseases, and how much more expensive food and all drugs are today, and how few supermarket chains there are (as you may have noticed if you have eyes) competing with each other. It is a known fact that every drug permitted to be sold today is, indeed, safe and effective, as proven to the FDA, and that everyone was forbidden to use it for many years prior to its FDA approval – many of whom died as a result of the FDA's prohibition on their purchasing drugs which, in many cases, many of them knew about and wanted.

The FDA claims, using <u>statistics alone</u>, that its actions save lives. The truth is, it has killed countless thousands who were deprived of the medications they wanted, not even including all who have been deprived of drugs whose manufacturers simply lacked the resources to run the FDA's gauntlet for approval. Apart from its fraudulent statistics, it cannot actually prove a single instance in which anything it did was of any value — except to parasites in and out of the government, including the FDA itself and its business-loathing, parasite employees.

In any event, the FDA fraudulently presents itself as performing various services for the public. It was formed based on massive fraud and deception and power grabbing by the federal government. Any service it actually pretends to perform could be better done by private businesses who don't have the powers to prevent people from buying what they want, or of putting people in jail who disagree with it. And the American public would benefit enormously if it were terminated immediately.

The idea that American citizens should be denied the right to buy whatever they want to ingest into their own bodies for their health is insulting to any notion of their being freemen.

The idea that any of us should have to beg permission from bureaucrats, who literally have the power of life and death over our fellow citizens in their hands, hands which have no capability whatsoever other than the power to harm anyone who stands in their way, without regard to morality, decency or even law itself, simply for the chance to be a guinea pig tells you all you need to know about the FDA and all legislation creating and enabling it.

All that legislation needs to be repealed. It is nothing but Bad Law, as explained in detail in chapter 5. It cannot be reformed. It has no business in a nation dedicated to individual liberty. And it is all utterly unconstitutional, as also proven in Chapter 11.

### The SEC

The SEC was formed in 1933 as part of FDR's New Deal. Like the FDA, all of the arguments in favor of forming it were completely fraudulent, even if that fact was not well-known at the time. The legislation which created and empowered the SEC (the various federal securities laws) sweepingly authorizes it dictatorially to "regulate," all corporate stocks and bonds, and all public companies which are their issuers, everyone involved in their sale at any time, and all markets in which they are sold.

What the SEC really does is impose all sorts of utterly-worthless, dictatorial mandates and directives, supposedly based on the nonsensical notion that bureaucrats have the ability, godlike, to "improve" markets it controls, markets which its very power over them necessarily distorts, corrupts, and destroys, as shown in the next chapter, all supposedly for the benefit of market participants.

It imposes mindless controls, and endless, worthless, and expensive bureaucratic red tape, on all communications and actions of all market participants, including stock-issuing corporations, traders of all kinds, brokers, dealers etc., "legal" controls all backed up by endless criminal and civil sanctions on market participants, in violation of multiple provisions of the Constitution, including the First Amendment prohibition on the regulation of speech.

It literally criminalizes otherwise perfectly-legal and harmless behavior and speech in its endlessly-hopeless and preposterous attempt to achieve a Marxist idea of "perfect" equality among all market participants — and to punish those who, in its radical bureaucrats' minds, simply make too much money, even where no identifiable victim of their doing so actually exists! It constantly expands the scope of its directives in an endless quest to justify its existence and expand its tyrannical power. It even has its own unconstitutional Star Chamber kangaroo "courts" it forces honest citizens in to contest its ruthless attacks, "courts" citizens have no chance for justice in — and where citizens literally never win.

Without getting into any technical details of the laws the SEC itself unconstitutionally creates – again, backed up by brutal civil and criminal sanctions – it literally outlaws and terrorizes all market participants for actions which actually harm no other actual market participant (any actual harm would be actionable under state tort and/or criminal law), based exclusively on completely-unproven, and unprovable, "economic" theories that such outlawed actions harm "the market as a whole" – a radical collectivist notion if ever there was one. And I am not exaggerating.

The underlying basis for creating the SEC was the nonsense claims that the Great Depression was caused by irresponsible trading of basically-fraudulent securities which ended up causing the great stock crash in 1929. Although there were indeed many people who harmed themselves in their mistaken stock trading, neither they, nor any stock-issuers, caused the Great Depression. Like all genuine market catastrophes, such could only happen because of the government imposing its brutal, endlessly-incompetent hand and wreaking havoc on the lives and fortunes of real markets and people.

But, as is always the case with government-caused disasters, its own culpability made it all the more important to find scapegoats – and that was the real purpose of blaming the stock crash of 1929, for the genuine horror which became the Great Depression, whose terrible longevity was also caused by massive government destructive intervention in real people's businesses and lives. And that was the real purpose for creating the SEC and its underlying legislation — to take massive government action consistent with that scapegoating, and to distract the public from the real culprit — government's inherently-destructive control over all aspects of the economy, including money itself.

Milton Friedman has conclusively proven – to the satisfaction of "economists" of all stripes – that the Great Depression was not caused by the stock crash, but rather primarily by actions by the (unconstitutional) Federal Reserve, and additional political mistakes by Pres. Hoover and the Republican Congress, political mistakes – a proposed huge income tax increase, and actually enacted massive tariff, increases which so destroyed the economy of Germany that the Weimar Republic collapsed and Hitler came to power – which certainly made it worse.

These mistakes were continued and magnified when FDR became president in 1933 and instituted The New Deal, including creating and empowering the SEC, all of which, as admitted by FDR's own treasury secretary in 1939, was an utter failure – and yet none of its liberty-and-prosperity-destroying legislation has ever been repealed to this day (except to the extent that the Supreme Court initially declared part of it unconstitutional). And yet all the admittedly-worthless, destructive agencies FDR created, including the SEC, live on — for what besides crushing markets and empowering parasites?

The idea behind the SEC on its face is nonsense: the notion is that sophisticated people buying and selling stock are too stupid to do so, and that stock markets, which had existed since the time of the Romans, needed government meddling to be "perfected." The SEC has always pretended that it has some magic formula to prevent fraud in stock markets. As always with such claims by government agencies, nothing could be further from the truth.

In fact, in its entire history, there is <u>not a single instance</u> when the SEC, notwithstanding its numerous enforcement lawyers and other functionaries, has ever actually detected and/or stopped <u>a single</u> massive securities fraud – such as Ponzi schemes – even in numerous instances, such as in the case of the Madoff fraud, when such schemes were <u>actually brought to its attention</u> long before others brought them down.

Again, the people who supposedly "require" the SEC's "services" are among the most sophisticated business people in the nation, people, that is with sufficient resources – and the desire – to purchase public-company stocks and securities with no "assistance" from an inherently tyrannical and incompetent agency. In real life, what the SEC has done has added enormous costs to any company choosing to go, and remain, public – costs forcibly born by its shareholders, inevitably, who are supposedly the people the SEC is assisting in supposedly preserving the value of their investments.

In fact, the enormity of the costs the supposed "beneficiaries" of the SEC are forced to bear guarantees that they get nothing of value from the SEC— and the securities they purchase necessarily <u>lose</u> value as a direct consequence of its actions and worthless (except to bureaucrats, morally-preening sanctimonious politicians, and other countless parasites, none of whom add any value whatsoever to the economy, nor to any of the securities under the SEC's dictatorial rule) requirements.

The SEC began its existence by imposing all sorts of burdens on issuers and sellers of securities, including formal stock-registration (with the SEC) requirements, and all sorts of other bells and whistles, including all the details of how stock issuers, investment bankers, and brokers may speak to others about any security – a clear violation of the First Amendment. None of the SEC's directives have ever actually added <u>any</u> value to any security. The SEC's argument in support of itself has always been its claim of preserving the integrity of markets and preventing fraud.

In fact, every state has long had its own anti-fraud laws which are more than adequate for all purposes, and no one is better able to oversee the integrity of a market <u>than its own participants</u>, participants who can sue if any of them are actually harmed.

Again, as in the case of the food and drug businesses discussed above, if market participants of any kind desire some kind of "regulator" to referee their activities, an exemption from the antitrust laws would permit them to create such themselves to their own satisfaction (and they are the only ones with an actual interest in this whole business). Unlike the SEC, whose interposition into markets is <u>forced</u> on the market participants whether they like it or not, and without regard to its competence or value (which is zero), those affected market participants could police such a regulator, which they are incapable of doing with the SEC except, at best, through political processes – which inherently are corrupt, in part because of the power over them of the SEC itself.

In any event, the only thing the SEC is able to bring to the table is its power to destroy anyone, including all markets, under its jurisdiction – a power it is constantly seeking to expand the more worthless everyone involved (secretly) knows it to be. The only beneficiaries of its presence are the countless lawyers and accountants and bureaucrats made necessary by its presence – none of whom add anything of any value to the actual economy or to the nation's wealth.

Among the uncountable, numerous, inherently-corrupting results of the SEC's intervention in security markets – always supposedly to make them "fairer" and more honest, particularly to small investors – has been that it has, since its creation, constantly come up with new rules for how those market should operate, rules which over time have become increasingly complex, particularly after computer trading entered the picture, to the point that the complexity alone of those rules creates trading opportunities for traders simply involved in what could be called regulatory arbitrage.

This has actually resulted in a never-ending process in which the SEC initially enacts market-regulating rules, traders take advantage of them, rather than trading securities based on genuine market considerations, followed by the SEC viewing those trading practices as evil and corrupt, often resulting in prosecutions of traders engaging in that activity – typically as show-trial victims – followed by a new set of rules by the SEC further complicating the market, resulting in new arbitrage trading opportunities, etc.

The net result of this today is that the SEC has itself undermined its self-proclaimed purpose in enacting all these rules, in that it has made trading by most ordinary individuals virtually impossible. Specifically, the SEC invariably investigates any investor who actually makes a noticeably-large profit in any market, on various theories, subjecting such successful investors to huge expenses and the personal nightmare of living through an endless investigation by a federal agency with no limits on its resources to harass investors – an agency, mind you, whose investigators' careers are enhanced by each "scalp" they are able to take from real people, based on the wholly-imaginary economic theories relied on by the SEC.

And that monstrous, tyrannical agency even forces targeted citizens into its own, unconstitutional, Star Chamber kangaroo courts which never fail to rule against those citizens.

Again, if the SEC were abolished today, and all of the unconstitutional federal securities "laws" (including the monstrous ones the SEC has written itself) were repealed – no constitutional amendment has ever been enacted permitting them – the real economy would benefit enormously, both in the value to companies of going public, and in the value added to the economy that fact alone could bring, resulting in stronger, more effective corporations, more employment, and untold economic growth.

And anyone who is <u>actually</u> defrauded or otherwise harmed by other stock market participants has more-than-sufficient remedies available to him under the law of every state in the nation – no federal law needed or Constitutionally-permitted at all.

## The FCC

The FCC violates multiple constitutional provisions by its mere existence. Like all the other alphabet agencies discussed here, the sole, legally-claimed Constitutional basis for its existence is the Commerce clause. As shown in Chapter 11, that claim is sheer, fraudulent nonsense.

The FCC's purpose for existence has always been to impose absolute, dictatorial federal control over every single business involved in every method of communication it is permitted, by its control, to socialize.

To those who object to that characterization: it is apparent that when an industry has to answer in every respect to federal overlords, the fact that its owners continue to be allowed to make financial profits (themselves subject to control by their federal master) cannot negate the fact that actual control — the most important property interest — of each company so regulated is, as a direct result of that "regulation," removed from its owners and executives and placed in the hands of the state, its politicians and unelected, faceless (to the public, but not to those whose businesses they control) bureaucrats. And make no mistake: control is <u>the single most important</u> attribute of ownership of any company, and particularly so for a company in the business of communicating information – or, when under the thumb of the FCC, disinformation, or even fraud.

You can call that federal control partial socialism, or fascism (it is indistinguishable from the tyrannical control over all businesses exercised by the Kaiser and Bismarck, Hitler and Mussolini) if you prefer.

As shown textually in chapter 6 below, because it demands confiscation by the state of all property, and absolute, dictatorial control over the operation of all "means of production" of all products and services in the nation – i.e., all businesses – Marxism can be boiled down to two simple messages: (1) the state, its functionaries/officeholders and the "experts" who provide them advice have a monopoly on wisdom, virtue and confidence, and (2) all businesses and businessmen are monstrous thieves. Yes, it really is that simple.

With those thoughts in mind, it is apparent that those two Marxist messages provide the underlying logic for federal control of the nation's broadcasting businesses – the sole function of the FCC. Belief in those Marxist messages permeates all employees of that agency and informs every aspect of their operations and control over the broadcasting industry.

Their ability to command the absolute loyalty – under implicit threat of catastrophic destruction to any broadcasting business for failure to follow the FCC's demands – literally puts that agency in the position of being what amounts to the leader of a mob – the mob being the broadcasting businesses themselves – all of which constantly militate in the messages and "news" provided to the public on behalf of promoting those two Marxist messages – all without the necessity that any individual involved in any of the businesses or the agency itself is actually aware of the Marxist origins of all their actions and demands.

To pretend that absolute FCC control of all broadcast businesses is consistent with a free nation, and that it does not eviscerate the First Amendment with respect to all the most powerful means of communication in the nation (broadcasting of all kinds), is preposterous. To pretend that it is moral is equally preposterous, as shown in the immediately-preceding chapter. And that control also provides no public benefit whatsoever since it invariably constricts the businesses so taken over, precludes new competitors, reduces the value of what the public gets from its broadcasters, and increases prices for a lesser product or service. What could be better than that?

And in 1913, when the FCC was formed, all these fundamental features of the FCC were well-known — and thereby instituted. The radical progressives ruling America at that time – after the election of Wilson and the campaign of Theodore Roosevelt – could not have been more intimidating to anyone and any business they targeted for control. And it was they who created the FCC and imposed it on all electronic means of communication in the nation – and on the public.

No one will ever know if the phone company – the first business subjected to its iron fist, which was turned into a monopoly thereby, with all the terrible consequences of such which the antitrust laws had been enacted supposedly to prevent – accepted that regulation voluntarily; as always, businesses simply have no choice but to collapse in the face of the state's lawless, existential threat because, as has long been observed, nothing so concentrates the mind as the prospect of the gallows.

In the chapter after this one, I explain how it is an inherent fact that no business, necessarily armed with nothing but market power, can ever survive when confronted by the power of violence commanded by the state – and how that confrontation always necessarily results in the destruction of the market itself, inflicting nothing but harm on the citizenry, as well as the businesses so commandeered by politicians and bureaucrats.

The FCC take-over of the very means of most effective communication throughout the nation is additionally monstrous because it is deliberately designed to preclude any actual, non-private, free speech over those very means of communication – violating the First Amendment. That is its purpose: nothing is more important to radical collectivists – which is what Progressives have always been – than silencing all opposition and flooding, and commandeering, those most-powerful communications to the public with propaganda, in this case made all that much more effective because it masquerades as mere privately-created entertainment or "the news," as opposed to just "news," suggesting some genuine objectivity in its images of society and events portrayed over those means of communication.

But as monstrous and tyrannical as all those aspects and attributes of the FCC have always been, all that only scratches the surface of its genuine evil – and the massive fraud on the public it has at least assisted in perpetrating, as discussed below.

This socialization – complete federal control stolen (that's what a taking of the single most important attribute of ownership without compensation unambiguously is) from private hands – so imposed was not only on the owners of the broadcast businesses: that socialization, like all federal takeovers, imposed a state-controlled, unassailable monopoly on all the very information – and, in reality, disinformation, and often outright fraud, which American citizens have been provided – or, rather, bombarded with – in the most powerful media for dissemination of such. That monopoly would still exist – had not private cable companies, and eventually the Internet, provided alternative sources of such information.

So the Obama FCC is now brazenly presuming to take over the Internet – in the face of actual legislation barring any federal regulation of it all – all while fraudulently pretending not to do so. And there is no guarantee that politicized, spineless courts will do anything to stop it. Only repealing all its enabling legislation can do so.

The FCC has rigidly controlled, directly and indirectly, not only the tiny number of broadcast networks – deliberately keeping the total number of privately-owned broadcast networks limited to three – but has also guaranteed that all privately-owned radio and TV stations must kowtow to its demands since none of them are actually owned by their "owners," but rather are simply licensed by the FCC, with all license revokable at its total discretion.

This monopoly control over all American broadcast media, tightly held by the FCC since 1913, ultimately resulted in the "news" heard by people everywhere on all FCC-controlled networks invariably being virtually identical – because all of it had to conform to the wishes of that radical-leftist, government control. Actual threats of destruction to the media by the FCC were never necessary. This was always because the danger from its control was always apparent to executives in charge of all such media and, over time, all career success by "journalists" required their conformity to the implicit demands of the truly-radical leftists who always controlled the FCC, and who populated its bureaucracy.

As shown in greater detail in a later chapter, the entire journalism profession, for various structural and pecuniary reasons, became enamored by Marxism in the 19th century, and has remained that way ever since, in most cases without most individual journalists even being aware of it. But journalists have known the approaches to the "news" they have needed to take in order to advance within their top-down, ideologically-controlled "profession," and have been taught to do so in university Journalism "professional" schools which, like all schools, have always held the implicit threat of career ruin through lower grades over ideologically-non-conforming students, and with faculties no less enamored with Marxism as the rest of the university since the 1840's.

And, like other professions, by the end of the 19th century, journalists began to claim that they, like other vocations, comprised a status-demanding "profession" and also, for the first time, began pretending that there was such a thing as a genuinely-objective description of facts which they as "professionals" — and supposed "experts" — possessed unique access and insights into, and that they could assemble all the important events of the day and objectively describe them to the public – as "the news," supposedly in contrast to opinion/advocacy journalism, or mere news.

The unanimity of descriptions of "facts" which invariably has emerged from broadcast "news" sources controlled by the FCC has served further to promote that notion (since all the "experts" on such matters agree on their "fact" descriptions, they must all be right), particularly when the hugely-powerful medium of television arrived in the 1950s.

Because of their overwhelmingly-Marxist orientation, journalists in America have consistently produced Marxist-biased (i.e., at least highly skeptical, if not inimical, to America, business, and to anti-collectivist politicians) "news." The claim of objectivity – that they were simply providing objectively-true "news," as opposed to opinion or propaganda – on top of the unanimity of their reporting has had the effect of providing the American public with a steady stream of Marxist propaganda from them made all the more powerful as propaganda because of its pretentious claims and seeming appearance of not being propaganda – unlike the explicitly-identified propaganda of various totalitarian regimes throughout the 20th century, which captive peoples had to at least cynically pretend to believe — or else.

The fact that all supposedly "mainstream" news sources invariably reported virtually identical "news" itself lent credence to the notion that that was indeed the news – since all apparent sources unanimously said it was and said the same things about it.

As discussed below, the FCC even enacted an explicit rule precluding honest broadcast media debates, a rule — "The Fairness Doctrine" was its Orwellian name — which it did not rescind until 1988. And that rule persisted under presidencies of both parties, with never a single president forcing them to rescind it.

I have shown in the previous chapter the complete immorality such theft through such "regulation" plainly is. In the chapters after this one, I show, through an analysis of how different types of law and markets operate in real life, that it is also utterly, and invariably, counterproductive to the broadcast business' customers (who are invariably promised magical benefits from the regulation), and everyone else legitimately contracting with those businesses for any purpose, including, particularly, their employees, whose opportunities for advancement in a growing and prospering business are radically curtailed by the "regulation."

Literally no one benefits other than politicians, bureaucrats and other assorted parasites who feed off of the multiple, perverse effects of the regulation. Washington DC and its suburbs today is populated by those parasites – lawyers, lobbyists, including former Congressman — officials who look forward to enormous compensation after leaving office exclusively for businesses to pay them for their political connections — countless bureaucrats, and the politicians who love the fact that the power they derive from the existence of the "regulations" enables them to extract rent/extortion of all kinds from the businesses so regulated – who either pay or die. Highway robbery would be a polite term for the entire process.

The FCC began its existence in 1913 when AT&T "agreed" to become a completely-regulated monopoly utility. The consequences of that were identical to those which occur every time any business – invariably one, like the railroads in 1887, sufficiently important that the politicians can't, if permitted, keep their hands off of it, as the businesses so-targeted are well aware – becomes subject to political and bureaucratic control in that manner: innovation and investment in the business, and all businesses that compete with it in some manner, come to a screeching halt, competitors are not allowed, and what had been a thriving, ever-improving business, whose prices kept getting better and better along with service, even if only out of fear a competitor would come along, effectively becomes a government-mandated-and-controlled monopoly or oligopoly, frozen in time.

The statute providing for the FCC regulating the phone company was modeled in all of its technical operations on the 1887 Interstate Commerce Act, which had similarly turned the railroad business into a ruined oligopoly that never improved, and whose prices never came down again. Railroad "regulation" was such a failure, from its very start, achieving nothing of benefit to the public, that it was "fixed" repeatedly by politicians pretending to know what they were doing – pretending, that is, to be smarter than God and knowing how to "regulate" a market – and none of those "fixes" ever worked. Even the Carter administration eventually acknowledged its complete failure.

By 1913, when the FCC was created, it was already obvious that regulating the railroads served only to benefit politicians, bureaucrats and parasites. Apparently that was reason enough for those same corrupt beneficiaries to impose a virtually-identical statute on the phone company which, like the railroad companies before it, was delivering a truly-transformative service for the public (spoken communication with anyone anywhere on the planet that had a phone – in real time) that would have been unimaginable previously – since banishment from Eden.

To give you some idea of how insane that FCC regulation was (and remains everywhere it infests any business), if you consider all of the remarkable developments in electronic communications which have occurred – cell phones, video conferencing on the Internet, you name it – and even the specific features of all the different types of telephones available now, consider the fact that they all probably could have been available at least 40 years earlier (all the technology was known then) but were prevented from doing so by the regulated monopoly of the phone company and its FCC federal controllers.

But the FCC has never been willing to limit its jurisdiction to the phone company. Indeed, it has invariably claimed the right to determine the nature and scope of its jurisdiction – and who and what it can subject to its control. It has always, since their invention, also completely controlled all broadcast media – radio and TV – but not cable, and, notwithstanding a gratuitous Supreme Court ruling to the contrary which has no rational basis – has cavalierly violated the First Amendment and sought to control both who was permitted to broadcast under any communication method it controlled, and the content of their communications (the latter by its complete, dictatorial control over all broadcasting companies, and by specifically forbidding certain types of communication).

Lest you have any doubts about this complete, dictatorial control of the FCC over every aspect of the broadcast industry: Remember when there were only three television networks? The FCC made sure that that was the case. And each of them was utterly beholden to its federal masters in political offices and at the FCC, with self-censorship of the content of its broadcasts to please those masters – including politically – inevitable.

But even that guaranteed self-censorship wasn't enough speech-restriction for the FCC: it had an explicit rule, until 1988, called the "fairness doctrine" which had the effect of precluding any honest and open political discussions on TV or radio. The <u>entire industry of talk radio</u> which grew up only after that monstrous, authoritarian rule, which the entire industry had had no choice but to accept, was repealed, had literally been <u>barred</u> by that rule from existing.

As a central feature of its existence, the FCC has always strictly controlled <u>who</u> was allowed to speak and what they were allowed to say in every single communication business it controlled – for fear of losing their license, licenses which are always subject to discretionary review by, and never "owned" by anyone but, the FCC.

And just as FCC regulation thwarted all technological innovation in the telephone business as long as it controlled it – until the 1980s – and grotesquely increased its costs to customers, it similarly thwarted technological improvements in televisions, for example: specifically, manufacturers have always been forced to abide by FCC dictates in the products they produce, which prevented them from providing the high-definition televisions, available now for over a decade, at least 30 years earlier, when the technology was known.

In 2015, the FCC, as demanded by the Obama administration, decided gratuitously to extend its jurisdiction in the most radical manner it had ever done: Over the last 15 years, it is apparent that the only sectors of the technology business that have flourished have been the recently substantially-deregulated phone businesses and all the various hardware and software businesses connected to the Internet, which, as directed by Congress, has never previously been controlled by the FCC. Rest assured: their flourishing has been the direct result of the fact that they have been subject to less "regulation" by tyrannical federal agencies than virtually any other businesses in the nation.

In 2015, the Obama administration made clear to the FCC that it wanted the Internet to be subject to its regulation, just like all the rest of the economy, and all other methods of communication in the nation. The FCC announced its compliance with that request, claiming the Internet is subject to the identical statutes which controlled the telephone company.

The cynicism of that step, including the extraordinary seizure of jurisdiction, recognizing no conceivable limiting principle, and the campaign that preceded it to lay the groundwork for that announcement, could not be more remarkable — and Constitutionally-outrageous.

Specifically, in its announcement of such regulatory seizure of the Internet, the FCC pretended to the public that it had the power and desire, selectively, to only apply those provisions of the telephone regulatory statute it chooses to apply, but not the whole thing. In fact, it has no such discretion to withhold application of the entire statute, if it can actually lawfully apply any of it. That is precisely why Obama demanded that the FCC seize complete control over the Internet under the telephone regulatory statute.

If applicable at all (it is not, as a 1996 statute expressly provides), the telephone-regulating "law" (which itself was completely unconstitutional all along, as shown in Chapter 11) would necessarily include controlling the content and all pricing of the Internet. The FCC is continuing to pretend that that is not the case, and that it has the power selectively to withhold imposing portions of a statute it supposedly may apply to the Internet, in its discretion.

Its efforts to generate at least the appearance of public support for this radical confiscation consisted of an extraordinary public relations campaign to promote the idea that the regulation was simply what it called "net neutrality," a concept it tried to sell particularly to the vast number of unemployed millennials who are ever searching for free stuff, with the FCC claiming they would get better prices (from the cable companies, who those millennials apparently detest) for their Internet service, and service comparable to that of major purchasers of Internet service, notwithstanding their insignificant payments for such, if "net neutrality" was established in law.

And the FCC has been pretending that that is all its "regulatory" Internet takeover ever was. Again, a "Big Lie" was used to sell a federal takeover of private property of an entire industry with the ability to effect communications to the public like none other – or to have such communication shut off or punished sometime in the future by a totalitarian government – that is, a government like the one that seized such control of the Internet with no Congressional authorization to do so whatsoever.

Like all other regulatory seizures of business, it is inconceivable that this will benefit the public in any manner. Business investment in the enormously-expensive Internet infrastructure has already decreased dramatically.

In the next chapter, I prove how this deliberate destruction of an actual market cannot possibly help anyone but parasites. It is literally the deliberate destruction of all genuine market forces and all genuinely-beneficial legal mechanisms which operate in its absence under the common law, as discussed at length below.

It is monstrous, immoral and unconstitutional. And in the case of the Internet, Congress did not even authorize the FCC to effect that seizure. The FCC simply did it unilaterally pretending that a statute that could not possibly have the Internet in mind empowers it to do so.

As always, once such regulatory control is imposed on a particular economic sector, its mere presence utterly corrupts the entire industry, and demands that the businesses involved in it play by the rules imposed on them, and game the system so that they can use it to their advantage against their competitors – instead of competing in a free market.

And rest assured: only determined political force will ever terminate the FCC's vice-like grip over the Internet and every other communications sector subjected to it. If the legislation authorizing the existence of the FCC and all the statutes it purports to regulate under are repealed tomorrow, the benefits to the nation will be incalculable in increasing our liberty and security and wealth.

## The FEC

The FEC was created by politicians in 1975 for the explicit purpose of imposing dictatorial federal control through a complex, compliance-demanding "regulatory" agency with massive power over all public speech, including all political campaigns of any kind, and over the power of all private citizens — other than journalists and FCC-controlled media — to use money in any manner to amplify their voices in the political/public marketplace/arena. The First Amendment absolutely forbids any such law "abridging" – that is, reducing or curtailing to any extent whatsoever – "the freedom of speech… Or the right of the people peaceably to assemble…"

Nothing but legal fiction fashioned out of whole cloth in a monstrous Supreme Court decision in 1976 permits either the creation of the FEC or any of the statutes it purports to enforce – combining the legislative, judicial and executive powers unconstitutionally in a single body, since it is authorized by Congress to itself legislate by adopting its own "regulations."

Policing political speech by citizens – that is, anyone who cannot afford to buy their own television station and claim to be a journalist, who would thereby be free from all FEC regulations – in the name of "fairness," or "cleaning up" politics – is what the FEC is all about. It presides over a maze of incomprehensibly-complex laws and procedures, navigating which has become a prerequisite for staying out of jail for anyone who wants to participate in the marketplace of political ideas in any manner. That criminally-enforced maze itself has become a major, chilling prior restraint on citizens exercising their supposedly-sacrosanct free-speech rights.

Politicians of all parties have voiced a variety of excuses for this abomination whose sole purpose is to force citizens to jump through hoops, and hire fantastically-expensive lawyers to navigate the unbelievably-complicated law that has been created in this area simply to exercise their First Amendment rights. Even the slightest deviation from what the FEC requires is deemed a crime, in many cases punishable by ruinous fines and lengthy jail time.

As always, the proponents of the law purport to be "equalizing" the rights of citizens in the marketplace of ideas – as if that were possible. In reality, it is a theft of citizens' ability to use their own money as they wish in a manner which only the monstrous federal election laws themselves (and they are endless) criminalize (you will find nothing in the 10 Commandments prohibiting any of the conduct which the federal election laws criminalize).

There has never been any public demand, let alone outcry, in favor of these laws. They are purely the product of noisy radical progressive journalists, do-gooder self-proclaimed "public interest" groups intent on manipulating the content of public speech by the creation of massively-complex rules effectively silencing large portions of the public, and cynical, self-serving politicians seeking to maximize their political advantages as incumbents through the creation of massively-complex rules whose bureaucracy they can preside over and thereby game the system to their advantage. It is utterly corrupt and utterly unconstitutional.

The federal election laws and the FEC use the sheer complexity of the laws themselves and the procedures they devise as a means to silence all citizens who cannot afford to navigate them. Those laws have not, as their proponents always magically promise, taken money out of politics. They have merely changed the rules of the game of all public speech in multiple unconstitutional manners which, like all "regulation" of any marketplace — in this case, the market of political ideas — benefits only the bureaucrats, incumbent politicians, and an entire industry of lobbyists, lawyers and money-raisers who have become essential employees of all types of political campaigns, if those engaged in the campaigns do not want to end up in jail.

Again, nothing in the Constitution permits this. Indeed, nothing in the Constitution, including the Commerce clause, even arguably permits Congress to have any such influence over any political campaigns whatsoever. The Constitution gives Congress <u>no power whatsoever</u> to enact legislation governing political contributions or speech in any political campaign – without regard to the First Amendment's absolute prohibition on such.

And again, the Commerce clause, is what is relied on to uphold the claimed "Constitutionality" of all this legislation and the FEC itself, based on its endless, deliberate misinterpretation by the courts. And again, as shown below, the claim that the Commerce clause is support for any regulation over any citizens' conduct is based on a patently-fraudulent reading of that clause manufactured out of thin air which, if it were to have any validity at all, would require a constitutional amendment to accomplish it – an amendment which has never been proposed or adopted, and so does not exist.

And under Article V, the combined, repeated unconstitutional misconduct of all three branches of government in this regard are not competent nor sufficient to actually amend the Constitution.

<u>Basic Facts about Federal Bureaucracies</u>

A few words about the nature of any federal bureaucracy – and yes, everything said here is true for every single one of them.

Each such bureaucracy, and all of its bureaucrat functionaries, is legally-empowered to control, forbid, or otherwise micromanage, behavior by citizens and their businesses, behavior which would otherwise be perfectly lawful, and so free from federal interference, in the absence of dictates from that bureaucracy, or the underlying federal law it is empowered to enforce. Moreover, each such bureaucracy is empowered to <u>add</u> to that underlying law, by writing its own "regulations."

To any who think otherwise, that is a precise description of what all such bureaucracies do. That is their purpose – to control, direct and otherwise restrict the liberty, of all the citizenry the agency claims jurisdiction over, in a deliberately ad hoc manner, inherently requiring the bureaucrats' permission for any citizen not wishing to run afoul of the bureaucracy to obtain. Each of them, accordingly, functions in a manner indistinguishable from the tyrannical Court of Star Chamber, which our English forebears fought a 20-year-long revolution/Civil War to eliminate.

We all know how irritating, or worse, it is to have to deal with any bureaucracy, let alone a federal one empowered to completely destroy anyone under its jurisdiction – and with the bureaucrats who populate it. Paperwork of various kinds they invariably impose on everyone subject to their jurisdiction is commonly referred to, euphemistically actually, as "red tape." But that is only the beginning of their power.

There are actually two types of people subject to each federal bureaucracy's power: (1) the citizens, and their businesses, which it is legally authorized, plus those it simply claims the power, in its discretion, to impose its policing powers on, and (2) the bureaucrats who work within the bureaucracy itself.

Astonishingly, at least to anyone who believes that we are in a free country, the power of the bureaucracy and its bureaucrats <u>over private citizens is far greater</u> than the power it is able to exercise over its own employees, even though it is only the employees who voluntarily subject themselves to its jurisdiction.

Specifically, what lawyers call the "burden of proof" imposed on parties seeking to prevail in court is far greater for any citizen seeking to undo any action by a federal agency, than the proof burden imposed on any agency employee, in order to undo any agency action harmful to either of them. Although all the facts described herein, including that one, have been obfuscated by statutes, rules and actions by federal employees in all branches of the government, I will describe the reality of all these situations to you in plain English.

First of all, under numerous rulings of the United States Supreme Court, all actions of federal bureaucracies, and the bureaucrats within them, which have any effect on any citizen are legally <u>final</u>, and subject to <u>no</u> further review by any court, unless a court considers such actions to be "abuses of discretion" on the part of the agency (yes,all such bureaucrats are automatically granted discretionary powers over citizens), based on that agency's own, potentially-gratuitous, determination of applicable facts and so-called "expert" analysis, no matter how intrusive on private property or other rights the agency's actions or "regulatory" directives may be, and even if there is very substantial proof that the agency's action is foolish and harmful and has no genuine public benefit.

Under those Supreme Court rulings, any private citizen seeking to overturn any action by any federal bureaucracy must prove "by clear and convincing evidence" — which is just shy of "beyond a reasonable doubt"— that the complained-of action of the agency is an abuse of its discretion.

In real life, particularly because of the ongoing power of such agencies, over anyone they simply claim power over, to impose draconian (literally ruinous) fines on any noncompliance with their directives, those Court rulings effectively give bureaucracies power without any real limits over private citizens.

And moreover, each such bureaucracy is empowered to <u>add</u> to that underlying law affecting citizens and their businesses, by writing its own "regulations."

In plain English, what that means is that any private citizen seeking to undo any action by any federal agency is forced to bear a crippling "burden of proof," and overcome an overwhelming presumption of legitimacy and correctness on the part of the agency, in order to prevail.

And any citizen who is subject to the agency's jurisdiction on an ongoing basis inevitably is particularly reluctant to challenge any of its actions, since he risks complete personal destruction, or the destruction of his business, simply from questioning its authority, since it inevitably has that kind of discretionary power over him and his business. When it comes to agency actions, that power precludes any freedom of speech — or appeal -- by those subject to it.

On the other hand, if an agency employee-bureaucrat is unhappy with his treatment at the hands of the agency, rather than the burden being on him against the agency to prevail, because of federal employee unionization and multiple bureaucrat-protecting federal statutes, if an employee-bureaucrat complains, the burden effectively is on the agency to prove the legitimacy of its actions adverse to the employee-bureaucrat.

As a practical matter, this results in those federal employee-bureaucrats having the power of effective immunity from termination and virtual employment for life, regardless of their incompetence – and regardless of the untold damage they may cause.

If only private citizens had a fraction of that power relative to the agencies they are forced to be subject to. And we all suffer tyranny whenever any of our fellow citizens do.

Another invariable feature of bureaucracies: although when they are created by politicians, the politicians paint them as "expert," politically-neutral arbiters for the good of all citizens, who selflessly enforce the laws they are charged with enforcing, all those claims are sheer nonsense.

In reality, each bureaucracy, and the bureaucrats within it, are keenly aware of their own personal interest both in enhancing their own power, in preventing anyone from restricting it, and in exercising it without regard to any genuine public benefit. The cynicism with which agencies operate in real life is invariably apparent to anyone who has to deal with them.

Examples of this are legion.

The most obvious example is the fact that notwithstanding the creation of countless hundreds of agencies by the federal government, particularly since 1906, the only one which has ever actually been taken out of business was the Interstate Commerce Commission – and it took 100 years of readily-observable failures, non-achievement, monumental expense, countless legislative "fixes," none of which worked and, with all that, the only way it was finally legislated away was a result of the fact that the railroad industry it was originally created to rule over had <u>declined in importance</u> because of the growth of other, alternative means of transportation (trucks, cars, airplanes).

A more formidable example is the fact that during the 1930s in the Roosevelt administration, dozens of administrative agencies were created as part of the New Deal, each of which agencies have the kind of bureaucratic power over aspects of citizens and their businesses described above – and so dramatically reduced citizens' freedom and, inevitably, the nation's prosperity.

On May 9, 1939, Henry Morganthau, who had been FDR's friend, an architect of the New Deal, and FDR's Secretary Of Treasury, testified before Congress that, after all its intrusions in the economy and in people's lives, the entire New Deal had failed to achieve anything of real value and could be considered a complete failure. These are his words:

> *"I want to see this country prosperous. I want to see people get a job. I want to see people get enough to eat. We have never made good on our promises.... We have tried spending money. We are spending more than we have ever spent before and it does not work....I say after eight years of this Administration we have just as much unemployment as when we started. ... And an enormous debt to boot!"*

Nevertheless, not a single federal agency created as part of it has <u>ever</u> been eliminated, and the more worthless they are, the more they have strived to enhance their power and the reach of their jurisdiction to create new "problems" for them to solve – and so to become, at least in their own view, indispensable. And that is, quite simply, what federal bureaucracies invariably do: if they serve any genuinely-public interest, that is no more than a mere byproduct of their primary focus which is to serve their own, power-enhancing interest, at the expense of everyone else.

In pursuit of ever more power for themselves, they invariably seek more and more "problems" to "fix," and the only risks to them are posed by potential, publicity-creating disasters which they can be blamed for. In order to curtail the possibility of such problems, bureaucracies inevitably follow the "precautionary" principle. That is, if a particular problem is <u>even imaginable</u> from a given set of facts, they will take it upon themselves to do <u>whatever it takes</u> — in precaution — to minimize the risk of that problem materializing.

Unfortunately for those under its jurisdiction, that translates into maximizing the bureaucrats" power over their subjects' lives to minimize the risk of such a problem surfacing – for the bureaucracy. And there are <u>no</u> market constraints on their actions – nor any logical nor legal constraints as a practical matter.

To better understand this phenomenon: imagine a bureaucracy created with the goal of maximizing automobile safety, without regard to any real cost/benefit analysis. In pursuing the "precautionary" principle, that agency will constantly seek out new "safety" devices, recommended by "experts," and will simultaneously attempt to discover "hidden risks" in all cars. Its actions will invariably be the banning of all existing cars, and to set up standards for cars in the future which will be vastly more expensive and will have all kinds of features which customers in real life have no interest in whatsoever.

Unfortunately, that is not just an imaginary situation: it is exactly the situation all car purchasers in America are confronted with today, since automobiles are subject to multiple federal agencies dictating every aspect of their design and manufacture, which is the reason why cars are now only made by a relatively tiny number of companies, why all modern cars look practically the same, and why the prices of cars are many multiples of what they were, in constant dollars, a mere 40 years ago.

And as bad as all that is, those are simply the practical monstrosities produced by bureaucracies. The fact that they also promote lawlessness and cronyism due to their patently unconstitutional nature is discussed and proven in a later chapter below. The nature of the Bad Laws under which they arise and operate is deconstructed in Chapter 5 below.

## The Constitutional "Authority" Which The Supreme Court Has Claimed Since the Mid-1930s Authorizes Federal "Regulatory" Administrative Agencies

It is important for you to know – as all law school graduates do if they paid any attention in their Constitutional Law classes – that our Constitution provides for a federal government of limited, specified (primarily in Article I, section 8 of the Constitution) powers, and that the particular, enumerated, Constitutional power that the Supreme Court has purported to rely on in all cases – which began in the mid-1930s – gratuitously reversing its previous, contrary decisions, in upholding the constitutionality of any of these alphabet agencies, and their underlying laws, is known as the "Commerce" Clause, which reads as follows:

> "the Congress shall have power... To regulate Commerce with foreign Nations, and <u>among the several States</u>, and with the Indian Tribes [emphases added]"

The substance of the Supreme Court's basis for ruling that all these federal policing agencies are supposedly legal and Constitutional <u>under that clause</u> alone is that, since the word Commerce is used in that clause, and so is the word "regulating," the words "among the several states" <u>can effectively be ignored</u>, together with all of the 18th and 19th century written records plainly showing what those who wrote that clause <u>clearly and unambiguously meant</u> by it, and so, according to the Supreme Court, that clause can be interpreted to mean that Congress can regulate – or comprehensively rule over – any aspect of commerce – or anything which can be considered "commerce" – and pretty much any other aspect of American life, as much and in any way it wants anywhere in the United States.

Since, as is apparent, virtually <u>all interactions</u> between human beings can be accurately claimed to be one or another form of "commerce," it is obvious that that interpretation of that clause effectively means that there is effectively no limit on the power of Congress thereunder to impose a federal police power on any aspect of human life in this country – in other words, that that clause grants the federal government in the Constitution, in utter violation of any notion of a highly-limited government, what is known as a general police power – over literally every activity American citizens might engage in that can be characterized as "commerce."

Additionally, in upholding the power of Congress to delegate this plenary policing power to bureaucracies/agencies it chooses to create incident to that power, together with any legislation adopted by states similarly directing how any business must conduct its affairs, the Supreme Court found it necessary effectively to <u>unilaterally delete</u> another clause (along with the "among the several states" language in the Commerce clause) in the Constitution, known as the "Contract" clause, which provides as follows:

> "<u>No State shall</u> enter into any Treaty, Alliance, or Confederation; grant Letters of Marque and Reprisal; coin Money; emit Bills of Credit; make any Thing but gold and silver Coin a Tender in Payment of Debts; pass any Bill of Attainder, ex post facto Law, <u>or Law impairing the Obligation of Contracts</u> [emphases added],"

In this context it should be noted that all of the express guarantees of individual liberty precluding various actions by the federal and state governments – freedom of speech, press, etc. – were, unlike the Contract clause, <u>not included in the original</u> text of the Constitution but were, rather, added immediately after its adoption in the first 10 amendments to it, known as the Bill of Rights. The Contract clause was included <u>in the original Constitution itself,</u> precluding any state from passing any law which could interfere in any manner with the terms of any contract entered into among people — i.e. exactly what <u>every action by every federal alphabet agency consists of</u> — except as had been permitted previously under the common law of contracts.

And if you read through all of the powers permitted to the federal government specified in Article I section 8, <u>none</u> of those powers would permit any interference by the federal government at all with any contract rights either – unless you think the Commerce clause could do so, in direct contradiction of the very purpose of the American Revolution itself, and of every gloss on that clause's meaning by all Founders, as the Supreme Court has, since the mid-1930s, repeatedly ruled it does; and all Americans knew to a certainty prior to 1887 that that clause meant nothing of the kind. I will prove that to you in Chapters 5, 8 and 11 below.

Indeed, it is a historical fact that <u>nothing</u> was more important to the founders of this nation in the creation of the federal government then that it be dedicated to protecting the nation from invasions and insurrections, <u>and</u> preserve and protect the property and contract rights of all Americans, and do nothing in any way to hinder, impede or encumber the growth of all commerce, ingenuity, inventions, businesses and trades of all Americans – and that it do nothing to permit the debasement of our currency which was to be based on gold and silver to preserve its soundness, with the federal government to have no part, let alone monopoly power, over any paper currency that was to be created. All this is discussed in detail in later chapters.

Indeed, counterfeiting is one of the very few crimes the Constitution expressly authorizes the federal government to police at all – an authorization which would be superfluous if the federal government actually possessed anything resembling the general policing powers the Supreme Court has claimed the Commerce clause authorizes.

The Contract clause was expressly included in the Constitution to prevent the states from in any way harming citizens' contract rights, and the "taking" clause was included in the Fifth Amendment to the Constitution expressly to prevent the government from ever taking anyone's property – including any rights over such property – except by paying its owner the full value taken, and only after due process of law supervised in judicial proceedings.

In fact, as clearly shown in a later chapter, the Commerce clause was included in the Constitution not to grant Congress the power to regulate or supervise citizens' commercial (or other) activities, but rather solely to impose a federal role in supervising actions by the states affecting the trading of goods (note the use of the words "among the several states" In the Commerce Clause) as a way of federally preventing the states from harming or impinging on any citizens' commercial trading activities or rights under the common law, including by any state attempting to impose laws which would have the effect of protecting or favoring the businesses of that state from competition by businesses from other states.

I will prove to you that this is the only correct reading of the Commerce clause by showing you unambiguous written statements on this precise point by multiple founders who participated directly in drafting the Commerce clause – with no dissenting statement to be found anywhere from any other founder, nor indeed from any American until 1887. The Supreme Court's rulings directly to the contrary since the mid-1930s are nothing short of gratuitous, completely-unconstitutional, purported-"amendments" to the Constitution which literally turn it on its head.

Article V of the Constitution alone provides for the methods of amending it, none of which include unilateral action by the Supreme Court – even when heartily approved of by the two other branches of the government. And simply trampling on the Constitution, as the Supreme Court has done in those rulings, creates no precedent authorizing the trampling. Otherwise, the Constitution would be a meaningless piece of paper.

In other words, the last thing the founders had in mind in creating the Constitution was to grant Congress a general policing power over any activity American citizens or businesses might engage in. if the Commerce clause actually created such a general police power over citizens and their businesses, such would literally <u>completely nullify</u> any concept of limited federal powers – the entire purpose of the American Revolution and of the entire Constitution itself – and create a constitutional loophole, solely for the benefit of the federal government, at the expense of the citizenry, big enough to fly a 747 through.

in reality, the Contract clause was deemed, by the founders, together with the Fifth Amendment's prohibition on any state "taking" of any citizens' property except for fair compensation and pursuant to judicial proceedings, of absolutely central importance to the Constitution's central purposes of <u>preserving</u> property and contract rights and severely <u>limiting</u> the power of the federal and state governments. And the purpose of the Commerce clause was plainly to serve solely as a policing mechanism on behalf of citizens and their businesses<u> to protect their business and contract rights from invasion by the states.</u>

Further<u> textual</u> support for this reading of the Commerce clause is provided by simply looking at what other entities the clause specifies granting federal authority to "regulate commerce <u>with</u> [emphasis added]" with respect to – foreign <u>nations</u> and Indian <u>tribes, not</u> the commerce engaged in by foreign nationals specifically nor individual Indians.

The description I have just given you of the actual, intended purpose of both the Contract clause and the Commerce clause is, moreover, confirmed by all authoritative interpretations of the Commerce clause (I am unaware of any disputes in the 19th century of the meaning of the Contract clause, as described above) during the 19th century prior to 1870 – which interpretations came from the pens of both presidents and the Chief Justice of the United States Supreme Court, with the presidents making such interpretation being none other than James Madison and James Monroe, the Constitution's principle author and another Founder. The most important of these authorities are discussed and quoted in detail in Chapter 11.

Moreover, the history of the republic for 100 years further proves that this was the clear understanding of what those clauses meant.

I will show you all I have promised to show you, conclusively proving the utter frivolousness of the Supreme Court's purely politically-motivated "reading" of the Commerce clause,. It has relied on that "reading" as the exclusive, purported legal authorization for every single federal administrative agency and department (other than the IRS). My proof of the frivolousness of that "reading" involves legal and historical analysis and discussion – in which I do indeed prove everything I have promised to prove in that regard.

Before proceeding with that discussion, in Part II I will lay out my structural analysis of the two different types of (1) power), (2) citizen-policing laws, (3) revolution, (4) nations and (5) politicians.

Another Pernicious Feature of Federal Bureaucracies:
Record Obfuscation And Falsification.

As discussed in detail in Chapter 4, regardless of his position in or out of any organization, private or government, it is impossible for any individual not to act in his own interest at any time. That does not mean the individual acts without regard to applicable law, morality and ethics. But the idea that federal bureaucrats act exclusively selflessly and in the "public interest" (whatever that is) is sheer fantasy. They are all humans, and so are just as self-interested as anyone else.

For them, in real life, that self-interest can and does affect their actions – all of which affect private citizens – in multiple ways, ways which can be truly tyrannical even if they are arguably following the law, which grants them enormous discretion in their actions anyway, and which can morph into genuine monstrous evil in a variety of ways.

Like other employees, it is to their career advantage in the bureaucracy to please their supervisors to whom they report, and who formally, and bureaucratically, evaluate their performance. In many cases, pleasing the union which they almost all belong to can also result in their career advancement – even if doing so is extremely harmful to private citizens.

Because, again, of the extraordinary discretion they are permitted, they often can truly harm private citizens in a manner close to the very edge, or even beyond, what even that discretionary law permits. In many cases, this can result in the selective application of harm to some citizens, often for political reasons, and the selective withholding of such harms to other citizens.

Some of the most powerful and dangerous federal bureaucratic employees – such as attorneys in the Justice Department – often have no choice but to apply extremely harmful laws selectively against particular citizens. As monstrous as that may sound (James II was removed from the throne of England for doing precisely that), their doing so may not even violate any law, and may be demanded by department policy.

Indeed, there are now such a virtually infinite supply of federal criminal laws, arising from "regulations" adopted by any of the countless administrative agencies, that it would be impossible for the Justice Department even to attempt to prosecute everyone potentially guilty of any such laws. It has become virtually impossible for any private citizen involved in any business of any size to avoid completely committing crimes under one or another of those regulations – at least weekly, if not more often.

For one thing, although all citizens are charged with knowledge of all those regulations and the criminal penalties for violating them, no one alive could possibly actually know the contents of all federal laws as of 20 years ago; and they have grown exponentially since then. Moreover, many of those federal crimes can be committed virtually unknowingly, with no real "willfulness" requirement, as used to be fundamental to criminal liability.

And, of course, none of those multiple crimes are forbidden in the 10 Commandments. They are all literally the criminalization of otherwise perfectly lawful conduct.

And Congress did not even pass most of them, as is unambiguously required by the Constitution. And every single one of those multiple "regulatory" agencies pass their own laws routinely, criminalizing ever more of real citizens' lives – without any possibility of them even knowing about that.

These particular facts illustrate a number of features of federal bureaucracies – among others, their legal arbitrariness, their potential for political-weaponization in the hands of partisan bureaucrats, particularly ones who genuinely hate citizens who do not share their political views, the extraordinary danger all of this poses to private citizens, and the incredible reach of the discretion to harm private citizens which bureaucrats have at their disposal.

Another feature of bureaucrats to be borne in mind is that people who choose federal bureaucracy as a career are often filled with self-righteousness, belief in their own moral purity, and are as ambitious as anyone. As discussed at length in Chapter 17, an entire movement led and conducted by determined Marxists in the 20th century dedicated most of its efforts to recruiting other highly-educated and fanatically-dedicated Marxists specifically to populate the various federal bureaucracies and use them to impose radical Marxist policies on the nation through those bureaucracies – a stealthy, largely-hidden revolution effected in briefcases and on paper. That movement was extremely successful in so doing.

As it happens, one of the favorite means of personal advancement available to federal bureaucrats is when their aggression results in them "getting scalps" of private citizens, particularly those who their own supervisors detest, who are often selected primarily because of their success in business – triumphs which please those supervisors and others higher up in the bureaucratic food chain. Not incidentally, all this abusive bureaucratic behavior can occur completely within the bounds of "law," and completely consistent with department policies.

The Justice Department is charged with prosecuting all crimes resulting from all violations of all federal laws, including those enacted solely by other bureaucracies. Each federal agency has its own policies regarding prosecution of crimes against the laws it administers, policies the Justice Department follows consistent with its own policies, and many of those agencies also have a specific policy of purely-selective prosecution of any crimes connected to it.

For example, the IRS is typical of many such agencies in having the explicit policy of prosecuting crimes in a deliberately arbitrary and capricious manner, so that the prosecution of tax crimes is invariably unpredictable, and has nothing to do necessarily with the severity of the crime nor anything else that would seem logical. The deliberate policy is to frighten everyone who potentially violates tax statutes – criminal liability for which can be triggered under any of the numerous tax crimes extremely easily, as a technical matter – with a view literally to frighten everyone to maximize through terror citizens' tax compliance, since they never know when they might be the target of an arbitrary tax prosecution.

Fewer than 3000 people a year are prosecuted for tax crimes, notwithstanding the millions who could be. The idea is to put the fear of the Lord in everyone – a deliberate policy of selective, arbitrary prosecution by that brutal agency.

This is all to give people unfamiliar with the federal bureaucracy a tiny idea of the danger it poses on a daily basis to all citizens. And I have only been describing bureaucrat behavior which does not technically exceed what is legally permissible. A direct consequence of this enormous power bestowed on those bureaucrats I have now given you an indication of is that they can become drunk on it – and go well beyond even the extraordinary bounds of permissible behavior for them in deliberately harming citizens for whatever motive.

It happens that just as there are virtually-infinite federal criminal laws citizens can run afoul of, federal bureaucrats are subject to other criminal statutes intended to prevent them from exceeding their powers. Virtually any violation of any of those statutes by any of them is a felony, with each such technical violation an additional felony. Any false statement by any of them in a report, for example, is a felony. And they prepare and file untold numbers of reports in connection with everything they do.

The numerous record-keeping requirements they are subject to are supposed to make their actions infinitely transparent and make it possible for private citizens to learn of all such actions through properly-drafted Freedom of Information Act claims, among others. Additionally, every federal agency has its own Inspector General who is supposed to be able to investigate all officials' actions independently.

In reality, federal bureaucrats routinely learn how to defeat unwanted investigations into their behavior – particularly when it goes beyond the bounds of what is permissible. In recent days, the public has acquired information concerning two former senior federal executives – Lois Lerner, who was a very senior, political appointee administering the IRS exempt organizations group, and Hillary Clinton who was Secretary of State.

The public record is replete already with multiple instances of crimes committed by both of them in the form of falsification of their record, deliberate destruction, or attempted destruction, of records they were required to keep, under numerous statutes, false statements made by each of them in connection with inquiries concerning all of that, mishandling of confidential documents and information – and that is simply a small list of the multiple crimes apparent to any knowledgeable observer from what is known in the public record.

Both of them are seasoned bureaucratic operators who knew exactly what they were required to do, what they were not permitted to do, and what they could get away with, as a practical matter, based on many factors, including their political status and the de facto immunity it provided them from inherently-political Justice Department prosecution, and when it came to falsifying records of what they were doing. It is notable that both of them have effectively been absolved of any possibility of prosecution in manifestly-political decisions by the Justice Department: a lesser bureaucrat committing the same acts that either of them did, would already be in jail, and all their personal assets seized – a routine, prejudgment federal action.

What this brief discussion of routine federal bureaucrat actions and misconduct plainly shows is the extraordinary power those bureaucrats have to harm citizens and evade detection, let alone any adverse consequences to themselves, from even the most despicable misconduct (much of which has actually been ruled "legal," under Supreme Court rulings), and some indication of the brutal actions they can take to anyone who crosses them – something that is certain to happen by an entire bureaucracy if and when it is threatened with extinction.

That is precisely why every single one of these agencies need to be extinguished at one time, deprived of power instantaneously – as Congress can do at any time simply by refusing to fund them at all, even without legislation repealing the legislation that creates them.

In later chapters, I discuss the concept advanced by Rousseau in the 18th century which animated the French, and all subsequent collectivist, revolutions – the notion of a general will, or Gestalt consciousness of a self-identified group. It happens, that that is precisely what actually occurs in virtually all federal bureaucracies: the bureaucracy as a whole has a clear idea of its interests and acts in accord with them against all who attempt to cross it.

# BOOK PART TWO:

## STRUCTURAL ANALYSIS OF THE TWO TYPES EACH OF POWER, LAW, REVOLUTION, NATIONS AND POLITICIANS

# Chapter 4

## Rules, Power, Markets And the State

The following chapters describe and explain my analysis of the structural features of politics, power, law, revolutions and their ideologies, and society. In addition to exposing the underlying architecture of all those phenomena, this analysis is intended to provide a judgment yardstick, equally applicable to any nation at any time, for the express purpose of appraising and evaluating whether, and to what extent, that nation's laws actually promote, or harm, the prosperity and individual liberty of its people.

Uniquely among all nations throughout all history, those values — legally-maximizing, and protecting from tyranny, individual liberty and citizen prosperity — have always been, since its founding, the primary, Constitutionally-protected values of America. As important as our security has also been, we have always viewed it as a phenomenon which results from the preservation and success of those values. Empire has never had the slightest interest to us (except in the fevered brain of Theodore Roosevelt) – unlike any other nation that has ever achieved power even remotely comparable to ours.

As shown in the chapters following those devoted to this structural analysis, the source of all our nation's problems can be simply described: politicians in all three branches (executive, legislative and judicial) authorized by the Constitution have created monstrous laws over a long period of time, laws forbidden in multiple provisions of the Constitution and for multiple reasons, laws which are – and which were deliberately designed by their European tyrant originators, for – choking off citizens' freedoms and the operation and control of all the actual, commercial sources of our nation's prosperity – and in many cases, even our ability to defend ourselves militarily.

Whatever popularity those politicians may have been able to gin up at the time of each such law' s enactment, they have done so largely through fraud, misdirection, and demagoguery – and Americans have never actually voted for any, let alone all of these laws, laws whose enactments which, particularly when viewed together, have constituted nothing short of a Counterrevolution.

The legal and political history of France, England and America, which illuminates the real-life nature, origins and destructiveness, of those monstrous laws and the Counterrevolution they represent, is described and shown in the chapters which follow this structural analysis, an analysis which explains in detail precisely why it is that those laws are indeed so malignant (no exaggeration) – and why there is only one way to rid ourselves of them, and reinstate our Constitution which they so grotesquely violate and insult.

My structural analysis begins as follows:

I have concluded that there are two, profoundly-different, types of each of the most important things affecting the structural features of politics, law, and society: specifically, I can clearly identify, and discuss at length below and in the three subsequent chapters, two, completely different types of each of the following:

(1) of power (market power, and the power of violence),

(2) of citizen-policing laws (those which define civil and criminal misconduct and compel compensation to victims, and/or penalize misconduct, only against its actual perpetrators, and only after it is fairly adjudicated to have been committed, and laws which restrain conduct by everyone in advance, and forbid everything until politicians grant permission),

(3) of revolution ((1) those promoting collectivism/socialism, and inevitably ending in dictatorship/tyranny, and (2) those promoting individual liberty),

(4) of nations (happy and miserable), and

(5) of politicians (ones willing, cold-bloodedly to defraud the people by using the "big lie," and those who will not do so).

What follows here, and in the next-following chapters, are my more-detailed thoughts regarding each of these matters.

Again, I claim expertise in nothing. God alone is an expert, and none of us is that smart – nor anything like omniscient. As shown in Chapter 1: learning a single, previously-unperceived "fact" is enough to completely transform any judgment by any supposedly-"expert" human about anything.

And none of us ever know absolutely everything about anything. That's why there are no real flesh and blood human experts on anything — only pretenders.

Everything you read in this chapter, and those that follow, was well-known to America's founders, based on their own experiences, and their deep understanding of the writings, in particular, of Plato, Aristotle, Thucydides, Thomas Hobbes, John Locke, Adam Smith, and Charles-Louis Montesquieu. And that understanding informed all their remarkable actions, including fighting our Revolution against the most powerful (and actually then-least-tyrannical) European nation, with a crystal-clear understanding of the wholly-unprecedented nation they were creating, which they very-deliberately legally-institutionalized in all our founding documents, including the Declaration of Independence and the Constitution.

Necessity alone urges me to bring all this to your attention: the Counterrevolution could never have succeeded to the extent it has without many among us ignoring or forgetting all that follows here.

### Basic Features of All Human Interactions

First of all, three things are always present in all interactions between human beings –

(1) rules of some kind – and, underlying them, moral principles of some kind on which those rules are, in turn, based – governing the interactions: either someone or some set of objective principles govern each interaction;

(2) the self-interest of each participant (none of us are angels, nor mindless, self-less drones, in any situation, and anyone claiming complete selflessness at any time is either an idiot, a fraud, or both); and

(3) power of some kind (as discussed in detail below, there are two basic types – (1) market power and (2) violence power) – which is always unequal among the participants, and which all humans possess, in one form, and to some degree, or another.

### Rules and Morals

Regarding the (inevitable in all human interactions) rules: their specific content varies enormously and, in each situation, depends on whether, in that particular interaction, there is a rule of law (as opposed to rule by individuals) and, if so, what kind – i.e., whether Good Law or Bad Law, both discussed in detail in Chapter 5, prevails.

And do not doubt: there are always rules of some kind in any interpersonal, or inter-governmental, situation. Even when things seem utterly chaotic, chaos itself has rules. The first and most basic step in understanding anything that is going on between people and nations at any time is knowing what rules are governing their interactions – even if one or more of the parties are oblivious to them, and act as if a completely different set of rules governs. Those who are blind to the real rules in play are certain to fail in all their interactions – catastrophically so if their opponents are dangerous monsters.

### The Rule of Law Versus The Rule of Men And Terror

First, as just mentioned, if, in a particular setting or, in lawyerspeak, "jurisdiction," there is no rule of law, interactions are nevertheless still governed by rules (of a sort). In that case, including seeming total chaos, the law of the jungle alone applies, meaning that the simple, inherently-tyrannical and brutal, <u>purely-discre-tionary</u>, arbitrary and gratuitous power, however obtained, possessed by one or another of the individual participants, to <u>inflict violence</u> against, and so terrorize, the others <u>alone</u> rules. Invariably, the only limit, or limiting principle, applicable to such terrorizing power is if it is forcibly confronted and stopped by another whose violence/terrorizing power is simply greater.

This is all true regardless of the number of participants involved. Any govern-mental body or official having discretionary power over citizens necessarily possesses violence/terrorizing power indistinguishable from this law of the jungle. That is because the mere existence of any official's discretionary power over any citizen necessarily creates an existential danger to the citizen: when state power is discretionary, its possessor becomes a law unto himself because of the unlimited violence he can inflict, as a practical, even if not a purely-legal, matter against those subject to his discretion: his subjects (that's what they are) are simply under his thumb, even when he technically exceeds what he is legal-ly-permitted to do.

That is because any official, always backed by the Violence Power of the state, further armed with discretionary, power over his subjects, effectively has ab-solute power over them, power which inherently has the effect of forcing silence on any complaints they might have. The very discretionary nature of his power, quite simply, renders impotent any laws otherwise purporting to impose limits on him.

The power (violence power alone, and <u>never</u> market power) underlying Bad Law (again, explained, defined and discussed at length in the next chapter) is indistin-guishable from that of the law of the jungle: however detailed, and even intermi-nable, the written, Bad Law involved may be, its (inevitably) discretionary nature makes it, in fact, the rule by men, and not of law at all.

Thus, Bad Law, just like the law of the jungle, terrorizes its subjects, however cheerfully they may pretend to accept it. And it always provides precisely this tyrannical, <u>discretionary</u> power (there is no other way to administer it) over all subject to it, power possessed by the government, its politicians and unelected bureaucrat functionaries.

Indeed, as discussed in later chapters, the absolute, tyrannical European mon-archs who invented, and first enacted, Bad Law had that very terrorizing, ty-rannical effect as its intended goal — <u>precisely</u> to choke off any rivalry to their hereditary, claimed-absolute, power from the then-recent, growing wealth of non-feudal, commoner merchants (artisans, shippers and traders, and bankers, e.g.), by forcing them into requiring state permission to function – and to prevent them from achieving extraordinary political/military power like the Medici bankers, the Venetian merchants, and the formerly-Spanish-ruled Dutch Republic had already achieved.

Bad Law always accomplishes, as its sole effect, that liberty-and-industry/wealth-crushing result — and with flying colors. Those absolute monarchs were willing to risk impoverishing their own kingdoms, and so reduce their own, desperately-needed wealth, simply to preserve their existential power over their subjects. And that has always been what Bad Law is really all about.

Good Law <u>alone</u> does not rule by terror, and, if it alone is present, with no Bad Law at all, it actually liberates and empowers the citizenry and provides the necessary, uncorrupt, legal foundation and environment for them to enjoy maximum safety, liberty and prosperity. Good Law prevails automatically, among small groups of participants, where no (government) enforcement mechanism exists, when the participants all simply voluntarily conform to the 10 Commandments.

However, because the most aggressive participant in any interacting group (no matter how large) invariably dictates the operative rules for everyone, if any of the participants violates any of the 10 Commandments in his interactions with the others (and so elects to operate under the law of the jungle), and his misconduct goes unpunished, Good Law ceases: absent government/Violence Power-enforcement of Good Law, the worst, most violent participant inevitably picks the applicable rules.

That is also true in all dealings among nations.

<u>Underlying Moral Principles</u>

Secondly, regarding the (similarly-inevitable in all rules) <u>underlying moral/policy principles</u>: all particular governing rules are necessarily an expression of an underlying (if sometimes unspoken) policy, and/or moral, foundation. And the moral/policy foundation they express is, in turn, always derived exclusively from one of two possible sources – (1) in the case of the law of the jungle, from whoever simply has power over the others, the single, situationally-ruling human; or, in the case of Bad Law, from the politicians or collective of humans which impose it on the citizenry, or (2) in the case of Good Law, from Jesus' command to "Love your neighbor as yourself," concisely summarizing the 10 Commandments given by God who, in the Western world, including America, is uniquely the God of the Old and New Testament (in the world of Islam, a very different God is said by his, Allah's, followers to prevail, a subject outside the scope of this book).

Knowing the source for the moral/policy authority underlying any law is critical for making any value judgment concerning that law. Furthering that policy is the law's purpose. The value of its result depends on its success in achieving that purpose and its effect on the liberty and prosperity of the people it applies to. Good Laws seek to expand that liberty and prosperity; Bad Laws have precisely the opposite purpose.

The underlying morals/policy for both Bad Law and the law of the jungle can be characterized as an <u>anti-</u>morality, contemptuous of any external limiting principle – limiting principles being what morals and laws are supposed to be – constraining the ruler from when and how he may exercise his power of violence over those subject to it/him. And a discretionary ruler who recognizes <u>no</u> limiting principle has no market power whatsoever, as explained below.

The particular policy/morals which are the foundation for any particular Bad Law vary enormously, but always have the following elements: (1) indifference to, or even contempt for, Jesus' just-quoted command and the 10 Commandments it summarizes as a moral authority for law, and for any other limiting principles whatsoever (including any supposed rights of those subject to the Bad Law) restricting the reach of the particular Bad Law and its enforcers, and similar contempt for the intelligence and worth of those subject to the particular Bad Law; and (2) claims/promises, by its proponents, to justify its liberty-destruction, that the particular Bad Law – and its supposedly "selfless," "expert" administrators – will vastly improve, if not actually perfect, all areas of citizen life subjected to it.

### Self-Interest: Everyone Has It – Everyone.

No idea is more pernicious – and patently false – than the notion that any human being ever acts without self-interest. That does not mean that, in so doing, humans who respect moral authority do not follow that moral authority limiting their actions in pursuing their self-interest. Indeed, moral beings may well consider it <u>part of pursuing their self-interest</u> to follow the moral authority they recognize — for the sake of their own immortal souls, to facilitate the rule of Good Law by not violating it, and/or even simply as an example for others.

Again, as indicated above, there are always rules of some sort, including rules which individuals choose for themselves based on morality as a vehicle for self-liberation, self-realization and personal salvation.

One of the great collectivist/socialist/Marxist slanders of markets and business people is that when people (but somehow never the Marxists) act pursuant to their self-interest, they necessarily do so merely based on "greed." Greed, of course, is one of the so-called seven deadly sins – and, accordingly, is viewed as immoral by all who accept that particular moral principle (which, interestingly, is not *per se* expressed in the 10 Commandments).

Understood within the context of Christian/Jewish morality contained in the 10 Commandments and Jesus' above-command, it is fair to say that <u>morally-forbidden</u> greed actually consists only of self-interest practiced with disregard for the dictates of those Commandments – i.e., disrespect for the intelligence, person and property of others, which obviously are inconsistent with loving them and all those commands.

For example, if one covets property of another, one is indeed being "greedy" and violating the Commandment forbidding envy. Similarly, if one is willing to steal, murder or defraud, and does so, to obtain property, that acquisition is appropriately characterized as "greedy."

However, if one is simply endlessly energetic in pursuit of one's vocation/work/ business and in honestly acquiring wealth for himself, and obeys all of the 10 Commandments in doing so, it would be a grotesque mischaracterization to call that "greed." Indeed, all men's greatest accomplishments and inventions, providing untold benefits to all of us, have resulted precisely from their ambition and from their taking enormous pains and risks to truly accomplish something. Smearing/slandering such actions and achievements as "greed" is simply a Big Lie – a "false witness."

It is also critically important to understand that, like everyone else, government functionaries and politicians are always acting in their own interests even when they are supposedly using their office for "public service." Indeed the louder they claim to be selfless in doing so, the more dangerous and fraudulent – and genuinely greedy in seeking power and acclaim they do not deserve – they are.

Quite simply, self-interest is what motivates us all to do things. Doing things morally, energetically, with every resource available, and without violating the 10 Commandments, is, literally, a moral blessing to all and the means whereby all human progress is made, and the wealth of the nation is enhanced.

Since none of us is a mindless, utterly-selfless automaton, each and all of us have needs and wants which we have the self-interest to fulfill and, of no less importance, we each have capabilities we have a desire both to fulfill for our own personal satisfaction and growth, and to use in whatever manner will provide us the greatest benefit, including wealth, wealth whose existence actually is a boon to all, and not evil booty as Marxists claim — for everyone else's wealth, that is, but never their's, all of which truly is stolen.

When we use/exercise our abilities and capabilities we are engaging in what is known as our work, or vocation, or profession – or business. As discussed below, that is also how we each cultivate our own Market Power, which is, <u>by its very nature, inherently-beneficial</u> to all, as shown below.

The Two Types of Power

In addition to each participant's (1) <u>self-interest,</u> and whatever (2) <u>rules</u> govern his interactions with others, each inter-acting person/participant has some kind of (3) <u>power</u> he always brings to bear (even if he himself does not realize it), with all three of these elements interacting with his choices to produce the particular outcome each participant derives from each voluntary transaction he participates in. All such transactions occur in a Market.

1) Market Power

Market power is, quite simply, whatever capabilities we each have <u>which produce something which others would like to acquire from us</u> to satisfy their own desires. Quite simply, it is the sum total of everything any of us is able and willing to offer <u>to others</u> lawfully to enhance those others' lives, harming no one (although competitors unable or unwilling successfully to compete may suffer disappointment).

In the terms of Economics jargon, our Market Power consists of the Supply of whatever we have on offer for which there is Demand from others. Quite simply, the greater that Demand, the greater our Market Power. And, of course, it includes all financial resources we are able and willing to command to purchase what others produce.

Remarkably, Market power's value in any business setting (as opposed to purely amatory ones, which also involve their own market power) can always be precisely measured in <u>purely-monetary</u> dollar terms: it is precisely the price <u>in money</u> as of any moment which those who want what we have on offer – including services they want from us – <u>are willing to pay for it</u>. Quite simply: the more others are willing to pay us for what we have which they want, the greater our market power. And money itself always has Market Power for its owner identical to its purchasing power, a.k.a. its monetary value.

It is indeed the great value of money in civil society that it provides both (1) a clear <u>measurement</u> of all Market Power, and (2) a <u>means of exchange</u> for purchases of whatever goods and/or services participants desire from each other. The greater the certainty the participants have about the stability of the value of money itself, the greater its value to those participants as a means to provide clear understanding regarding all aspects of the market – "market signals," as such information is often characterized.

Thus, <u>completely unlike</u> Violence/terror Power, Market Power has <u>nothing what-soever</u> to do with the ability to <u>harm</u> others – those others being our potential customers and other transactional counter-parties (e.g. employers or employees, business partners, and even lovers and/or marriage partners). Instead, it consists <u>exclusively</u> of our <u>power</u>, with respect to each such counter-party, in that other's, subjective view, <u>to benefit that other person,</u> and <u>serve his</u> self-interest, which <u>attracts that other person voluntarily</u> to interact and transact with us.

Indeed, it is precisely the purchasers, sellers, employees or any other transacting parties, whose desire for what we are offering itself literally <u>creates our</u> Market Power; and it is they alone, who place, or voluntarily agree to, the value of whatever we have to offer – in the market for whatever those goods or services are.

In short, our Market Power consists of the purely-subjective value placed on whatever we have to offer by those who want it.

It is literally the case that only someone who despises voluntary actions and exchanges by citizens would find anything objectionable, let alone sinister, in Market Power – or confuse it with its opposite, which is the Power to inflict Violence/terror. That very confusion is precisely what Karl Marx and his socialist followers (whether they even know that is what they are – let alone admit to it) manifest – and literally obsess about. That utter loathing of the individual and his liberty is the very heart of Marxism. Thus they demand an end to all private property — always except for themselves! — and dictatorial state control over absolutely everything.

State control of any market necessarily limits — drastically — the number of those willing to participate in it. The more market participants there are, the more choices and opportunities of every kind there are for everyone.

The explicit goal of Marxism is to eliminate all free markets, and thus all voluntary market participants, and render everyone a slave to the state, which alone commands all goods and services it can force them to provide — force being the only incentive for them to do so, since Marxists forbid all profits. The mass death and brutality Marxism always produces aside, it also inevitably impoverishes and imprisons everyone except for the tiny few who politically-dominate everyone else, for the simple reason that humans produce the most when they are freest, and able to reap the rewards — profits — which their productions justly entitle them to – the very conditions precluded in a Marxist society.

The subject people in Marxist societies are always destitute (e.g., in Cuba today, $20 per month is the maximum permissible legal salary!), and there are few goods for them to purchase anyway, because, although whatever wealth the politician rulers permit the subjects/slaves to retain is distributed equally among them, no one has any incentive to produce any goods for anyone to purchase (and the ruling elite alone purchase the goods they desire in countries outside the hell hole prison nation they rule over).

In their utter contempt for individuals to make their own choices in life, and their utter loathing of all businesses and businessmen, Marxists completely confuse Market Power (literally the power to benefit others voluntarily) with Violence Power – its opposite. Indeed, that particular confusion is the very heart and foundation of Marxism, together with Marxists' complete inability to understand that any power other than Violence Power even exists.

For that reason, they view all profits derived by market participants as inherently evil and corrupt — as forcibly stolen. They do not comprehend that all profits are actually the result, in a free market, exclusively of voluntary choices, with each transaction participant choosing to make each trade he engages in. Each market participant necessarily believes that, in his every transaction, what he receives is of greater value – to him – than what he is giving up. He simply has no other reason to complete the transaction, which he is free to walk away from.

Absolutely nothing but his own choice, based on his belief that he will enjoy that added value, requires him to contract for any transaction.

Thus, in real, non-Marxist life, profit is, quite simply, the measure of that additional value experienced subjectively by each (i.e. on all sides of any transaction) market transaction participant. That profit increases the wealth both of each market participant – a genuine win/win – and of the nation itself, as Adam Smith taught us centuries ago.

And it is precisely that profit – that genuine, voluntarily-created boon to all – which Marxists, in their utter, deluded confusion, consider <u>evil</u> incarnate! They believe that all profit can only exist by being <u>stolen from others</u> (employees, customers) when, in reality, as I have just proven, it is inherent that it can <u>only</u> occur in purely-voluntary transactions since it consists of, by definition, the purely-subjective, but nevertheless monetarily-measurable, net benefit each market participant experiences from each transaction he engages in.

It is also literally the case that if anyone does not want what we are offering, its market value <u>to them</u> is zero – regardless what it may be worth to others. Market value is inherently subjective – always a matter of individual choice.

Accordingly, market power is, in short, <u>our power to enhance the lives of others</u> in some manner. The greater that power, the more its value. By definition, it <u>never</u> harms any other transaction participant, whose participation is purely voluntary (within whatever rules govern the transaction, including distortions caused by state interference), in any market unadulterated and uncorrupted by government Violence Power and its inevitable favoritism/intervention/bullying.

As shown above, Market Power <u>cannot exist without a demand from others</u> for whatever (including money) we each have to offer. Other market participants may offer similar, or in some way competing, products or services to those we offer. In a market, which always has aspects of scarcity (since no product or service exists in infinite supply), all things being equal, if demand for our offerings is greater than for that of our competitors, those competitors may feel personally harmed by our Market Power. They may even experience envy – the one emotion forbidden in the 10 Commandments – at our success.

But, within the rules of Good Law and the market, as long as we are committing no fraud, theft, assault or other tortious misconduct, <u>that's a Just outcome — the way things are supposed to be</u>: there are winners and losers, but the losers' harm suffered is supposed to provide an additional incentive for the loser(s) to try some other venture, or work that much harder – which will ultimately result in further improved offerings of the kind we are temporarily privileged to be dominant in, enhancing the value of offerings of that nature for the buyers who, in turn, necessarily must produce something of value themselves in order to pay for what we have to offer.

I have been describing a market operating under the rule of Good Law, uncorrupted by Bad Law and the government intervention/Violence Power it inevitably grants its functionaries to impose political obstacles and corruption on market participants. Quite simply, Good Law, and the complete absence of Bad Law, is the most basic requirement for an uncorrupted, truly free market.

It was Karl Marx who, intending to besmirch such a free market which was the object of his fanatical loathing, coined the term Capitalism (as an insult) to characterize it, absolutely convinced that it was some purely violence-and-ideology-driven perversion of inter-human activities — rather than, as in actuality, simply what happens when free people are free to interact under Good Law and literally be and offer all which they can for others, and be fairly, and voluntarily, compensated for their offerings – and so enrich everyone's life <u>at no one's involuntary expense</u>.

It is no exaggeration to say that this fundamental, ontological confusion about markets, Market Power, and profit, which lies at the very heart of Marxism, can fairly be characterized as a form of pathological delusion.

In Marx's perverted bizarro world view, nothing is more monstrous than that free market I have just described. He and his followers are utterly unable to comprehend that, as I have just shown, Profit, and the expectation of realizing it, is the engine – the invisible hand – which drives the entire mutually-satisfying and always-agreed-to results of the voluntary exchanges which take place in the market.

Marx and all his followers find all those concepts utterly incomprehensible and, in their literally insane view of the world, characterize all profit as <u>evil</u> (within the pseudo-morality of his religion-hating militant atheism) and necessarily exploitative – even though, in real life, as described above, profit is always simply the measure and consequence of the mutual satisfaction between humans acting exclusively according to their individual desires within the market and under the rule of Good Law.

As Adam Smith explained brilliantly over 200 years ago, the subjective profit <u>always</u> realized by <u>each</u> participant in every voluntary market exchange, together with the increased value of all market offerings resulting from competition among the participants, both have the effect of increasing the wealth of the entire nation in which these transactions occur. <u>The combined profits each voluntary exchanger realizes from each exchange is the very measure of that increase in wealth</u> – to them and to the nation. The supply of money can grow without inflation in an amount dollar for dollar equal to the sum of all such profits realized in the nation, <u>because it reflects genuine value added to the wealth of the nation</u>.

Bear in mind: Karl Marx pretended – and continues today to be accepted by numerous "intellectuals" – to reach his conclusions based on his supposedly serious, reasoned analysis as a supposedly-sophisticated social "scientist" and economist. His patently nonsensical claim that profit is evil is literally as insane as proclaiming that the air in your lungs is harmful to your health. And tens of millions have died as sacrificial lambs by followers of his in pursuit of the new-Eden he insisted his profoundly-evil, and utterly nonsensical ideas would pave the way for.

A market consisting of willing participants subject to the rule of Good Law alone is one in which Market Power <u>alone</u> determines all participants' choices, opportunities and outcomes. It is the only uncorrupted market. Any involvement by the state and its officeholders – who inevitably use the Violent/terrorizing Power of the state for their own advantage to threaten harm to market participants – beyond simply enforcing Good Law, always corrupts — and even destroys — the market and reduces its value to all its legitimate participants. And that is always the true, intended purpose for such state Bad Law involvement — or "regulation," as it is euphemistically called.

(2)  State/Political Intervention In And Control/Regulation/Corruption Of the Market; The Power to Inflict Violence

The easiest way to understand the nature of any intervention by the state, when it exceeds its necessary role of being the Good Law enforcement mechanism, is:

Consider a playground where two children are happily playing a game involving some kind of competition: they each employ whatever skill they have involved in playing the game, a game which has its own rules, with neither of them able or interested in employing violence against the other.

A bully enters the playground determined to intervene and, through the use or threat of physical violence, he completely disrupts and, indeed, destroys the game. It does not matter whether one of the hapless children may have invited the bully, or if he enters on his own gratuitously. He can threaten to beat up one or both of the children, but he can never improve the quality of the game.

If he takes the side of one of the children, he deliberately rigs the game against the other player, effectively forcing that player to lose – or just quit the game altogether. The bully's presence will also prevent any additional children from choosing to participate in the game, leaving any child with whom the bully sided alone to play the game himself, with all potential other, new players moving on to find some completely different game where the bully is absent.

What happens when there is any — and I do mean any — participation by the government in a market in which participants offer to buy and/or sell goods or services, participants who otherwise, as in any market, compete with each other, if the government then takes any role other than being the Good Law enforcement mechanism? Because the only thing any government can bring to any market is its Violence Power, its sole involvement, beyond that mere enforcement of Good Law, necessarily is that of a bully – and only that of a bully.

This is because, as an automatic monopolist/dictator, it is inherently impossible for the government ever to produce any good or service anyone would voluntarily want to purchase, even after stealing a formerly-thriving business from its owners (simply consider Cuba's economy since 1960 if you doubt this fact) – so it inherently can never possess any Market power whatsoever within the market itself; its only power always is that of violence, including its threat, against the actual market participants.

Only when the government only monopolizes violence, and acts exclusively as the enforcer of Good Law, thereby discouraging, and punishing only after-the-fact, violence committed by market participants against others, is its Violence Power put to its only possible good use.

If any market participant succeeds (always corruptly) in bringing in politicians and the state, with their violence/bullying power, to intercede on his behalf against competitors, the entire, then newly-"regulated" (by Bad Law) market is ruined (although its incumbents will continue in business, corruptly-surviving under political, rather than market, control), with value reduced or destroyed for all existing, and especially any potential new participants — any manufacturers, employees, buyers and sellers — and subjected to the discretionary tyranny of politicians, bureaucrats and Bad Law. Cronyism, or crony capitalism or socialism, is the name for that corrupted former market and its continuing participants and, to moral market participants, it is poison.

The seeming benefits which governmental market intrusion can bring particular participants who believe they will thereby be advantaged over others, and so desire it, can seem appealing, in the short term, particularly to those currently in management (who may reap the benefit of the short-term advantage the bully provides them, and retire before the inevitable damage arises), politicians and other parasites.

Other, honorable market participants opposed to such, armed only with even the most Market Power, simply never can overcome the inherent Violence Power of the state once its politicians decide, especially if, as does corruptly happen, they are invited in by other market participants, to enter any market.

That is precisely why the only means of preventing such entry into markets by the government is opposing, more powerful Violence Power – in the form of actually-enforceable, Constitutional prohibitions on such and, ideally, further supported by moral taboos. And that was indeed the precise purpose our Founders intended to achieve and institute legally and morally in our own Constitution. No other nation on the planet has ever been blessed with such clear, constitutional prohibitions on government/politician/crony competitor market-destroying power – and no other nation, since the 17th Century has ever been able to resist its inevitable tyranny.

Quite simply, if the government is not absolutely and forcibly forbidden to intrude on markets, it is certain that it will do so and, notwithstanding its pretensions of being able to limit that intrusion, ultimately it will recognize no limits on its power, once it jumps any rails preventing its entry.

The state and its officeholders – politicians and bureaucrats – have no market power at all since they are inherently incapable of producing any good or service anyone would want (if you doubt that, just remember the Soviet Union and think of present day Cuba, Venezuela and North Korea and all the things they manufacture which you are dying to buy). They do have one power however – the power to inflict violence, or to threaten it.

"Political power grows out of the barrel of a gun."That is how Mao allegedly put it. And for once he actually spoke the truth – and got something right.

Quite simply, producing goods and/or services is what citizens do in their businesses; that is what any business is — the work and professional vehicle for the individuals involved in it. The real, productive business of the state and its functionaries has nothing whatsoever to do with any production of that nature — other than in a socialist tyranny, with its inevitably worthless – and yet scarce – "products".

The state's <u>sole</u>, actual, non-tyrannical business is, pure and simple, to monopolize violence, enforce Good Law, and protect citizens' money and property and the nation as a whole from traitors and external enemies – precisely as provided for in our unique Constitution.

Politicians, like everyone else, always act in their own interests. The more they insistently and loudly claim to be disinterested, selfless public servants, the more they are to be disbelieved as frauds. That is why it is critical for a constitution to strictly limit what they can and cannot do – and why it is equally critical that they obey those limitations.

Quite simply, politicians' selfish, personal interests are served if they can increase their violence power – the only kind they command as politicians — over the citizenry. The most predatory among them seek office precisely to maximize that tyrannical violence power, and its reach into markets, to the greatest extent they can get away with. And any increase in politicians' power is always obtained, as a zero-sum proposition, at the expense of the freedom and prosperity of the citizenry. Those are simply undeniable facts, as discussed in detail in the next chapter.

When politicians are able to abuse their offices to impose government/violence power – power which they themselves wield, supposedly on behalf of at least some of the citizenry – over the economy, markets and citizens' businesses, they can, and often do, further abuse that power to extract forced payments, and personal loyalty, from those subjected to that power, and so increase their personal wealth.

They extract these corrupt personal benefits, quite simply, by using the power of violence they wield, from market participants who possess market power <u>alone</u>, market power which is always unable to withstand assault from state/violence power. Quite simply, the sword and the jackboot invariably overwhelm mere producers of goods and services of even the greatest value.

And politicians who extract those personal benefits, always without contributing anything of actual value, are able to extort those benefits from honest market participants who have no choice but to obey the politicians — politicians who are armed with their existential, Violence Power — in order for the honest to survive at all.

Additionally, in a democracy, if allowed to do so, politicians can deploy their (fraudulent) promises to "improve" the real economy through their forced state intervention into it, as a powerful means to also increase their popularity with voters. That is, quite simply, what demagoguery (and fascism) means. Democracy is far from a guarantee against tyranny. It does, however, provide a non-violent means to completely undo tyranny – whenever the people wake up and see it is upon them. As Lincoln observed, "You can fool…"

There is no easier way for politicians to achieve personal benefits from forced interventions in the real economy, than to claim – invariably gratuitously and falsely – that, in the absence of such intervention, a market for a particular good or service is "defective," or has "failed" in some respect, and to propose and implement state – that is, bullying/violence power wielded by politicians and bureaucrats – intervention in that market, purportedly to "improve" it (a complete impossibility, as proven below), and so supposedly cure that purported market "defect."

Again, politicians will invariably accomplish this market intervention and force it on the market participants (under threat of violence if they resist) unless they are legally and forcibly prevented – by constitutional limitations and taboos against violating them alone – from doing so. Again, that is precisely what our Constitution was written to accomplish – an accomplishment which even extremely ambitious politicians feared — and refrained from — violating for the first 100 years of the Republic.

It is a fact: If politicians want to find something to complain about in any market, they can always find something. To a hammer, everything looks like a nail. Marx gave them a menu of complaints they can always bring against any market in a free country – complaints demagogues are always ready to use — and which they can get away with, if the people have not been educated to know that all those complaints are nothing but anti-constitutional, Marxist nonsense.

As discussed in Chapter 14 below, for numerous, structural reasons, multiple, highly-influential professions in America – journalism, entertainers of all types, university professors, the legal profession, clergymen – have invariably cheered on, and even instigated, political interventions in the economy against other citizens' property and businesses, since the 1840s, interventions those professions' members personally, invariably benefited from, along with the politicians, all at the expense of the real, productive market participants — including all businesses' employees and customers, even if the harm to them was successfully obfuscated.

And politicians can always find many citizens they promise magically to please by, as a pretext for, their market interventions – whether customers who claim to have been overcharged (always in a transaction they voluntarily consented to, by the way, for a good or service they indeed wanted), market competitors unhappy with their market position who blame the market, rather than their own inadequacies, for such, or some other claimed "victim" nursing some grievance.

Politicians know: someone will, at least initially, be happy if they are permitted to, and do, intervene – and they will reap the benefit of pleasing those newly-happy constituents who will owe them in some manner, and enhance their power to extract further tribute in the future by virtue of their control seized over the market.

And politicians also know that once they determine to intervene in and control any market, any market participant who attempts to stand in their way does so at his peril. Again, mere Market Power can never withstand the force of state/Violence Power. Only other, state/Violence Power has the power to do so – precisely what a Constitution and articulate, opposing politicians, are supposed to accomplish.

Once forced on any market, political control will, in turn, generate work that pays for bureaucrats, lawyers, lobbyists and other parasites (an accurate description) who, along with the corrupted incumbent businesses, personally benefit from the presence of the government market intervention – again, euphemistically called "regulation" – all of whom will together become a corrupted "regulation"-supporting constituency, who are happy it has been imposed on the market, and none of whom will produce any product or service of actually enhancing the value of the nation's wealth, unlike genuine market participants.

The only highly-visible victims of the "regulation" are the honest market participants whose transactions become subject to the weight and huge costs of that government /Violence Power intervention and its numerous compliance and tribute costs. Less honest, corruptible market participants may, as mentioned above, welcome the intervention as market incumbents, insulated by that intervention from future competitors, competitors who never can thereafter materialize and who, accordingly, themselves are invisible victims of the "regulation."

That is because those potential competitors are now barred, as a practical matter, from participating in the "regulated," violence-corrupted market.

Additional, typically-unsuspecting, invisible victims are the public, who politicians invariably pretend will benefit from the "regulation," but who, in reality, never do – because the intervention is incapable of doing anything other than subtracting, rather than adding, value to all enterprises affected, other than parasitism. In reality the public thereafter miss out on the numerous benefits (which they formerly took for granted) of an uncorrupted market – those being the formerly, now lost, continuing improvement in the now-"regulated" product or service, the previous continued reductions in price, and in enhanced choice.

All those real, and inevitable, benefits of free markets are lost when the market becomes controlled by the state, its politicians and bureaucrats. And that control is an enormous cost forced on the public who, as customers, inevitably must pay for it (if the affected businesses cannot pass those costs on to their customers, those businesses go bankrupt and disappear), in addition to what is left of the good or services they still want which is now "regulated."

Any political effort to reduce any supposed market "inadequacies" – such as to disappointed or envious competitors – caused by the healthy functioning of the inherently-and-beneficially competitive market, inevitably results in damage to the market's integrity, and to the wealth and liberty of all participants – and in corruption, resulting from what, incident to such market-"fixing" efforts, inevitably turns what had previously been a normal, healthy market into a rigged game.

That rigging, as discussed above, inevitably harms all honest and productive market participants, and benefits no one but those politicians and other parasites who control, or lobby or otherwise intercede with those who control, and those market participants who corruptly participate in, the rigging – and definitely not the customers or employees of any formerly-free business.

As mentioned above, such "regulatory-fixing" of any market also has the de-structive (to wealth and freedom) effect of discouraging new market partic-ipants from entering the market at all and competing against the incumbent ones, since the incumbents inevitably have all the advantages in a rigged game – rigging which can only occur when the government intervenes in — and de-stroys — the market.

Notwithstanding claims by power-seeking politicians, there has never been a single, actual instance in history in which any market participant, armed with nothing but Market Power alone, succeeded in similarly-rigging any free market, or even in controlling it as a monopolist for any significant amount of time – in the absence of government facilitating such rigging and/or monopolization.

Once demanded by always self-serving politicians, the incumbent businesses invariably agree to the rigging, whether voluntarily or involuntarily. Basically, they really have no choice about this: as mentioned above, if the state decides to intervene and "regulate" a market, and politicians are determined to do so, the incumbents' mere market power simply cannot stop the politicians' assault and, with their own shareholders in mind, especially if they are public companies, they are forced to make the best of the corrupt, tyrannical situation.

Again, the most fundamental feature of the two types of power – Market Power and Violence Power – is that Market Power is, quite simply, powerless in the face of Violence Power and has no choice but to yield to it. The only power comparable to violence power is other, stronger Violence Power equipped to overwhelm it. That is the role our Constitution was consciously intended to play in the Republic — as a forced restraint on politicians' and their inevitable power grabs.

The second most fundamental feature of the two types of power is the fact that political complaints about markets, including their typical complaints that some particular market participants' market power has become supposedly so great as to endanger the public, all actually arise out of confusing Market Power (which is simply the power to benefit others, as shown above) with its <u>opposite</u> Violence Power (which is the power to do harm – the <u>opposite</u> of Market Power).

## Antitrust Laws

Indeed, that particular confusion – which is the very heart of Marxism, as discussed above – is what gave rise to antitrust laws, first in Europe, where one would expect such nonsense, and in America in 1890. Those laws, quite simply, declare illegal the accumulation of "too much" (whatever that is – and no one knows, by the way) Market Power in the hands of any company. They also declare it illegal for ostensible competitors to collude with each other and fix prices and otherwise engage in joint, anti-competitive activity.

However, regarding antitrust laws' civil and criminal prohibitions on bid-rigging, boycotts, price-fixing and other anti-competitive activity: Common-Law business torts in existence in the laws of every single state in the nation <u>prior to</u> the antitrust laws' enactment already rendered tortious, <u>all</u> such anti-competitive behavior, making it actionable in state court, with anyone who is actually harmed by that anticompetitive behavior entitled to sue for damages for such.

To the extent such anticompetitive misconduct constituted fraud or theft of some kind, it had also long been actionable, with no need for any additional, federal antitrust or other laws, as both a civil and criminal matter in all states.

The very idea that anyone can have <u>too much</u> pure Market Power is preposterous <u>on its face</u>: how can anyone ever have <u>too much power to benefit others</u>?

In reality, no matter how great it may be for any market participant at any one time, the Market Power of any single player is, by definition, power that disappears immediately when some other player/s is/are able to benefit others <u>better</u>, or when the benefit otherwise disappears. <u>It is inherently incapable of harming anyone</u> other than competitors unable to compete with it — competitors who can only complain about, and be rewarded for, that consequence of their own inadequacies in a politically-rigged game.

The 1890 federal Antitrust Law's legislators/enactors promised the impossible — that it would never be used simply to benefit politicians or competitors, and that its sole purpose was to benefit customers.

In fact, antitrust laws'<u>only</u> real-life, actual effects have been <u>precisely the opposite</u> of those promises: other than as a Violence Power vehicle for political-crony competitors to corrupt a market, and for politicians to panic, and extract tribute from, market participants, due to those laws' inherently-arbitrary, discretionary nature, they are economically-worthless and have <u>always only</u> been used corruptly by demagogue politicians personally, and to facilitate unearned competitive, short-term benefits to competitors who invoke politicians' power under those laws to harm their competitors corruptly.

Because of its vacuous, supposed "economic" underlying rationale, antitrust law is today, as it always has been, simply an open-ended threat politicians can use against businesses whenever they want to harm them – always for political reasons – or simply to extort/blackmail them. No one has ever been able to make a credible, substantive economic justification for its existence based on anything other than theoretical constructs, all of which are proved pure nonsense by simple common sense understanding of markets.

Unlike laws against fraud, antitrust laws — because it is based on the bogus notion that too much Market Power is even possible — simply have no coherent moral or intellectual underlying basis. That, and their draconian penalties, including criminal liability, is why antitrust laws have always been so frightening to businesses: they are an open-ended weapon politicians can use against them, in a purely discretionary and arbitrary manner, with the ability to destroy those businesses, as a threat the politicians personally thereby wield.

It was, in fact, the then-unprecedented, manic threats of massive antitrust prosecutions announced, and pursued, by Theodore Roosevelt after his first actual election as president in 1904 that led to the panic of 1906 which, in turn, was used by politicians later to justify politically nationalizing the very currency through the creation of the disastrous and utterly unconstitutional (as shown in later chapters) Federal Reserve.

Whatever incumbent market participants' motive for buying in to their own "regulation," its presence always serves to preserve their own positions corruptly by freezing out competition from new market entrants. And the bureaucrats who enforce the rigging have their own motives (yes, the bureaucrats too always act based on their own self-interest) in order to preserve their own positions – and self-interestedly exercise power over all market participants.

The politicians and bureaucrats imposing market "regulation" inevitably engage in a corrupt bargain with market incumbents – to preserve their own bureaucratic positions and to make sure the incumbents' businesses are not fatally damaged. They must prevent such fatal damage to market participants to preserve their own power: because the public will not tolerate the complete loss of the services and/or goods the incumbents are providing. If the regulation were to completely destroy the product/service producers, that would literally kill the Golden goose – an outcome neither the bureaucrats nor the politicians can accept – for their own self-preservation, the interest they invariably serve.

The state-intervention-created rigged game constitutes a classic barrier to competition. That is, indeed, one of its major purposes. Those who want such "fixing" in any market invariably are either fools or knaves because they either do not understand the value – to both the freedom and prosperity of all – of a genuinely-free market and competition itself, or simply desire such corruption for the non-market Violence Power it produces – as a feature, not a bug.

### How Real, Free People/Markets Function – And Why They Always Benefit Everyone

Fundamental to the entire <u>non</u>-corrupted, free market process is the ability of all its participants voluntarily to engage in private <u>contracts</u> with each other to purchase and/or sell whatever the other contracting party wants. As mentioned above, <u>all</u> market participants have the (beneficial) self-interested incentive to maximize the value of what they are offering to others – their market power – in whatever way they can – using all their capabilities to do so. The more participants there are on each transactional side – prospective buyers and sellers of whatever is being offered – the more competitive the market.

In the simplest case — where two people bargain between themselves and come to an agreement to buy/sell a particular item or service at an agreed-to price — there is always a willing buyer and a willing seller, with each getting what is acceptable (even if not wishfully-ideal) for himself out of the interaction and, at the very least, coming away from it better off in his own view than prior to the interaction. And we know this last point for a fact <u>because each could have turned the deal down</u> and been left with the status quo ante — had that choice seemed preferable to him.

There are a few other things to remember about markets. First, a market of some sort is present in <u>every single</u> interaction between human beings in which they each have something the other desires — for whatever reason — and regardless how unlike the pure market described above they may appear.

### The State As Market Participant

For example: Lets say that my driver's license is expired and I need a new one. I go to the Department of Motor Vehicles and, after waiting endlessly and pointlessly, interact with a bureaucrat who couldn't care less about me and derives no benefit whatsoever from the money I pay for my new license since the money does not go to him, unless he steals it, and his compensation is unaffected by my satisfaction with his performance, or lack thereof.

In that situation there are three market participants in reality – me, the bureaucrat and the (unseen) government agency which actually issues the license and pays the bureaucrat his salary (undoubtedly without any regard to his performance in providing me the "service" of providing me my license).

In that situation, the state has a monopoly on the product I want – the license – and I have no choice but to put up with whatever it charges me and however it and its functionary act towards me. But it is also important to remember that the government functionary is not some selfless angel: he has his own interests, whatever they may be, which may include using his position to bully me, even if only by wasting my time excessively. This last point, regarding the power of government and its functionaries, is of critical importance: they produce <u>no</u> goods or services that have any value, and so have no market power, but they always have the power to harm, which includes the power to threaten but withhold harm.

Because the state – and its functionary – can also harm me directly by either refusing to let me purchase its "product" – the license – by fining, or even jailing me and otherwise depriving me of the ability to drive. It has <u>both</u> violence-infliction, and a kind of violence-created market power over me: it can fine and/or jail me if I don't buy its "product," and can charge me whatever it wants, without any concern of competition from others for the monopoly "product" it has to offer – a "product" I would not even buy if I wasn't legally forced to.

That is what is unique about the state: unlike real citizen market participants, it – and its officeholders – always have the power – which it is the state's job to monopolize and prevent others from having – <u>to inflict harm</u>; but other than licenses which it may demand we obtain simply to do things we wish to do, it is incapable of producing any goods or services anyone would want without being forced to accept such.

That is because the state has no "talent" for producing any goods or services – other than the violence it uniquely has the power to monopolize and inflict.

Nevertheless, whenever the state injects itself into any transaction, it, together with any of his functionaries through whom it acts, become <u>additional, always self-interested</u> participants in any such transaction and, simply by virtue of their presence in the transaction in any manner, reduce its value to all of its voluntary, actual market participants – especially with respect to any participants it chooses forcibly to impose its will against by overruling theirs (forcibly forbidding their real choices) in the transaction.

There is one way and <u>one way alone</u> in which the state and its officeholders can maximize the wealth and freedom of its citizens and the value of all market transactions to the market participants: by being the impartial enforcer of all Good Law which, by its nature, as discussed in the next Chapter, both, under the Common-Law, provides the beneficial, necessary, underpinning rule of law enforcing the property and contract rights underlying all market transactions, and provides the various additional market value protections authorized under the Constitution (preserving free trade, the value of the currency, intellectual and all other property rights, etc.).

Any other action by the state — and, as always, its functionaries — beyond that can do nothing but harm the market and citizens, increase corruption, and reduce the wealth and freedom of the entire nation.

As just mentioned, there is only one circumstance in which the state has any market power/value – as opposed to the power of physical violence – at all: when it provides the necessary, underlying service as the just-enforcer of Good Law – and absolutely nothing else. To the precise extent to which the state attempts to involve itself in any market in any manner beyond that, its presence is inherently destructive to all legitimate market forces and participants. And the only power it ever wields is its power to inflict violence/terror – the power to harm. It is incapable of ever being a normal market participant – even if it pretends to provide any particular goods or services to actual market participants – i.e., non-state actors.

Government involvement in/control over markets, always as a bully – what is euphemistically called "regulation" – was a phenomenon well-known to the founders: it was the very form taken by the tyranny absolute monarchs, such as the French Bourbons, imposed on their own economies, and which the British monarchy had been forcefully <u>prevented</u> from then-imposing on the English by Parliament in the English Civil War/revolution of the 1640s and 1650s. That victory against centrally-imposed tyranny from that earlier English revolution was precisely what our founders expected to build on in our Revolution: they did not expect that that revolution would have to be <u>fought again</u> 200 years later – i.e. here, now.

Power in the central government even approaching that type of micromanagement of citizens' actions was, as shown in later chapters, what all the Founders <u>thought they had Constitutionally outlawed for the federal government,</u> in its enumeration of specific powers, its procedural provisions, the Contract clause, and the Takings clause of the Fifth Amendment – which outlawing was recognized, followed and respected even by America's most ambitious politicians, with respect to every single American market and industry — until 1887.

The first instance of such involvement – the creation of the Interstate Commerce Commission in 1887, through virtually unopposed congressional legislation, as discussed below – paradigmatically illustrates the confluence of political forces that invariably come together to produce every such federal market-takeover – and its inevitable purely-destructive results — except, arguably, for the incumbent market participants, whose complete control of the market ends up being guaranteed by the mechanism of "regulating": they alone can afford the compliance costs, and the regulators end up needing them alive because the public will continue to demand the service they provide – and no new market participants will attempt to overcome the entry barriers posed by the existence of the regulators and the legally-entrenched position of those very incumbents.

To summarize that process: for some time prior to seeking legislation authorizing such "regulation," an industry produces media headlines involving, often falsely, alleged financial scandals of various sorts, scandals sometimes arising, as in the case of the railroads, out of (often perfectly-legal) federal funding of some of the market participants' projects. Since that funding necessarily benefits some of those market participants, inevitably at the expense of other citizens, and such promotes the jealousy of non-participants, including members of the public, who are stuck with the bill for the allegedly-corrupt subsidy, it is deeply resented by at least some members of the public who expect to be able to themselves get some special benefit when they employ the services of the subsidized business.

Alleged windfall profits for one or more of the federal fund beneficiaries are noisily touted in the press, with the suggestion that if those profits were diminished, others would benefit – with no evidence for that whatsoever. Customers of the subsidized business complain to politicians, who pretend to be their advocates and promote "regulation" of the industry. "Regulation" eventually is imposed, which has the effect of forcing all market participants to comply with commands, and seek permission for all their actions, from federal bureaucrats. That has the effect of freezing out any new competitors, guaranteeing the incumbents – who alone perform the service which the public continues to demand – their exclusive, now oligopoly, market control, and virtually precluding any further innovation by those market participants for the two reasons that (1) any further innovation would require obtaining permission for such from the "regulators" and, (2) since they end up with virtually-guaranteed, if reduced, profit margins, they simply have no incentive to change things in any respect.

The public derives no benefit whatsoever: although some members of the public may have joined in the clamor for the "regulation" based on the promise that their prices would be reduced for the same product, in fact prices never come down, and the product ceases any further improvements.

Other than the incumbent industries whose incumbency and control of the industry inevitably becomes guaranteed – their monopoly or oligopoly position, which can only be obtained and continued indefinitely by such state interposition in the market – the only real beneficiaries of this entire process are politicians who are empowered by the regulation and can hold the regulated industries hostage to paying them "campaign contributions" or, in crasser situations, simply bribes, to fend off the destruction of their businesses which the regulators ultimately have the power to effect, bureaucrats, and numerous non-government parasites.

Those other, parasite beneficiaries are lawyers and lobbyists who become necessary intermediaries for obtaining all permissions required from regulators for the system to operate thereafter. Their fees must be paid – ultimately increasing prices paid by the public, without any improved service. Their fees are part of the total compliance costs. Again, customers and potential competitors are deeply harmed by all this and only corrupt politicians and lobbyists, lawyers and other parasites benefit.

And the total wealth of the nation suffers from all this.

The nation has seen this process unfold repeatedly since 1887 – always with the same initiating processes, and the same results: complete destruction of the market subjected to federal "regulation," damaging all present and future prospective participants in it – including the public at large who are the customers (and market participants), and all existing and prospective employees, of the numerous businesses which are adversely affected both directly and indirectly by the "regulation."

## An Example of "Regulatory" Harm: The SEC

As discussed in the previous Chapter, "regulation" of the securities industry, instituted beginning with the Securities Act of 1933, affects every single corporation in America, particularly any public ones, whose stock is available for anyone to purchase, in addition to the multiple industries involved in selling stock, bonds, and options for such, at any stage of their existence, including initial offerings and secondary markets, stock exchanges of all kinds, all other financial institutions (banks etc.), and everyone who buys or sells securities anywhere in the world – securities whose value, incidentally, is inherently <u>reduced</u> by built-in compliance costs for the issuers' complying with the multiple layers of federal regulation.

The original, politically-announced supposed purpose of such regulation, of course, was to prevent fraud etc. and, supposedly, to "help" stock market investors. <u>It has never done either of those</u>: for example, <u>never once</u> has the SEC detected an actual major securities fraud with significant market consequences (such as the numerous Ponzi schemes, etc., that have made headlines over the years) prior to its exposure by non-government victims – even when SEC bureaucrats were actually, repeatedly notified specifically of particular schemes which, burdened with their own bureaucratic incompetence, they ended up ignoring.

Always stretching to define some argument for its continued existence, the SEC has spent most of its efforts inventing rules which have no basis in morality or the common law (which, by itself, is more than adequate to address any actual frauds etc.), which provide a convenient way for the government to prosecute — and, in reality, simply persecute —people for doing no more than engaging in normal business transactions – "regulations" based on unprovable theories devised by self-proclaimed "economists," which, in fact, other economists have shown to be utterly bogus in real life.

The truth is, the more worthless the SEC has proven itself to be, the more ardently it has sought to justify its existence by inventing fake "harms" it can torture individual American citizens with for supposedly having subjected their fellow citizens to – notwithstanding the fact that anyone <u>actually harmed</u> in a market can obtain damages against the wrongdoer under state business tort and corporate law, laws which exist in every American jurisdiction. Things that are genuinely harmful have long been against state law – both criminal and civil – with never any need for the SEC to police such at all.

The only thing the SEC really does in that regard is create new crimes and wrongs out of thin air, criminalizing previously legal, and always harmless, behavior by citizens, and benefiting no one but the SEC and its bureaucratic interest in surviving long past the time it served any legitimate purpose — and all the lawyers and other parasites necessary to protect citizens in dealing with the SEC and its "regulations."

## The Employment Market

One particular type of market requires special mention – if only to clarify massive, widely-held, (Marxist) confusion about it, and so dispel the mountains of mis-information and disinformation that have been heaped on it for hundreds of years. I am talking about the market(s) between employers and employees and potential employees. This particular market is like any other: each participant brings whatever value each actual or prospective counter-party places on him – no more and no less.

That value, of course, can be affected substantially by competing bidders for what each party has on offer (employers offer compensation for employment; their counter-parties offer their services): it is an obvious fact that the more bidders there are – and the greater their incentive for bidding – for what any other party has to offer, the greater the always-subjective and objective market value of what that party is offering.

Thus, it is always to each employee's or prospective employee's advantage for there to be as many potential employers incentivized to bid for his services – and subject to minimal disincentives to do so. Left undisturbed by government intervention, markets automatically expand, as suppliers of goods and services compete against each other and so necessarily improve what they are supplying, and purchasers multiply as the value of what is being supplied increases, while prices decline; and the purchasers' financial resources to pay for such increase as the overall economy expands, with the resulting expansion of profits for sellers, which profits invariably increase the wealth of the nation (and alone result in the economy's growth).

The greatest disincentives to employers to want to hire anyone are federal market interventions in the form of directives, compliance obligations and costs, and prohibitions on their otherwise legal actions which distort business decisions of all kinds, without any wealth production whatsoever, and reduce any incentive to expand the business by hiring new employees.

All those disincentives are precisely what all laws and agencies policing any aspect of employment markets in the nation – other than the Common Law ad-ministered by states – do. They literally do nothing else, in fact, other than harm all market participants in the labor market — including the employees and pro-spective employees they falsely pretend to help — and in fact immensely harm by limiting, if not eliminating, their employment opportunities.

I am talking about <u>every single</u> law and regulation administered by, among others, the federal Department of Labor, and all so-called minimum-wage laws, whose only purpose and effect is to outlaw people from working for less than the stated minimum-wage amount — even if that is all their skills are worth. All those laws and agencies were created under the pretense that they would "help" the "little guy" – employees or prospective employees (always called, in Marxist language, "workers") – in their dealings with employers. For the reasons just shown, all those laws all have precisely the opposite effect.

This is because the one thing any employee or prospective employee should actually want is for the government to interject itself into the economy <u>as little as possible</u>, so that his employment opportunities will be greatest. Any time the government says it is doing something to "protect" employees or otherwise "help" them in their dealings with lawyers, the opposite is inevitably the case, because the government action has the automatic effect of reducing demand for the employee's services.

An employee's market value clearly is also directly affected by the business prospects for his employer within the market in which the employer himself competes to sell his own goods or services: the greater the demand for what the employer is selling in his market, the greater his need and desire for employees. And that market, in turn, is directly affected by the overall relative favorability of the legal climate in which his business operates: the more oppressive that climate is to his business, the more costs and less profitability he can expect, which in turn would reduce the amount he is willing to pay for any employee and the number of employees of any kind he is willing to even contemplate hiring.

This means that each employee's own market value to prospective employers increases to the extent that the business-profitability climate for each prospective employer's own business improves. The more employees an employer desires, the greater the market value of each employee becomes to him – all other things being equal.

Additionally, if an employer decides to retain the services of a particular prospective employee, he will be willing to pay the most for that employee depending on whether that employee has competing offers of employment: the more excited the bidding war for that employee's services among prospective employers – each of whom necessarily places a different maximum subjective dollar value on those services depending on such prospective employer's own needs – the more pay that employee can demand.

Accordingly, it is always to an employee's advantage for there to be as many bidding, prospective employers, each of whom value his services as highly, as possible, which value in turn increases as the overall business climate increases.

Normally an employer would want to pay an employee as little as (subjectively) possible so that the employer can maximize the per-employee profit he anticipates deriving from that employee. It is in fact to each of his employees' advantage for him to exercise great discipline in not overpaying employees: his ability to profit from his business is essential to its continuation because, if it fails, all his employees loses their jobs.

The better the overall business climate for his services, the more likely the former employee is to replace a lost job. If all employers are subject to onerous "regulatory" compliance obligations concerning employees, obligations necessarily reducing the per-employee profitability, their incentives for hiring are reduced accordingly — and often eliminated.

Nevertheless, the fact that it is in the employer's interest for an employee to maximize his profitability for the employer, a fact which only a complete idiot would consider in a vacuum, led Karl Marx to claim – as a fundamental element, by the way of all his "teachings" – that all employees are virtual slaves of their employer who necessarily "steals" from them the entire profit (Marx called this, in his typical abuse of language, "surplus value" – and by telling you this I am sparing you reading his psychopathic drivel) he is able to derive allocable to their services.

And Marx alleges further, based on the benefit to the employer of maximizing his employee's profitability to him, that there is always <u>inherent abusiveness</u> in every employer-employee relationship, abusiveness which can only be cured by the state completely confiscating the employer's business from him (by his employees themselves, or by the state acting on their behalf, supposedly): by claiming that employers, to maximize this "surplus value", invariably pay employees no more than bare subsistence wages, which, Marx (nonsensically) claims, the employees never have any choice but to take whatever any employer offers them – all based on the assumption that there are never any other competing employers for their service.

That scarcity of need for employees is precisely what happens when employers are subject to a lawless state which does not recognize their property rights over their business – and the weaker their property rights are concerning their business, the less interested they would be in employing anyone. It is obvious that Marx's prescribed cure – confiscation of the business from its owner – is guaranteed to eliminate any incentive for any employer to hire anyone, and to foreclose all employment except by the state itself — necessarily producing nothing of any value.

In real life this produces the Soviet reality for all its state employees: "We pretend to work, and they pretend to pay us."

It is no exaggeration to say that Karl Marx's "solution" to the inherent, supposed "abusiveness" of the employer-employee relationship is simply to destroy it completely and eliminate employers altogether – other than the state itself, which is inherently more powerful relative to its "employees" than any human employer could possibly be. That is an undeniable fact, since the state, unlike any citizen, has the legal power to exercise violence of any kind against them or anyone else – that being the only attribute in which it is unique.

The world has seen the results of carrying out Marx's brilliant solutions – in the Soviet Union and every communist country that has ever existed.

For decades, European nations and the United States have taken half-Marxist measures regarding employers – using all-powerful bureaucracies to control all employers' decisions regarding operating their businesses and the terms of their arrangements with employees, through "regulations" and "mandates," but not formally confiscating the entire business. Although those legal measures taken by European nations since the 18th century, and by America since the 1930s, are themselves "half-Marxist," the underlying analysis and judgments regarding the employment market on which they are based is the pure Marxist nonsense described in the immediately-preceding paragraphs.

This has resulted in steadily declining employment opportunities in every nation that has done so for all would-be employees, steadily declining business opportunities for business owners because of their compliance costs, if nothing else, resulting in ever-expanding fiscal deficits for those nations resorting to welfare type policies they cannot afford to provide substitutes for earned livelihoods for the unemployed and the underemployed who inevitably proliferate in such an adverse business environment. When further borrowing to fund all that becomes impossible, catastrophe ensues. Hello Greece.

As preposterous as it may seem, American politicians' substantively agreeing with those preposterous accusations from Karl Marx regarding the inherent abusiveness of all employers has led to the enactment in the 20th century of thousands of pages of American law devoted to "fixing" those features of the employment market – features which almost never exist in real life and, indeed, to the extent they do exist, could best be minimized by encouraging employers to proliferate, and business profits to be maximized (further increasing their incentive to hire new employees) by minimizing employers' compliance obligations in hiring employees – rather than burdening them with such compliance obligations resulting simply from their ownership of the business (laws inherently presuming that business ownership is an evil thing, rather than the opposite), as all that law unambiguously and deliberately does.

This is most unfortunate because Marx's accusations could not be more ludicrous: no employer can have the monopoly power Marx's accusations necessarily presume, unless the state – which alone has the non-market power to harm sufficient to do so – has destroyed the business of all actual or prospective competitors of such employer, since no monopoly can exist for employment, in particular, in the absence of such monopoly-creating market destruction by the state.

Quite simply, in the long run, no monopoly can exist in any market unless the state creates or requires its existence and, in the absence of that state imposition in the market, the "long run" becomes shorter and shorter the more potential market participants there are – participants and competitors who can materialize in unpredictable ways if they are not barred, or at least discouraged, from participating in the market by state market intervention and monopoly creation.

Although it is true that, like any market participant, an employer never wants to pay more than he has to (which might include enhanced amounts to keep the employee happy and maximize his productivity, and not simply retain his disgruntled services) for the employment service he is purchasing, market forces alone are sufficiently powerful to force him to increase the amount he must pay for those services if there are market incentives for him to do so, including competing bidders for those services.

And, since an employee Is a human being, who the employer has every incentive to keep happy in his employment to enhance his productivity, even in the absence of competing bidders, the employer has that additional consideration affecting the amount he is willing to pay.

In any event, the employee can never be worth more than the maximum amount his prospective employer is willing to pay – which may not, in fact, be limited to the break-even amount of allocable profit the employer can expect: a particular employee may have services to offer which would justify an employer, in his own interest, paying that employee an amount which would not in fact result in any profit to the employer. Like any other market good or service on offer, an employee's services' value to his employer is inherently subjective.

# CHAPTER 5

## The Two Types of Law

As discussed at length in the chapters devoted to its history in Part IV below, the American Counterrevolution has truly been multi-faceted, manifesting itself not only in federal law, but also throughout our society – throughout the spheres of entertainment, education, the so-called learned professions, journalism, America's churches, and any other sphere of influence or activity you can think of in the nation.

That very ubiquity of its presence, throughout every sphere of activity of the citizenry and our businesses it has been able to penetrate, dominate and even vanquish into servitude to the collectivist Cause, is a major point of difference between it and our founders' original Revolutionary aspirations: free Americans were supposed to be able to live their lives, each pursuing his own ideas of happiness, unencumbered by any forced religion, ideology, unconstitutional government intrusion of any kind, nor any other outside influence.

Specifically, the founders intended their/our Revolution, and the Constitution it produced, both to establish a new, non-monarchical, non-tyrannical central government, and simultaneously to narrowly-constrict and confine its powers and influence over civil society to only those few, specifically-defined, purely-legal functions/activities, specified in the Constitution, functions which would facilitate the new Republic's security from invasion, the soundness of our currency, and the individual liberty, property, including intellectual property, and opportunities for enterprise and prosperity of all the citizenry.

They intended their/our Revolution to manifest itself in federal law <u>alone</u>, with the least possible influence of federal officials — and ideologues of all kinds — otherwise on civil society, in citizens' lives, and on the sovereign operations of the several states. The Revolution's value to all was to speak for itself from its own, particular, narrowly-defined works and results – with that minimal role enforced by the legal strictures of the Constitution.

The Counterrevolution, as described in Part IV has, on the other hand, drawn massive power from its massively-intrusive influence throughout all American society, enabling it constantly to interject and promote itself and to effect and promote the changes it has sought in citizens' very thought-processes (changes necessary for free citizens to buy into its collectivist logic), as well as in federal law. Even just those Counterrevolutionary legal changes have been profound, involving the enactment in America of tens of thousands of pages of federal laws whose <u>very structural, forensic nature</u>, as discussed below, was radically different from what is Constitutionally permitted; indeed, all laws of that very nature are deliberately precluded under the Constitution.

Since their very first enactment in 1887, those clearly-unconstitutional (as shown in Chapters 8 and 11), Counterrevolutionary laws have had the effect of seizing crushingly-intrusive policing powers for the federal government, its politicians and bureaucrats, over the citizens, their businesses and virtually all our activities, markets, lands and even dictating in minute detail products of all kinds the federal government unconstitutionally, and increasingly, permits, forbids and, most monstrously, even forces us to buy.

Taken together, those laws, and the federal, virtual-Star Chamber alphabet agencies and federal departments – and their unelected bureaucrats – those laws purport to create and empower have had the effect of transforming the nation from one in which there <u>used</u> to be a rule of law, into one in which there is now a rule of politicians and unelected bureaucrats whose discretionary power in enforcing – and even creating – federal law has no real limits.

That inherent lack of any real limits on all those agencies and their bureaucrats <u>alone</u>, without regard to the legal arguments shown in chapters 8 and 11 below, announces their utter unconstitutionality: it is an undeniable historical fact that the whole purpose of our Constitution was severely to limit the scope of the federal government. In short, as mentioned above, all those laws and agencies are of a completely different forensic and operational nature from anything contemplated in, or permitted under, the Constitution. That is what is explained in this chapter below.

### There Are Two, Completely Different Types of Citizen-Policing Laws

Because structurally, there isn't just one type of law: when it comes to laws <u>policing citizens' behavior</u> and actions, there are in fact <u>two</u>. One type of such policing law (Good Law) provides the necessary societal underpinnings in which free people can pursue happiness, secure in their lives, liberty and property, to the maximum extent law can actually provide. Laws of that nature are the only ones permitted under our Constitution.

The other type of citizen-policing law – Bad Law – consists of all other policing laws that don't qualify as Good Law.

In this chapter I will describe to you in detail all the structural elements of Good Law, and what Bad Law has consisted of historically in all the places it has arisen –

throughout the tyrannies of continental Europe ever since the 17th century, and here in America, as the Counterrevolution has succeeded in imposing it on us, bit-by-bit, beginning in 1887.

The key structural differences between Good Law and Bad Law invariably manifest themselves in two, different ways:

(1)  who is subject to prior restraints on their actions under the law – the government and all its officeholders under Good Law, and the citizens, their lands and other property, including every aspect of their businesses, under Bad Law; and

(2)  what agency imposes legal sanctions and/or dictates on citizens directly under the law – due process-constrained judicial courts alone, with very-limited discretion, under Good Law, and unelected bureaucrats, including always-politicized criminal prosecutors, each with his own career interests and other agendas, all with virtually-unlimited discretion under Bad Law.

This nation was blessed with Good Law alone (other than the federal laws legalizing the slavery which, in fact, had existed in all nations since the Stone Age) at the time of its founding in 1789 – nothing further of that nature needed nor permitted. The Counterrevolution has been cursing us with freedom-and-prosperity-destroying laws which are, without exception, Bad Law. And, as shown beyond dispute in Chapters 8 and 11, none of the federal agencies – other than the IRS – manufactured by politicians in Washington to enforce that Bad Law are permitted under the Constitution.

Every law reduces citizens' freedom: that is, quite simply, what law does. Laws that do so tyrannically, unconstitutionally, and with no genuine benefit to the nation's prosperity and the security of citizens, with the sole, actual consequence of empowering politicians and bureaucrats and other parasites at the expense of the citizens and their businesses – as all Bad Law does – have no place in this Republic.

The founders included multiple provisions in the Constitution to prevent Bad Law from being enacted by either the state or federal governments here. That was, indeed, one of the Constitution's most fundamental purposes – enshrining in our only fundamental law all the victories for individual liberty won in our Revolution — and those won in each of the English revolutions which had proceeded it since the 12th century. Chapters 8 and 11 prove that legal proposition, and the fact that all the purported legal/Constitutional arguments advanced by proponents of Bad Law in support of its supposed legitimacy, arguments monstrously and illegally adopted by the hyper-politicized federal judiciary in the 1930's, are not only meritless: they are patently frivolous.

In a nutshell, Good Law has two elements:

(1)  the unique American Constitution itself, which polices, and strictly-constricts, not private citizens, but rather the permissible activities of the central

government and its officials by, among other things, explicitly imposing <u>prior restraints</u> on that government and all those officials, and

(2)  the Common Law (much of which has been statutorily-codified) in each state which <u>alone</u> was intended by the founders and the Constitution to police America's private citizens' behavior (and that of their businesses). The Common Law was developed case-by-case over many centuries by the English courts articulating legal principles applicable to real-life situations based on, and limited to, precisely what God Himself mandates in the 10 Commandments. In accord with the 10 Commandments, as shown in Chapter 2, it criminalizes and penalizes everything the 10 Commandments demand – and, consistent with those Commandments unambiguously-implied requirement, provides for citizens' complete, unfettered freedom to do everything else.

<u>The federal Constitution</u> portion of Good Law contains each of the following:

(1)  bright-line rules describing the specific, <u>limited</u> powers and jurisdictions of each of the three —and only three -- Constitutionally-created branches of the central, federal government and its officers, and rules prescribing in detail mandatory procedures for all such officials' acquisition of and, when applicable, their forced-ouster from, their offices,

(2)  express <u>prohibitions</u> on certain specifically-described state and federal actions, described in the various provisions of Article I section 9 and 10, and and in the Bill of Rights contained in the first 10 Amendments to the Constitution, and the Civil War Amendments 13 through 15, including prohibitions on states' issuing paper money, imposing impediments on commerce, engaging in any foreign policy actions, "impairing the Obligation of Contracts, or grant[ing] any Title of Nobility." The Constitution also forbids any title of nobility to be granted "by the United States…"

(3)  specific, carefully-described procedures which must be rigorously followed in order for any "law" actually to be law, for the Constitution to be amended in any respect, and in order for new states to be added to the nation.

(4)  a precise enumeration of <u>each and every criminal-policing law</u> the federal government is authorized to enact and enforce ("Piracies and Felonies committed on the high Seas, and Offenses against the Law of Nations", "counterfeiting the securities and current Coin of the United States…" "Exclusive Legislation in all Cases whatsoever, over [what became the District of Columbia]… And to exercise like Authority over all Places purchased… For the Direction of Forts, magazines, arsenals, dockyards and other needful Buildings…" and "Treason against the United States…").

Since those particular areas of criminal-policing law are specified as the <u>only</u> ones which the federal government has power to enact and enforce, it is manifest that they are <u>exclusive</u>: the federal government is <u>forbidden</u> to criminalize any other citizen actions without an amendment to the Constitution permitting such. No such amendment has ever been explicitly enacted (including, interestingly, with respect to the income tax authorized in the 16th Amendment), although the Civil War amendments XIII through XV contain broad enabling language permitting their enforcement by "appropriate legislation."

(5)   unambiguous provisions to force politicians in all three branches of government to conform both to all of the Constitution's directives – rendering a legal nullity of any action of any kind they may take which fails to do so – and to force them explicitly to seek and obtain all Constitutionally-necessary, mandated consents to any amendment of any kind to any of its provisions. Those provisions both preserve the Constitution's timeless integrity and value, and permit its modification – but only when overwhelming super-majorities of all the people and the states genuinely desire and force such. In our Constitution, these provisions consist of its explicit Article VI statement that it alone is the "supreme Law of the Land," which automatically repeals and repudiates any violation of its terms, and the provisions of its Article V providing for the exclusive means for amending it. Under these provisions all misconduct by any politician which violates them in any manner – such as if any, or even all, of the political branches violate, and so purport to amend, any Constitutional provisions without conforming to the provisions of Article V – has no validity whatsoever at any time, and can be legally repudiated at any time by anyone in the nation, under the express provisions of the 9th and 10th Amendments which, as Jefferson himself proclaimed at the time of their creation, incorporate all the natural rights provisions announced in the Declaration Of Independence, which he knew something about.

A Constitution like ours has, in all world history, only existed and been enacted in the United States.

As just mentioned, it uniquely sets up explicit, self-enforcing (by automatically rendering all violations legal nullities) prior restraints on the federal government itself, and on all federal officials, and specifies the only powers available to each of the three branches of the federal government, and formally precludes it, and its officeholders, from taking any official action outside the powers specifically granted them in the Constitution.

The Common Law is the other necessary component of Good Law. It constitutes all the citizen-policing laws of every state (which is virtually identical in all states, and has existed with few changes in England and here since long prior to the Revolution), applies to all citizens equally, and describes clearly and simply all conduct which is prohibited, under the criminal and civil laws, to protect the life, liberty and property of all citizens, together with rules regarding property rights specifically.

The Common Law, unlike Bad Law, in no way prescribes any actions citizens are required to take: it contains all the legislation necessary to codify God's requirements for law in the 10 Commandments and since, as shown in chapter 2 above, those Commandments specify all conduct forbidden for free men in a free society, they are necessarily exclusive, and implicitly forbid any laws forbidding any conduct not described therein.

The Common Law simply tells citizens actions they are prohibited from taking – e.g. murder, theft, defrauding others, assault, trespass, false imprisonment, business misconduct, etc. – and prescribes both civil and criminal consequences for such misbehavior — after it has, by due process, been adjudicated to have been committed by someone. Civil (tort) liability thereunder, if adjudicated, provides any and all actual victims (definitely not including political activists claiming to act on behalf of "the public", or "the planet" or "the environment") of such misbehavior with compensatory and, where applicable, punitive, damages payable by anyone who has harmed them.

And, as indicated above, in stark contrast to Bad Law, the Common Law never applies as a discretionary prior restraint on citizens' actions: citizens are always free, in the first instance, to act as they desire, but will face the law's adverse consequences if they are later adjudicated to have engaged in prohibited misconduct. Under that judicially-created law, prior restraints – known as injunctions – against other citizens can only be obtained after first convincing a judge they are genuinely required in the particular circumstances for justice to prevail.

And judges and juries alone have the power to impose fines and punishments and directives on citizens under Good Law; no bureaucrats, let alone invisible, unelected ones, have any such power thereunder. And, under the Constitution's Article III, no federal court is permitted to exercise any jurisdiction/power over any citizen unless an actual "case or controversy" — necessarily arising from someone's actual, past conduct — is before it. And Congress alone has all legislative power, with no power to delegate it specified anywhere in the Constitution.

## Bad Law – What It Is

The other type of law (Bad Law) is what the 10 Commandments implicitly forbids any moral state to enact. This is because, as shown in Chapter 2, in those Commandments, God specifies all conduct He orders to be forbidden – thereby implicitly ordering that, for citizens to be free, everything else must be legally-permitted.

Bad Law is, quite simply, all law whose enactment procedurally, or whose contents substantively, is forbidden in the Constitution, all law forbidding conduct by citizens not forbidden by the 10 Commandments, and all laws dictating that citizens act in a particular manner – laws I have characterized as prior restraints, or tyrannical directives, on citizens, as opposed to officials acting in a public capacity, who alone are subject to any such restraints and directives under the Constitution.

Bad Law turns out to be the opposite in virtually every respect of Good Law. By Bad Laws' very micromanaging nature, they are invariably complex and difficult to understand – with full comprehension of them well beyond the capabilities of anyone lacking specialized, legal understanding of them, They supposedly "protect" the citizens from all injuries which can be imagined from any source – including themselves. Bad Law literally treats citizens like stupid, incompetent children — or presumptively evil, in need of constant restraint and active supervision by bureaucratic masters.

And Bad Law pretends, preposterously, that the bureaucrats with unfettered discretion to enforce, and even create, it against the citizenry are both wiser than judges and all the citizens themselves — and virtually selfless, to boot!

In stark contrast with Good Law policing laws, rather than applying only <u>after</u> they are adjudicated to have been violated, Bad Laws invariably operate as <u>prior restraints</u> on citizens' behavior, with citizens needing to obtain permission from bureaucrats for any action which they fear could run afoul of them – because the consequences of violation, even if inadvertent, are often dire, including crushing fines and jail time.

By their very nature, Bad Laws cannot be administered like Good Laws – by ordinary policeman and courts. Instead, they are invariably administered by specialized governmental agencies – i.e., all the federal alphabet agencies and departments – which invariably claim "expert" knowledge, supposedly to maximize public safety. Because of their inevitable complexity, Bad Laws are unable ever to respect the individuality – and dignity – of citizens and, instead, inevitably create "one-size-fits-all solutions" for everything their unelected bureaucrat administrators contemplate to be a "problem" requiring their interposition. And, once empowered at all, there is never an end to the "problems" they insist on addressing — until they are forcibly stopped,

The complexity of the Bad Laws, each of which inevitably operates on the "precautionary principle" (discussed below) invariably results in the specialized government agencies which enforce them being granted the legislative power regarding such laws to formulate additional, euphemistically-named, "regulations" — which themselves have the force of law also — supposedly "interpreting" them, as applicable to the endless real-life circumstances which can arise, <u>plus</u> the combined executive-and-judicial power to actually <u>enforce</u> such laws against the citizenry, with fines and jail. The effect of this combination of state power in such agencies can be summarized in one word – tyranny.

If there is any doubt about this point, consider the following quote from James Madison in *the Federalist* no. 47 in which he, the Constitution's principal author, both defines tyranny as consisting of precisely that accumulation of powers by a single person or agency, and expressly repudiates the notion that the Constitution he was advocating therein permits such ever to occur:

"The accumulation of all powers legislative, executive and judiciary in the same hands, whether of one, a few or many, and whether hereditary, self appointed, or elective, may justly be pronounced the very definition of tyranny. Were the federal constitution therefore really chargeable with this accumulation of power or with a mixture of powers having a dangerous tendency to such an accumulation, no further arguments would be necessary to inspire a universal reprobation of the system."

## The Founders Well-Knew What Bad Law Is — and Forbade it in the Constitution

Both types of law – the Good and the Bad – were well known to our founders at the time of the drafting of the Constitution and, indeed, during the Revolution which preceded and paved the way for it. And they had a clear understanding of which type of law they wanted to permit the new Republic's federal government under the Constitution to enact – and to provide the strongest mechanisms they knew to devise in the Constitution to forbid the enactment of any Bad Law.

The Constitution was conceived by them as a written, legal constraint on central, federal and state power. The founders were well aware that in it they were creating such a document for the first time in legal history for an entire nation (many of its provisions were based on a similar mechanism Massachusetts had then-recently adopted, much of which was devised and drafted by John Adams) precisely to forbid the federal government from enacting any Bad Law.

That is the precise reason they defined with such specificity the few areas the federal government is permitted to legislate in – primarily in the Constitution's Article I section 8: to create guardrails severely limiting actions the federal government could take which would have any affect on all the liberties of the citizenry – including impairing their property and contract rights above all. The last thing on earth they wanted was a central federal government with the power to dictate to individual citizens or their businesses how they should conduct themselves, or operate their lands or other property, in any manner whatsoever.

And Article I of the Constitution prescribes in very-specific detail how any law can become a law – requirements that can never be met by any "regulation" manufactured by any executive agency. And the Constitution specifies how the only citizens authorized to adjudicate cases against other citizens – judges – are to be appointed; no other citizen – let alone a bureaucrat within the executive department – is authorized to impose any directives or punishment against citizens of any kind.

The founders deliberately separated the various powers of the federal government (legislative, executive and judicial) into three separate branches, and defined with such precision how the legislative branch should conduct its affairs: it was always to act openly, and never in the dark, with full disclosure of everything to the citizenry; the Constitution prescribes very-specific procedures governing how all those persons who alone were authorized to participate at all in the actual, law-making legislative process should be selected. The Constitution could not have been clearer in that regard: only those persons who were so elected and publicly known to be so were authorized to participate in the legislative process in any official manner, by providing explicitly in Article I Section 1 of the Constitution,

> "All legislative Powers herein granted shall be vested in a Congress of the United States, which shall consist of a Senate and House of Representatives [emphases added]."

Article I section 8 specifies all the legislative powers Congress is granted. It is forbidden to do anything not so granted. None of those powers include any power to delegate any portion of its legislative power to anyone – particularly to some unnamed, unelected bureaucrats, and particularly to anyone in the executive branch.

The founders were, specifically, well-aware both of the actual virtues of certain aspects of English law, which the English had secured for themselves uniquely among European nations over many hundreds of years (the English Common Law and the freedoms the English people and its Parliament had been able to extract from the King since the 12th century, including particularly freedom from Courts of Star Chamber, and other freedoms extracted from the King in the Civil War/ Revolution of 1640-1660, and the so-called Glorious Revolution of 1688), and all the evils of Bad Law – including the manner in which it was invariably created and enforced – both of which they were determined to preclude in the Constitution.

Quite simply, Bad Law – and the unelected bureaucrats it empowers – tell citizens what they must do, and so turns them into servants, serfs and even slaves of the state – and of the politicians and bureaucrats who run it. We know this as a historically-proven fact today, as shown in the chapters devoted to history below, because Bad Law is what tyrants have always used to enslave their people in the West – beginning with Louis XIV and other monarchs claiming absolute power over their citizens.

And, although they – the two types of law – have certain things in common (primarily the requirement that people obey them – or else) and are both called "the law," they are actually as different from each other as night is from day.

Indeed, as history has revealed, and as discussed below, to the extent that Bad Law exists at all in a nation it institutionalizes state tyranny and corrupt cronyism over the citizenry; such has invariably been the norm for all continental Europe; and the American Counterrevolution has been imposing Bad Law here as its primary mission.

Once Bad Law is enacted in a nation, it overwhelms and destroys the Good Law – and has the effect of crushing all the benefits of Good Law. This occurs inevitably because Bad Law smothers all property rights and, accordingly, all liberty and prosperity of the citizens which depend on the substantiality of those property rights. And, unlike Good Law, it reaches far beyond the legal arena; for numerous reasons discussed above/below, its tentacles extend throughout all civil society, securing absolute control by the state over every aspect of its citizens' lives.

As a result, Bad Law, while invariably claiming to secure safety for the citizenry as an excuse for its enactment, in fact destroys all legal and other safety and security of the citizenry by, among other things, destroying citizens' property and contract rights and choices of all kinds, and subjecting the citizens directly affected by it to constant fear of prosecution – prosecution resulting from their having simply engaged in conduct which is specifically not forbidden by the 10 Commandments, and which, accordingly, Bad Law, and its bureaucrat-enforcers, alone endlessly, and gratuitously, criminalize.

The only actual, even arguable, beneficiaries of Bad Law in a republic or democracy, are personally-ambitious politicians, lobbyists, lawyers, bureaucrats and other parasites who feed off its presence. It gives the government so much dictatorial power over the citizens that they need those intermediaries simply to survive. That has always been its purpose – a feature, not a bug.

Today, the wealthiest counties in the nation surround Washington, D.C., populated almost exclusively by such people, all whose wealth is derived from performing work made possible by Bad Law alone, none of which work adds any actual value to the nation's wealth and, indeed, all of which simply drains and harms the real economy's strength, restricting and/or even preventing its growth — and the freedom of those who produce all goods and services actually desired by the citizens — including those virtual parasites themselves.

Nothing in the Constitution permits the federal government to police behavior by American citizens and their work/businesses (with extremely limited exceptions, as specified above – e.g., treason, counterfeiting, piracy) – which is precisely what Bad Law does.

Good Law alone provides all the necessary underpinnings of a truly free and prosperous society. In all recorded history it has been the ruling law to any extent in only a handful of (English-speaking) nations, and it has been fully present only in one nation – the United States. it has invariably come under attack – from politicians who despise the constrictions it imposes on them and on their ability to curry favor to be used to amass power for themselves. Those guardrails which Good Law does indeed impose on the federal government and its politicians are the single most important feature – its underlying foundation or Constitution – of this virtuous law.

## What Good Law Does

When fully present, as the founders of the United States consciously intended, Good Law does each and every one of the following:

(1)   it provides rules which the citizens and, most importantly, in its Constitutional provisions, the state, at all levels, and all public officials (whether elected or appointed) without exception themselves must live under, all to guarantee that the citizens, the state and its officers each respect the sanctity of all individuals' person and property, including,

(2)   making sure that all non-criminal (under Good Law) promises citizens make to each other intended to be binding among the parties to such agreements are indeed enforceable, under the principles developed under the Common Law, as contracts – and are not subject to being disturbed in any manner by the state,

(3)   protecting all legally-acquired property from theft, fraud or invasion by others, including the state and its officials,

(4)   clearly describing all misconduct which constitutes crimes and civil misconduct (torts), all of which are sanctionable against each wrongdoer after the fact of their commission, and only after being adjudicated as such pursuant to genuine, even-handed judicial due process, including trial by jury if requested, with monetary damages payable to actual victims due from adjudicated wrongdoers,

(5)   rules, including the Constitution itself, which describe with specificity all the powers which the federal government and each state, and each separate portion of each of them, may lawfully exercise, and expressly precluding any government and its agents from exercising any other power,

(6)   laws prescribing all the procedures the state and its agents/officers must follow in exercising each of its legitimate functions (executive, legislative and judicial) and,

(7)   laws describing with specificity all the procedures which must be followed for the selection of each of the state's officeholders who alone are permitted to act as its agents, and to do so solely in the capacity of their specific office – precisely so that neither the state itself, nor any of its agents, exceed the boundaries set for it/them.

Failure by the state and any of its agents to obey the bright-line boundaries so set for them inevitably results in such state becoming what virtually all other states have become throughout history – a tyranny governed under the discretionary power of men, and not the rule of law, a tyranny whose subjects – and that is indeed what they become, at best – can best be described as servants of the state and its functionaries, if not their slaves or serfs, instead of as freemen.

As described above, Good Law is easy to recognize: other than its Constitutional provisions which act as prior restraints at all times only on the federal government and its officers and agents, the Good Law – Common Law – applicable to individuals only actively comes into play, from an enforcement point of view, after the fact of its actual or claimed violation by someone. Under Good Law, all citizens are treated like responsible adults, fully capable of internalizing the requirements of the Good Law, and it is only when they have actually been fairly adjudicated to have violated it – which often requires a jury finding that they did so – that it comes into play to actually impose justice (a money judgment, an injunction, a conviction, for example) against them.

For example, although Common Law contract law (an example of Good Law) informs the process of people entering into a contract, it is only if and when one of them are alleged to have breached that contract that the state gets involved – and only through its courts – at all.

What Bad Law Does

Bad law is also easy to recognize — once its invariable features are understood: it is, quite simply, all law that is not Good Law, and is always recognizable, particularly, by when it applies: as mentioned, it, and the bureaucratic governmental agencies inevitably created to enforce it, act as a prior restraint against citizens' actions and enterprises, rather than coming into play only after it is violated, like the Good Law.

Because those empowered to enforce Bad Law invariably, and inevitably, are granted discretion in such enforcement, discretion whose potential reach is often unpredictable by those subjected to the law, Bad Law invariably has the effect of forcing those so subjected to it to seek permission from government functionaries in order for them (who such Bad Law thereby reduces to serfs) to engage in actions subject to it which they otherwise wish to pursue – even though such actions in fact pose no actual, identifiable harm to any other citizen.

Indeed, the discretionary enforcement of Bad Law by those empowered to do so is what turns each government functionary so empowered into a lawless tyrant (true rule of law requires those enforcing it to do so only pursuant to judicial processes, with no discretion in the application of genuine justice – which, as the ancient Greeks recognized, must be blind).

For example, there was no shortage of laws, which those enforcing them had practically unlimited discretion in doing so, most, if not all of which laws were enacted according to (at least arguably) technically-legal, prescribed procedures, in Nazi Germany and the Soviet Union (and in present-day Cuba, Communist China and Vietnam and North Korea) – laws explicitly relied on by each of those monstrous tyrannies to kill millions, and to enslave their entire populations

The Constitution is written in plain English, easy for anyone to understand – with no need for any assistance from a lawyer, judge or any other claimed "expert."' Its authors were well-known at the time (principally James Madison), as were its intended consequences – discussed at length in the widely-published *the Federalist*, and in other writings by the founders— as was their very clear and self-consciously held understanding of its absolutely unique place in world history, and its historical roots in the various uniquely-English revolutions which they were well-aware had preceded it, beginning with the Magna Carta, followed by the English Revolution, known as the Civil War, of 1640 through 1660, which had, in turn, been followed by the so-called Glorious Revolution of 1688.

Our own unique Revolution was consciously intended to absorb and retain all the liberalizing victories won through the blood and efforts of all those previous English revolutionary events, each extracting additional individual liberties from the crown/state beyond those won previously, with our Revolution guaranteeing equality before the law and multiple additional individual liberties from state power to a greater extent than had ever achieved previously in known history.

More on Bad Law

There were actually three, specific types of Bad Law which the founders were personally familiar with (many of them had spent considerable time in Bourbon France witnessing its crushing effects, including Franklin and Adams, both of whom were active participants in the drafting of the Constitution, and Jefferson who, though in France at that time, communicated always with Madison, the Constitution's principle author, and was personally actively involved in the drafting of the Bill of Rights) and wanted to prevent.

The first type of such Bad Law – what we would call bureaucratic regulatory law and enforcement – was what prevailed throughout continental Europe by the end of the 18th century. As discussed throughout this book, that particular type of Bad Law was the creation of absolute monarchs determined to subjugate their people completely under their absolute authority.

The Bourbons first created and wrote it, and imposed it with particular effectiveness, and with the most elaborate bureaucracy for enforcement of such at that time, on the French people, very consciously under Louis XIV in the 17th century. Those laws continued unchanged under his Bourbon successors and, with almost no substantive changes whatsoever, even after the French Revolution. This it did under both the Reign of Terror under the Committee of Public Safety of Robespierre and guillotine notoriety, and again, with little change other than its name – the Napoleonic Code, as it was thereafter called – under the totalitarian military dictatorship of Napoleon and, unfortunately for the French, and for all the rest of continental Europe which imitated it, for the rest of their history, including today.

And, far from incidentally, the founders were well aware that the English had had their own experience with Kings claiming absolute authority over their people – James I and Charles I – who punished their political enemies in secret tribunals (the Court of Star Chamber) they alone controlled through their cronies, and who made what efforts they could to similarly impose the kind of central, absolute bureaucratic authority over their people perfected by the Bourbons in France in the 17th and 18th century.

And the founders also knew only too well that the English and their Parliament had fought a bloody revolution/civil war literally for decades, beginning in the 1640s specifically to end Star Chamber and the other absolutist claims of this nature made by Charles I, who they ended up beheading, permitting his son, Charles II to ascend to the throne only after his commitment to major constitutional concessions precluding precisely such absolutist claims (including tyrannical Courts of Star Chamber).

Thus, the founders, who saw themselves self-consciously as building on the previous two revolutions in England of the 17th century in their own Revolution, clearly viewed preventing this type of Bad Law as having been a constitutional, individual-liberty achievement of the English over 150 years earlier, an achievement they wanted to make sure in the Constitution did not have to be fought for in blood again.

Although it has now become our task to once again win that victory over Bad Law which our founders hoped we could avoid under the Constitution, its remarkable provisions make it unnecessary to shed blood once again to do so.

### The Second And Third Types of Bad Law

But there was a second type of Bad Law which the founders also had an intimate experience of under the British – and which they also wanted to forbid or, at least, make extremely difficult to enact, by the federal Congress. This type of Bad Law was the type of law Parliament was continuing to pass, and the king to enforce brutally, prior to our Revolution, all as described in many of the enumerated instances of British tyranny described in the bill of particulars portion of the Declaration of Independence.

This type of Bad Law consisted of Parliament – the legislative branch in England – passing special laws corruptly to provide benefits to some of their constituents// cronies – at the expense of other citizens. These laws were the direct result of Parliament and its members themselves becoming drunk with their own power derived in the revolutions of the previous century: they would pass special laws – taxes (including the Stamp Act, and the tax particularly on tea which had given rise to the famous Boston Tea Party), for example – intended to benefit particular constituents or businesses to the detriment of other citizens – the American colonists, for example – in exchange for corrupt payoffs of some kind to the legislators themselves.

Again, the explicit rules for openness – what we would call today complete transparency – regarding all the details of selecting Congressional members and how they were required to conduct and publicize all official proceedings, as prescribed in detail in Article I of our Constitution, were intended to at least make it extremely difficult for Congressman to engage in such corrupt activities without the public (and the state legislatures, who originally controlled Senate represen-tation) knowing about it – and so having the ability to remove them at their next opportunity.

It is the inherently corrupt nature of such law, including the cronyism/favoritism involved in it, coupled with the political and/or even financial payoffs to legis-lators that make it so difficult for it to be enacted except in secret – something the Constitution was designed to completely forbid, or at least make extremely difficult, if not impossible.

The consciously-divided federal nature of all government in the nation – in which the states retained their sovereignty over all police powers affecting individuals and their property, while the central, federal government had only very specific tasks assigned to it, and was precluded from doing anything else — was also intended to minimize the risks of such special laws, by preventing the central government from showing favoritism to particular regions or states in the nation, and preventing, to the extent possible, states from favoring their own citizens over citizens of other states – policing which was the sole intended purpose (as I clearly prove below from the actual text of formal writings by multiple founders, with no contrary writings by any founders) of the Constitution's Commerce clause and the Contract clause.

A third type of Bad Law was also well known to the founders – through their knowledge of its enactment in continental European countries, typically through mere decrees by absolute monarchs, prior to 1789 – and the founders also wanted to preclude its enactment in the Constitution. This type of law consisted of inherently-intrusive, confiscatory taxes on citizens' income.

The founders wanted the federal government to be able to have sufficient revenue to defend the nation – the principal expense expected for the federal government contemplated in the Constitution – even in the face of potentially existential military danger posed by the European superpowers of the day – En-gland and France, either of which had more than sufficient military capability to conquer us. But they were determined that the taxing power of the nation not permit anything like an income tax, nor any other tax that could fall unevenly among the citizenry (such as favoring one portion of the country over another). And that is why the provisions of the Constitution regarding taxing were drafted the way they were.

England had never enacted an income tax as of the time of our Constitution – and did not do so at all until faced with the dire military emergency posed by Napoleon early in the next, 19th, century, a tax which initially lasted only during that Napoleonic emergency, and was repealed within years.

But our founders knew what an income tax was because they were aware that Louis XIV had, unilaterally, imposed an income tax of 10% on all French citizens who were not nobles (the commoners), on top of all the other taxes they were subjected to, in his fruitless efforts to fund his extravagant government (which nevertheless defaulted several times technically). And the major purpose of Louis XVI in taking the steps which ended up resulting in the French Revolution was to try to get the nobility and the church hierarchy in France to go along with also being subjected to an income tax (the clergy and church possessed, and nobility itself provided, complete immunity from all taxes in France prior to the Revolution).

The income tax could only be enforced by intruding into all the personal affairs of taxpayers – and so was a particularly humiliating, though income-producing, tax – and was seen in France as akin to an attribute of serfdom (even though it was continued with a vengeance after the Revolution). A major reason commoners in France who were financially able to do so purchased titles of nobility from the crown prior to the Revolution was to obtain complete exemption from taxes – including the income tax – by doing so.

Quite simply, our founders wanted all citizens in this nation to have a dignity and status comparable to that of only the nobles in both France and England (by the time of our revolution, English nobles had significantly less actual legal/juridical privileges, as opposed to mere social standing, which they clearly enjoyed, over commoners, than the French nobility with similar titles). Although, as discussed below, a temporary income tax was indeed passed as an extraordinary emergency measure during our Civil War, as discussed below, it took a constitutional amendment – the 16th amendment – to permit its institution here in 1913. And it has indeed proven to be the abomination our founders were determined for us to avoid.

### Bad Law in Operation

To fully understand how monstrous – and genuinely-enslaving – Bad law is, all one need do is consider how it actually operates in real life — in contradistinction to Good Law, whose rule is essential for citizens who obey its simple demands to obtain and maintain their freedom and personal security.

To illustrate this, consider the following situation:

I own X acres of land in the countryside where I have my house and conduct various types of farming operations, including raising animals and growing crops of various kinds in different years, all of which I am able to do profitably because of my astute agricultural management – without any government assistance. Immediately adjacent to my land is land owned by Mr. Evil. I learned that Mr. Evil is going to conduct a number of activities on his land which I fear might harm my land, including opening and operating a mine expected to produce multiple minerals, and operating an industrial-type animal-breeding and raising business that will produce massive amounts of animal waste.

If Good law governs exclusively, we each are free to do what we want with our land: our property ownership is secure and absolute; however, if either of us creates a nuisance on our land which affects our neighbors' land adversely, the landowner who is harmed is entitled to sue the nuisance creator under the common law for all damages and, if the nuisance was created deliberately or knowingly, the wrongdoer (tortfeasor, in legalese) can become liable to the injured landowner for punitive damages as well.

In addition, also under Good law, if the person whose land will be adversely affected becomes aware of his neighbor's intended nuisance-creation misconduct, and has the ability to prove the irreparable damage that will befall his own land if the neighbor follows through on that misconduct, to the satisfaction of a judge (no jury for this type of proceeding, though there is for a damages claim), he can obtain an <u>injunction</u>, or legal <u>prior restraint</u>, barring his neighbor from engaging in such injurious misconduct.

<u>But he must first actually prove</u> that he is actually entitled to that in order to obtain that prior restraint on his neighbor's activities; and, as free men, neither I nor Mr. Evil is ever required to seek the others' permission in his use of his land – nor anyone else's permission, including the government's, and we are each entitled to the full enjoyment and value of our own land, without having to grease the pocket of anyone.

In other words, unless I or Mr. Evil can genuinely <u>prove to a judge</u> that the other of us is about to engage in conduct certain to harm our homeland, we each are free to develop and utilize our land to its full potential and reap the financial and personal benefits from doing so, and provide whatever we produce on the land for purchase by would-be buyers in a free market, and so increase our own wealth and, as Adam Smith proved, the total wealth of our nation.

Again, if it turns out that either of us actually harms the other or his land – and can prove that to the satisfaction of the jury – the injured party is permitted to sue and obtain full compensation for such harm as legal damages, including possible punitive damages for being such a tort victim. That is what all happens under Good law.

Under Bad law, neither of us is able to use our land with any security that the state will not destroy us, without first obtaining the permission of numerous "regulatory" agencies, each staffed by bureaucrats who have <u>their own </u>career and other considerations – including possibly political considerations – in mind when they review our requests – requests for permission for us to use what is supposedly our own land.

Under the multiple agencies that exist at the present time, depending on the precise nature of the activities we plan, our activities on what is supposedly our own land would be subject to prior restraint by at least the following agencies – the Environmental Protection Agency, the federal Department of Agriculture, if we have any employees, the Department of Labor, with its own additional multiple agencies, the Internal Revenue Service and numerous other agencies (the Equal Employment Opportunity Commission, OSHA and numerous other ones.

Bureaucrats in each of these agencies have passed their own "regulations", which are actually <u>laws by another name</u>, violation of any of which can result in massive fines and even criminal conviction and sanctions (even though Congress never itself enacted the actual statute defining any such crime we could be subject to, and it was created exclusively by unnamed, unseen and unelected bureaucrats).

Because of their power to harm us if we run afoul of their regulatory dictates, the only way either I or Mr. Evil can do anything on what is supposedly our own land is if we begged the permission – employing and paying lawyers, lobbyists and other intermediaries, at our own enormous expense, who we have no choice but to use if our interests are to be protected at all against the power of the state – of each of the multiple regulatory agencies and obtain that permission.

Accordingly, what this entire circumstance we are each faced with under Bad law amounts to is that the massive prior restraints on all of our conduct it imposes – even though all we want to do is utilize land we supposedly own – is indistinguishable from the injunction forbidding us to act which only our neighbor could obtain under Good law and, in that case, he alone could do so only <u>after first legally</u> convincing a judge to first rule that we were about to commit some grotesque misconduct on our land that would irreparably harm him.

Under Bad law, it is as if we are operating as someone who is <u>automatically pre-judged</u> to have engaged in misconduct worthy of an injunction against us – before we have done anything with our land at all — and with no <u>actual</u> foreseeable victim of any misconduct by us even complaining.

In other words, Bad law transforms us from actual ownership of our land into effectively a serf who must do the bidding of overlords – the various bureaucrats whose permission we require to act – in utilizing our land at all. Additionally, because of the huge transaction costs involved in obtaining such permission – and the potentially enormous amounts of time potentially involved – the value of anything we produce from our efforts from our land is substantially reduced, if not destroyed, by the need to engage in such compliance costs and activity in order even to get to square one. And the nation's wealth is diminished *pro tanto*.

And today, in America, every business in the nation, particularly those with any employees, is subject to that same micromanagement from multiple federal agencies and their bureaucrat functionaries – who have become the true masters of all our businesses.

<u>Bad Law's Inevitable Liberty-and Prosperity-Destroying Handmaidens – The Precautionary Principle And The Criminalization Of Virtually All Conduct</u>

<u>The Precautionary Principle</u>

As shown above, Bad Law always is administered to control the behavior of citizens <u>prior to</u> their engaging in any conduct its administrators choose to forbid

– regardless of their particular rationale for their so forbidding it. That rationale invariably consists of claims that the forbidden behavior will supposedly result, typically based on claimed "expert" predictions, in some harm – to other citizens, the environment, the government, you name it.

The most-flattering claim for Bad Law's purpose is inherently utopian and preposterous — to prevent all imaginable harms from ever occurring at all, not simply to punish them after the fact – although typically it does that as well, and in draconian in fashion (truly-extraordinarily-high fines, e.g.). Since its only real result is always to radically empower tyranny, it strains credulity to believe that is not at least its other purpose.

Quite simply, the underlying enabling mandate legally-imposed on each such agency – to anticipate and prevent all harms even arguably within its purview – results in its inherently needing to forbid all conduct posing even the slightest chance of resulting in any such harm – even if only as a matter of self-protection from any oversight by Congress, for example.

Specifically, no federal bureaucrat wants to be called on the carpet before a Congressional hearing and accused of permitting some horrible, theoretically-preventable, in hindsight, tragedy from occurring. Each bureaucrat, of course, reports to his superiors within his particular agency, superiors who impose that duty on their support always for the most-restrictive citizen -action mandates, even if only for their self protection from their own superiors.

Accordingly, simply to fulfill its duty of "protecting from," and so preventing, all harms within its jurisdiction from occurring, the agency has no alternative but to take the most extreme precautions necessary to forbid any citizen conduct which could lead to any conceivable harm – however unlikely – which its "experts" might imagine. Quite simply, the agencies never suffer any adverse consequences from forbidding behavior of citizens unnecessarily,purportedly always to prevent improbable harms; they are reprimanded only if some conceivable harm eventually actually occurs.

Thus the behavior they forbid – and criminalize, to enforce such forbidding – is done by casting a very very broad net. The very purpose of the agency is to limit citizens' freedom, never to enhance it.

Fulfilling the agency's mandated duty is one reason it necessarily employs the precautionary principle as its guiding principle for restricting citizen behavior. But there is an additional reason why it does so with enthusiasm: bureaucrats always want to make themselves as indispensable as possible and to expand their power over the citizenry. Indeed, they typically constantly expand the scope of the jurisdiction. The precautionary principle provides a readily available excuse for them to do so.

Quite simply, the bureaucracy only encounters adverse reactions when it permits some harm to occur – never when it over-restricts citizens' freedom.

The Criminalization of Virtually All Conduct

Federal bureaucracies have been churning out tens of thousands of pages of "regulations" on endless subjects, every single page of which is enforceable by criminal prosecutions. As mentioned above, since all crimes actually forbidden in the 10 Commandments have been forbidden under the states' Common-Law since we were simply colonies of Britain, it is obvious that all of these <u>additional</u> agency-decreed crimes criminalize behavior that is otherwise perfectly legal — and always perfectly moral under the 10 Commandments. As more and more behavior is criminalized, less and less behavior is legal.

This fact has multiple consequences. First of all, it empowers the federal Justice Department and its bureaucrats to literally decide who they want to prosecute, without regard to the genuine criminality of their conduct, simply because they cannot possibly prosecute everyone who has violated some regulation – typically without even knowing it existed – and so have no choice but to make all prosecutions highly-selective.

In that circumstance, not only is it purely a matter of their arbitrary discretion what particular crimes — among the millions possible —they choose to prosecute, but also who, since they have the virtually-unlimited resources of federal prosecutors at their disposal – the FBI, numerous lawyers and accountants, and the sheer terror that any such mere federal investigation, let alone an actual prosecution after indictment, inspires in its targets.

The federal bureaucrats risk nothing from going after someone who they simply choose to destroy, while their target risks everything in even trying to oppose them. They can typically seize his assets, destroy his business and credit, frog march him on camera — all without ever actually convicting him of anything.

Indeed, it is fair to say that since they can prosecute people based on who they are, rather than what they did, and make their lives miserable in the process, there is no limit to the harm they can inflict on any citizen they simply choose to harm in that manner. This fact literally makes America today, and for several decades past, increasingly what can only be called a police state.

That in itself creates a reign of terror among the citizens – at least those who are aware of this fact. Because they never know when they might become a federal target and, if they are, even if they are not actually indicted, the process of defending themselves is typically financially ruinous, as well as being emotionally devastating.

# CHAPTER 6

## The Two Types of Revolution

The state of our nation today cannot be understood without appreciating (1) the differences between our unique American Revolution, and the diametrically-different collectivist ones, beginning with the French Revolution, (2) the particular mental state – promoting its always-weaponized, anti-religious and anti-individual attitudes intrinsic to its cause – deployed by collectivist revolutions everywhere, including our own Counterrevolution, and (3) the "teachings" of Karl Marx, whose writings, beginning in the 1840s, did so much to inspire and inform all subsequent collectivist revolutions – including the American Counterrevolution (though its individual proponents invariably disclaim being Marxists, sometimes truthfully). This chapter addresses all those topics.

Just as there are two types of power and of citizen-policing law, over the past 1000 years or so in the Western world, <u>there have been two completely different types of revolutions</u>. Many, if not most, of those who participated in both types of revolutions have had, if anyone had asked them, <u>identical goals</u>: virtually all of the active participants in all such revolutions would say they were fighting (for fighting, violence, physical suffering, death and blood – and often plenty of it – is indeed what has always accompanied a revolution) to obtain liberty from bondage and tyranny which had become unbearable, and which they had no doubt they were suffering under.

But throughout recorded history, only one type of revolution has <u>actually had that genuinely-liberating result</u>. The other, collectivist type of revolution – everywhere other than in America's Counterrevolution (so far)— invariably descended into a tyrannical, bloody abomination. Collectivist revolutions have always simply removed the tyrants in charge of the pre-revolutionary state and replaced them with new, dictatorial masters – administering Bad Laws at least as tyrannical as, and often, as in France, <u>identical</u> to, those of the ousted regime.

In America, the Counterrevolution has sought, and succeeded in, the gradual, piece-by-piece imposition of dictatorial Bad Law, where such had simply not existed previously. Notwithstanding the counterrevolution's undeniable "successes," it remains very-much an unfinished project. If you dislike its results so far, rest assured: it will only get worse – and probably more brutal – until it is actually defeated, like the British at Yorktown, and the South at Appomattox.

All revolutions have a few things in common, notwithstanding their completely disparate goals and effects. The common features of all revolutions, including our Counterrevolution, are:

> They are all initiated, consciously fought for, and led by a core-group of ardent, true believers who, prior to the revolution's victory, are deeply dissatisfied with the prevailing political regime/order, seeing it as hopelessly flawed. Those revolutionary leaders personally commit themselves to overthrowing the existing regime's power over them, without regard to its apparent invincibility – the very invincibility they see as so overwhelming as to make it impervious to any reform whatsoever: pre-revolution, the old regime always is omnipresent and utterly omnipotent – until it isn't. Those are pretty much the only things the two different types of Revolution have in common.

The differences between the two types are numerous. The most profound difference, from which all others result, has been whether they believe in, or explicitly repudiate, God and religion. All their resulting views of man, his rights and their origin, and the state depend on, and follow from, that their basic religious (or not) epistemology.

## God, Man, Revolution and Government

Each of us either believes in God – or not. Each of us in America either believes every single individual human is infinitely valuable, a divine soul, worthy in the eyes of God Himself of salvation by the agonizing sacrifice on the cross of His own son – or not.

It turns out that to believe in the infinite value of each individual, one must also believe that each individual has an immortal soul; and that belief, in turn, requires a belief in God (no particular religion required), as the eternal progenitor. Absent that belief, the individual has never been seen as having inherent value. Yes, it is that simple.

Since the end of the 18th century, the fundamental question whose answer has determined the character of every new, post-revolutionary government ruling any nation has been: is that government – and its officeholders – presumed by all (the people and those government officials) to be the servant, and subordinate to, both God and its citizens – and therefore answerable to both Him and them morally and legally — or not?

Prior to that time, everywhere in the West, regardless of the form of the government, there was unqualified, official certainty regarding the first part of this question, to wit, that God – or, in the cases of ancient Greece and Rome, possibly multiple gods – indeed ruled supreme. Even the worst, previous European tyrants had invariably claimed, however improbably, that God's selection of them — based on their lineage— as monarch was the basis for their legitimacy.

Belief in God's ultimate rule was never, prior to the French Revolution, doubted anywhere in the Western world (with the possible exceptions of Nero, Caligula and a few other Julians – exceptions which, in their own way, proved the rule).

Also prior to then, the citizenry had ruled supreme over the state itself in none but the rarest and briefest moments of Western history – in ancient Democratic Athens, at some point in ancient Jerusalem, perhaps when Rome was a true Republic. Nowhere else even arguably.

Only in America, after our Revolution and the adoption of our Constitution, were the government, and its officeholders, legally-compelled (the only means of achieving such) in the Constitution, to be the servants of both God (no official religion necessary or permitted) and the citizens who, in our Revolution, had thrown off the yoke of being "subjects."

The French Revolution, on the other hand, for the first time in history, raised the question whether God indeed ruled the government/ruler.

Indeed, even more remarkably, the regicide Jacobins who completely took over that Revolution by 1793, for the first time ever anywhere in the West announced affirmatively that not only was God <u>not</u> in charge of their new state – even if He existed at all which, also for the first time, they officially and institutionally <u>denied</u> – the salvation and, indeed, the achievement of "liberty" by all in the state actually, according to them, depended on His institutionally-presumed <u>nonex-</u>istence and, therefore, on the complete and final legal and moral omnipotence of the state and its rulers over everyone and everything. This, the essence of the Jacobins' collectivist notion of "liberty" – radically different from the individual liberty championed in the American Revolution – is discussed and explained below.

But although, in the French Revolution, the new rulers claimed to govern in accord with the peoples' will (no election necessary), they simultaneously demanded unqualified allegiance of each citizen to the government, making that loyalty an absolute prerequisite to his life having any value whatsoever. Quite simply, without the belief in God, the belief in any divine value of the individual and his soul evaporated.

That has also been the fundamental ontological fact of every Collectivist revolution which followed the French, including all the socialist/Marxist/Communist ones – and including our own Counterrevolution, whose ever-proliferating policies and massive dictates we Americans have long been passively tolerating, with no serious, strategic, political party opposition, as an experiment on our economy, our institutions, our lives and fortunes, particularly since 1906.

Attempting to institutionalize this identical, ontological theory (institutional atheism and denial of the individual citizen's divine value) – and getting the people to actually accept it – has, similarly, been the determined goal of American Collectivists in their ongoing Counterrevolutionary efforts to undo the unique achievements of the American Revolution. Indeed, American collectivists have been attempting to re-create here their understanding and vision of the French Revolution, its so-called "Age of Reason" Enlightenment aspirations, and, as shown below, many, though not all, of Marx's ideas.

Those very Collectivist efforts' success has alone created all the misery in America today resulting from the Bad Law it has now imposed on all citizens' purchasing choices, their property and on all genuinely-productive people and elements in the nation (i.e., all American land and businesses). Each of the multiple federal alphabet agencies they have created through that Bad Law, and all of them together, exercise unchecked, monstrous, dictatorial, politically-weaponized power over the citizens, power unconstitutionally usurped by officials in all three branches of the federal government, and unelected bureaucrats, since 1887; and yet every bit of that Counterrevolutionary "success" can be undone at any time, and our Constitution resurrected.

That is because of both (1) the true content of our Constitution and (2) the fact that American citizens — unlike Europeans and, contrary to the Counterrev-olutionaries' endless best efforts, deploying all the inherently-coercive power over students of virtually all our schools and universities, which they tightly control, the power of law and the so-called "learned professions," all the news and entertainment sectors of all media, and even clergyman of all faiths — still believe in God, our Constitution, and the infinite value of the individual citizen and his soul. And that the Counterrevolution has never either tolerated — nor defeated.

Americans' combined belief in God and individual liberty, and in our Consti-tution, remain the as-yet unstoppable sources from which our national salvation will arrive: No matter how much corruption and injury to citizens' liberty it may have succeeded so far in inflicting, the American Counterrevolution has never been able to succeed in winning over the American people themselves, and the Counterrevolutionaries have never, fearing certain defeat, dared forthrightly to try to amend (except for the 16th amendment legitimizing the income tax) the Constitution to make their "successes" Constitutional and legitimate; accordingly, all the Counterrevolution's usurped "achievements" are completely undoable at any time, as soon as the people simply wake up and demand it.

### The Collectivist And American Revolutions' Differing Views of "Liberty"

The Jacobin-led French Revolution claimed it had achieved "liberty", as well as equality and fraternity, for the people, by ousting the king, the church and God Himself, and replacing them with rulers whose actions reflected (it claimed) the collective General Will of all the people, even though none of them obtained office through an election, including those who, while in office, had absolute, dictatorial power, such as Napoleon and Robespierre.

Instead of promoting individual liberty <u>versus state power</u>, as is the essence of the American Revolution, for the Jacobins, and the French Revolution which they ultimately led, "liberty" has actually had a nonsensical bizarro meaning: they actually used the term "liberty" to mean freedom exclusively <u>from any religious constraints</u>. As part of that their bizarro concept of "liberty", they simultaneously demanded absolute conformity with the dictates of their "collective's" own "moral imperatives," all based on its pseudo-religion: for them, the term "liberty" has always had that purely collectivist meaning, derived directly from the morally-and intellectually-incoherent, and fundamentally anti-religious, writings of Rousseau, discussed below.

To further clarify, to the extent that it has any meaning at all, French revolutionary "liberty" refers to what could be called purely-human-derived anti-clerical/anti-Catholic <u>"liberty"/conformity for the nation as a whole collectively</u>, in which its leaders, believing themselves freed, as a result of their fanatical devotion to the "cause," of original sin and so purportedly able to provide the path, itself purportedly based on scientifically-derived "reason," supposedly leading to achieving human perfection, all which supposedly provided moral authority for them to compel, and so guarantee to all citizens, universal adherence to the nation's General Will (as determined by them alone) – supposedly for the good of everyone. And no, I am neither kidding nor exaggerating.

These critically-important features of the always-transnational French Revolution – everywhere it manifests itself – are most clearly understood in contra-distinction with the 180°-different principles underlying the American Republic:

To wit, America, in all its founding documents, based all of its values on the supremacy of God over <u>all</u> men (though uniquely without any established church dictating how to worship Him), as the creator of both each individual's infinitely-valuable immortal soul, and of all rights with which each soul/person is endowed – rights which the state is forbidden, and ultimately powerless, to revoke, except through the unjust, improper usurpation and abuse of its power of violence. And all men have the inalienable right, actively exercised by the American revolutionaries against England, forcibly to reclaim all such natural rights if the state purports to usurp/take them away.

The French Revolution in all its manifestations is <u>the very opposite</u>: in throwing off the Bourbon absolute monarchy which, based on its claims of divine-right, had imposed virtually-total centralized control over all citizens' activities, and replacing it with a militantly atheistic totalitarian dictatorship imposing control <u>virtually-identical</u> to that of the deposed Bourbons over the citizenry, it perceives God, all religion, and any state whose legitimacy is based on the blessing of any religion or religious ideals, as the very definition of tyranny, and insists that the sole path to "liberty" – and ultimately to supposed perfection, through the supposed application of scientific principles to human life – is for all the citizens, rather than

God, <u>together</u> to be the sole source of state power, absolute allegiance to which is mandated for each citizen, supposedly for the good of the citizenry as a whole – none of whom have immortal souls and none of whom are individually important.

The idea is that when all citizens are compelled to conform to such General Will that enables all citizens to achieve a kind of collective heaven-on-Earth free of the constraints imposed by any church and any <u>other</u> authority (such as the Church and the Bourbon kings).

Unlike the Americans, the French revolutionaries simply had no quarrel with the secular, centralized state controlling all aspects of life, perhaps assuming that such absolute state power could not be avoided in a civilized nation, and that, in any event, such control was positively <u>non</u>-tyrannical and desirable as long as its leaders supposedly reflected the General Will – and, as importantly, were not the Bourbons. It is as if the American concept of individual liberty free of state constraints literally never crossed their minds as a possibility.

As a practical matter, for the French citizens, revolutionary Jacobin "liberty" simply meant that a supposedly more-popular, fundamentally anti-Catholic, totalitarian legal regime replaced a very Catholic (and religiously moral) one, with no actual increase in individual liberty whatsoever achieved for the citizens – nor even sought.

The tragedy of the French Revolution, as brilliantly described by de Tocqueville in his *The Old Regime and the French Revolution* (1856), was precisely the fact that it began as a perfectly-rational revolt against a totalitarian regime (which, incidentally, was actually extremely popular, rather than detested, when the process began in 1787), but it completely lacked any concept of individual liberty at all – as if the spirit of the American Revolution, which the French of all classes were well aware of <u>and which itself was wildly popular in France</u> while it was occurring (succeeding, by the way, only thanks to the French monarchy and its gunships at Yorktown), was, quite simply, <u>utterly incomprehensible</u> to the long-suffering French people for themselves, people who had been subjected to one form of serfdom or other totalitarian control for over 900 years.

Nothing so perfectly describes all these features of the French Revolution as the words of Maximilian Robespierre, its then-leader, as leading member of the Committee of Public Safety which had totalitarian control of France in 1794, in his writing explicitly to justify the bloody Reign of Terror he was presiding over, included in his writing titled <u>On the Moral and Political Principles of Domestic Policy, Justification of the Use of Terror</u>:

> "But as <u>the essence of the republic or of democracy is equality</u>, it follows that the love of country necessarily includes the love of equality. It is also true that <u>this sublime sentiment assumes a preference for the public interest over every particular interest</u>....

From all this let us deduce a great truth: the characteristic of popular government is confidence in the people and severity towards itself....

This great purity of the French revolution's basis, the very sublimity of its objective, is precisely what causes both our strength and our weakness. Our strength, because it gives to us truth's ascendancy over imposture, and the rights of the public interest over private interests....

We must smother the internal and external enemies of the Republic or perish with it; now in this situation, the first maxim of your policy ought to be to lead the people by reason and the people's enemies by terror.

If the spring of popular government in time of peace is virtue, the springs of popular government in revolution are at once virtue and terror: virtue, without which terror is fatal; terror, without which virtue is powerless. Terror is nothing other than justice, prompt, severe, inflexible; it is therefore an emanation of virtue; it is not so much a special principle as it is a consequence of the general principle of democracy applied to our country's most urgent needs.

It has been said that terror is the principle of despotic government. Does your government therefore resemble despotism? Yes, as the sword that gleams in the hands of the heroes of liberty resembles that with which the henchmen of tyranny are armed. Let the despot govern by terror his brutalized subjects; he is right, as a despot. Subdue by terror the enemies of liberty, and you will be right, as founders of the Republic. The government of the revolution is liberty's despotism against tyranny [emphases added]."

This brief quotation from Robespierre who, at the time he wrote this was the leader of the 12 members of the Committee of Public Safety holding dictatorial powers over the entire French nation: In it he literally articulates the very essence of the French Revolution as of that moment, shortly after the Revolution's murder of the king and queen, brazenly flaunting some of its most remarkable features – features revealed by considering these words in their legal historical context, features which the French Revolution retained, initiated, and shared with all collectivist revolutions thereafter. Those eternal collectivist revolution features can be summarized as follows (in our own American Counterrevolution, its politically-attuned leaders have usually taken pains to mask these blatantly-totalitarian features from public view, though they have always been just below the surface, and have even begun to appear in public, for the first time, during the Obama administration):

(1)  its messianic, totalitarian zeal to utterly eradicate all who oppose it in any manner – and literally to terrorize, and completely subjugate, the entire population so that none may dare oppose it in any manner;

(2)  the absolute exaltation of purported "equality" above all other consider-
     ations/values, with individual liberty – "private interest" – completely deval-
     ued and effectively vilified, as an opponent of the quasi-deified "public inter-
     est" of promoting the Revolution itself;

(3)  any opposition to the Revolution – in whatever form, including mere thought
     – requires the brutal death penalty without delay – "justice, prompt, severe,
     inflexible…" This is the classic description of <u>thought crime</u> as itself the most
     serious, heretical capital offense, no trial necessary;

(4)  the "Cause" of the Revolution must be obeyed and pursued with absolute de-
     votion and fanatical zeal, with no limiting principle applicable or permissible,
     even though in reality that "cause" involved imposing authoritarian (Bad Law,
     in my terminology) laws on the people, substantively indistinguishable from
     those of their previous, Bourbon absolute monarchs.

In the French Revolution, the only real political/legal change was that the Bourbon
dynasty itself was removed and replaced by new, purportedly popularly-chosen
(no election necessary) rulers – "Legislators," in Rousseau's terminology, as discussed below – and the mandatory anti-religion was established, completely
replacing the Catholic Church in France as a political force (e.g., everything in society derived from non-secular sources was renamed, including the days of week,
the names of months, and even the calculation of what year it was).

And, with all the blood, violence and dislocation it has spawned, all the French
Revolution has ever delivered wherever it has manifested outside France has
been what I have called Bad Law, stifling all freedom, originality and individuality,
and all economic growth and prosperity – as completely as the Bourbons had
done so effectively in France before the first French Revolution.

As Robespierre made clear: subordinating the individual to the interest of the
state – as the Bourbons had done so effectively for their monarchy since Louis XIV
– was a central purpose of that revolution, with the revolutionary state explicitly
subject to <u>no limiting principle</u> on the violence it was authorized to inflict against
its own people to effect such subordination. A clearer declaration than his of <u>total
opposition to individual liberty</u>, and of relentless totalitarianism, would be difficult to imagine.

All subsequent Collectivist revolutions, in other continental European nations, in
Russia and in China, Cuba, various nations in South America, Asia and Africa, and
elsewhere, to the extent they had any intellectual coherence at all (ideological
claims, that is, by the brutal, lawless thugs who actually prevailed) did the same
as the French Revolution – that is, they both empowered new rulers who were
officially atheistic, and therefore answerable to <u>no</u> superior, moral authority
whatsoever, and who claimed that that very fact – and their totalitarian powers
– themselves provided true liberation for the people. Each such collectivist revolution had its own particular features (the Nazis had Jew-hatred and German

nationalism, e.g.) but those were <u>in addition</u> to those of the French Revolution, which have remained constants.

The American Revolution could not have been more different: it presumed the rule of God (no official religion necessary, desired nor permitted here) — that the government and all of its officials are morally subordinate to Him, that all rights of the people are derived from Him, and that the people, acting pursuant to their God-derived rights to do so, imposed specific constraints limiting, and explicitly confining, the powers of government officials and the federal government (and the state governments as well) in the terms of the written (for the first time in any nation) Constitution.

In stark contrast with the French Revolution and its numerous Collectivist followers, the American Revolution and Constitution explicitly presumed that the people's freedom <u>depended on</u> both the subordination of the rulers to God and on the Constitution's explicit constraints on, and the narrow-delineation of, the power of the state and all of its officeholders. All American officeholders have been required, as a precondition to assuming office, to take affirmations or oaths in the Lord's name swearing to serve the people and the Constitution alone, oaths which would be morally meaningless if taken by a nonbeliever.

Which of these two, radically-different, approaches to government and the citizenry itself would any rational people desiring either individual liberty or prosperity, let alone both, choose? Armed with even the slightest knowledge of history, the question answers itself: notwithstanding the American Collectivists' Counterrevolutionary assaults on the American Revolution and on the value of individual liberty itself since the middle of the 19th century, America alone (together, to a lesser extent, with other English-speaking nations) has both flourished economically and provided genuine freedom for its people – facts further proven by the desire of people from all the rest of the world to emigrate to America, notwithstanding the constant insults and calumny thrown its way by the rest of the world – and by many in its own self-proclaimed "intelligentsia."

<u>The English (And The American) Revolutions</u>

Our American Revolution was actually a continuation of the ongoing, episodically-active English revolution which began in the 13th century. In that first episode, English barons extracted from King John his commitment, memorialized in the Magna Carta, to recognize the legal substantiality (which he had previously denied) of their property rights. That concession forced from the king meant that he could never, as he had claimed the right to do previously, take away those rights gratuitously, and without what came to be called due (judicial) process of law. Magna Carta further established the legal principle that the king could impose no taxes on his barons (who were the only free men in England at that time, after the Norman conquest in the 11th century) without their consent (in Parliament).

Prior to Magna Carta, the Norman English kings, following William's conquest, had claimed that their power over the entire (defeated) kingdom was absolute and that no one but the king himself could really "own" property. Although the actual events were more complicated than just described, this was how the Magna Carta legacy was understood in the early 17th century, when the second major episode of the English Revolution took place between 1640 and 1660. That extraordinary, and obviously lengthy, Civil War is today known as the English Revolution and involved multiple intellectual, religious and political events – including the trial and regicide for the only time in English history of a king – King Charles I – who prior to his death, unlike other, deposed English monarchs (e.g. Richard III), had had an uncontested claim to the throne.

As directly relevant to the American Revolution, the mid-17th century English Revolution, building on the Magna Carta, further restricted the rights of the monarch relative to his subjects beyond those restrictions won in the 13th century – which additional restrictions are of enormous importance again today. Those restrictions were numerous, including precluding the King from creating any laws without Parliament's approval, outlawing his selectively refusing to enforce laws, and – of particularly enormous importance today – banning both his special, crown-controlled kangaroo courts (known as Star Chamber) and his attempts to extend centralized, bureaucratic control over most aspects of British life.

Permitting the continuation of Charles' Star Chamber and that central, bureaucratic control, which the English Civil War prevented, would have effectively forced all English subjects back into virtual serfdom, which no longer existed in England at that time, by forcing them to first obtain permission from the crown (through local bureaucrats the king intended to appoint for purposes of administering his tyrannical control) in order to engage in multiple activities. Of equal importance today, and directly connected to that banning of central, bureaucratic control, was the banning of the hated Star Chamber, which the tyrannical Henry VIII had started.

Star Chamber functioned outside the normal judicial courts of England. Its power, under the thumb of the king, who completely controlled every aspect of it, amounted to a combination of executive, legislative and judicial power — exactly what our Constitution, building on that 17th-century victory for liberty, was later intended to preclude here.

All modern federal administrative agencies function exactly like Star Chamber, possessing unlimited – as a practical, if not a purely legal, matter – existential power over everyone subjected to their jurisdiction. Their power over their subjects – Individuals and businesses, primarily, but ultimately including all of us – is always unlimited as a practical matter, because they have the powers to invent, then apply laws, and gratuitously to enmesh their subjects in endless legal expenses and red-tape, and destroy them financially, if they choose.

After Charles I was executed, England had no king at all and was ruled by a so-called Lord Protector (initially Oliver Cromwell), with Parliament as its legislative branch and the Common Law and Equity courts as the judicial branch, until 1660 when Charles II was permitted to ascend to the throne (the Restoration) only after he agreed to explicit restrictions on his power, including his renunciation of Star Chamber courts, his recognition of Parliament as the exclusive legislative branch of government, and his recognition of his obligation as executive to enforce <u>all</u> duly-enacted laws, without any power on his part to permit the selective <u>non</u>-enforcement of such laws (as English kings had previously done).

When Charles II's son, James II, who succeeded him, failed to abide by all his father's commitments which had permitted the Restoration, and flagrantly engaged in the selective non-enforcement of laws, Parliament arranged for his legal removal from the throne, in 1688, and his replacement by his cousin, William of Orange, in what is known today as the Glorious Revolution.

The true believers in the later, 18th century American Revolution were many in number – probably the overwhelming majority of those who literally risked everything by joining the fight against the British superpower of the day in Washington's Continental Army, together with the numerous other self-identified Patriots who otherwise actively promoted its cause.

In the French Revolution, as in all Collectivist ones to follow, the true believers/leaders were a small, often-changing (guillotined, like Robespierre and St. Just themselves, when they fell out of favor) group, who self-consciously viewed themselves as a morally-and-intellectually-superior, elite avant-garde entitled to use any means they could to excite the loyalty of their subjects, who they contemptuously viewed as "the shoeless ones," for "The Cause." Though noisily proclaiming themselves radical egalitarians, for them, equality was strictly for their subjects, who were always to be under their authoritarian, elitist thumb. The leaders, as always, were MORE equal.

As noted above, the American revolutionaries self-consciously viewed themselves as continuing a revolutionary process unique to the English, beginning with Magna Carta in the 13th century, with each successive revolutionary outbreak achieving greater and greater victories, forcibly-extracted from the crown/central state, for individual liberty/property rights for more and more citizens, and with each such victory secured by successively-stronger, quasi-constitutional legal guarantees, ultimately culminating in our Constitution.

Our Constitution was, and continues to be, completely unique in that it is written, and is so in clear, easy-to-read, plain English (lawyers were never to be required to understand it), in one document, and in the substance of its provisions. The American Civil War, which secured such legal rights for the few Americans who had previously been left out – the black slaves — technically completed the process of obtaining at least nominally-required legal equality for all Americans (although, because of a corrupt ruling by the Supreme Court – *Plessy v Ferguson* –

and the corrupt, racist Democrat, one-party rule in the South, post-Reconstruction enforcement of that legal equality was absent until the mid-20th century).

As also noted above, the American revolutionaries knew throughout their struggle that there were features of English law which they were determined to retain – specifically, the Common Law, and all of the victories for individual liberty secured in the earlier eruptions of the English Revolution – along with the Americans' revolutionary new creation – equality before the law for all citizens (unfortunately, initially, not including black slaves), resulting in equality of opportunity (but not of results) in all respects – all ultimately secured in the Constitution itself.

Their goals of promoting individual liberty, property rights and equality before the law were actually quite clear and foremost in their mind throughout their Revolutionary years of struggle, as clearly shown in the Declaration of Independence, which was their revolutionary manifesto.

### The French Revolution

The Jacobins – those among the French revolutionaries who came to dominate it – uniquely among Collectivist revolutionaries, initially had little clarity regarding where they intended to take the revolution, other than profound hatred for things in France as they were (particularly the absolute Bourbon monarchy itself, and the easily-ridiculed, often corrupt, Catholic Church which the Bourbons had promoted, often with enormous brutality), regarding the type of government they would create. Rousseau had pointed the way, as discussed below.

Unlike the Americans, they had no prior French revolutionary tradition whatsoever to draw on and, indeed, were far more radical than the American revolutionaries in the extent of the break they wanted with their past: they explicitly sought to eradicate practically everything (even renaming the months of the year!) from their French past, with the French revolutionaries eventually expressing deep contempt, anger and resentment for most of France's ancient institutions and traditions (although, ironically, ultimately they ended up embracing the most repressive, bureaucratic, Bad Law aspects of Old Regime France which the Bourbons had created).

The French revolutionaries also did not consider drawing on the English revolutionary tradition at all, including the then-recent American Revolution, which they were very-well aware of, beyond their desire to break from their own past in a revolutionary manner.

Unlike the American version of revolution, the French Revolution turned out to be utterly contemptuous of the concepts of individualism, individual liberty and of equality for citizens solely of opportunity and under the law; instead, radical egalitarianism of results came to be their goal, a goal which, together with their collectivism and bureaucratic, dictatorial central direction, coupled with complete subordination of all individuals to that direction, ultimately sacrificed and eliminated all individual liberty, economic growth, and prosperity, for all citizens.

By its very nature, since everyone has different skills and attributes, equality of re-sults, as opposed to equality of opportunity and before the law, must be imposed on the citizens/subjects by dictatorial force by the state from above, disrupting and undoing the results of free human interactions which, left to themselves, can never produce that result. It precludes anyone from retaining the fruits of his own successful efforts and, accordingly, destroys any incentive for anyone to exert such efforts, and so guarantees equal poverty for all since no one has any incentive to produce anything knowing that if he does so, it will simply be stolen from him by the state and redistributed to others who are so rewarded precisely because of their failure to similarly produce value.

The French revolutionary state's only real legal difference from the most authoritarian aspects of the monarchy overthrown by it was that the new, absolute rulers repudiated God and the church — and were no longer the Bourbons. Within a few years they had subjected themselves – voluntarily – to the absolutist military dictatorship of Napoleon, whose expansionist wars took the lives of millions of their young men, ultimately for nothing.

How did the French Revolution so differ from the American Revolution, which itself was well-known to the French revolutionaries – and was even known by the French revolutionaries to be succeeding in providing new-found liberty for the Americans already at the time the French began their Revolution in the 1790s?

Both the American and French revolutionaries all considered and believed themselves involved in a profoundly-moral quest in favor of liberty against tyranny – as they each defined those. The ultimate, defining difference between them turned out to be the particular, diametrically-different, moral authority on which they each based their moral claims – and their revolutionary goals.

The American revolutionaries' moral claims are spelled out in the Declaration of Independence and were explicitly derived from their expressed belief that God alone is the source of all moral authority for all purposes, and that all political rights are granted by Him, and not by the state nor by any ruler.

The particular textual sources they derived their views explicitly expressed in the Declaration from, in addition to the English Common Law (itself based on the Old Testament 10 Commandments) and the English revolutionary tradition, which had extracted explicit legal concessions from the English kings – all in conformity with divine demands, as the American Revolutionaries saw it – were then-recent writers, particularly John Locke, Adam Smith, and Montesquieu, himself a French political philosopher for whom the French revolutionaries showed utter disregard.

On the other hand, the French revolutionaries' moral authority was, quite simply, Jean Jacques Rousseau.

Rousseau came up with what he claimed was a moral basis for government authority derived not from God, but rather, according to him, solely from the people who would themselves be subject to that government, as a whole. He claimed that the ordered society which would result, based on the General Will of the governed themselves, alone would provide them "liberty."

In fact, and in practice, his utopian vision in the Jacobins' hands (consistent with his writings) was for a top-down centrally-directed state whose bureaucratic details ended up looking indistinguishable from those of the Bourbon French Kings – the most recent of whom those revolutionaries cheerfully guillotined – except that the Bourbons had claimed the absolute authority to impose such absolute control over all the subjects based on their claim to have been appointed for such purpose by God – in sharp contrast to Rousseau's explicitly-non-divine, human, collective origin of such power for the state.

In attempting, through all-pervasive regulatory law and bureaucracy, to micromanage every detail within their kingdoms, the absolutist monarchs in France (and elsewhere in continental Europe, including Russia, Austria, Sweden and Prussia) had viewed themselves as simply administering their own property – their kingdoms over which they claimed God-mandated absolute control – and not as appropriators of the property of their subjects; on the other hand, in the totalitarian vision of Rousseau and the Jacobins, all subjects and all their property were simply 100% subject to the supposed purely-human "general will" of their nation – no God or morality involved or wanted.

Rousseau and His Writings

In 1762, in *A Treatise on the Social Compact...*, his book spelling out his views I have been describing, which book was literally to shake the world ever after, beginning in 1789, Jean-Jacques Rousseau wrote, "Man is born free, and yet is universally enslaved." He proclaimed his purpose in writing that book was that he had discovered the secret of how to liberate people from their previously-perpetual slavery.

He was absolutely correct about one thing: throughout history, including in then-present-day France, virtually all men have indeed spent their lives in a state of both dire poverty and servitude, prevented from even beginning to realize their potential – from owning property or pursuing happiness for themselves and their families – by the force of crushing laws empowering masters over them.

As to the "solutions" contemplated by Rousseau, in fact, the opposite of such liberation turned out to be the lot for those subjected to the world created by the (French and other) politicians who followed his teachings. Indeed, the slavery/serfdom most Europeans had indeed endured to varying degrees in different countries for about 900 years, or more, prior to 1789 was idyllic and benign compared to what was to follow.

In that book, which was instantly proclaimed a work of political-philosophical genius by most among the self-proclaimed intelligentsia of Paris at the time, and became an instant bestseller, Rousseau was understood to proclaim both the moral virtues/superiority (no exaggeration) of both all <u>collectives</u> of any kind (the family, the tribe, the city, a nation) of people over the individuals who comprise such collectives, and, indeed, of revolution itself to force the government to comply with the "general will" of the nation's people as a whole. Such is at least what most understood he meant, to the extent that any of his ideas can be identified with any specificity in light of their actual, complete intellectual confusion and incoherence.

Additionally, he was understood to argue cogently for the propositions that all the large nations of Europe, including the France of his time – the mid-18th century – unlike his native Geneva — a city-state he proclaimed an example supposedly of good governance — so enslaved their people that the people were worse off than they would have been <u>without any government at all</u> in the lawless so-called state of nature, described by Thomas Hobbes as one in which human life is "nasty, brutish and short."

Although variously proclaiming himself a believer in both monarchy and aristocracy, as optimal forms of government for a large nation (among his claims is that the larger the nation, the smaller the number of persons who govern should be – one of the few relatively clear positions he takes in his fundamentally anti-systematic, and fundamentally incoherent, work of supposed political philosophy), he also proclaimed the unquestionable need for a bureaucracy dictating virtually all aspects of life (what actually <u>already existed </u>throughout continental Europe at the time, including in pre-Revolutionary France), in conformity with the dictates of the "Legislator" (his word) who supposedly had clairvoyant understanding of the "General Will" of the people, as an absolute necessity for the (mythical) sovereign adequately to control the (inherently dangerous) actions and desires of the individual citizens/subjects.

He further proclaims the need for absolute equality, and insists that all of these ingredients – completely equality of the citizenry and their complete subjugation to the "General Will" of the collective (which he claims might not actually be even a majority of the people – go figure) is the <u>sole</u> moral way for the citizenry to become free and not enslaved.

Reduced to its bare essentials, Rousseau claims that true freedom for the citizenry requires radical collectivism with the complete subjugation of individuals to the state, which is responsible for imposing bureaucratic control over all their actions and absolute equality in the administration of its dictates. It happens that this turned out to be a recipe for precisely what the Jacobins – the most radical of all the French revolutionaries who increasingly took control over their Revolution – had in mind and eventually imposed on the nation – and, under Napoleon, on most of Europe.

The truth is, Rousseau's book – with little exaggeration, the Jacobins' Bible – is so filled with internal contradictions and intellectual confusion that any effort to actually derive any coherent political philosophy from it is doomed to failure.

Nevertheless it was wildly popular for the last half of the 18th century in France, particularly with the French intelligentsia and "fashionable" upper classes – people, that is, who were most likely to suffer after the real-life imposition of such radical, revolutionary ideas – with the ultimate take-away from it the notions that since the people as a whole are always sovereign, they have an inalienable right to revolt against any government that pretends to be their master and to replace that government with one which properly expresses their gestalt (a word he doesn't use, but which, alone, would seem to express his concept) "general will" which must always be followed for the state to be legitimate.

Why, you doubtless ask, am I spending so much time describing the ultimately-nonsensical views of M. Rousseau, who few but graduate students bother to read anymore? Because, quite simply, his writings and moral/philosophical/political views are the ultimate source for all subsequent socialist/collectivist and, yes, Progressive writers and ideologues – and politicians, and revolutionaries – including Karl Marx and all the revolutions and movements his writings inspired and, yes, the American Counterrevolutionary Collectivists who have variously named themselves Progressives and, sometimes, Liberals (beginning with the Progressive Democrat FDR, who appropriated that term based on his opposition to Prohibition, enactment of which had poisoned the name "Progressive" because of their advocacy for it).

## Rousseau And His Malignant Legacy

However improbable it is that any, supposedly-rational people could be won over by the incoherent nonsense of Rousseau, this all matters enormously now, today, in the United States, which, unlike Europe, remained largely immune to the cancer which Rousseau's ideas indeed created, until they were injected into our nation and all its institutions beginning in the mid-19th century. That cancer has been growing and metastasizing ever since, tolerated largely by America's invariably-generous and bighearted people as a mostly-avoidable, though increasingly-corrupt, nuisance – until now, when its growth has reached the point throughout our laws, culture, civil society and government that, to preserve our most dearly-held individual liberties, it must indeed be both unmistakably recognized for what it is and eradicated as the utterly vile parasitic cancer it is.

Rousseau's manifest indifference and contempt for individuals as individuals is obviously irreconcilably different from fundamental Christian theology in which the life, death and resurrection of Jesus Christ is proclaimed as the very vehicle provided by God Himself which provides the sole path for the individual immortal soul's salvation – all of which would be pointless if the individual and his soul were not supremely important—an importance Rousseau categorically rejects.

Although very few Americans today, or even during and after his lifetime, have ever actually read anything Rousseau wrote (this is also true for the similarly-important and malignant writings of Karl Marx, discussed below), once the full scope and nature of his "contribution" in his writings to all Western civilization is fully appreciated, and seen for what it is, it becomes apparent how profound his ideas' influence has been, to the point that literally nothing important that has happened in American politics, journalism, educational institutions, the legal profession, and even established religions since the latter decades of the 19th century and, increasingly, after the 1950s, popular culture, can be fully understood and appreciated for what it is without understanding Rousseau's "contribution."

Indeed, if more of those who have, usually-unknowingly, been profoundly influenced by him actually read, analyzed and thought about his books (and those of Karl Marx), they would realize how utterly idiotic, nonsensical, intellectually dishonest and vapid they are – and how delusional, destructive and, yes, anti-human (as well as anti-God) and, accordingly, genuinely evil it is to take anything he (or Marx) said seriously and to heart.

Although Rousseau himself never directly attacked religion, and even claimed (almost certainly dishonestly) that he was a believing Christian and that he intended to promote both liberty for everyone and morality in his writings, the truth is, his ideas simply cannot be reconciled with a belief in God – particularly the Judeo-Christian God. That is because his totalitarian position regarding the complete primacy of the group over the individual necessarily has the effect of denying the primacy of God and has each of the following effects, none of which can be reconciled with belief in that Judeo-Christian God – nor ultimately in the fundamental Christian concept that each individual has an immortal soul, which Jesus sacrificed His divine life to save:

1.  Because the individual must subordinate himself completely to the commands of the "general will," he necessarily must be deprived of free choice in his actions and so of any moral responsibility for them;

2.  Because the "general will" is, by definition, the will of men alone, and not of God, Rousseau demands that men become the supreme moral and legal authority and alone rule under it without reference to God's moral demands;

3.  The necessary denial of any independent rights of individuals as individuals, who are effectively slaves to the "general will," means no one in the society has any independent right to his own life, liberty and property since all such are required to be subordinated to the "general will."

4.  Since the state/general will is required to be all-powerful with respect to all, it has no obligation to respect any of the 10 Commandments – which demand respect for the life, liberty, property and dignity of all individuals in society – nor the substantively-identical commandments of Jesus to "love your neighbor as yourself" and to render unto Caesar only that which is Caesar's, and

unto God what is God's: Rousseau's requirement for absolute obedience to Caesar means <u>everything</u> is Caesar's, and <u>nothing</u> is God's.

5.   Because absolute obedience to the necessarily-man-made "general will" by each individual is mandatory – supposedly to guarantee the "liberty" of all – that requirement in itself is indistinguishable from a religious requirement and so effectively forces a man-made, and inherently evil, <u>anti</u>-religion on all members of the group.

Rousseau's "contribution," in a nutshell: he originated the concept in the West of a purely-secular, millenarian/messianic <u>political</u> ideology/religion believed in by its advocates and followers with a zeal, fanaticism and, indeed, ruthlessness never seen previously except in the most bigoted followers of a religion who insisted that all others follow the same religion – or else. He literally created the notion of a political movement as a secular religion – all the more fanatical because of its claims to be based solely on the application of pure reason – materializing, first in Revolutionary France, and later elsewhere, and resulting in fanatical hatred of Christianity and particularly, in France, the Catholic Church.

In other words, it could fairly be called an <u>anti-religion</u> religion, in practice both driven by and <u>fueling</u> fanatical anger, resentment and envy against everyone and everything outside the particular "group" who is not, for whatever reason, in con- formity with the group's "general will" – with envy itself being the <u>sole emotion</u> categorically <u>forbidden</u> in the 10 Commandments.

Although Rousseau did not use the term "collectivism" for what he was preaching, that is as good a name for it as any. That is because its fundamental feature in- volves resolving <u>all</u> issues <u>always</u> on the side of the group – or collective – and its "general will" in answer to the question of: who is more important, the individual or the group (necessarily consisting of multiple individuals) he is identified with?

Since the collective – the group – is invariably deemed of primary importance, requiring the subordination of the individual and his wants and desires, this is literally the opposite of individualism — with God-believing individualism, the <u>opposite</u> of Rousseau's atheistic collectivism, being the most accurate name for the American Revolution's philosophy.

According to Rousseau himself, subscribing to his collectivist position does not automatically tell you <u>how</u> one is to determine what the collective's "general will" is at any time. Is Democratic majority rule mandated? Some might think so, but that was not the position of Rousseau – nor of the French revolutionary Jacobins.

Rousseau even takes the position that the collective majority may often <u>not even know what its true true will is</u>.

This is what leads him to the concept of the Legislator – the person or persons who divine the group's collective general will at any time, with the optimal number of persons or person who comprise this Legislator diminishing as the size of the group it rules over expands, with a nation the size of France necessarily demanding a <u>single</u> individual for that position. Since the Legislator is granted such overwhelming power over each individual in the collective he is charged with determining the will of and directing, clearly Rousseau is providing justification for absolute dictatorship – something that, in practice ends up looking and sounding an awful like the Emperor Napoleon Bonaparte – or any other, tyrannical dictator in history you can name (e.g, Stalin, Hitler, Pol Pot, Mao, Castro).

## The Ramifications of Collectivism

As indicated above, the anti-religion portion of the French Revolution arose from numerous sources, historical and literary, the former including the cruel persecution of non-Catholics by Louis XIV, and the latter most notoriously contained in the very popular writings of the prolific writer in numerous literary genres (poetry, plays, novels, letters even) known as Voltaire (the pen name for François Marie Arouet), in addition to Rousseau's writings.

Coupled with the radical, vehemently anti-religion (particularly anti-Catholic) ideology which the Jacobins, the first explicit followers of Rousseau's teachings, marinated in and accepted as true teachings of the other prophet of the French Revolution – Voltaire – the radical, messianic ideology of what can fairly be called collectivism (ultimately synonymous with anti-individualism) was born.

But if any society accepts collectivism as a legitimate, moral and political concept, it literally spreads like a weed – or cancer – assuming many additional manifestations, forms, mind-sets, and rules.

## The Radical, Unchristian Notion of Collective Guilt

For example, under <u>non</u>-collectivist Judeo-Christian morality, it Is always the individual <u>alone</u> who can either be guilty or innocent concerning any misdeed -- or credited with any particular achievement. Thus the idea of assigning guilt, innocence or victimhood to an entire <u>group</u> of people is morally abhorrent under the concepts of Judeo-Christian justice – and similar concepts of justice under the English/American Common Law which was self-consciously based on it, and also under the laws of Golden age Athens (as described by Plato, very similar in practice to the English Common-Law).

But once <u>collectivism as an idea is accepted as legitimate</u> by a society, instead of being reviled as taboo, the idea of <u>group guilt or victimhood necessarily follows</u> logically from that acceptance, and can, when invoked accusingly, itself be used as a form of intellectual and moral <u>weapon</u> — and a tool for further spreading acceptance of collectivism, breeding unquenchable resentment, and vilification of entire groups of people. Racial discrimination of any kind, including so-called "affirmative action," is an obvious example of this kind of projected, group victim deification/vilification. But there are other similar examples.

For example, is this not exactly what racial agitators in America's black and radical leftist communities – Al Sharpton, for example – are claiming when they say that all blacks alive today have been victimized by all whites and "their" society, because of slavery which individual, all now-dead, blacks indeed endured in previous centuries – even though not a single black alive today in America, nor probably even his parents or grandparents, were themselves slaves. And none of today's whites, who he accuses of collective guilt, were involved in any of that.

And, of course, countless, white Americans who are second and third generation immigrants had parents or grandparents who themselves escaped from monstrous tyrannical circumstances (Nazi Germany, e.g.) – far worse than those of Blacks who grew up in Jim Crow America.

And note how collectivist/Marxist grievance promoters in America – asserting both collective guilt against entire races, and collective victimhood of others, all based on purely-racist, evidence-free assumptions – claim, gratuitously, that all whites are racial victimizers just because of their race. Those assertions are examples of blatant, weaponized collectivism in action. And, of course, there is certainly not a single white person alive today in America who owned any such slaves.

And, in the context of alleged group victimhood, why should American blacks, solely because of their color, be considered to be inherently racial victims to a greater extent than, say, white American Jews whose relatives were actual victims of the Nazi Holocaust in very recent times, or Vietnamese Americans who escaped actual persecution from Vietnamese Communists, or Chinese who escaped from the mass death inflicted during the reign of Mao – and countless other refugees from government evil around the world?

Yet Al Sharpton – as simply one, very-prominent example due, to his being actively promoted and endorsed as legitimate by the President, Obama – in his anti-American grievance-mongering, demands of the black community that all its members, for their own legitimacy, consider themselves to be victims inherently by virtue solely of their color, and be so considered by all others in society, and demands that all Blacks should be filled with rage and resentment at all white society – and be entitled to special, privileged treatment by that society today, in supposed group recompense for whatever group harm they are imagined to have suffered.

And this nonsense is taught as gospel at major American universities, with entire departments dedicated to this anti-American, collectivist poison (what do you think they do in black studies and women studies and gay studies departments?).

These racial accusations (all identically made by Marx, incidentally), though frequent, are far from the most significant claims of collective guilt asserted by the

American Counterrevolution. Instead, that distinction belongs to the targeted vilification of businesses and businessmen of all types, against whom American collectivists have invariably asserted the collectivist Marxist claims that they are all simply thieves victimizing their customers and employees, victims who can only be protected by means of the state taking absolute control over all those businesses. That is the invariable claim asserted to justify each of the federal alphabet agencies — and their effect.

Similarly, a determined collectivist typically would always seek to divide the people of a larger society into multiple groups of supposed victims and supposed oppressors – each of whose status as such is a function purely of belonging to a particular, supposedly-identifiable segment of the larger population. Some groups are to be accorded special privileges based on their supposed victimhood, entitling them to say or do things no one else is permitted to do, and to make claims on others' property that would be offensive from anyone else. And even to be considered blameless victims when they commit crimes – so that, if jailed, they should be considered political prisoners – even after a jury unanimously found them guilty!

This is a Marxist/collectivist propagandist strategy for filling a society with resentment and victimhood – supposed "class consciousness," even where no juridical classes actually exist – for purposes of having it embrace a collectivist ideology. It is literally a strategy of divide and conquer, identifying "villains" in groups (the Jews in Nazi Germany, for example), and otherwise legitimizing the anti-individual notion of group identification.

Collectivist claims and accusations of this sort are used to obtain absolute bureaucratic control over (in the case of all businesses in America), and to obtain emotional hold over the population to have it embrace the larger ideology of collectivism. Thus collectivism becomes a <u>tactic</u> – a means to an end – as well as the end itself.

Though the phenomenon that resulted from the combination of the ideas of Rousseau marinated in the anti-religious bile of Voltaire has appeared in many forms, and under many names, masks and guises, ever since then it is, in reality, always the same, anti-individual, anti-Christian poison.

<u>Collectivism's Tautological Cohesiveness</u>

As mentioned, to an external observer of the phenomenon, one of the most remarkable features of Collectivism as an ideology, and the Collective it has indeed both spawned and energized transnationally, is the extent to which it does indeed generate – as Rousseau claimed exists for each nation – a kind of collective, or gestalt, consciousness among all its members resulting in their holding uncannily similar, if not identical, views on a remarkable range of subjects – even if discussing any of those topics to arrive at particular opinions regarding any of them, let alone all of them, rarely if ever occurs.

This phenomenon invariably manifests, in all nations, and among all sociologi-cally-identifiable Collectivism-subscribing groups, including all bureaucracies: it is as if the Collective had convened and consciously agreed/conspired to hold certain views on a vast range of subjects – without the members needing ever to actually discuss them at all.

This phenomenon, in turn, has multiple consequences both in reinforcing in mul-tiple ways its adherents' virtually-religious loyalty to the Collective – and their in-tolerant hatred for any perceived opponents – and in the particular proselytizing arguments and other efforts made by those adherents to win new converts to the Cause.

This phenomenon manifests itself in a number of emotionally-connected core beliefs subscribed to by virtually all Collective adherents, almost immediately upon their becoming convinced of their personal – there is no other word for it – profound, often desperate, need to become a Collective member. Most such members value that membership far more than ordinary party loyalty – as a means to feeling personally fulfilled or, in many cases, redeemed from what they experience as guilt (notwithstanding their non-belief in any God). Eric Hoffer wrote brilliantly about this phenomenon in his discussion of what he called Mass Movements.

The Collective also secures the loyalty of many through terror, precisely as pre-scribed by Robespierre. This is particularly true of businesses and businessmen under the thumb of federal regulatory agencies, many of whom are forced into living lives of doublethink and doublespeak in order to make a living and survive under that thumb. That is particularly true of corporate executives of public com-panies today in America, who have a duty to maximize their shareholders' stock value, which is literally impossible under the weight of the multiple bureaucracies they are forced to answer to, unless they at least give the appearance – through doublespeak and doublethink – of loyalty to the collectivist cause enforced by those agencies – and to the anti-business, usually Marxist, bureaucrats who wield discretionary power over those executives and their companies.

The most important of such invariable collectivist core beliefs can be summarized as follows:

1.  All Western religions are absurd, irrational fairytales and nonsense, and none of their moral directives have any validity or value: there is no God anyway – nor any objective reality.

2.  All Western civilization prior to the French Revolution was evil, irrational (primar-ily because, in their description, it was informed by foolish, superstitious, Bronze Age Christianity), and enslaving of all who came into contact with it, including particularly all lands and people colonized by any European nation who, inci-dent to such colonization, were necessarily enslaved and brutalized far beyond the experience of conquered nations anywhere else in the world previously

(they have no idea that different European nations colonized in profoundly different ways – particularly the British, who valued their empire as a free-trade zone, and not as a collection of conquered peoples: previous governments all remained, subject to English protection and peacekeeping and its Common Law – e.g., widow-burning in India was considered murder and outlawed).

3.   The individual must always be subordinated to the group, even if that means sacrificing all his life, liberty and property – which sacrifice would inevitably be for the greater good.

4.   "Experts'" opinions on all matters – including all the details of how people and all businesses should conduct all their affairs – are authoritative, and individuals who do not accept that authority must be suppressed and forced to agree – or be silenced. "Experts" are identifiable as such by the degrees and awards they receive from accrediting institutions, such as universities, professional organizations, and other credential-bestowing institutions admired by the Collective – and its already-acknowledged Experts. The facts that such "experts" have been demonstrably-proven wrong on multiple occasions previously, and/or that other "experts" disagree with them, are deemed irrelevant by the collective.

5.   The American Constitution is a monstrous document because it does nothing but constrain the power of government, as written (Justice Ginsburg has unambiguously expressed this precise view in public!), and so serves only to restrict the power of the people as a Collective – and implicitly requires America and all its resources and people to be the enemy of all Collectivist revolutions everywhere. Subverting the restrictions on government power in the American Constitution by any means available is required by the force of history for the American Counterrevolution, and by the inherently-liberating moral imperative of all Collectivist adherents, including those in America who populate its courts, legal system and the Constitutionally-authorized and created branches of the federal government.

6.   The beliefs and principles of the Collective do not constitute any particular ideology but are rather simply a scientifically-based, rational and pragmatic set of principles and views for the betterment of everyone's life. It is what everyone who is decent, good, rational and intelligent – always an overwhelming majority, regardless what any polls may say – believes and favors, and all who disagree with it in any manner are monstrous, Neanderthal idiots intent on harming normal people – particularly all minorities, women and all victimized groups in society.

7.   Members of the Collective are the coolest, hippest, smartest and all round best people around, intent on obtaining maximum liberty for themselves and everyone; and everyone opposed to, or who disagrees with, the Collective is uncool and monstrous and intent on destroying the freedom of everyone – including particularly those in the Collective.

8. No action by any member of the Collective, particularly its leaders, or any victimized group it champions within society, is evil or wrong and, to the extent it is condemned or punished by the rest of society, that is inherently an act of injustice – without regard to what the action so condemned consisted of (including murder – unless it is murder of a fellow Collective member – or any other action otherwise considered a crime). This is why all Blacks who are in prison in America today effectively are deemed to be political prisoners, victims of a system inflicting injustice on them. Similarly, since all women are inherently victims of society, it is impossible for their choice to kill their unborn fetus to be condemned in any way, and everyone opposed to their right to kill that fetus at any time is inherently anti-woman.

9. Any Collectivist-inspired government whose officers are democratically elected should have unlimited power – effectively an elected dictatorship – so that the People's will will be effectuated as quickly and easily as possible; because its election was democratic, it is never to be considered a tyranny. On the other hand, any government, individual, or party dedicated to individual liberty must be opposed, silenced and defeated by any means necessary, even if it is supported by an overwhelming majority of its people.

## And, After The Influence Of Karl Marx Beginning In The Mid-19Th Century, The Following Additional Beliefs:

1. All businesses and businessmen are thieves and scoundrels, seeking only profit for its own sake – and to steal it (profit's only source) from all who they contract with (all employees and all customers) – with all such theft-produced profit being evil and adding nothing to a nation's wealth. The more the state imposes its will, demands and directives on businesses of all kinds, the better. This belief is the foundation of all Marxist thought – and also the underlying basis justifying all of the federal alphabet agencies in America, with each such agency dedicated to attacking businesses and businessmen from its own particular angle.

2. Western civilization, particularly the United States, constitutes a direct insult to the entire earthly Environment (land, atmosphere and all water), with that insult increasing exponentially with each technological innovation, all exploitation of all oil, gas and minerals, and every innovation in the financing of business projects of any kind, so that every effort to retard or reverse any and all of those developments must be supported by the state, using every coercive or deadly power it has. Suppressing economic growth and technical innovation to the greatest extent possible are absolutely demanded – by any means necessary, including deploying fraudulent "scientific" or "expert" claims requiring action to accomplish that. And

3. Everyone who claims that any of this is not true, and/ or that Western civilization does not pose an existential threat to the planet, must be silenced and opposed by the full power of the state in any way possible. All claims of threatened environmental disaster at the hands of Western civilization must be ac-

cepted as true at all times, all who disagree must be silenced, and the full power of the state must be used, without regard to any private rights whatsoever, to minimize or reverse this existential risk – even if such efforts are likely to have virtually no actual impact. This quasi-religious devotion to "environmentalism" has been particularly prominent since the 1970s and, since the collapse of the Soviet Union in 1990, has become a virtually-religious endeavor.

Similarly remarkable features observable among virtually all Collectivist true believers are:

(1)  their certainty that they do not in fact subscribe to any ideology whatsoever, but simply are interested in purely-pragmatic solutions to the multiple social and political problems which they are always confident can be solved only through central government action (the problems they identify are legion, never actually solved, and ever-expanding – and there is always only that one solution);

(2)  they are invariably confident that all views held by them on all subjects are, as they would describe them, "mainstream and middle-of-the-road," and that all who disagree with them on any subject are, by virtue of that disagreement alone, beyond-the-pale radical extremist "kooks." This absolute certainty – both regarding the validity of their own views, and the inherent worthlessness/evil of all who disagree with them – arises from, and is continually reinforced by the unanimity of agreement they experience from multiple sources whose "expertise" regarding such matters they similarly consider beyond rational dispute.

These just-referred-to sources include multiple persons whom organizations they view as beyond reproach (i.e., universities) have credentialed as "experts", all journalists and other media sources they encounter – which invariably express identical views regarding the similarly-identical "news" and opinions they report or otherwise express. Any contrary ideas, opinions, or even news stories, are repudiated or simply ignored by all those media sources, and confidently viewed by the Collective as simply misinformation, or even lies, unworthy of consideration at all by any decent people.

That unanimity of views among what the Collective members consider a vast cross-section of sources in turn confirms their certainty of the unquestionable correctness of such views: since everyone who they encounter, in person or otherwise, seems to agree, how could any of them be wrong in any respect?

This entire phenomenon generates an effect similar to the experience of one experiencing "virtual reality": while experiencing it, even if one knows intellectually that what one is so experiencing is, in fact, not real, maintaining that belief in its unreality is almost impossible until the entire virtual reality effect is over: one finds oneself irresistibly "believing" everything one is seeing/hearing etc., literally overwhelmed by the illusion. That is precisely what doublethink is.

(3) they genuinely believe that they are on the side of promoting liberty and virtue.

(4) they not only are convinced that their views are held by an overwhelming majority of all citizens – without regard to what actual polling data, which they otherwise consider sacrosanct, may indicate – all voices from every Collective invariably unanimously announce that conviction to all, resulting in many who in fact disagree with all the Collective's views invariably considering themselves a minority – an effect which is also powerfully discouraging to all who <u>oppose</u> the Collective who, in fact, have always been an overwhelming majority in the United States, though not in the European countries in which it began.

## Karl Marx in a Nutshell

Although he pretended to be a multi-faceted intellectual – supposedly a sociologist, a philosopher and economist, in addition to being a prolific journalist – few ideas in Karl Marx' s voluminous writings are original to him. But there is no question that his influence as a propagandist for socialism and Communist revolution has been profound, represented in, or influencing, every revolution in Europe, Russia, Asia and South America, and in our Counterrevolution, since his notorious *The Communist Manifesto* first appeared in 1848.

He was communism/socialism's most ardent propagandist – at least in the 19th century – and spent most of his time in his writings attempting to formulate supposedly-rational arguments supporting communism/socialism, "proving" its historical inevitability, and fulminating against America and its revolution, which he absolutely loathed. That anti-American loathing was, and has always been, in fact, the underlying emotional engine for Marxism. This was because he – correctly – perceived America, in its then-pre-Progressive state, and its Revolution as being utterly antithetical to the radical collectivism, begun with the original Jacobin revolution in France, which he, also correctly, saw himself as the leading advocate for in his day.

He viewed America and its Revolution as the mortal enemy with which he and Collectivism were eternally at war – regardless what actions America took – so long as it was not a communist dictatorship.

To spare you the utter tedium and unpleasantness of wading through his voluminous drivel I will summarize it for you, as follows:

> All businessmen and other owners of property are thieves who have acquired everything they own solely through what amounts to theft (or worse) from their employees (who he called "workers", to differentiate them from the supposed parasites who employed – or, in his view, effectively enslaved – them) and their customers; God does not exist, and all religions are fraudulent, but there is a non-divine, ever-present force compelling all human activity forward – history itself, which compels humans toward a particular political

arrangement – socialism/communism – inevitable momentum towards which is appropriately called "Progress," initially requiring absolute control over the entire economy and all human activity by an all-powerful state, ultimately resulting in the "improvement" and transformation of human beings and their very nature itself, into totally selfless automatons, thereafter – and only then – rendering the state unnecessary.

Marx was, accordingly, well aware that the socialism/communism he propagandized for, together with the all-powerful state required to impose it (all representing the supposed will of the "workers", like the General Will of Rousseau), was utterly inimical to inherent human nature, individual liberty of all kinds, and opposed by all religions and their morality.

The following are Marx's own words regarding what he wanted, quoted from his most famous work:

"And the abolition of this [non-communist society] state of things is called by the bourgeois, abolition of individuality and freedom! And rightly so. The abolition of bourgeois individuality, bourgeois independence, and bourgeois freedom is undoubtedly aimed at [by Marx and the Communists].... In one word, you reproach us with intending to do away with your property. Precisely so; that is just what we intend....

"... In the most advanced countries [Britain and America] the following will be pretty generally applicable [to implement the communist revolution].

1. Abolition of property in land and application of all rents of the land to public purposes.

2. A heavy progressive or graduated income tax.

3. Abolition of all rights of inheritance.

4. Confiscation of the property of all emigrants and rebels.

5. Centralisation of credit in the hands of the State, by means of a national bank with State capital and an exclusive monopoly.

6. Centralisation of the means of communication and transport in the hands of the State.

7. Extension of factories and instruments of production owned by the State; the bringing into cultivation of waste-lands, and the improvement of the soil generally in accordance with a common plan.

8. Equal liability of all to labour. Establishment of industrial armies, especially for agriculture.

9.  Combination of agriculture with manufacturing industries; gradual abolition of the distinction between town and country, by a more equable distribution of the population over the country.

10. Free education for all children in public schools. Abolition of children's factory labour in its present form. Combination of education with industrial production"

— Excerpts From: Karl Marx. "The Communist Manifesto."

First note how many of these Marxist proposals have indeed been implemented, even if only partially so far, in the United States:

> "a heavy progressive or graduated income tax," a confiscatory (55% for large estates) estate tax, a federal environmental agency with virtually unlimited power to direct the use by citizens of all rivers, land and air in the nation, the establishment of the Federal Reserve and multiple financial regulatory agencies with total, often conflicting, control over all financial businesses in America, regulatory agencies which have had complete control over the railroad, radio, telephone and television businesses, including what products are permissible to be sold and by who, and is now claiming similar control over the Internet, and multiple federal agencies controlling all aspects of employment in the nation, including granting special privileges to labor unions, and public schools, with mandatory attendance, run by the states and by the teachers unions, and multiple federal agencies "regulating" all aspects of business, employment and products sold in the nation – including prescribing what products can be sold, by who and to whom – with power to destroy anyone in any business under their jurisdiction.

And that remarkable list of Marxist "achievements" in America does not even include the frontal assaults on traditional marriage by the Supreme Court, rampant "political correctness"-policing by the government and private businesses, anti-American proselytizing and "diversity"-inspired grievance promotion in all our education institutions, including universities whose accreditation has become essential for anyone to enter any of the professions and management in any corporation in the nation, and the transformative attacks on the family and traditional morals which have become constants of our culture, along with having businessman, rather than gangsters, monsters, or guys in black hats, depicted as the invariable villains in cartoons, movies, novels, and television.

Query: have we not already been completely taken over by a Marxist state?

Marx viewed the complete transformation of human nature necessary, as he acknowledged, to achieve the supposedly-historically driven utopia he envisioned as itself a worthy goal: he was convinced he had come up with a brainstorm for improving human beings at the most fundamental level: he literally thought he was smarter than God.

Of equal importance to him was the desire to overthrow, as inherently antithetical to the socialist/communist revolution he yearned for, America and its revolution. Indeed, as mentioned, virulent anti-Americanism has always been the most powerful, emotional engine energizing Marxism.

To that end he initiated what has become a tradition among all subsequent Marxists, and other collectivist/socialist, revolutionaries – looking for features of America he could criticize as supposedly deeply immoral, even for a professed atheist like him.

His principal target in that regard, like that of all who have followed in his footsteps, was the then-slavery of black Americans prior to our Civil War, with his followers in the 20th century harping on the (technically-unconstitutional, after the 13th, 14th and 15th Amendments) mistreatment blacks continued to suffer under Jim Crow laws until they were federally dismantled in 1965, and the miserable conditions of the ghettos that have continued thereafter – with the claim that that misery is exclusively blamable on other, white Americans living today.

As a deep believer in collectivism, Marx freely and voluminously alleged collective guilt for the mistreatment of blacks against all white Americans, and claimed black slavery was the sole, actual underlying rationale of the American Revolution itself, and the sole source of all American wealth (which had dwarfed the wealth of any European nation by the mid-19th century). He also claimed Americans had victimized American Indians and all other nations we had come in contact with. He invariably claimed the misery of Europeans who already lived under various government-controlling bureaucracies was due to their having insufficient communism.

As obviously preposterous as all these anti-American arguments he trotted out were, they have all remained a staple of anti-American collectivists around the world – and in America itself, where they have been the "bloody shirt" such collectivists have eternally waived in asserting their own moral superiority and loathing of the individual liberty required by our Constitution.

### Socialism's Fraud, Thuggery And Anti-Human Nature

The fraud and false utopianism which are the very heart of Marxist thinking are revealed by a simple, grammatical analysis of the all-purpose, central Communist/socialist slogan Marx popularized (like everything else in his writings, all of which are utterly unoriginal, he was not its original author) as his version of summarizing what happens under communism:

"From each according to his ability, to each according to his needs."

Those are the precise words used by Karl Marx, and numerous other Communists/socialists, as their party slogan.

That slogan announces the supposedly idealistic, non-demanding generosity of communism – it's supposed upside – while deliberately, fraudulently, concealing everything substantive about it and the totalitarian power it requires to be vested in the politicians who use that ideology as the justification to use all the power of violence of the state to exercise absolute power over the citizenry. The slogan is literally communist happy talk.

That deceptive concealment is revealed grammatically by the simple fact that the slogan omits any grammatical subject or predicate in what would otherwise be a completed sentence for the slogan. The hidden subject, grammatically, is "the state and its officeholders", and there are two hidden predicates – "takes," followed by "distributes."

Accordingly, when the slogan is turned into a complete sentence with all of its missing parts supplied, what it really says is obviously far more menacing:

> "The state, and its officeholders who act in its name, take whatever they want, with no limiting principle, from each according to their assessment of his ability to provide such, indifferent to his desires, and the state and those officeholders distribute whatever they want out of such taking, to each according to their gratuitous assessment of his needs."

When socialism/collectivism prevails over a particular property – including, as is common, particular businesses (some property or duties of citizens may be socialized at a moment in time, while others are not – yet), a citizen is only allowed to keep, control or use whatever such property – regardless whether he was at one time it's true,100% owner – as the state permits: the state, and not he, has replaced him as its real, 100% owner/master when such property is socialized.

In a lawless society – one where the so-called law of the jungle prevails, no one has property rights at all. Property rights' substantiality depends completely on laws' protection of them – a central feature of the English/American Common-Law. Socialism/collectivism is a legal scheme diametrically antithetical to laws protecting citizens' property rights: in a zero-sum process, to the extent socialism/collectivism prevails under law, that law necessarily abrogates and repeals the very laws on which property rights depend, and so obliterates them.

Thus, if socialism/collectivism prevails, replacing common-law property rights, the rights of citizens are stripped away and reduced to what they were in a completely lawless "law of the jungle" society.

Moreover, even if – as has been the case in the United States since 1887 – it enters the bloodstream of a nation very gradually, once collectivism/socialism becomes accepted to any extent in the society, it is only a matter of time before anything at odds with it – such as all citizens' property rights, and self-support/improvement duties – is completely eradicated, because in all history, collectivism/socialism has never respected any limiting principle on its expansion.

Deliberate, forceful opposition alone is what socialists/collectivists fear – and the only thing that will stop or reverse their attempt to engulf any society their monstrous ideology penetrates.

And, as the even partially collectivism-accepting/driven state expands its control over citizens' property – and, necessarily, their livelihoods – those citizens' possible opposition to further state power expansion is silenced because of its existential control over them – and their families' well-being: "He who controls the piper calls the tune."

Moreover, the ability to achieve all the socialists' <u>functional</u> objectives of complete nationalization of entire business sectors simply by obtaining that <u>existential control over</u> them through "regulation" was explicitly recognized by American socialists – deceptively calling themselves "Progressives" – even prior to the 20th century. Indeed, using that existential control, through "regulation," to obtain the virtual, functional equivalent of nationalization became their explicit goal, as publicly announced by, among others, Woodrow Wilson in his prolific writings prior to winning his presidency.

But socialists/collectivist/Progressives have always had two problems (among others) in imposing their genuinely-radical views on America:

(1)  our Constitution has always precluded every avenue for their doing so and, although they have indeed forced their desired program on almost the entire American economy through the unconstitutional collusion of politicians in all three branches of the federal government, everything they have achieved in that regard since 1887 is subject to instantaneous repeal by any principled action by Congress and/or the president, or the Supreme Court unilaterally courageously upholding the actual Constitution, at any time – and American collectivists have never had the nerve even to propose actual amendments to the Constitution which, if ratified, would actually legitimize their "achievement"; and

(2)  human nature itself, when not coercively suppressed, revolts at the very idea of socialism/collectivism – and its necessary complete destruction of all property rights of citizens – as do the most fundamental teachings of the Bible, which 70% of Americans continue to believe in, all as discussed below.

<u>First, with respect to human nature:</u>

"Mine." That is invariably one of the very first words every infant says – no teaching or prompting needed, no parental discouragement capable of limiting, let alone ending, its frequent repetition. A word, in short, filled with extraordinarily-profound subliminal meaning, striking chords within the innermost psyche no less profound and basic to human nature itself – and permanent – as "mommy" or "daddy."

Is any further proof needed to demonstrate the fundamental importance to each of us of our property? Even animals have a similar sentiment – wild animals which are keenly aware of "their" territory, which they are famous for "marking," and even domestic pets who often guard what is "theirs" – food, toys, etc. – against actual or perceived rivals. The desire – indeed, the need – of every living being for his own property is basic and, indeed, essential to survival.

At the most basic level, you would literally starve to death if you did not have "your" food to eat and, if you do not have "your" own shelter, you are either being provided such by someone to whom you are necessarily subservient or you are, literally, "homeless."

Thus, the desire to have one's own property is, without exaggeration, basic to human nature. And anyone who thinks that is a problem that can or should be "fixed" is a hypocrite and fraud (how does he intend to survive without himself owning anything – including the food he requires?) and someone with a deep antipathy for other humans.

The need/desire for property <u>of one's own</u> is an inherent, inalienable attribute of all humans – "hardwired in," in the pompous, clinical language of so-called social or anthropological "scientists."

That fact alone suffices to prove the utter impossibility of socialism/collectivism succeeding as a supposedly-beneficial political/economic/legal regime: It is a direct insult to the human psyche and to human nature.

That is why, whenever given the chance explicitly to vote for or against it, Americans have invariably overwhelmingly rejected it. Other, than in continental Europe where serfdom has existed with no material interruption in one form or another for most people for over 1000 years – and so became a kind of generally-tolerated mental habit long ago – there is no chance freemen would ever voluntarily and happily choose socialism/collectivism for themselves in the absence of fraud, trickery and overwhelming physical coercion (i.e., threats of death, torture, imprisonment, or even utter personal financial destruction).

That is because, quite simply, socialism/collectivism's very existence depends on the total vulnerability of <u>all</u> property rights to taking/"regulation" by the state. This taking, or taking over, is done by politicians and their functionaries using their public office as weaponry against the citizenry. This they do to feed their own desire for power for its own sake, and envy for other people's property, always claiming they can put it to better use, on behalf of the nation, than its actual owners.

However dressed up it may be with happy talk and utopian promises, socialism/collectivism is, quite simply, politically-organized theft of everything formerly-free people hold dearest.

This is because socialism/collectivism, which never does, nor can, actually deliver on any of its nonsense utopian promises, always involves two things:

(1) the state/political rulers taking, or taking over, whatever lands/business/property – which taking can be "limited" to complete, existential control over its management and use by its actual owners – they want from those who have earned or inherited it, usually dispensing crumbs out of it to those they pretend to be rescuing from some alleged victimhood – and invariably managing to keep for themselves and/or destroy, the rest. Socialists/collectivists always promise, among other things, equal "sharing" of everything by everyone; but, as Orwell observed, in *Animal Farm*, some in the socialist/collectivist paradise always are "more equal" than the rest; and

(2) all, or at least most, duties, obligations, the provision of goods and services, education, housing, food, drugs and healthcare, and even morally-inspired undertakings (e.g., charity care for the personally-helpless – pre-school children, incapacitated adults and elderly – inspections and "quality" certifications of all sorts) are assumed and/or taken over by the state, with citizens limited or precluded from doing any of the same.

# CHAPTER 7

## Two Types of Countries and of Politicians

### The Two Types of Countries

"What can be said at all can be said clearly; and whereof one cannot speak thereof one must be silent."– Ludvig Wittgenstein, *Tractatus Logico-Philosophicus*

Happy countries are all alike. Unhappy countries are each miserable in their own way.

In the millennia since God banished man from the Garden of Eden (definitively ending the possibility of utopia for all time) the times when there has been even a single happy country anywhere on this beloved planet have been so rare as to barely merit an asterisk when considered as a percentage of the human race's entire history.

Happy countries are always, like everything human, imperfect and, obeying God's mandated prohibition, do not attempt to become utopias, but are nevertheless happy (unlike all the other nations) because all happy nations' people both (1) each enjoy and possess individual liberty and (2) are able to interact, flourish and grow in as much safety from injury from others as is possible, under laws that do not attempt to do more than law is capable of achieving; and so, together with the officials and institutions necessary to enforce them, such civil and criminal laws provide all the protection actually possible for the citizens, their property and their families— protection, that is, from violence, trespass, business misconduct, including fraud, and oppression from their fellow citizens – and from the government and its officeholders.

Happy citizens are legally-free, and so fully able, to obey the commandments of God to "be fruitful and multiply," and to follow and obey those of the 10 Commandments which forbid specifically-described actions (e.g., theft, murder, fraud) and a single emotion – envy – harmful to fellow citizens and their property, succinctly summarized by Jesus as, "love your neighbor as yourself," secure in the knowledge that they can legally defend themselves, and that the law and their government will also protect them to the extent they are able to do so, from harmful violations of those commandments by others – including public officials.

Happy citizens live under a government duty-bound to protect them only from those dangers which government is actually capable of protecting against without doing more harm than good – dangers such as would-be foreign invaders, counterfeiters, traitors, and violations of each citizen's life, liberty and property. The happy citizens' government administers all laws equally to all (blindly, like the Greek goddess Justice) and, in so doing, provides liberty and justice for all – and no special benefit or privilege for anyone.

Happy citizens are promised both legal equality and justice based solely on their own, and others', actions, and equal opportunity to succeed (or fail) based solely on their own attributes, abilities and deeds.

Happy citizens understand that each person has his own definition of success for himself, and that any extra boost or handicap provided by the government — and its politicians — to assist, reduce or otherwise alter the success (or failure) any citizen achieves for himself is inherently corrupt and insulting to citizens' dignity and honor – and constitutionally-forbidden, due to its inevitable favoritism, in happy countries.

Happy citizens are free at all times to say or do anything they choose, no matter what anyone else thinks about their action's danger or wisdom (that pre-action judgment is left to the citizen, with the citizen knowing he will reap all its consequences, good and bad, including all resulting benefits, and any civil and/ or criminal legal liability to anyone he harms); happy citizens need permission before acting from no one, being presumed to be law-abiding, moral adults, with the government, following the law, intruding to discipline them and/or any of their fellow citizens in their lives only if, and after, they are proven, in fairly-operating courts of law, to have harmed others, and violated a law forbidding such harm, in some manner.

Rejoicing in the prosperity and peace that inevitably result from their own work in such an environment, happy citizens also rejoice in choosing to extend charity to those very few among them who are unable to escape poverty or other hardship even in the happy country – charity which is accepted with gratitude and joy by its recipients, whose numbers become fewer and fewer as the happy country inevitably prospers from its citizens' freedom more and more.

All happy citizens render unto the state (Caesar) only that which the state can rightly and legally claim from them in taxes (which the state spends only pursuant to strict constitutional provisions and limitations, and only as legally budgeted and authorized) and in obedience to the law, and unto God what is God's.

In happy countries, no result is guaranteed to anyone for any action they take (other than imposition of any law they violate); everything is earned or inherited from family who pass it on lawfully to them. True justice prevails for all to the extent possible on this planet – as prescribed in those of the 10 Commandments which forbid specific actions harmful to fellow citizens and to their property.

All laws in happy countries are short, simple and easy to understand (no lawyer needed) and are themselves enacted under constitutionally-prescribed procedures openly, by duly-elected and publicly-identified legislators, with favoritism to no one. No government official or agency can exercise more than one government power (legislative, judicial and executive).

In happy countries, no "benefit" is ever provided by the state to any of its citizens other than as justice requires, such as when courts award prevailing parties judgments in their favor pursuant to the requirements of blind justice rooted in widely-accepted legal and moral principles: nothing is ever gratuitously "given" by the state to any citizen, nor taken from any citizen (as would necessarily be required for the state to bestow any gratuitous "benefit" to any other citizen) except that which justice requires, with the genuine rule of law and the climate of liberty and prosperity and safety it creates being the one true benefit for all citizens which is promised and granted to all equally, with no special privileges or rules or favoritism for anyone.

All happy citizens and their government understand that if the state and its officers ever take any actions affecting citizens that differ from what justice specifically requires, in doing so, the state necessarily does <u>in</u>justice, which is forbidden in the happy country.

Regarding unhappy countries: to the precise extent to which each such country differs from a happy country (and the degree to which unhappy countries do so varies enormously), political power — and its office-holding, and other, parasitical beneficiaries — prevail over all, the power of individual citizens relative to the state and its functionaries is reduced (to the point that citizens can be reduced to serfs), and constant, existential fear is ever-present, even for the few among the populace who seemingly benefit from the oppression of all others.

Everyone in unhappy countries is subject to the whims of someone else to whom they must answer and whose permission must be obtained for them to take any action – except, in the unhappiest countries, for the ultimate dictator, who himself also lives in terror of being deposed.

But the details of the particular oppression that prevails in unhappy countries always differ according to the particular ruler/tyrant/kleptocracy who (temporarily) holds sway at any time. In unhappy countries, the state and those who act in its name (invariably proclaiming themselves virtuous, selfless "public servants") assume power over as many activities as they can claim for themselves – or rather, as many such activities as the public officials who hold offices in it and use the power of the state against their fellow citizens can take for themselves. Their reason for assuming such power – invariably at the *pro tanto* expense of the power of the people – is always the same: they claim the safety and/or security of the citizenry or some other claimed emergency urgently requires their doing so.

And the more such power the state assumes for itself, the more attractive holding public office in it becomes to sociopaths who despise their fellow citizens and yearn to hold power over them.

Happy countries are the most hated – and feared – countries on the planet at any time. This is because most, if not all, the other countries are unhappy; and the rulers of the unhappy countries are, for a multitude of reasons, unable to tolerate the very existence of the happy countries; and those rulers both do everything in their power – without regard to law, morality or decency – to induce their own subjects to share that hatred.

Rulers of unhappy countries care only about the magnitude of their power over everyone, always blaming their inevitable failures on others, including foreigners and/or identifiable groups within their subjects, and incite hatred and envy among their subjects to divide them into groups warring with each other.

### The Two Types of Politicians

People who <u>actively</u> seek public office in a republic or democracy – otherwise known as politicians – have one of the following two motives for doing so: (1) they either genuinely feel some calling to what they consider to be public service, and have personal integrity/morality ranging from high to barely passable, or (2) they are genuine, utterly amoral sociopaths obsessed with acquiring power over others, who will say and do anything – and can be counted on to tell big lies constantly and never to speak the truth about anything, nor ever to honestly reveal anything — about themselves, their actions and, particularly, their true motives for doing anything.

Unfortunately, the more power over citizens the state is given, or simply takes, the more power it also provides for those who purport to act in its name as its agents – and the more likely it is to attract the worst sociopaths to seek public office in order to wield that power over others.

To protect itself from these monsters, most of a republic's citizenry – and, at a minimum, all recognized political parties – must be able to recognize any such sociopaths for what they are, and create barriers to preclude them from entering any position of power. If any sociopaths are allowed to get past any such taboos or other barriers excluding them, particularly in a democracy, they are likely, unfortunately, to succeed in their quest for power.

Indeed, if any sociopaths at all are able to achieve any legitimacy as candidates for any public office, the worst of the worst of them are certain to rise to power. This is because both of the perceived "charm" sociopaths (pathological narcissists) invariably project, at least to many, and their complete indifference to any moral, ethical, and even legal, constraints, necessarily puts any non-malignant opponents at an impossible strategic and tactical disadvantage. Because the sociopath is willing to say and do absolutely anything to win, the constraints any decent opponent respects and follows have the effect of completely disarming him against his unprincipled sociopath opponent: he finds himself in a gunfight with no gun, and with both hands tied behind his back – against an opponent who is armed to the teeth and perfectly happy to commit murder.

Thus, nothing is more dangerous to a republic then for any sociopaths to be (mistakenly) accepted – by the electorate, or by any ostensibly-legitimate political party – as legitimate political candidates or leaders, and so avoid the total ostracism they deserve – and the republic, for its own health, requires – on the merits.

Because of their obsessive need for power over others, their inherent contempt both for morality and for those they rule over, when given any chance to do so, sociopaths are willing to say and do absolutely anything they imagine they can get away with, including making "big lies" on the model described, and used, by Hitler – lies which are simply too big to be disbelieved by too many decent people.

This dynamic can be described as it has been by Lord Acton: power corrupts and absolute power corrupts absolutely. An additional observation: the corruption that occurs and increases with the growth of state power permeates to society at all levels — including to all businesses — the providers of all needed and desired goods and services — subjected to overwhelming state power.

Those businesses so subjected simply have no choice but to engage in the corruption — in order to survive without being crushed. So too, the corruption spreads to the media which people rely on for information, media which need to participate in the corruption, even if only to continue to have access to information from the state – even though it becomes nothing but disinformation and misinformation as relayed to the public. And it engulfs popular entertainment, schools at all levels and, let us not forget, the so-called learned professions such as law and the social sciences whose members actually, parasitically, profit from their participation in the corruption, and who pride themselves on their intellectual ability to split hairs and rationalize any action.

In Chapters 14, I describe how all these corrupting processes have transpired here in America, particularly since 1906.

How could this possibly have happened? What follows is my structural answer to that question; later chapters contain my description of the actual history of these events.

As humans, we each have our own, psychological blind spots which, even when we are intellectually aware of them, are virtually impossible to overcome. For example, if you suffer from serious, chronic illness, do you find it difficult, if not impossible to fully remember what it was like to be healthy? Or conversely, if you are relatively young and healthy, do you find it difficult, if not impossible, on some level, to fully comprehend serious, chronic illness – even when it seems to stare you in the face in the company of a desperately sick parent or loved one?

Similarly, decent, moral people (i.e., most of us) find it difficult, if not simply impossible, to comprehend someone who is truly evil and morally malignant. We may even feel guilty when so characterizing anyone – even when the evidence for such is overwhelming.

Even when we know for a fact intellectually that the evil person – a proven, serial liar, for example – is almost certainly brazenly lying, it is incredibly hard, if not impossible, for us to fully comprehend that, yes, <u>everything</u> he is saying now (and likely has ever said) really is a lie – an inescapable conclusion based on his own, known past, fraudulent moral depravity.

We normal people feel compelled to project onto the sociopath how <u>we</u> would behave if we had engaged in the particular misconduct we know for a fact he previously committed, misconduct which, in our case, we would have considered personal failings, deviations from who we truly are.

But, as a scorpion is always a scorpion, a sociopath is always a sociopath, and his bad deeds are not, as with the rest of us, aberrational failings. They are his norm, what the sociopath always does, and expressions of his very nature. Any explanation he gives for any of his conduct is always a lie designed to hide his true motives and agenda, which are invariably amoral and/or malignant. He always wears a mask regardless what he is doing or saying. Nothing so terrifies him as honesty, and the possibility of being truly recognized and understood by others.

On the other hand, our experience of the sociopath is analogous to the experience of very high-quality virtual reality: even while telling yourself intellectually it is all a pure illusion, it is virtually impossible to abandon the experience of believing the genuine reality of what you are seeing and hearing – until physically removing the equipment creating the illusion.

Indeed, because it forces us to experience this phenomenon – and so teaches us this our remarkable psychological vulnerability to the total-believability effect of artificial hallucination — the technological development of virtual reality may do more to preserve future generations from mass madness than anything since Jesus Christ's resurrection (not that the two are otherwise equivalent).

Sociopaths know how to exploit and manipulate these our hallucinatory blind spots. They exploit that knowledge, together with their own total amorality, to obtain power over decent citizens, cold-bloodedly seeking to control citizens' thoughts and actions.

And if the sociopath can generate a mob – as through "community organizing" – angrily demanding support from all for his most radical proposals, he is happy to use that mob to sweep away any and all who oppose him.

Entire nations – including the most modern, intelligent, highly-educated and sophisticated – can fall victim to genuinely-evil, cynical manipulation via such emotional/intellectual blind spots, and become absolutely convinced of the sheerest nonsense and, succumbing to such manipulated beliefs, say and do things they would otherwise consider inconceivable.

Sociopathic politicians force the public into the position of having to either believe them, or not, about something the politician claims is profoundly important to everyone. Even when the evidence is abundant that the politician cannot be trusted in anything and is, indeed, a pathological narcissist – that is, a psychopath or sociopath (the terms are synonymous) – normal decent people simply have a hard time getting their brains around the idea that someone is lying to their face about something profoundly important. It is that basic unwillingness to disbelieve that the sociopath preys upon.

Think not? Consider the case of Germany in the 1930s and 1940s.

There was a nation in the heart of Europe, as educated, cultured (the home of, among others, Beethoven, Johan Sebastian Bach, Goethe, Emanuel Kant) and, yes, as Christian (a nation filled with spectacular churches, and at least 1500 years of Christian history) as any country had ever been. And yet we know beyond any doubt the blood-thirsty Nazi barbarism they descended into – ultimately supported by the overwhelming majority of the Germans.

And it was not simply the uneducated: although many professionals doubtless joined the Nazi party solely for selfish, career reasons in order to obtain advancement, without necessarily being true believers, some of the most highly-educated and brilliant of all were indeed true believers – Martin Heidegger for example, as prominent a professional philosopher as lived in any nation during the 20th century – and a genuinely committed Nazi. Was he simply fooled?

The sociopaths Hitler and Joseph Goebbels, Hitler's propaganda minister, unabashedly revealed one of their most potent weapons (in a remarkable instance of self-confessed liars telling the truth for once) – the big lie. This was how Hitler put it in *Mein Kampf*:

> "...in the big lie there is always a certain force of credibility; because the broad masses of a nation are always more easily corrupted in the deeper strata of their emotional nature than consciously or voluntarily; and thus in the primitive simplicity of their minds they more readily fall victims to the big lie than the small lie, since they themselves often tell small lies in little matters but would be ashamed to resort to large-scale falsehoods. It would never come into their heads to fabricate colossal untruths, and they would not believe that others could have the impudence to distort the truth so infamously...."

165

Among the many ways America was absolutely unique in all human history, aside from the Constitutional absolute prohibition on the status of nobility for anyone, and its attendant prohibition on any citizen having any hereditary claim to any public office, were (1) the Constitution's combined strict restrictions on public officials' actions and transparency and disclosure requirements for all official actions (to minimize secret, self-serving dealings among politicians harmful to the public), and (2) the genuine hope that the combination of very-limited power available to federal officials, and patriotism arising from public awareness of the unique individual liberty created for our citizens legally, would result in many, if not most, federal officials taking office genuinely as a public service, with little or no hope of advancing their own careers by doing so.

The checks and balances and power-restrictions in the Constitution were designed to maximize our safety from all politicians who might actively seek public office, with impeachment and removal of true sociopaths, with no need for military action, specifically-contemplated and made available. And the hope that true, patriotic, liberty-loving public servants would indeed take public offices seemed truly realizable by the example of George Washington – an example which men of honor succeeding him — until Teddy Roosevelt— would be embarrassed to betray.

But, alas, sociopaths are always so difficult for decent people to spot, and once any of them gain entry to power, nothing but the power of violence can remove them from the scene. And once they obtain political office, they will use that office to expand their own power, and the power of the state they wield as its officers, as massively as they are permitted to do. And that is precisely what politicians in America have been doing for well over 100 years.

# BOOK PART THREE:

## AMERICA'S FOUNDING AND ITS AFTERMATH – A POLITICAL AND LEGAL HISTORY

# CHAPTER 8

## The Founders and Our Constitution

Our nation was founded as the result of a revolution – a military one involving a real shooting war and, indeed, a long war of attrition, fought by our founders on our own soil, against the greatest superpower of that day, resulting in many deaths, property damage and great hardship for all who participated in it for many years, until it ended in the American victory at Yorktown in 1783 (It began no later than 1775 with the actions in and around Boston, including the Battle of Bunker Hill).

In fighting, and eventually defeating, the British (who, not long before the American Revolution, we had considered fellow countrymen who, in the Seven Years/French and Indian War, we had fought alongside of against the French and their Indian allies), and in drafting and adopting our Constitution, our Founders were keenly aware of both what they wanted to preserve of the legal traditions which had been ours under the British, and what they wanted to forbid our new government to engage in. That was the explicit purpose of adopting the Constitution – to describe as simply and clearly as possible what activities the federal government and its officeholders were allowed to do – and forbidding them from doing certain, specified things, along with anything not explicitly allowed.

We Americans, their successors, have always known exactly what they had in mind, both in choosing to take up arms and risk everything against the British, and in the very precise provisions – all written in clear, simple English requiring no lawyer for analysis or explanation – of the Constitution. Throughout the period of our Revolution and founding, our founders described with crystal clarity what they intended by their actions – and why.

The Declaration of Independence was explicit in containing <u>a bill of particulars</u> enumerating the actions that the British government – the King and Parliament – to whom they had previously sworn loyalty, had taken which they found so intolerable that they were willing to fight the greatest superpower of the day to the death to escape such actions. Few, including courts and law professors claiming to analyze the terms of the Constitution, take the time and effort anymore to consider specifically what the founders included in the Declaration's bill of particulars – and what they did not.

Yet understanding our founding documents – the Declaration and the Constitution – requires careful attention to every word in those documents, including the details of the Declaration's bill of particulars, together with familiarity with a few historical facts which the founders plainly had in mind in preparing both those documents.

The easiest way to understand the bill of particulars in the Declaration is to understand the political actions taken in Britain which gave rise to the actions our founders had found intolerable. The Declaration declares intolerable a series of actions taken by Parliament as a result of what we would call today cronyism or crony capitalism, in which Parliament enacted laws demanding that the American colonists pay taxes and submit to various governmental mandates which members of Parliament had passed for purposes of favoring certain citizens in Britain, and their commercial activities, at the expense of other British citizens – us, the Americans – all without the consent of the Americans, with the British relying on brutal enforcement methods for such favoritism-promoting legislation.

Both that parliamentary legislative cronyism, and its brutal enforcement methods were explicitly included as grievances in the Declaration's bill of particulars – and forbidden to the new American government in multiple provisions of the Constitution, including the Bill of Rights.

In other words, the founders knew only too well that politicians would serve their own interests by corruptly passing laws and taxes favoring some constituents – inevitably at the expense of others – unless they were legally forbidden to do so. The structure and words of our Constitution were designed precisely to prevent such legislative political misconduct – and make it impossible for politicians, if they obeyed the Constitution, to hide if it occurred.

Specifically, the Constitution requires full disclosure of all actions taken by the legislative branch in particular, including who could belong to that branch, how they were to be elected, a budget, and itemization of all public money spent, which could only be spent with the express permission of that legislative branch.

And the Constitution's Article I explicitly precludes anyone ("_All_ legislative _Powers herein granted_ shall be vested in a Congress of the United States, _which shall consist of_ a Senate and House of Representatives [emphases added].") not elected to _actual membership in_, and so outside of, the legislative branch, from having any "powers" to make any laws whatsoever.

_Nowhere_ is Congress granted any power to offload or delegate that power to anyone not elected to its actual membership, pursuant to its explicitly-described election procedures, and acting pursuant to the disclosure rules of Article I. And the Constitution explicitly specifies the _full extent_ of Congress' powers, precluding it from acting outside them.

Article I section 7 prescribes very specific steps which must be taken for any proposed or contemplated law to actually become a law — even if it otherwise qualified as constitutional. Several alternatives are permitted in that section, but every one of them require the actual vote for the proposed law by both houses of Congress, at a minimum. The specificity of those procedures makes clear that any pretense that Congress can delegate its legislative power is null and void because any "law" supposedly produced by any such delegate can never meet the very specific requirements of Article I section 7. And no other provision in the constitution grants any federal branch, including Congress, any power to delegate any of its powers to anyone.

And falsely claiming a law is simply a "regulation" simply doesn't do the trick. If the "regulation" is to have the force of law it is a law and, because it was not passed pursuant to the Constitution's strict requirements it is nothing at all.

We know exactly what the founders' intent was – to absolutely forbid the federal government from intruding in any manner into private business' affairs, and specifically to prevent it from doing what the corrupt Parliament they had fought the revolution against had been doing – granting "benefits" to some citizens and/or businesses, at the inevitable expense of others.

And every single step taken, even by the lawfully-elected senators and congressmen alone, in producing legislation of any kind, including the identity of each elected official participating in such, is required by the Constitution to be publicly disclosed.

The idea of unelected bureaucrats – particularly ones employed and directed exclusively by the separate, executive branch – creating and passing laws, with their identities obfuscated, if not actively hidden, from the public – which is what every single one of the multiple federal "regulatory" agencies do – is plainly Constitutionally-forbidden by these provisions in Article I, as it even was in Britain at the time of our Revolution.

Moreover, the states alone were to exercise all police powers with respect to the citizenry and their businesses, under the Common Law which existed in every state, with contract rights explicitly Constitutionally-guaranteed by the federal government from intrusion by the states, and all laws policing citizens and their businesses to be administered in accord with due process, by the courts alone – with no Star Chamber courts permitted.

None of this is even seriously debatable, with the slightest knowledge of relevant history and the text of the Constitution and the Declaration.

The federal government was to be the guarantor and protector, against any lawless encroachment on such by any state, of the private property and contract rights of all citizens and their businesses, and to do everything in its power to foster commerce, property rights – including intellectual property – and the monetary soundness of our currency, the medium of exchange. Again, none of this is seriously debatable.

The founders had perfect understanding of the fact that between the power of the federal government and individuals, it was a zero-sum game, and the sole purpose of empowering the federal government in any respect was to protect individuals and their individual liberty — including their property and contract rights — both domestically from state takings, and against foreign invaders.

The founders were also highly-aware of the tyrannical, permission-requiring type of bureaucratic/Star Chamber law that governed all activities in continental European countries in the 18th century, such as France. Montesquieu, who they knew well, respected, and explicitly cited with approval (*Federalist* No. 47) as a genuine authority on political philosophy, wrote extensively about the tyranny of the French administrative state in which administrators dictate and act as prior restraints against private business activities by virtue of combining the legislative, executive and judicial powers in performing their administrative functions – and he was explicit in exposing that combination of powers as being as he described it, "the very definition of tyranny."

Our founders had this understanding foremost in their minds in providing for the separation of powers in the first three Articles of the Constitution.

Moreover, as mentioned above, they could not have been more explicit in mandating what we would call "absolute transparency" in every single respect regarding the creation of all laws in the new Republic in their provisions in Article I of the Constitution – including public knowledge and selection of each individual who was to be allowed to be involved in that specifically-prescribed process – and forbidding anyone else to do so.

Quite simply, we know for a fact that it was their intention to absolutely forbid anything resembling the administrative state which governed all activities in 18th century continental European countries, particularly France, and which English monarchs in the 17th century, claiming absolute power like Louis XIV, had attempted to establish in England — until they were prevented from doing so in the two revolutions which took place in England during the 17th century.

We know this by virtue of that history, including the text of the Declaration itself, numerous published writings, including portions of The Federalist, and letters by the founders, and the specific provisions contained in the Constitution itself – and in the debates and actions which those who had been involved in creating the Constitution took both in the new Republic after the Constitution was adopted in 1789, and for almost a century thereafter, with relatively minor deviations beginning only in 1887, and genuinely monumental, devastating ones beginning only in 1906 during the presidency of Teddy Roosevelt.

Today, most of us take for granted – and generations of law students have been propagandized by their own textbooks to believe – the proposition, formally adopted by the U.S. Supreme Court in the 1930s, that the federal government has the power to "regulate" virtually any activity of its citizens and their businesses, and that Congress has the power (which is nowhere in the Constitution) to create government agencies with the power to rule over any citizens subject to their discretionary jurisdiction, in a purely discretionary manner, and to create their own laws, which they are also empowered to adjudicate against the citizenry, again, in a purely discretionary, ad hoc manner – exactly like the tyrannical bureaucracies in France at the time of our Revolution (and ever since).

It is precisely that dictatorial "regulation" – including its combined, purely-discretionary, legislative, executive and judicial powers, necessary for it to function as the dictatorship it cannot avoid being – which the founders intended, and put multiple provisions, both procedural and substantive, in the Constitution, to absolutely <u>preclude</u>.

It is no accident that no such "regulation" of any business by the federal government of any kind was even attempted until 1887.

### <u>The Constitutional Questionability Of the First Bank of the United States</u>

Consider the first issue remotely related to all this which was actively debated between two of the founders – Alexander Hamilton and Thomas Jefferson – in the cabinet of a third founder, President George Washington.

That issue was whether it was Constitutional for the federal government even simply to hold 20% of the stock of a non-regulatory banking institution – a bank like any other – simply for purposes of managing financial matters for the Department of Treasury, which had the duty of arranging for the finances of the government, including paying its obligations and those which each of the states had incurred during the Revolution which the federal government had accepted as its own obligations in the Constitution itself.

Treasury Secretary Hamilton, one of the principal advocates for the Constitution during the period when the states were considering whether to adopt it (he was one of the three authors of *the Federalist*), very much wanted the federal government to hold that minority interest in the Bank of the United States, solely for purposes of managing its own finances – and in no way to intrude on the banking business or any other business of private institutions except possibly by its presence.

Secretary of State Jefferson, principal author of the Declaration of Independence and the Bill of Rights and close friend and political ally of James Madison, himself the principal author of the Constitution, was absolutely convinced that the Constitution unambiguously forbade any connection by the federal government to such an institution at all. They each wrote detailed memoranda to Pres. Washington presenting their arguments for their positions – memoranda which remain public and well-known to anyone interested in reading them. Those memoranda are discussed below.

It is a pity more people – especially more law students – do not read both of those memoranda by those two brilliant Founders today. They leave no doubt that it was at least doubtful whether the federal government could have the power to even issue a charter for that bank, and own 20% of the stock, notwithstanding its potential utility, and that even if it could do so, it was a very close question.

The undeniable closeness of the question meant that even that very-limited, federal use of that bank, if Constitutional at all, represented the absolute outer reaches of federal power to intrude on the private economy.

The idea that that bank, let alone any other federal executive agency, would have the power to "regulate"/dictate to any other bank or any other private activity or business would have been considered utterly shocking to all such Founders.

All of them well-understood that the federal government could only do those particular things it was authorized to do specifically in Article I Section 8, and the last thing any of those powers included was the power to intrude into any private business affairs of any person or institution in the nation.

### The Constitution As Our Fundamental Law – What That Has Always Meant

Our Constitution, by its express terms constitutes the nation's fundamental, all-controlling law which must be followed meticulously in all other laws of the nation and by all public officials, officials who, throughout this nation's history, including the present, are required to swear an oath to follow and uphold it throughout their term in office.

Any doubt about this fact is unambiguously resolved in its Article VI which expressly declares it "the supreme Law of the Land…" thereby automatically rendering a legal nullity any action by any federal official – including any purported "law", or "regulation" whose content or enactment violates the Constitution in any manner. Its terms are simple and direct and mean precisely what they denote, with no alteration in that fact permissible except pursuant to its own terms providing for its amendment, unambiguously contained in its Article V.

There is no gray area here: the Constitution must be obeyed and conformed to as written by all the nation's public officials and by all laws – if it is indeed the fundamental law it is specifically proclaimed to be in its own text. Again, by virtue of that absolute supremacy, any supposed law or official action which violates the Constitution is necessarily a legal nullity and unenforceable, as is any unconstitutional action or directive from any public official who, by engaging in such action, necessarily violates his own oath of office.

These principles, made explicit in the Constitution's text, have been repeated by all American public officials, including in countless written opinions by the Su-

174

preme Court of the United States, since its formal ratification, also announced in its text, in 1789. Even those, such as Woodrow Wilson, who have presumed publicly in their own writings to criticize it and even call for its repudiation and repeal, have acknowledged its validity as the duly-enacted Constitution of the United States.

As a purported argument to overcome this clear, Constitutional barrier to achieving any of the federal confiscation of all directional authority over all American businesses which Wilson unambiguously demanded, he promoted the facially-nonsensical and unconstitutional claim that, contrary to its express terms, the Constitution was an infinitely-malleable, "living" document – his terminology – with no actual meaning that could not be altered by any branch of the federal government as it deemed appropriate purportedly to "update" it – no actual amendment necessary. This usurpation of the authority of the Constitution has been adopted by the United States Supreme Court beginning in the mid-1930s.

In fact, Article V of the Constitution provides the only procedures permitting any amendment to the Constitution. Such procedures are defined in that Article with precision, in plain English that, by design, is readily-understandable by anyone who can read – no lawyer required except, through fraudulent casuistry, to undo it.

Significantly, in light of our nation's history over the last 100+ years, those Article V procedures include neither (1) the ratification, with or without active collusion, by all three branches of government created in the first three Articles of the Constitution, of any laws or actions not expressly permitted in the Constitution, even if that unconstitutional ratification is repeated frequently over long periods of time; (2) nor does any violation of the Constitution create a "legal precedent" which can appropriately be followed thereafter based on its supposedly having been validated by the mere fact of its being a precedent.

Otherwise, the Constitution would have no force at all as the nation's fundamental law since the mere violation of its express terms WOULD ITSELF VALIDATE the violation itself – a facially preposterous notion.

That notion is preposterous – and it is monstrous that such now requires any explanation – because, were it true, it would not merely render the Constitution a legal nullity, instead of the supreme law of the land, but rather would actually encourage such violations, since their mere occurrence would automatically become their own reward, rather than an inherently reversible and punishable act of grotesque misconduct against the fundamental law of the nation – which is plainly what they are.

Our Constitution was written by a group of our Founders who were formally authorized to do so by each of the 13 states which comprised the United States in the late 1780s after our Revolution achieved military victory over our British colonial masters. We know the identities of the Constitution's authors, the legal/political philosophies they deeply believed in (and for which they had only recently engaged in many years of unimaginably-difficult armed conflict against Britain, the greatest superpower of its day) and the authors, including some Constitution writers themselves – James Madison, Alexander Hamilton, and others – of such philosophies.

We even know from many sources the extremely precise and sophisticated understanding which the authors of our Constitution had of (1) history, particularly British history, (2) the place they were self-consciously making for themselves and for the nation in developing a particular, explicitly-revolutionary theme of that history, both in our Revolution against the British and in the text and adoption of our Constitution and, most importantly, (3) the fundamental principles they intended to express in the Constitution and the nature of the federal government it was intended to create – and, of no less importance, the nature of the type of laws (Bad Law) and government it was specifically designed to <u>prevent,</u> which they were well aware of.

In addition, in connection with all the information described in the immediately preceding paragraph which clearly provides a contemporaneous gloss on the Constitution offering deep insights into how it should be applied in particular practical circumstances, prior to its official adoption by the nation, Hamilton, Madison and John Jay wrote a series of essays known today as *the Federalist* which contained a detailed explication of various provisions in the Constitution providing arguments that were widely published contemporaneously advocating the adoption of the Constitution.

All this information summarized in the immediately preceding two paragraphs has been widely available and known since 1789, together with the text of the Constitution itself which, though incorporating some terminology which had particular legal meanings at the time, was, as indicated above, written in the clearest, plainest and most articulate English so as to be readily understandable without the need for any legal priesthood to preside over its interpretation.

That being the case, one would think that any time a legal case arose raising Constitutional questions, or some federal or state action was proposed which was in any way questionable Constitutionality, immediate resort would be had to the plain text of the Constitution itself and, if further explication were necessary, to that vast body of literary gloss on it to resolve any such constitutional issue.

Amazingly, at least so it has always been to me, if one looks over what is called constitutional law – which is actually nothing but the judicial decisions on constitutional cases – there is barely a mention in any of it of any of those genuine authorities.

Indeed, one of the most astonishing things about law school, to me, was learning that what is called "Constitutional Law" is really just a bunch of gratuitous opinions by Supreme Court justices pretending to "interpret" the Constitution and, instead, over time, twisting it into saying things it manifestly does not say, and even purporting to strike out and eliminate actual language in the Constitution's text – to the point that today, and since the mid 1930's, it is routinely assumed that the Constitution provides for a general federal police power over all businesses, indeed, over anything that can be called "commerce," whereas it is an undeniable fact that the authors of the Constitution fought a revolution precisely to prevent the central government from engaging in any such activity, which is inherently, and invariably, corrupt and tyrannical, as our founders were well aware.

They enumerated the corrupt practices by Parliament they were revolting against in the Declaration of Independence, and they were, in particular, well aware of the English Civil War their revolution was building on, in which the English Parliament revolutionaries fought against <u>precisely</u> that kind of centralized police power from the central government and government agencies – including courts of Star Chamber – which had tyrannically claimed the power to make up laws – legislate – and impose them on whoever the king wanted, with the judicial power completely under the thumb of the executive, combining all three government powers in one government body – the very definition of tyranny, as our founders plainly announced in *Federalist* No. 47.

And that is what we have today, imposed on us by corrupt politicians, and rubber-stamped by the Supreme Court with full knowledge of its unconstitutionality, poisoning every aspect of the economy and our lives – and the entire legal profession itself, which has knowingly acquiesced in this politically-motivated, utter subversion of the Constitution by the courts.

For over 100 years after its adoption, it is fair to say that, until1887, for the most part, the Constitution as written and as understood by all who participated in its adoption – and, indeed, by virtually all public officials throughout the 19th century – was faithfully followed.

However, during the first three decades of the 20th century, particularly beginning in 1906, each of the three branches of the federal government took formal, radical steps which together effectively constituted a counterrevolution against the Constitution and the Revolution it had grown out of – steps which all who participated in them well knew at the time had the effect of literally turning the long-known meaning of the Constitution on its head.

The Supreme Court withheld its participation in this iteration of the Constitution until the mid-1930s – and then joined in in the Counterrevolution, gratuitously reversing its own, long-standing cases, and trampling on the Constitution's long-known meaning as authority for further such trampling.

Even its most ardent apologists on the Supreme Court itself for such monstrous behavior have never been able to articulate any coherent legally and historically supportable argument for these actions. To the extent they even pretend that any 19th-century Supreme Court cases support the Counterrevolution, they claim to rely on *Gibbons v. Ogden*. As I show below in Chapter 11, that case plainly stands for <u>precisely the opposite</u> proposition, to wit, that the Commerce clause, on which <u>alone</u> the Supreme Court has relied in its participation in the Counter-revolution, permits <u>no</u> police power over businesses whatsoever.

That Counterrevolution by all three branches of the federal government has, as discussed below, had a profoundly corrupting influence on all aspects of American society, including the courts themselves and the entire legal pro-fession, including the law schools in which it trains its members.

And it has burdened the decent, moral, patient American people with moun-tains of unconstitutional law, all of the endless federal bureaucratic "regulatory" agencies which do nothing but violate the liberty and prosperity of the nation and its citizens, resulting in every single financial disaster that has occurred since 1900, and the weakening of America militarily as a result, which greatly endanger the nation and exposed us to the dangers of two world wars, each of which could have been prevented had America maintained the financial and military strength it would otherwise have had in the absence of those self-defeating, destructive agencies preying on the American people.

An overview description of the political and constitutional history of the nation follows.

# Chapter 9

## Louis XIV and the Welfare/Administrative State

Strange as it may seem, the two (and possibly more) most important and seminal events directly affecting all the most important and radical developments of the United States federal government, particularly since 1906 – and they have been many and extraordinary in their magnitude – occurred in Paris, France during the late 1640s. Those two events involved a young boy who at the time was nominally Louis XIV, King of France, a title he inherited following the death of his officially-declared father, Louis XIII. His kingship at the time was nominal only because until he turned 20, France was actually ruled by the Regent, his mother, Queen Anne and her long-time lover (possibly Louis' real father) Cardinal Mazarin, with Mazarin actually running things.

However, during the late 1640s – and continuing until 1653 – saying that any of those three – Anne, Mazarin or Louis – were actually running anything in France would be a bit of an overstatement of their actual condition: a civil war of sorts was, in fact, going on in France during that time, with a significant portion of the very powerful French nobles in active revolt against the King, with those nobles deliberately agitating mobs in Paris and elsewhere in the country to commit violence – including, on those two (at least) occasions referred to above, when such Parisian mobs threatened the very life of nominal King Louis XIV, his brother, and his mother to the point that they were forced to flee from the nation's capital itself, Paris, and were lucky to be able do so and escape alive.

The condition of Louis, his younger brother and their mother was so desperate due to the revolting nobles and Parisian mobs that, on one occasion, the Queen literally had to pawn royal jewelry to be able to feed her family.

What could these events in a country so unlike ours, so far away and so long ago, involving people so unlike any of us, have to do with us and our government? Practically everything.

These terrifying events Louis XIV experienced as a child convinced him that the country he was supposedly king of was at war with him, a war he was determined to win at all costs – a project he devoted the rest of his life and his very long reign (the longest of any king in French history) to achieving. It was his method in achieving that victory over his own nation which became the institutional predecessor of what our own federal government has become since 1900 – and which leaves no doubt of the true nature of the changes effected in our federal government during that time – and the enormity of the betrayal of the promises of our Constitution, which our founders fought a bloody revolution to achieve for us, to protect individual liberty, and to shield us from state tyranny, which that transformation of the federal government has effected.

Let me explain. During the 17th and 18th century, most of the kings of the various countries in Europe claimed their right to be absolute, all-powerful monarchs over their kingdoms, to whom everyone and everything in their realm was utterly subservient. Louis XIV was preeminent among all European monarchs in asserting and institutionalizing such claim for himself. His childhood experiences of powerlessness steeled his determination to completely subjugate his nation, subjecting every activity and every person in his kingdom to his oversight and complete domination through his agents.

To achieve this complete subjugation of his people – including the nobles who had revolted against his father and himself – he did two, interrelated things, and thereby created the first administrative/welfare state the Western world has ever seen – the original model for what the federal government has become in the U.S. today.

The welfare portion of what he created consisted of building the most extraordinary, lavish, gilded cage the world has ever seen for all the nobility in France – known today as the Palace of Versailles. He compelled them to move in there into lavish apartments he provided for them, and he paid them annuities and wined and dined them there, providing extravagant entertainment and parties for them constantly – so long as they remained his coddled prisoners there, utterly subservient to him, literally fighting among themselves over who could carry his candle, for example.

He provided for all their needs and wants – as long as they remained his captives and servants, and refrained from plotting against him in any manner. He mercilessly punished any nobles who failed to go along with that program. They were his prisoners in their gilded cage – exactly as he intended. And that was precisely the purpose of the welfare he "coddled" them with – just as such has always been the purpose of welfare here – to turn its recipients into virtual serfs, who cannot make a move without the approval of their master/provider. He left it to his administrators to impose that virtual serfdom on the rest of the population, who previously had been subjects of the nobility, nobility who, under Louis, were forcibly housed at Versailles away from their own estates.

The administrative portion of his subjugation of France consisted of his recruiting and sending all over the nation his direct, personal representatives, entitled Intendants, who worked to act on his behalf in supervising and regulating literally all activities of everyone in France, supplanting all the local administrators who had previously, historically, been in charge throughout the kingdom. He created elaborate new laws detailing how everything was to be done, and how nothing could be done without his approval anywhere, in France, with each local Intendants acting on his behalf to control all the people not housed at Versailles, everywhere.

So extensive was his micromanagement in this respect that, for example, if the roof of a building was destroyed and needed to be replaced, the approval of his Intendant would have to be obtained to do so. That was true for the roof of anyone – from the poorest peasant in the nation to the richest noble.

Thus, Louis used his version of the welfare state – the golden cage of Versailles – to cement existential power over the French nobility. But he was equally determined to secure that absolute control over any potential threat to rival his power from the phenomenon which had been emerging in late medieval Europe, principally in northern Italy (Venice, Florence, and other city states there) and in the lands of present-day Belgium and the Netherlands – and in England. That particular phenomenon I am referring to consisted of the rapidly-growing wealth of non-feudal merchants (artisans, shippers and traders, and bankers, e.g.).

Louis was painfully aware that that growing wealth had financed the development of navies and other political and military power (including the capture of the papacy itself!), and even foreign empires and colonies, from those relatively-minuscule political entities, wealth and power rivaling that of major kingdoms – including France itself. In 1667-1668 Louis fought a bloody and costly (virtually bankrupting Louis) war – the Dutch War of Devolution – in which the tiny Dutch Republic, which had split off from being ruled by the Kingdom of Spain in 1581, successfully defended itself from conquest by Louis' own army. The very fact that the Dutch Republic even existed proved the power of that merchant-created wealth to successfully revolt against its former Spanish overlord.

By the 17th century, the tiny Dutch Republic was already establishing its own foreign empire through its seafaring prowess – further enhancing its wealth-creating capabilities through the trade, which was its principal purpose for establishing that Empire – as was also true of the English with the empire they were creating.

Today, the so-called Renaissance is famous particularly for the art, including spectacular architecture, literature and high culture associated with it. It is no accident that most of those phenomena were centered in those same Dutch and Italian merchant-empowered city states and republics. Always jealous of others' rivalry to French "glory" in culture, political power, etc., Louis deeply resented the success of those "upstarts" and was determined to prevent any similar rise of power by the merchants of France.

It was precisely to constrain the wealth-generation and power of his own merchant class – commoners who were developing wealth and power equal or greater than that of the old feudal aristocracy – that Louis instituted the first and most-controlling Bad Laws, and the bureaucracy to enforce it throughout his kingdom. They did what such laws and bureaucracy always do – they forced absolute control by the crown over all businesses in France, severely limiting the growth of the French economy compared to that of England and Holland,

Although Louis XIV claimed always to have the best interests of all of his kingdom at heart, his rule was an absolute tyranny over his subjects – and that was what they were, not citizens of anything resembling a free nation – with incredible brutality visited on anyone who failed to knuckle under to his will.

For example, at one point he decided to transform France from the most religiously pluralistic nation in Europe, where Protestants for over 100 years had flourished and were allowed to worship in peace in a kingdom ruled by a Catholic monarch, into a virtual Catholic theocracy. At that point, he decided that it was no longer legal for Protestants to live in France at all, and that everyone had be a Catholic; and he brutally punished any Protestants who disobeyed and, when tens of thousands of them fled the country, he even made it illegal for them to do that any longer. And anyone who attempted to do so and was caught was immediately sentenced to serve as a galley slave for life (a sentence of brutal torture, and very early death, as a practical matter).

The legal code administered by Louis's Intendants throughout France was so detailed and complex that its administration created a whole new nobility, or ruling class, of lawyers and other intermediaries necessary for its administration. that code created a situation in which the only way anyone could act in any manner with any safety from brutal punishments under the legal system which Louis XIV instituted in France throughout his reign was to first seek and obtain permission from the local Intendant – almost always requiring one of the powerful lawyers/lobbyists to succeed.

This all-encompassing, bureaucratic, permission-requiring legal regime is exactly what has been created in the United States in the 20th century. And it could not be more offensive to everything our founders risked their lives to fight for, against a much less brutal tyranny than Louis XIV – King George III and his Parliament – and violative of the Constitution they created for us.

But even Louis XIV, notwithstanding his absolute, tyrannical rule over his people, was limited in one significant way which our federal government has not been so limited since 1913 (it had been so limited before then): Louis was very restricted in the taxes he could impose and, specifically, was unable to impose any taxes at all on the wealthiest people in his kingdom – the nobles – and the only income tax he ever even attempted was at the rate of 10% and it only applied to peasants.

Because of the extravagance of the welfare he bestowed on his nobles and the expense of the numerous wars he engaged in, Louis XIV was constantly in financial difficulty, as were his successors Louis XV and Louis XVI, both of whom continued his palatial domestication of the nobility at Versailles and his micro-managing, bureaucratic, all-pervasive central ruling through the local intendants. And like all economies forced to operate under administrative bureaucracies, the French economy never grew, and so made extracting revenue from his people for Louis that much more difficult.

It simply never occurred to him to permit the economic freedom occurring across the English Channel which was turning England into a wealthy nation, far wealthier per-capita than France, a fact which has continued ever after.

Louis XIV imposed this brutal, bureaucratic permission-requiring rule on his people (it applied to the nobility as well as the peasantry, although the nobles were smothered in luxury – whether they like it or not!) for the purpose of utterly subjugating them to his will, literally like a conquered people. But, like all promoters of Bad Law, he also, hubristically, almost certainly imagined that his micromanagement of their lives and businesses would actually promote their prosperity – and his. It did the opposite, as it always does.

And this same, claimed utilitarian/materialistic and protective purpose is what American politicians have invariably claimed they would achieve and were promoting as they instituted each of the pieces of the all-encompassing bureaucracy the federal government has become over the 20th century.

But the only thing that has ever been achieved by the imposition of this kind of permission-requiring bureaucracy by the central government has been empowering the state, always at the expense of the liberty of the people, and restricting the people's liberty, prosperity and the growth of the economy.

Louis XIV was, by all accounts, a genuinely brilliant man who surrounded himself with highly intelligent advisors and ministers, all of whom were intent on using all the powers over their subjects at their disposal with their ability to micromanage all business and agricultural activities in the nation to promote the overall French economy and the wealth of the nation, a not insignificant side-effect of which would be to increase their own wealth and tax receipts necessary to fund the fabulously-expensive welfare state (whose "beneficiaries" were the nobility alone) he created and his foreign wars. In other words, Louis wanted to have it both ways: to completely defeat and subjugate his nation and also to enhance its wealth – and his own.

Unfortunately for Louis XIV and his successors, the only results of his regulatory control of the nation was a static, primitive agricultural economy for the most part, the channeling of talented, educated Frenchman into various roles connected to the administration of the elaborate regulatory state he created, instead of their engaging in genuinely-constructive activities (profitable trade, growing businesses etc.), with the overwhelming portion of the population remaining peasant farmers employing primitive agricultural techniques leaving them existentially vulnerable to adverse weather conditions – including extreme cold weather that occurred throughout the 18th century in what has been called a mini Ice Age.

Thus, his elaborate micromanagement of the economy did not increase the general prosperity of the French economy and, given the technological limitations of the time, most people remained destitute, and the monarchy went from financial crisis to financial crisis under Louis XIV, Louis XV and Louis XVI, with the latter two continuing all of the Bad Law policies Louis XIV had begun.

Eventually, in the last decade of the 18th century, the unhappiness of the French nation, suffocating under poverty, debt, and the complete absence of liberty for everyone, culminated in a revolution against the king, the church, the nobility – everything. The famous slogan of the French Revolution was "liberty, equality and fraternity" – none of which the revolutionaries had felt existed under the monarchy with its micromanagement of everything and prosperity for very very few.

And, for a brief period after the French Revolution began, in the early 1790s, the entire French Bad Law welfare/regulatory state vanished.

But, as discussed in detail in other chapters, it was soon reinstated in every respect, including it's brutality (the guillotine was invented and used liberally to silence all opposition) and, after years of chaos and what can only be called totalitarian democracy, when Napoleon came to power as Emperor, the entire regulatory regime was reconstituted in a manner almost identical to that which Louis XIV had created, with the laws he had enacted reinstituted under Napoleon with very few changes in 1804, and called the Napoleonic Code, which Napoleon set about imposing throughout continental Europe as he conquered it, and which has remained the underlying legal system in France and, indeed, in most of continental Europe, ever since.

The contrast between the liberty available in America throughout the 19th century with the complete lack of it under the repressive, permission-requiring regimes in every single European country other than Britain throughout that century, was what created the huge incentive for Europeans who were able to do so to leave everything behind and emigrate to America, not simply because they hoped to find more prosperity here, which they did, but for the liberty which we had – uniquely in the world.

# CHAPTER 10

## The American Welfare/Administrative State — an Introduction

Quite simply, America is no longer the land of the free in real life. Not even close.

Although the tyrannical edifice that prevails here now was erected, piece by piece, by public officials elected by our countrymen, never once has that edifice itself been voted on by the people. This is no accident, no mere oversight: if the officials who genuinely desire this edifice for all of us thought they could win such a vote from the people themselves, they would not hesitate to propose it – something no politician has ever done.

For each piece of this edifice oppresses all of us, even when, as is invariably the case, its control over our choices and lives is deliberately obfuscated and masked through the laws' sheer complexity and endlessness, and the multiple frauds and misdirections of its proponents, so that it may appear to many not to affect us directly.

The closest thing to such a vote that has ever occurred in America was the presidential election of 1912 in which Woodrow Wilson and Theodore Roosevelt together won almost 2/3 of the total votes, with both of them being ardent advocates for the administrative state, and Wilson emerging victorious in the race. The only other instances in American history in which any politician explicitly and forthrightly proposed any of the major elements of the administrative/welfare state have been those rare occasions when self-identified socialist and/or communist candidates have run for office. The best showing for any such candidate who ran for president was that of Eugene Debs, a relatively charismatic socialist, who ran for president in five elections in the early 20th century – and never received more than the 915,000 votes he received in 1920.

Indeed, ask any politician in American history who has ever publicly announced himself as a proponent of the welfare/administrative state whether he is a socialist or Marxist (assuming *arguendo* there is any difference between the two) and, in virtually every case, beginning with the early 20th century, he is likely not only to vehemently deny such (and to shout insults at you), but also to insist he is simply a practical intellectual, interested only in "what works," subscribing to no known ideology which is why, if his life depends on it, he is willing to call himself a Progressive – and sometimes a liberal. However, as the saying goes, if the shoe fits, wear it.

Karl Marx did not originate the idea of socialism or communism – or, indeed, pretty much anything else (despite the enormous amount he wrote, I defy anyone to identify a single original idea in any of it – or, indeed, to read large amounts of his scribblings applying anything resembling common sense while reading them without coming away with the certaintude that he was a raving idiot who no intelligent, moderately-educated, rational person could take seriously. If only.) Notwithstanding the fact that his name is always linked to those terms, and so remains extremely useful as a confusion-dispersing analytical device and appellation for that ideology/religion, the idea of socialism, and each of its multiple elements, long predated him.

Let us calmly and intelligently analyze, in this context (in addition to my exposition of Marx's writings themselves, in Chapter 6) what socialism is, accepting the fact that communism is simply the most radical, no-holds-barred version of it. It is worth noting and emphasizing that this analytical process is invariably something socialists pretending to be something other than that (as American socialists almost invariably have always done) resist, oppose, and spare no energy to prevent from occurring. They inevitably attempt to silence those who publicly engage in this process.

It is no accident that they do so: forceful silencing of all opposition to socialism has always been one of its most salient features since its birth as an organized political movement, like its parent, revolutionary France in 1793, when the Committee of Public Safety, as it named itself, assumed absolute power – and made the guillotine famous.

Socialism's continuing need, for its very survival, even when supported by a well-armed police state (as in communist USSR), by propagating and insisting on intellectual and linguistic confusion was beautifully named and described by George Orwell (himself a socialist – go figure) in *1984* with his novelized depiction of "doublespeak," "Newspeak" and "doublethink" and "thought crime" – the existential need in a radical socialist society for the state to demand that everyone lie to others and to oneself about virtually everything – to genuinely believe two things simultaneously, one being a nonsense description of claimed reality, while knowing the truth, which is its opposite – and to criminalize and silence anyone who fails to do so.

Quite simply, as shown in Chapter 6, socialism cannot be tolerated by observant, awake, real people in the real world who experience it directly, and who wish to retain any semblance of sanity for themselves, without this deliberate linguistic violence (doublespeak) and self-deception (doublethink). They become thought criminals when the socialist state recognizes their inability to do so. Real-life socialism requires this deliberate confusion and fraud, quite simply, because everything about it is utterly contrary to human nature, logic and common sense.

So what was socialism's agenda for enactment in a free, Christian America? First of all, except in a violent revolution, such as Russia's or Cuba's, radically imposing it on society, its full force is never imposed all at once. In that sense, its initial stages can be considered a "movement" or trend which can occur in any society, or any aspect of that society, gradually or all at once – depending on who has the power in that society.

Socialism can be said to occur in a society or nation whenever any particular right, duty or obligation which otherwise would reside in an individual is taken over by the state. Examples of this are the expropriation of complete, or at least equitable, or practical, ownership of privately-owned businesses or other property, resulting in their actual, or effective, ownership by the state, and/or the assumption by the state of the duty to provide any good for individuals which they would otherwise have to provide for themselves, such as healthcare, housing, food, money, etc.

In America, the piece by piece imposition of socialism, involving the political appropriation here of control over one business sector, and numerous other aspects of American life, at a time, has only been accomplished by its proponents pretending that their actions were permitted under our Constitution, with them relying exclusively on the Commerce clause as the sole textual basis for all their actions in that regard.

The following chapters are an accurate (you can check it yourself if you have any doubts, and read all the referenced documents, all of which are readily available on the Internet with minimal effort to find them) description of the relevant history of the Commerce clause, Illuminating its undeniable historical context, including discussions of French and English history and institutions our founders bore directly in mind in drafting the entire Constitution, including the Commerce clause, and the legal history of that clause itself, discussing and quoting from every single 18th and 19th-century document addressing its content and meaning.

Thereafter, BOOK PART FOUR contains my description of various aspects of American history bearing on and outlining major features of the progress of the collectivist/socialist Counterrevolution.

# CHAPTER 11

## The Real Meaning of the Commerce Clause –
## From the Founders Themselves

It is apparent to anyone applying common sense that the plain meaning of the words employed in the Constitution's Commerce clause, on their face, together with the entire, undeniable, historically-individual-property rights-promoting rationale for the American Revolution, render utterly preposterous the current, post-1935, "reading" by the Supreme Court of that clause, acceptance of that non-sense "reading" being required to pretend there is any Constitutional legitimacy to <u>any</u> of the federal policing of citizens and businesses since 1887.

And yet, as accurately described above, that hyper-political, fraudulent "reading" of the Commerce clause, and the Commerce clause <u>alone</u> (and no, that is not hyperbole) constitutes the <u>sole</u>, supposed Constitutional authority authorizing <u>every single one</u> of the hundreds of federal "regulatory" administrative agencies, including entire cabinet departments and bureaus — <u>other than</u> the IRS, thanks to the 16th Amendment.

And again, to be clear, that "reading" <u>alone</u> constitutes the <u>entire</u> supposed-ly-Constitutional authority for the federal government to seize, through all those administrative "regulatory" bodies, powers over American citizens and their businesses identical to those which were the real enforcement tools of unabashedly totalitarian states – such as the France of Louis XIV, Louis XVI and Napoleon, the pre-revolutionary Russian Czars and the German Kaisers. Total political control over all the nation's sources of goods and services ("the means of production," as Marx called it), taken piece by piece, has always been all those administrative agencies' express purpose – just as demanded by Karl Marx in *The Communist Manifesto*, as quoted in Chapter 6 above.

In short, the Supreme Court's post-1935 "reading" of the Commerce clause amounts to the claim – preposterous on its face to anyone with the slightest understanding of the American Revolution – that that Clause amounts to a wholesale grant of authority to the federal government to establish itself as a fascist, totalitarian dictatorship with power to dictate every detail of all citizens' lives – since <u>all</u> human interactions of any kind are "commerce." Even purporting to "limit" that, its own "reading," of the Commerce clause to transactions in which any party thereto is seeking a profit, the Supreme Court would effectively adopt the purely-Marxist notions that profit is per se evil, and that the Marxist state must have the power to eradicate it, or at least absolutely control it.

The idea that the Constitution empowers a Marxist or fascist state – which the Supreme Court has implicitly ruled is the case under the Commerce clause – is as absurd as it is monstrous. And, as shown below, it is a reading plainly repudiated by the many, undeniably-authoritative founders who described the actual meaning of that clause, including presidents and John Marshall, the most famous and highly-regarded Chief Justice of the Supreme Court in history. And there is not a single statement by any Founder, nor any public figure prior to 1870, which fails to utterly repudiate the reading of the Commerce clause imposed on us by the Supreme Court since the mid-1930s.

Their unconstitutionality and immorality aside, even the purported practical "benefits" to the public promised by politicians when each such agency is created never materialize – with minor exceptions sometimes that are always insignificant compared to the destruction of freedom and prosperity directly caused by each of those agencies. And on the rare occasions when any such agency actually accomplishes its supposed "purpose," rather than disbanding, it recognizes no limits on its power and inevitably seeks to expand its power and to find new "problems" to "fix" – all at the expense of the liberty and prosperity of real people whose lives it oppresses.

And the politicians' inevitable answer to each of their failures is either to increase the agency's power, add additional agencies on top of the already-failed ones, or both, all "authorized" by clearly-unconstitutional Bad Law.

In fact, as this book proves, the Supreme Court's post-1935 "reading"/rewriting of the Commerce clause, on which so much legal weight rests, is utterly frivolous, gratuitous – and truly monstrous – and literally the opposite of the Commerce clause's true meaning.

The patent falsity of that reading is proven by the fundamental purpose of the American Revolution, the Commerce clause's own text, writings by the founders on this precise subject I will show you here (with no contrary writings whatsoever from any other founders), all pre-1870 19th-century Supreme Court decisions bearing on the Commerce clause, and the limits on federal power which even personally-ambitious American politicians recognized – and obeyed – up through 1887.

It happens that we have extensive knowledge of publicly-available writings, going back to the administration of George Washington itself, authored by numerous, prominent founders. Those writings address with great specificity what they viewed as the outer boundaries of federal Constitutional authority for the federal government to involve itself in the private economy.

As mentioned above, those writings include memoranda by Alexander Hamilton and Thomas Jefferson in the Washington administration, definitive Supreme Court rulings on the subject by Supreme Court Chief Justice John Marshall, an official, written message as president by James Madison vetoing legislation passed by both houses of Congress during his administration, in which he explicitly defines the outer parameters of the Commerce clause and all other potentially-relevant constitutional provisions, and a lengthy legal memorandum on this precise subject by Pres. James Monroe.

All of these written authorities, by eminent founders one and all, on this precise issue are discussed in this chapter below, in the chronological order in which they arose. These issues were first addressed by founders in the executive branch, and only later by their judiciary branch counterpart John Marshall.

None of these actual, written authorities on the subject are challenged, let alone refuted, in any way, in any of the numerous Supreme Court opinions proclaiming Constitutional even the most-radical, liberty/property-destroying legislation Congress has enacted since 1906. The Supreme Court, and its cheerleaders in the legal profession, simply ignore, and pretend away, all these authorities and spout nonsense in support of their rulings on this subject (even more than on other subjects).

Indeed, they presume to pretend away the Constitution itself, including its Article V which provides the exclusive means for amending the Constitution, an Article effectively stricken from the Constitution by the Supreme Court when it unilaterally appropriates and usurps the right to amend the Constitution, and even pretends to have the power unilaterally to undo the plain meaning of the Commerce clause, and turn it into a plenary grant of unlimited power for the federal government to dictate everything about the operations of every business – or anything that could be characterized as having any relation to "commerce."

Pres. Madison's pronouncement on the outer limits of the Commerce clause is quoted below *in toto*.

It is a historical fact that even among the founders, no one had more thorough understanding of The Constitution than James Madison, recognized as its principal author, together with Alexander Hamilton and Jefferson (Jefferson was not involved in drafting the Constitution, other than the Bill of Rights, since he was in France as our ambassador, but he and Madison exchanged extensive correspondence throughout their lives, including then, and Jefferson of course was the principal author of the Declaration of Independence).

### The Washington Administration – Controversy regarding the First Bank of the United States

George Washington was, of course, our first president, and in his cabinet were Alexander Hamilton, Treasury Secretary, and Thomas Jefferson, his Secretary of State. At that time, the United States Treasury had only the extremely restricted taxing powers under the Constitution as originally drafted (prior to the 16th amendment permitting an income tax). It also had significant financial obligations, including the obligation assumed by the federal government in the Constitution itself to pay the debts of all the colonies which they had incurred during the Revolution.

Treasury Secretary Alexander Hamilton, who himself was also both a lawyer and a banker, determined that it would be extremely advantageous as a means of managing the financial affairs of the government if the federal government created its own bank, or rather, acquired a 20% minority shareholder interest in such a bank, to give it some official stature. Plainly, since that was his purpose, he viewed any greater federal intrusion in the economy – say, a 50%-federally-owned bank – completely beyond the pale and out of the question.

Now bear in mind, the last thing anyone intended or thought of with respect to this institution, to be named the Bank of the United States, was that it would impose its will on, let alone supervise and/or "regulate" any <u>other</u> financial institutions in the nation. It was not even supposed to have any competitive advantage over any purely-private banks. And the federal government was to be a mere 20% shareholder in it. This was to be nothing remotely like the Federal Reserve Bank in any respect.

The sole function of the Bank was to facilitate the financial operations of the Treasury. It would have the ability to issue banknotes – like any other bank in the country prior to 1913. In that regard, note: the issuance of banknotes, all backed by specie, by private banks was how <u>all</u> paper money was generated <u>prior to 1913</u> in the United States. And the country then prospered, enjoying more rapid GDP and income growth than it ever has since 1913 – with no inflation whatsoever. Imagine that! That fact alone proves what an utter, practical disaster – apart from its manifest unconstitutionality and immoral taking/nationalization of the nation's currency – the Federal Reserve has been, with not a single redeeming virtue.

Secretary of State Thomas Jefferson, and Atty. Gen. Edmund Randolph (in a cabinet with only four members) both wrote detailed legal memoranda, still available for all to see today, to Pres. Washington providing compelling arguments to the effect that the Constitution absolutely forbade the federal government from creating, or owning any stock in, <u>any</u> corporation, including such a bank. Their position was that none of the enumerated powers in the Constitution's Article I section 8 specified authority to create any corporation for any purpose; and that it was imperative that the Constitution be interpreted strictly so that the clear boundaries of government never be breached.

Needless to say, Jefferson and Randolph did not view the Commerce clause as granting the federal government any power whatsoever to involve itself in the private economy in any manner – including the mere creation of the Bank of the United States, in which the government was to be a minority shareholder.

Jefferson and Randolph argued that the 10th Amendment requires the strictest confinement of federal powers because it provides expressly "that all powers not delegated to the United States by the Constitution, nor prohibited to it by the states, are reserved for the states, or to the people." Thus, under that Amendment, any claim by the federal government to power not specifically granted to it in the Constitution would necessarily be an unauthorized usurpation of the power of the states and/or of individuals.

In opposing them, Hamilton did not claim that anything in the Constitution, including the Commerce clause, specifically authorized the creation of any corporation for any purpose. The idea that the Commerce clause would permit any actual federal intrusion on the private economy, including into the activities of private banks – as the modern Supreme Court routinely and cavalierly pretends – plainly was utterly unthinkable to him. And the Constitution has never been amended since then, nor at any time, to permit any federal power of that nature.

Instead, while Hamilton did not pretend that any explicit Constitutional power permitted the creation of the bank, he argued that if its creation could "be employed as an instrument or mean of carrying into execution any of the specified powers," that would legitimize it as simply a means to attain a constitutionally-authorized end. Hamilton argued for a broad meaning to the notion of what the Constitution means by "necessary and proper" to carry out a specifically-enumerated power, whereas Jefferson and Randolph argued that necessity alone could never justify the federal government taking any action if it is not specifically authorized as an enumerated power.

None of these men, including Hamilton, all of whom possessed authoritative knowledge on this very subject, thought for a minute that the Commerce clause authorized the creation of a bank – let alone any "regulation" of private banks, nor of any citizens nor other businesses at all!

Still further from the thoughts of any of them – including Hamilton – was any notion that anything resembling the Federal Reserve, unconstitutionally created in 1913, which prints paper money and controls the entire banking system in the United States – paper money which has not been backed by any specie whatsoever since Pres. Nixon unilaterally repudiated the gold standard – could possibly be constitutional. With respect to any federal power to issue money of any kind, Constitution Article I Section 8 grants power to Congress only "to coin the money [emphasis added]..." Thus Congress had no power whatsoever to permit the issuance of any paper money by the United States under the Constitution.

And that explicit, Constitutional refusal to authorize the federal government to issue paper money was no oversight. The founders were extremely well aware of the so-called early-18th century Mississippi bubble involving the Scottish economist/financier John Law, the Duke of Orleans while Regent of France during the minority of Louis XV, and France's enormous then-colony in America known as Louisiana.

Without getting into all the multiple levels of complexity involved in all that, suffice it to say that in connection with all that, France, for the first time, established its own national bank which issued its own paper currency based on the theories (which were far from crazy, by the way) of John Law, together with stock in a private company – the Mississippi Company – chartered by France to exploit, operate and populate its Louisiana colony, all of which ended up creating both a huge financial bubble in the stock of the Mississippi Company and a paper currency which initially showed promise of ameliorating the serious indebtedness of France and which, though theoretically backed by property of enormous value (though not specie) ended up suffering catastrophic inflation."

With that then-recent fiasco vividly in mind, the founders had no desire whatsoever to permit the federal government to have the ability to issue paper currency, knowing full well that it could be manipulated under the political power of the state, if permitted, to inflate away federal debts and otherwise cause grave damage to the property of citizens. It was for that precise reason that the federal government was given the power, with respect to the issuance of money, only to "coin" such – that is, to make its own money out of metals, including gold, silver and copper, but absolutely not to be able to create anything resembling a national bank, nor to issue any paper money whatsoever.

There was no problem with private banks issuing paper currency – bank notes – because if they were not fully backed by specie the bank would simply go bankrupt. Because unlike the government, private banks were subject to market forces which prevented them from doing any harm to the currency or the public when simply acting on their own, under the Common Law.

Hamilton argued that "necessary and proper" for purposes of permitting the very limited federal activity involved in its minority share ownership in the private bank effectively meant "helpful" in advancing any specifically-authorized Constitutional power, and that since Congress was specifically authorized to receive and spend money, and to supervise efforts by the states to regulate trade (somewhat-confusingly called "Commerce" in the Constitution), and to declare and wage war, a bank would be helpful in furthering each of those specifically-authorized powers.

He did not claim that the "necessary and proper" clause of the Constitution by itself permitted the federal government to create any corporation – unless it was to further actual, specifically-authorized activities.

## Hamilton's Description of the Scope of the Commerce Clause

"Thus," Hamilton wrote, "a corporation may not be erected by Congress for superintending the police of the city of Philadelphia, because they [i.e. the federal government] <u>are not authorized to regulate the police</u> of that city. But one may be erected in relation to the collection of taxes, or to the <u>trade</u> with foreign countries, or to the <u>trade</u> between the States, or with the Indian tribes [emphases added];"

This passage leaves no doubt that Hamilton viewed all aspects of the police power of the citizens to be barred to the federal government, because, he explicitly states, policing the citizenry and the police who do so locally "are not authorized" activities for the federal government. And note his use of the word "trade" rather than "commerce" in his unambiguous gloss on the Commerce clause.

Specifically, note in this critical passage his argument <u>for</u> the constitutionality of the Bank, claiming that both the power to tax and the power to oversee what he calls "trade with foreign countries, or to the trade between the states, or with the Indian tribes," Hamilton plainly shows his (authoritative) view of the Commerce clause's true meaning: it actually uses the word "commerce" to mean "trade," and it only permitted federal regulation over any effort <u>by the states</u> to regulate "trade <u>between</u> the states [emphases added]" – all coupled with his specific, affirmative statement that the federal government is forbidden "to regulate the police" of Philadelphia.

Today, federal disrespect for its constitutional limits has reached the point where multiple city police forces are, in fact, micromanaged by the federal Justice Department – in manifest violation of the Constitution, with no constitutional amendment permitting such since the time of Hamilton.

But Hamilton had more to say about the Commerce clause in his argument in support of the Bank in 1791, statements by him that bear directly on what, if any, power it actually grants the federal government with respect to private businesses, as follows:

> "This making the regulation of commerce to consist in prescribing rules for buying and selling this, indeed, is a species of regulation of trade, <u>but is one which falls more aptly within the province of the local jurisdictions than within that of the general government, whose care they must be presumed to have been intended to be directed to those general political arrangements concerning trade on which its aggregated interests depend, rather than to the details of buying and selling. Accordingly, such only are the regulations to be found in the laws of the United States whose objects are to give encouragement to the enterprise of our own merchants, and to advance our navigation and manufactures. And it is in reference to these general relations of commerce,</u> that an establishment [such as the Bank] which furnishes facilities to circulation, and a convenient medium of exchange and alienation, is to be regarded as a regulation of trade [emphases added]."

It is clear and indisputable that what Hamilton is saying in this passage regarding the federal Commerce power is that the last thing on earth it empowered the federal government to do was <u>intrude</u> in any manner – let alone dictate rules, empowering bureaucrats, to override private control – on how private businesses conduct any of their own affairs regarding their employees, services, products and customers, including rules regarding markets in which they did so – "rules for buying and selling" — which he states should be left to the states alone – and that the sole role of the federal government is to consist of "general political arrangements concerning trade on which its aggregated interests depend, rather than to the details of buying and selling [emphasis added]."

And federal involvement in trade was to be limited solely to giving "encouragement to the enterprise of our own merchants…" – the very opposite of the constriction, micromanagement, criminalization and permission-requirement over their activities which occurs under every federal "regulatory" bureaucracy.

Again, Hamilton makes clear that the word "commerce" as used in the Commerce clause referred exclusively to "trade" between the states, and not what we would call commercial activities of private businesses at all.

Thus, according to Hamilton, under the Commerce clause, the federal government was only to encourage and facilitate all businesses and trade itself through its "regulation" of potential impositions on those businesses and trade by the states, or Indian tribes, and in no way restrict or dictate to private businesses about anything.

And bear in mind, that of the founders of the nation who actively participated in the writing of, and advocacy for (as a major author of *The Federalist*), the Constitution, and in American politics thereafter, Hamilton was the foremost proponent in his day of maximizing, within the Constitutional limitations, the size, scope and power of the federal government and, together with Adams, was the founder of what became the Federalist political party dedicated to that proposition.

Yet even for him, creating the Bank of the United States which was to have no power whatsoever over citizens or any of their businesses, constituted, as he himself recognized, the outer limits of what was permissible – and he further acknowledged that the Commerce clause by itself was not a sufficient basis for creating it.

Jefferson, the founder of the other political party created at the beginning of the Republic – the Democrat/Republican party, which the modern Democratic Party claims to be a continuation of – adamantly opposed, as unconstitutional, the creation of the Bank at all. And his view of the Commerce clause itself was identical to that of Hamilton – to wit, that it provided no authorization whatsoever for the federal government to intrude in the affairs of citizens and their businesses.

Jefferson was also absolutely convinced that any breach by the federal government of the Constitutional walls against its authority would lead to tyranny because once those walls are breached no limiting principle would remain other than what politicians and their sophistry could get away with in fooling the public to permit them to expand the power of the state – and, of course, their own.

President Washington ultimately sided with Hamilton and permitted the establishment of the Bank.

But note how close a question the Constitutionality of its establishment was – and the extraordinary authority as founders of those – Jefferson and Randolph – who considered its creation utterly unconstitutional, and how even Hamilton, in support of it, could not point to a single enumerated power, including the Commerce clause, which would permit its creation by itself.

In light of these arguments by these genuine, Constitutionally-authoritative founders regarding the outer limits of federal power, there can be no question that the gargantuan, 20th century stretching of the Commerce clause to authorize, all by itself, all of the hundreds of federal "regulatory" administrative bureaucracies has been an utter abomination and a grotesque mischaracterization of that provision.

Yet since the Supreme Court adopted that view of the Commerce clause (gratuitously reversing its own prior rulings directly to the contrary) in the 1930s, that view of it has been taken for granted in all supposedly-authoritative legal circles, including the Supreme Court and every American law school.

In adopting that position regarding the Commerce clause, the Supreme Court did so gratuitously, without any, authorizing Constitutional amendment, as provided for and permitted pursuant to the very specific procedures in Article V of the Constitution. it is not even debatable: no actual Article V amendment has ever occurred authorizing and legitimizing the gratuitous expansion of federal power in the 20th century purportedly based on the Commerce clause.

Nothing in Article V permits amendment except pursuant to its unambiguously-specified procedures; and even the unanimous concurrence of the three authorized branches of government on an otherwise unconstitutional proposition does not accomplish such an amendment and remains an unconstitutional abomination.

This process of Constitutional usurpation by the political branches of the federal government is best understood by looking at it from its beginnings and considering that process, as I do below, in connection with the history of American political parties after the Washington administration – and considering the clear, and clearly-authoritative, Constitutional pronouncements by Presidents James Madison and James Monroe addressing all these constitutional issues, and by the Supreme Court in two major decisions, pronouncing, in all respects consistently with Madison, on some of them – the cases of *McCulloch v. Maryland* and *Gibbons v. Ogden*.

## Politicians' First Attempts To Spend Federal Taxpayers' Money

Beginning in 1808, with increasing stridency, politicians of various stripes – most publicly, two senators, John C. Calhoun and Henry Clay – actively promoted federal government involvement, in self-conscious imitation of actions by the British government, in the building of roads and canals – activity they labeled "internal improvements" – and, in 1817, those two senators in particular came up with a scheme for federal funding for such activity (which activity everyone recognized could not by funded by taxpayer-provided federal money under the Constitution) by using money available for dividends from the second Bank of United States to pay for such, with both houses of Congress passing a bill – the so-called Bonus Bill – providing such indirect federal funding and promotion of those so-called internal improvements.

They pretended – for the first time – in passing that legislation, that the Constitution's Commerce clause and General Welfare clauses together provided Constitutional authority for such spending.

And, in the context of the radical, post-1930s "readings" of the Commerce clause purportedly authorizing all those federal agencies, each of which actively, discretionarily dictate the details of how all businesses and people under their direction must act, note how <u>limited</u> an intrusion into citizens' lives the mere spending of that dividend money on such "internal improvements" was.

And yet, Pres. Madison declared even that limited federal activity unconstitutional, explicitly declaring there was <u>no</u> support in the Commerce — nor any other — Constitutional clause for such.

Specifically, in his last official act as president, James Madison, principal author of the Constitution and, literally, the greatest authority on its meaning and intentions in all American history, <u>vetoed</u> that legislation and wrote an official gloss and pronouncement on both the Commerce clause and the General Welfare clause in his formal message in connection with that veto, which message left no doubt about all these matters, was respected by all branches of government until 1887, and which is reprinted here in toto – precisely because it leaves absolutely no doubt of the grotesque Constitutional misconduct which our federal politicians have been engaged in since 1887 – as follows:

### March 3, 1817

To the House of Representatives of the United States:

Having considered the bill this day presented to me entitled "An act to set apart and pledge certain funds for internal improvements," and which sets apart and pledges funds "for constructing roads and canals, and improving the navigation of water courses, in order to facilitate, promote, and give security to internal commerce among the several States, and to render more easy and less expensive the means and provisions for the common defense," I am constrained by the insuperable difficulty I feel in reconciling the bill with the Constitution of the United States to return it with that objection to the House of Representatives, in which it originated.

The legislative powers vested in Congress are specified and enumerated in the eighth section of the first article of the Constitution, and it does not appear that the power proposed to be exercised by the bill is among the enumerated powers, or that it falls by any just interpretation with the power to make laws necessary and proper for carrying into execution those or other powers vested by the Constitution in the Government of the United States.

"The power to regulate commerce among the several States" can not include a power to construct roads and canals, and to improve the navigation of water courses in order to facilitate, promote, and secure such commerce without a latitude of construction departing from the ordinary import of the terms strengthened by the known inconveniences which doubtless led to the grant of this remedial power to Congress.

To refer the power in question to the clause "to provide for common defense and general welfare" would be contrary to the established and consistent rules of interpretation, as rendering the special and careful enumeration of powers which follow the clause nugatory and improper. Such a view of the Constitution would have the effect of giving to Congress a general power of legislation instead of the defined and limited one hitherto understood to belong to them, the terms "common defense and general welfare" embracing every object and act within the purview of a legislative trust. It would have the effect of subjecting both the Constitution and laws of the several States in all cases not specifically exempted to be superseded by laws of Congress, it being expressly declared "that the Constitution of the United States and laws made in pursuance thereof shall be the supreme law of the land, and the judges of every state shall be bound thereby, anything in the constitution or laws of any State to the contrary notwithstanding." Such a view of the Constitution, finally, would have the effect of excluding the judicial authority of the United States from its participation in guarding the boundary between the legislative powers of the General and the State Governments, inasmuch as questions relating to the general welfare, being questions of policy and expediency, are unsusceptible of judicial cognizance and decision.

A restriction of the power "to provide for the common defense and general welfare" to cases which are to be provided for by the expenditure of money would still leave within the legislative power of Congress all the great and most important measures of Government, money being the ordinary and necessary means of carrying them into execution.

If a general power to construct roads and canals, and to improve the navigation of water courses, with the train of powers incident thereto, be not possessed by Congress, the assent of the States in the mode provided in the bill can not confer the power. The only cases in which the consent and cession of particular States can extend the power of Congress are those specified and provided for in the Constitution.

I am not unaware of the great importance of roads and canals and the improved navigation of water courses, and that a power in the National Legislature to provide for them might be exercised with signal advantage to the general prosperity. But seeing that such a power is not expressly given by the Constitution, and believing that it can not be deduced from any part of it without an inadmissible latitude of construction and reliance on insufficient precedents; believing also that the permanent success of the Constitution depends on a definite partition of powers between the General and the State Governments, and that no adequate landmarks would be left by the constructive extension of the powers of Congress as proposed in the bill, I have no option but to withhold my signature from it, and to cherishing the hope that its beneficial objects may be attained by a resort for the necessary powers to the same wisdom and virtue in the nation which established the Constitution in its actual form and providently marked out in the instrument itself a safe and practicable mode of improving it as experience might suggest.

James Madison,

President of the United States

As powerful and authoritative a repudiation of <u>any</u> federal power under the Constitution to engage in such "internal improvements" in any manner – including simply facilitating funding for such – as Madison's just-quoted veto message undeniably was, apparently political pressure for such spending was so intense that his Democrat-Republican successor, James Monroe, after initially agreeing in all respects with Madison's veto message, and continuing to oppose any "internal improvements" legislation, eventually announced what he attempted to present as a slight modification in his views in a detailed, scholarly, very-lengthy formal Statement in 1822.

That 1822 written statement by Pres. Monroe is of enormous interest for many reasons in this context.

In Pres. Monroe's Statement in 1822, his bottom-line conclusion was that the Constitution does permit the spending of money by Congress, so long as it is spent on behalf of the nation's defense and/or "general welfare," and does not simply subsidize any citizens at the expense of others, and the federal government plays no role whatsoever in whatever the money is spent on – unless the money is spent on the military or some other Constitutionally-authorized purpose.

Pres. Monroe reached that conclusion in his 1822 official statement based on his detailed analysis therein of the Constitution and its history, including its roots in the Revolution itself, the necessary scope of federal power in dealing with foreign nations, and the Constitution's roots in the Articles of Confederation, all of which he knew from personal experience and involvement.

In a detailed analysis and explanation of all the enumerated powers in the Constitution, Pres. Monroe explicitly rejects any claim that any provision of the Constitution other than the spending power permits any such action. He explicitly and affirmatively rejects any notion that the Commerce clause permits such funding.

Indeed, in a detailed explication of the Commerce clause, he makes clear that that clause is extremely limited in its scope, arising from particular problems which had occurred under the Articles of Confederation in which tariffs on goods enacted by individual states concerning foreign trade had acted at cross purposes. Specifically, he makes plain that the Commerce clause contemplates no federal power other than supervising what we would call "the trade of goods" between the states, as opposed to the broader term "commerce" per se.

While Pres. Monroe continued to maintain that Congress could not itself establish, operate or preside in any manner over any "system" of internal improvements, he accepted the notion that Congress had discretion to appropriate money to fund such and, with that formal announcement, the last bastion of the limited-government Democrat Republican party opposition to such federal involvement in those activities ended.

Notwithstanding his clear efforts to narrowly-limit any federal power over anything claimed therein, Monroe's 1822 statement had the effect, ultimately, while clearly intending the precise opposite, of opening the Pandora's box of eventual federal involvement in the economy.

Pres. Monroe opened that box in his 1822 Statement by announcing that the Spending power in the Constitution alone permitted Congress to authorize spending on anything it claimed was in the national interest – but it could do so in its absolute discretion.

This permission for the federal government discretionarily to spend federal funds constituted a Pandora's box precisely because, as anomalous and paradoxical as it may seem, as discussed in detail below, the single most dangerous power any democratically-elected government can have is the power to provide any supposed "benefit," including money or any service it claims to perform on behalf of all or any part of the nation – anything that is, beyond simply funding and enforcing the powers actually enumerated in the Constitution which, as

Presidents Jefferson, Madison and even Monroe unanimously agreed, <u>do not</u> <u>include the power to perform "internal improvements"</u> and do not permit providing any benefit to any citizen – because any such benefit must be paid for by other citizens.

It is, indeed, the very attractiveness of the promises which the discretionary power to spend, if available at all, permits politicians to make that makes it so dangerous – and so politically impossible to control.

This is because if politicians are <u>allowed at all</u> to provide funding for "benefits" out of public funds, <u>there will never be any limit to the demands on them to do</u> <u>so</u> and, to the extent any of them attempt to refuse to spend such funds, their position inherently becomes politically unsustainable since they will always be accused of simply being niggardly and cruel.

In his 1822 statement, Pres. Monroe went to great lengths to describe why he believed that granting politicians the power to provide funding for anything they chose to fund in their discretion would pose no practical problem to the nation's freedoms: specifically, he stated he was confident they would all remain patriotic and respectful of the sacrifices made by the founders in our Revolution, and that political pressures of various kinds, including the desire to minimize taxes to fund such payments, would prevent politicians from spending such money unwisely and in a profligate manner.

In fact, precisely the opposite has always been the case: once the discretionary power to spend (other people's money) by politicians was unleashed, the political pressure to do so endlessly ultimately became irresistible – although, perhaps due to the very factors described by Monroe in his 1822 Statement, federal spending did remain pretty constrained, all things considered, and controlled – even when funding railroads, as discussed below, during the 1860s – until the 1930s – nearly 20 years after a federal income tax was authorized in the Constitution's 16th Amendment.

Prior to his issuing that statement, Pres. Monroe was effectively the last man standing among federal politicians actively opposed to spending federal money on "internal improvements." It may be that, although he fully believed everything in his Statement, he took its step to dramatically change his legal position on federal spending in the manner that he did – carefully attempting to limit its collateral damage in every way possible – with the idea that his ability to keep back the overwhelming political pressures to permit such expenditures had become a hopeless cause politically, actually in an attempt to constrain it to the greatest extent possible in that Statement. It is possible that his discussion therein of why he doubted politicians would abuse the power was more an expression of hope, reminding them of their duties etc., than of his true, political expectations.

Soon after Pres. Monroe issued his statement, legislation providing for funding for canals and other "internal improvements" (initially just highways) passed both houses of Congress with little opposition and the cause of promoting federal involvement in those activities effectively continued unabated for 50 years thereafter, with similar federal involvement in railroad construction and funding as soon as that truly-revolutionary invention became practicable.

There was, however, a huge difference between providing funding for the "internal improvements" contemplated by Pres. Monroe – canals and roads which would facilitate commerce engaged in by citizens, but would not themselves be a part of the economy – and funding railroads, which were themselves commercial enterprises. It was the federal funding later provided for the construction of national railroads that was the true first involvement of the federal government in the private economy itself.

### The Most Dangerous Power

As between the individual citizen's liberty, and the police power of the state, it is always a zero-sum proposition: each can only be increased by diminishing the other. This fundamental fact, which our founders were keenly aware of, requires keeping the police power of a state to the absolute, barest minimum if individual liberty is to be maximized.

The founders were also keenly aware that, particularly in a large nation such as ours has been since its very beginning, precluding any power in the central government to police the citizens (except for the very-few crimes described with careful specificity in the Constitution, as the central government's sole, permissible targets) has always been an absolute necessity, with all such citizen-policing power permissible only for the states. There are several reasons for this.

First of all, any law policing citizen behavior would, once enacted, inevitably attract its own supporters, particularly officeholders in the central government, who would relish the power such law gives them over other citizens. That support would make it particularly difficult to undo such laws in a very large country, where the national government is always more remote than more-local governments, making it that much less responsive to individual citizen grievances arising from its policies.

It is always imperative, in the interest of freedom, that laws restricting citizens' freedom – the very purpose of policing laws – be administered only by that government which is closest to the people, and so most responsive to them. The fact that all the states already had Common-Law policing laws at the time the Republic was founded armed them with all such laws that were needed in a free Republic. Any additional criminal laws imposed by the federal government would either be duplicative of those state laws, or necessarily excessive, and so inimical to individual liberty, immoral and tyrannical: as shown in chapter 2, God has already given us all the policing laws necessary to keep us free; and no one is smarter than God.

Secondly, the central government would never have any particular competence to protect the citizenry, that being the sole purpose of policing laws – beyond protecting the nation, again, from those specific crimes identified in the Constitution. Indeed, as America's Counterrevolutionaries understood long ago, unconstitutionally maximizing policing laws at the federal level would make undoing them particularly difficult – and preclude a major point of competition among the states.

Specifically, the founders, in setting up our federal system, deliberately contemplated that the states would compete with each other in the nature and content of their laws, and so have an incentive to maximize the freedom of their citizens – consistent with their safety and prosperity. Any state that overstepped what citizens wanted would risk losing its population to other more-attractive states.

However, when it is the federal government dictating policing laws, citizens literally have nowhere to go to escape – and that fact guaranteed that any policing laws it enacted would be administered in the most tyrannical manner. There is, quite simply, no purpose for citizen-policing laws to be at the federal level other than that – again, other than those crimes specified in the Constitution itself.

Our Constitution, intent on preserving individual liberty as its deliberate, overriding purpose, permits the federal government – the central state entity – to exercise only those very-specifically-described powers enumerated in the Constitution itself – primarily in its Article I §8 – and none others.

As mentioned above, none of those enumerated powers permit the policing of the citizenry except with respect to very-specifically described types of citizen misconduct – "counterfeiting the Securities and current coin of the United States," and "Piracies and Felonies committed on the high seas, and Offenses against the Law of Nations." The only other crime Congress is granted legislative authority to provide punishment for is the crime of treason, addressed, and provided for, in Article III §3.

It is a fundamental principle of statutory construction that the enumeration of those specific powers in this manner precludes any inference that any others exist. Specifically these few provisions contained in Article I and III specifying the only crimes which Congress is granted power to punish necessarily comprise a comprehensive list of _all_ police powers the Constitution permits the federal government to wield against the citizenry.

As Thomas Jefferson explicitly pointed out in writing to Pres. Washington, because the 9th and 10th amendments leave to the citizens and the states all powers not explicitly granted to the federal government in the Constitution, any assumption of any not-so-specified power by the federal government would necessarily infringe on, and usurp, powers reserved to the states and the citizenry.

But the most dangerous power the state or any politician can be allowed is the power to spend taxpayer money and claim he is doing so to "benefit" some of the citizens – inevitably at the expense of others who must pay for it.

Because the nature of all state power is that, in real life, it is wielded by government officeholders officially vested with the authority to act in the name of the state. It is an inherent and unavoidable fact that all actions by the state involve the actual, or threatened, use of violence against citizens who are the subject of such actions. There is no other possibility: it is precisely the monopolization of violence that is the state's one attribute. That is how taxes are collected.

And it is only through the collection of taxes that the state can spend any money at all (even if it pays current expenses through loans, those loans will need to be repaid from taxes at some point), since it is only through the forced extraction of money from some citizens that the state has the power to spend it on others. And unless the expenditure is exclusively for something which truly benefits the nation in general – such as paying for the national defense – it inevitably is paid only to its particular recipients.

Although the state does have a real existence, like any entity, it can only act through its human agents – its officeholders, whether elected or appointed. And those officeholders – politicians and bureaucrats – use their official positions as their personal instruments of power over citizens subject to their jurisdiction.

Indeed, those positions become weapons in their hands, particularly if the power they have over the citizens is discretionary to any extent. Quite simply, the more discretionary power they may have, the more tyrannical and dangerous they become to the citizens.

There are many reasons why it is so dangerous and destructive for the state – necessarily acting through its office holder/agents, who invariably seek to claim credit for themselves – to purport to provide "benefits" of any kind gratuitously for its citizens, or any group of them. The history of the nation proves this destructiveness since it is the source of all corruption, cronyism and everything citizens despise about government.

First of all, if any such "benefit" consists of a purported "service" provided for the citizenry – such as supposedly "protecting" citizens from some claimed misconduct, potential or actual, from other citizens or entities — the federal government is inherently incapable of performing any such service competently.

Because there are only a few things the state is actually capable of doing – including monopolizing violence, to be used constructively in connection with the enforcement of the common law and powers vested in the Constitution (all of which are specified in the Constitution's Article I §8), and protecting the nation from genuine threats, such as from foreign or domestic enemies.

The reason it can do nothing beyond those with any competence is because any other "services" it performs which could otherwise be of value are best performed by individuals acting independent of government in the market, since only market participants – other than the state – are able to compete with each other to provide services independent of political considerations.

Once the state is involved in providing services, it inevitably exercises monopoly power in doing so – with all the adverse consequences to everyone from that power, which has long been declared illegal and criminal if exercised by private companies.

But its involvement in the economy is even more corrupt and corrupting than that of a private monopoly, because its involvement inherently makes it impossible to avoid politics, as opposed to honest market demand and supply, in all its actions. That in turn results, automatically, in corruption and cronyism – and even further damage to any real market and the public, due to the bureaucrats acting in the state's name inevitably applying, for their own self-preservation, the "precautionary principle."

To the extent the state bestows money for funding any activity, other than those specified in the Constitution's Article I §8, since the state is incapable of itself producing the money in the manner non-state actors do, and since any money bestowed can only benefit some citizens, it is inherent that the source of the money must be from other citizens.

This is because the state has no money other than what it takes under threat of force from its own citizens, however legal the taxing authority it uses to do so may be.

It is, indeed, the very apparent attractiveness of the promises the discretionary power to spend, if available at all, permits politicians to make that makes it so dangerous – and so impossible to control.

In the 1830s, Pres. Andrew Jackson attempted to prevent any further such "internal improvements" spending and, at various times, described the problems such spending posed to what he called "the republican principle." He stated, at various times, that federal involvement in such "internal improvements" projects risk jurisdictional clashes with the states and that government investment in private transportation companies delegated public responsibilities to private agencies and led to charges of "favoritism and oppression." He also protested against the "flagicious [sic] logrolling" involved in legislating funds for such projects, and that the government involvement by itself distorted natural economic growth. But by then it was already too late.

As anyone with any understanding of what happens when the state/government gets involved in "assisting" or "funding" any private commercial activities, understanding its mere presence in all attendant transactions spreads corruption, incompetence and, inevitably, business disasters at some point. All these occurred in connection with all the "internal improvements" and, most notoriously, in the building of railroads throughout the United States – and in the corrupt cronyism which federal funding of the railroads injected into the economy for the first time.

Commerce Clause Rulings by the Supreme Court in the 19th Century

The Supreme Court of the United States twice had the occasion to consider the meaning and scope of the Commerce clause during the 19th century, in unanimous opinions written by Chief Justice John Marshall, who was appointed to the Court by John Adams, in whose cabinet he had served, and was himself among the nation's founders. To this day, Chief Justice Marshall is revered in the legal profession as one of its true, all-time "greats."

Indeed, uniquely among 19th-century Supreme Court justices, most of whom are long-forgotten and ignored, a number of Marshall's opinions – or rather, curiously-selected (by law professor authors of casebooks) excerpts from them – continue to be widely read by law students today, including excerpts from the two discussed below.

Rare, however, would be the law school class in which the utter irreconcilability of Marshall's actual, textually-provable views of the constitutional limits on federal power, discussed and shown textually below, and those of the modern Supreme Court (particularly since *Wickard vs. Filburn (1942)*) are even mentioned, let alone discussed at length.

For example, in the leading law school case books purporting to contain the text of the cases discussed below, <u>some of the most important language is never included</u>, whereas mere *dictum* in *Gibbons*, which some, including the late Justice Jackson erroneously, have believed authorizes virtually unlimited federal police power, when read out of context of specific language quoted below, invariably is so included.

It is no understatement to say that for decades, generations of law students' minds have been polluted by grotesque mischaracterizations of the decisions discussed below.

Specifically, neither of Marshall's two 19th century opinions discussed below provide the slightest support for any notion that the Commerce clause provides Congress with any police power whatsoever over any aspect of private businesses, let alone a general police power over <u>all</u> business operations, including all transactions with them by any person of any kind in the nation, as the Supreme Court has been interpreting that clause beginning in the mid-1930s.

Indeed, as shown below, Justice Marshall <u>specifically repudiated</u> the possibility of any such federal police power over businesses – and did so in a portion of his *Gibbons* opinion meant to highlight its precise holdings (what would be characterized in more modern decisions as the official Syllabus by the Court).

Indeed, it is clear that both of those Marshall opinions utterly <u>repudiate</u> the post-1930's Supreme Court Commerce clause "reading," and are themselves absolutely consistent in all respects with the views of the Commerce clause described above expressed by Sec. Hamilton, and Presidents Madison and Monroe, each of whom described that clause in a manner rendering the "modern" view of it by the Supreme Court as utter, Intellectually-Insulting nonsense and patently frivolous.

Unlike the presidents whose views of the Commerce clause are described above, in applying that clause to the circumstances of the cases it was deciding in the 19th century, the Supreme Court was limited to providing its legal ruling to the precise facts and issues before it in those cases.

*McCulloch vs. Maryland*, decided in 1819, was the first such Commerce clause case ruled on by the Supreme Court and, significantly, involved various constitutional issues raised by the second Bank of United States, which Pres. Madison had authorized after the War of 1812 exposed to him the difficulties of the federal government operating without such a bank in time of war, leaving him to end his opposition to such a bank based on his prior agreement with Jefferson in opposition to it. The *McCulloch* decision was issued two years after Pres. Madison's 1817 veto message's comprehensive description of the scope of the Commerce clause quoted above.

Not only did the Court's *McCulloch* decision intimate <u>nothing</u> in any way inconsistent with Pres. Madison's then-recent view of the Commerce clause, it made clear that the purpose of that clause was <u>precisely</u> as described by Madison and all the other founders and presidents described above: it provided Congress with a power <u>not over citizens'</u> businesses themselves, but rather over any actions <u>which the states</u> (who alone were to be policed under that clause) might take affecting trade among them of any kind, such as imposing taxes or rules affecting any interstate business.

The second Bank of the United States was similar to the first one, discussed above: it was by no means a central bank possessing any regulatory power over other banks or the currency, but rather was itself a private bank with a special relationship with the Treasury department which owned 20% of its stock, with the rest held by private persons. *McCulloch* arose after the state of Maryland had passed a law imposing taxes on all banks within Maryland as a prerequisite for them legally to operate there. The Bank of United States refused to pay the tax, claiming the tax was unconstitutional to be imposed against such a quasi-federal entity.

Justice Marshall decided two issues in the case: (1) the constitutionality of the Bank of United States itself and (2) the constitutionality of the Maryland tax imposed on it.

With respect to the first issue, Justice Marshall ruled the Bank was indeed constitutional, though acknowledging it was a very close question, in a lengthy opinion which was substantively identical to that of Hamilton's memo in support of the first such bank in 1791, described, and quoted from, above. Like Hamilton, he agreed with Jefferson that the Commerce clause <ins>in itself was insufficient</ins> to authorize the federal government to create such an institution, but that the Necessary and Proper clause permitted it as a useful vehicle for the federal government to carry out financial transactions it was necessarily involved in, including in regulating trade between the states pursuant to the Commerce clause.

Again, <ins>nothing</ins> in that decision provides the slightest support for the "modern" notion that the Commerce clause authorizes Congress to police <ins>citizens and their businesses</ins> in any manner. Indeed, the fact that that decision recognizes how <ins>close a question</ins> it was whether the mere federal involvement as a minority shareholder using the bank for various, limited, national purposes was itself even permissible shows how preposterous that "modern" interpretation would have been viewed – if anyone had even had the temerity to suggest it.

Regarding the second question presented in *McCulloch*, the Supreme Court ruled that the Maryland tax could not be constitutionally applied to the Bank as a quasi-federal instrumentality <ins>at all</ins> because, as the Court unambiguously ruled, "the power to tax is the power to destroy," and the Court ruled it was impermissible for any state to have power of that nature over the federal government or any of its instrumentalities — even one, like the Bank, in which the Treasury was a mere 20% shareholder.

It is apparent that that devastating characterization of the power of taxation would be equally, or even more, true of any power of "regulation" (as that term is used in the modern sense) of any business – in which unelected federal functionaries have the powers to write <ins>and</ins> administer <ins>and</ins> adjudicate (tyrannically, according to Montesquieu, and Madison in *the Federalist* number 47, by combining all three governmental powers in one body, with <ins>no</ins> separation) laws directing even minute details of the activities of businesses, and effectively hold existential power over such businesses and their officers if they dare to voice genuine objection to the gratuitous taking away of their actual authority over their business' affairs – had that issue been before the Court.

The second 19th century John Marshall-written Supreme Court decision involving the Commerce clause was issued in 1824 in *Gibbons vs. Ogden*. To the extent proponents of the "modern" view of the expansive policing power purportedly based on the Commerce clause claim that there is any support for it in Supreme Court decisions prior to the mid-1930s, they invariably cite *Gibbons*. The Supreme Court itself has done so.

In fact, *Gibbons* provides <ins>no support whatsoever</ins> for either that frivolous reading of the Constitution or of that case itself, and makes plain that the Commerce clause was intended to police only the extent to which <ins>states</ins> could impose any "regulations," limitations or other burdens on interstate trade or instrumentalities involved in it – such as the steamboat involved in *Gibbons*. Again, as shown textually below, that case clearly and unambiguously negates any federal police power over citizens or their businesses themselves.

Specifically, the clear, unambiguous actual holding of *Gibbons* is that once Congress had authorized a particular boat to operate in American waters, the Commerce clause precluded a state from attempting to supersede that federal authorization by the state purporting to forbid that boat from operating in waters within that state, which connected to waters in any other state and/or any foreign nation, which state forbidding was based on its purported grant of a monopoly to so operate in its waters to another steamboat.

In other words, the Supreme Court's ruling in the case was, quite simply, that Congress' undertaking to grant authority to one boat to operate in the potentially-interstate waters preempted the power of any state to grant a monopoly to any other boat.

In so ruling in *Gibbons*, the Supreme Court summarized what it officially characterized as its "Principles of Interpretation" of the Commerce clause, in a manner absolutely consistent with the reading of that clause by Sec. Hamilton and the two presidents Madison and Monroe described above, as exclusively limited to policing state actions affecting trade, and any instrumentalities involved in such, between the states and foreign nations, by ruling in part as follows:

> "The power of regulating commerce extends to the regulation of navigation. The power to regulate commerce extends to every species of commercial intercourse between the United States and foreign nations and among the several states....But it does not extend to a commerce which is completely internal [to a state].... State inspection laws, health laws and laws for regulating the internal commerce of the state, and those which respect turnpike roads, ferries etc. are not within the power granted to Congress [to regulate state actions] [emphases added]...." 22 U.S. at 3

Nothing could be clearer than the fact that in those words, the Supreme Court was confirming the very limited and precise scope of the federal power provided in the Commerce clause described by all the authorities – Hamilton, Madison and Monroe in particular – whose views are quoted and discussed above: that clause provides power only for the federal government to regulate the conduct of states, and not to police any purely intrastate matters, nor the actions of private businesses themselves, other than those involved in navigation, and only to the extent the states' actions could have an effect on trade among the states or with foreign nations.

And note that, even while permitting the federal government to regulate "navigation," that just-quoted language from *Gibbons* precludes any federal power in the nature of "inspection laws [or] health laws…" even, presumably, with respect to boats involved in "navigation." With that language in mind, it should be noted that the overwhelming justification for all federal "policing" regulatory laws has been supposedly to protect the nation's physical and financial "health" and to permit businesses to be "inspected."

Indeed, in the language highlighted above in the final "Principle of Interpretation", the Court could not be clearer in both specifically stating that it is only state laws and activities affecting trade – "intercourse" – which are subject to being regulated by Congress at all under the Commerce clause, and in specifically pre-cluding Congress from having any citizen-policing power whatsoever – including over the state laws themselves – by describing precisely the kind of laws normally considered as laws policing business – "inspection laws, health laws and laws for regulating the internal commerce of the state…" – and in explicitly stating that laws of that nature "are not within the power granted to Congress…"

Accordingly, the idea — baselessly espoused by the Supreme Court, all American law schools, and the entire legal profession since the mid-1930's — that *Gibbons* provides any authority whatsoever for the federal government, purporting to rely on the Commerce clause, to impose citizen-policing powers of any kind over any private businesses not involved in navigation, is utter nonsense, as the above quotation could not make more plain.

And nothing so proves the cynicism and fraud involved in the Supreme Court rulings pretending *Gibbons* actually supports its post-1935 readings of the Commerce clause, and the legal profession's fraudulent cheering for such, than the fact that, if you review the books prepared by supposedly-learned "experts" on what purports to be Constitutional law, books which are used to train future lawyers in Constitutional Law classes in law schools throughout the nation, you will not find a single one which, in purporting to include *Gibbons* as a case they pretend to present to their readers, includes that central, quoted, language which summarizes the entire, actual position of that case on the Commerce clause. And that has been the case at least since the 1960s in those casebooks.

It should be mentioned, in the context of 19th-century Supreme Court decisions on this subject that, after Chief Justice Marshall died in 1835 and, accordingly, left the Court, it no longer had any founders on it, and it has, ever since, been populated exclusively by politicians (though they pretend otherwise) of various sorts, including prominent members of the legal profession. Those justices have increasingly felt freer and freer to use their positions on the Court to advance their own political preferences, unconstrained by any possibility of being questioned, let alone repudiated (except perhaps in a law review article penned by an even more radical law professor), and increasingly indifferent to the actual, plain meaning of the Constitution. As Lord Acton observed, "power corrupts and absolute power corrupts absolutely."

This extraordinary, monstrous politicization of Supreme Court opinions, beginning in the 19th century, is apparent in the notorious 1857 *Dred Scott v. Sandford* case (gratuitously precluding both citizenship and any access to federal court to any slave <u>or free</u> "negro, whose ancestors were imported into [the U.S.], and sold as slaves," and precluding federal legal power concerning slavery outside the original 13 states), and in many cases after the Civil War. Other, similarly-purely-politically-motivated and legally-frivolous 19th Century rulings by the Supreme Court included the following:

(1) *The Slaughterhouse Cases (1873)*, famous for gratuitously reading the "privileges and immunities" clause out of the 14th Amendment, and so validating a blatantly-racist Louisiana-granted monopoly over an entire business sector (the slaughterhouse business);

(2) *Plessy v. Ferguson (1896)*, famous for validating, and so institutionalizing, official race-consciousness by state officials, and in state laws – in direct contradiction of the Civil War Amendments and the Civil Rights acts which immediately followed them – by proclaiming the Constitutional legitimacy of "separate but [supposedly] equal" apartheid treatment by states regarding all their actions over the citizens, including in public schools, public transportation, and in businesses – such as hotels and restaurants – serving the public, which businesses, under *Plessy*, could, and were, forced by state laws to discriminate in favor of one race over another, in plain violation of both the Civil War amendments and the Contract clause;

(3) *The Daniel Ball*, an 1870 case in which a hyper-politicized Supreme Court completely ignored the unambiguous teaching of Chief Justice Marshall quoted above from *Gibbons*, and instead ruled that the federal government has the power to license and inspect, without limitation – and so exercise a citizen-policing function ruled expressly forbidden by Marshall – over all boats navigating any waterways in the United States. As observed by the losing party in that case – the boat in question – that ruling effectively meant there was no limit on the police power of the federal government. Although the Court claimed it was limiting its ruling to boats operating on American waters, it did not deny that that would indeed be the effect of its ruling.

The cynicism of the *Ball* case is shown by the facts that it both fails even to mention the ruling by Marshall in *Gibbons*, which was directly contrary on this precise point and, in its purported detailed recitation of the parties' arguments, suggests no one even argued that Marshall's ruling on that issue should be followed – a highly improbable claim by the Court clearly attempting to provide cover and justification for its monstrous decision.

Obviously, the Supreme Court has no power to transform the Constitution as the *Dred Scott* and *Ball* case most-blatantly do, while pretending otherwise. Each of these cases' undeniable attempt to do so was itself an undeniable violation of the

Constitution – and a violation of his oath of office taken by each Supreme Court Justice who approved it.

Lest there be any doubt about this: Article VI of the Constitution explicitly establishes the Constitution as the fundamental, "supreme law of the Land," and requires that all federal laws must be made "in Pursuance [of the Constitution]", and that the Constitution and those permissible federal laws "shall be the supreme Law of the Land" with respect to all state laws. Although mere laws can be repealed or defunded at any time under Article I the Constitution, by its own, express terms, the Constitution itself can only be altered or amended pursuant to the very specific procedures prescribed in its Article V.

The legal effect of the combination of those provisions in Articles V and VI is that any purported "law" or official action inconsistent with the Constitution is a legal nullity. None of the Article V amendment procedures are met by a mere decision by the Supreme Court, even with the unanimous approval of both other branches of government.

The *Ball* case is, in its own way, as monstrous as *Dred Scott* and *Plessy* – and we are still awaiting a Supreme Court that will repudiate it as decisively as *Plessy* was repudiated in 1954. Instead, we have the absurd, legally-baseless rulings by the Supreme Court beginning in the 1930s plainly adopting the totalitarianism-validating proposition which even the *Ball* Court declined explicitly to adopt.

# CHAPTER 12

## 19th Century Political Debates And Developments

### An Overview Of Early Federal Economic Intrusions

Following the memorandum debate, detailed in the previous chapter, among his cabinet members, regarding the (first) Bank of the United States, President Washington decided to proceed with authorizing a federal corporate charter – and 20% stock-ownership by the government – for the bank, under which charter it had a limited life of 20 years. Once established, that bank handled the money issues Hamilton had wanted it to address – and made no effort whatsoever to "regulate" the business of the state-chartered private banks which, not incidentally, were the primary issuers of all American paper currency (banknotes – that is, written paper dollar promises to be redeemed upon presentation to their bank issuer with gold or silver) in the nation – which remained the case until 1913, as discussed below.

By the end of the Washington administration, there were 24 state-chartered banks in the nation, the Bank of the United States and an additional bank which Hamilton had originated in Philadelphia in 1782 named the Bank of North America.

After the first Bank of the United States ceased to exist under its 20-year-life provision of its charter, the Republic fought the British in the War of 1812 with no such institution. Pres. Madison, a stalwart ally of Jefferson – and, accordingly, similarly opposed to the first Bank of the United States – reluctantly concluded that lacking such a bank contributed to numerous serious inconveniences (including possibly even the burning of the White House) during that war, leading him to abandon his Jeffersonian view with respect to the bank and join in to promote a successor to it – The Second Bank of the United States – in 1816.

Again, that bank had no role of "regulating," in the modern sense, any other banks in the nation, and the banknotes it issued were promises similar to those of the state-chartered banks – promises to redeem the issued paper dollars with specie. The Supreme Court case involving that second bank – *McCulloch* – is discussed above.

Neither of these two Banks of the United States were federal agencies, although the federal government issued each of their charters and was a 20% stockholder in each of them. Nevertheless, both such Banks behaved arrogantly – no doubt because of their presumed special standing – in their dealings with other banks, often behaving in a non-commercial, abusive manner.

For example, on multiple occasions, both such banks made sudden specie-redemption demands of the other banks. These demands consisted of presenting banknotes for redemption to their issuing banks in a manner almost certainly calculated to damage the reputation of those other banks, and possibly to cause a run on them, because commercial banks normally maintained a supply of specie of about 20% of their outstanding bank notes' face value, a sound practice in normal circumstances.

Specifically, in each of these cases, the Bank of the United States first accumulated large numbers of banknotes issued by a particular bank, with a view to harming that bank (there was no legitimate business purpose for its actions), and presented the notes to such bank specifically for specie redemption in a manner well outside normal commercial practices deliberately to abuse its own capital advantages against those other banks.

The second Bank of the United States misbehaved in numerous of its ordinary banking practices for the first decade of its life and earned a reputation as a corrupt, incompetent institution (even after 1823 when Nicholas Biddle largely cleaned up its act), to the point that Andrew Jackson, the popular war hero and Democrat candidate for president, explicitly ran for office as an anti-Bank of the United States candidate and, when it's 20-year charter expired in 1836, refused to renew its charter claiming, among other things, that it was engaging in unconstitutional actions.

This he did not as a doctrinaire Jeffersonian small-government Democrat: Jackson had no problem intruding in the banking business, and, in fact, effectively caused the greatest financial panic in America of the 19th century by abruptly, and radically, demanding an end to the issuing by private banks of all paper currency!

As always, nothing is better calculated to lead to a financial panic than for popular political figures, with multiple prosecutorial and other violent weapons at their disposal, to make abrupt rule changes, or threatening business destruction – as Jackson clearly did in that circumstance, with nothing in the Constitution providing authority for him to do so. But private banks felt obligated to follow his directive out of fear of his destructive capabilities. As always, mere market participants are defenseless against the existential threat of violent, destructive government power.

And that was exactly what followed from Jackson's radical demand for the termination of all paper currency – a demand arising from his visceral hatred of the entire banking industry which then, as always, provided the lifeblood of all commerce in the nation, even more so than today: at that time, banks, and not the government, were the sole issuers of paper currency. And the multiple alternative sources of capital for businesses created by various aspects of the banking business, including the investment banking business, barely existed at all at that time.

Fortunately for the nation, between 1836 and the creation of the Federal Reserve in 1913, private banks were indeed able to issue paper banknote currency (always redeemable in specie) and that sound, privately-issued currency, with no federal institution able to intrude on the currency market, was a major factor, together with the general absence of federal involvement in the economy, with facilitating the amazing growth of the American economy in all respects for most of the rest of the 19th century.

The few economic busts amidst the boom throughout the 19th century were almost certainly enhanced, If not caused exclusively, by the federal policing/regulatory presence which first began in 1865 with the entire defeated South crushed under federal Reconstruction laws, laws enforced politically and with particular brutality and unpredictability by the Justice Department after its creation in 1870, followed in 1887 with the enactment of the Interstate Commerce Act, itself followed by the (terrifying) Sherman Antitrust Act of 1890, the first federal statute explicitly intended to apply against all businesses throughout the entire economy. And, as discussed above, Pres. Jackson caused the most serious panic in the entire century by his erratic, gratuitous demand that all paper currency be withdrawn from circulation.

The next, comparable financial panic did not occur until 1906, after Pres. Roosevelt similarly terrorized all American businesses with his threatened, manic persecution of them, particularly banking and oil businesses, under the antitrust acts, his effective federal-control takeover of all the multiple interstate food and drug businesses through the initiation of what later became named the FDA, briefly discussed in Chapter 3 above, and his creation, with no Constitutional authority whatsoever, of the FTC for purposes of engaging in ongoing fishing expeditions into all the affairs of all American businesses.

And all these actions were that much more terrifying to American businesses because they had been free from this kind of tyrannical government oppression throughout the 19th century, in dramatic contrast to the eternally-stagnant businesses throughout continental Europe which had long been subject to precisely such laws and tyranny – laws which Theodore Roosevelt greatly admired and wanted imposed throughout the American economy. And he had made himself an enormously popular – and thereby powerful and terrifying – public figure.

None of those radical, tyrannical federal statutes and agencies would have been considered constitutional by any of the founders, and none was explicitly held constitutional by the United States Supreme Court until the 20th century.

We know to a moral certainty that none of the founders would have found such statutes constitutional based on the authorities quoted and discussed above in the previous chapter – and on the fact that even the most ambitious federal politicians, always eager to empower the federal government and thereby empower themselves, did not dare to propose any laws remotely like the Interstate Commerce Act of 1887 for almost 100 years after the founding of the Republic..

Early American Politics and Political Parties

George Washington won the first two presidential elections without campaigning, and without opposition, with unanimous votes of the College of Electors (who some states even then picked by popular election, and others by selection by their legislatures).

Nevertheless, political parties began to develop during his first term along the lines indicated in the debate, described above, between Hamilton and Jefferson regarding the first Bank of the United States: Hamilton was in favor of having the federal government be as active as the Constitution permitted (in his view), including providing encouragement to the growth of the nation's economy; and Jefferson was convinced the federal government should play no role whatsoever in the domestic economy except to the extent absolutely necessary, and solely to prevent the states from intruding on it.

As shown above, Jefferson and Hamilton actually agreed completely on the Constitutional meaning and intention of the Commerce clause: the Constitution used the word "commerce" to mean what Hamilton explicitly called, and we would call today, to be precise, "trade," and was not by itself a grant of any federal power over business enterprises' operations whatsoever.

Indeed, as both men's written opinions regarding the bank make clear, they agreed that the Commerce clause was not by itself sufficient Constitutional authority even simply to authorize federally chartering a bank, like the Bank of the United States, in which the federal government simply would hold a minority (20%) shareholder interest.

Both of them plainly would have been horrified at the mere thought of the federal government doing anything that could in any way impose any burden whatsoever of any kind on any private enterprise – anything, that is, remotely resembling the dictatorial, central government, federal business "regulation", as that term has been used here since 1887 – and as it had been used for identical laws since the 17th century in the tyrannical, absolute monarchies of continental Europe (e.g., Bourbon France, Prussia, czarist Russia).

Indeed, as Jefferson, Hamilton and all the Founders were well aware, the very England whose tyranny (compared to what they wanted) they had waged a bloody revolution to rid themselves of, was itself relatively non-tyrannical, compared to those other European powers, precisely because freedom from such absolute, central authority was precisely what the English had achieved in their own two revolutions during the 17th century – an achievement the American revolutionaries self-consciously and deliberately were building on both in our Revolution and our Constitution, which was specifically designed to preclude, substantively, and through its procedures mandated for each branch, federal government claims to such power over the citizenry and their businesses.

With respect to the Bank of the United States, as also discussed above, Hamilton's and Jefferson's differences had solely to do, as a legal matter, with their differing views of the scope of the Constitution's "Necessary and Proper" clause, and not the Commerce clause.

Their principal difference regarding the Bank actually had to do with their legal-factual assessment of the substantive significance of the federal government's simply owning a mere 20% of the stock in any private corporation, including one like the Bank which it contemplated using solely to facilitate its own financial transactions: Hamilton viewed such minority stock ownership as Constitutionally trivial, although representing the outer reaches of what was constitutionally permissible; and Jefferson, doubtless with his direct, personal experience of pre-Revolutionary France's state-controlling tyranny in mind, viewed it as simply a bridge too far – and just too risky a step in the direction of inherently-tyrannical intrusions into private business matters for the Republic.

It took over 100 years for American politicians to join together in any legislation which realized any of Jefferson's fears in that regard with respect to any American business – legislation and smothering control which metastasized with increasing rapidity in 1906 and thereafter.

This federal "regulatory"/dictatorial control over one portion of the nation's economy at a time – the Bad Law component of our Counterrevolution – has never been seriously, ideologically opposed by any American political party since the Democrat-Republican party ceased actively to oppose any federal activities connected to the economy after James Monroe left the White House. And, as discussed below, since no later than the Woodrow Wilson administration in 1912, the Democrat party has actively promoted that Counterrevolution in a highly-disciplined manner, often with the very active assistance of the Republican Party, and never with any serious opposition from it or any other organized political party.

Nevertheless, the universal understanding of the Constitution's prohibitions on anything resembling federal "regulation" – consisting of executive agency legislating/controlling/policing – of any citizens and/or their businesses was so deep that it was not until decades later – in 1887 – that any actual federal legislation imposing such regulation on any part of the economy was even proposed.

From our perspective in 21st-century America, these Constitutional differences between the two original American political parties that formed around Hamilton and Adams, on one side, and Jefferson on the other, may seem so minor (there were indeed other, significant ideological issues between them, as discussed below) as to be virtually nonexistent.

But opposition between the two parties was indeed bitter, and Jefferson left the Washington Cabinet in 1793, and the parties' differences became increasingly hostile during the John Adams presidency (in which Jefferson was vice president) which followed Washington's – and, as always in America, a matter of vigorous public debate.

Each party had its advocates in the principal media for such debate at the time – consisting of various pamphlets and published periodicals. Periodical and other political authors made no pretense of political "objectivity" – in stark contrast to most, more recent, American journalists in newspapers and other media outlets who, as discussed in a later chapter, beginning particularly in the 20th century, have routinely at least pretended to be mere "objective reporters" of "the news." Politicians themselves often personally published powerful polemics, often under pen names, as had been the case among advocates for and against the Constitution prior to 1789 (most of the famous, pro-Constitution essays comprising the Federalist were published under the pen name Publius).

Hamilton's party, which included Washington's VP and successor president John Adams, were known as the Federalists, with the Jeffersonian opposition initially called the Anti-Federalists, and later the Democrat-Republicans.

The other major difference between the two parties, besides whether federal minority ownership in the Bank of United States was Constitutionally-permissible, arose from their very-different views of the then-contemporaneous French Revolution, Britain's eventual military opposition to such, and the implications of that European warfare, primarily for the safety and security of the new Republic. These differences resulted in enormous, additional Constitutional issues between the parties during the Adams administration – differences which, I believe, ultimately had the effect of destroying the Federalist party politically.

Regarding these additional differences between the two parties: It is often said, simplistically, that Federalists were simply Anglophiles who favored aligning our nation with Britain both as a trading partner and in its ongoing war against France, as the French Revolution progressed in its radicalism in all respects during the 1790s, including particularly its radical egalitarianism and expansionist military ambitions, which ultimately culminated in the European-wide military dictatorship/empire under Napoleon after 1800. Similarly, it is often said that the Democrat-Republicans simply remained staunchly anti-British, resulting in them having a romantic sympathy for the French Revolution and its claimed quest for "liberty" (discussed at length in Chapter 6) in all respects, and favoring its opposition to what they viewed as our common enemy of Britain who they feared continued to desire to reconquer our nation, among other things.

In fact, the war between Britain and France during the Adams administration (1797-1800) which war, of course, continued with few interruptions until Napoleon's final defeat in 1815, was very much on Americans minds, posing particular risks to American ships on the high seas, though thankfully not on our land itself – except in our War of 1812 with Britain.

President Adams and his party members in Congress were deeply concerned that the British War against the French Revolutionaries could come to America, and that the radical egalitarian/collectivist ideology of the French Revolution (discussed in detail above) could impose its monstrous tyranny on our own revolution.

Specifically, they, like Edmund Burke, who they largely agreed with, recognized the existential danger posed by the French Revolution precisely because of its inherently-expansionist and radical-egalitarian ideological nature, and the profound military danger that posed to our new Republic, in the form of possible invasion by the French from retaking their former colony in Canada – Québec – their potential alliance with American Indian tribes and, particularly, both the Federalists and Edmund Burke feared, with fifth-column supporters in our Republic, and in England, who might be drawn to the ideological claims of the French revolutionaries, whose very ideological nature made them inherently potentially transnational.

Edmund Burke spelled this all out brilliantly in his *Reflections on the Revolution in France* (1790) and in pamphlets, including particularly *Letters On a Regicide Peace* (1796), which were all well-known here, as well as in Britain.

These fears of an American fifth-column joining with radical French revolutionary ideologues from Québec, possibly assisted by the French Navy (the very navy whose gunboats had assured our own victory at Yorktown against the British) were enough to give rise to the same type of security concerns present today regarding Islamist terrorism, which has resulted in the modern federal government surveillance techniques many consider antithetical to our constitutional freedoms.

In the Adams administration, such fears gave rise to statutes named The Alien and Sedition Acts, which, in the name of obtaining security, criminalized many constitutionally-protected actions by citizens and resulted in the closure by the federal government of a number of newspapers and the jailing of numerous citizens – virtually all of whom were Democrat-Republicans. It was widely feared by the Democrat-Republicans that they were actually persecuted purely for their political opposition to the Adams administration and not out of any genuine, patriotic concern for the nation.

That criminalization of political opposition, further embittering the deep ideological divide between the two parties in this period, was a reflection of the debate in print, initially in Europe, between Edmund Burke, author, as mentioned above, of *Reflections on the Revolution in France* (1790), and Thomas Paine whose pamphlet *Common Sense* (1776), had earlier powerfully propagandized for our own revolution, and who became a powerful propagandist/apologist for the French Revolution in his *The Rights of Man* (1791) and *The Age of Reason* (1793-4) (an extraordinary diatribe against Christianity). Edmund Burke had actually supported our own Revolution as a Whig member In the English Parliament.

Neither the Federalist nor the Democrat/Republican party was organized in anything resembling the modern sense of political parties – with platforms, conventions etc.

Both political parties had elected members in state offices and in both houses of Congress, with different regions of the country showing marked preferences for one party over the other (Federalists were overwhelmingly represented in the northeast, and Democrat-Republicans in the South, with some variations), with the Democrat-Republicans alone winning the presidency from 1800 on, and the Federalists essentially imploding as a party when their generally pro-British (against the French) sentiments became politically impossible in the War of 1812.

The nation was not a one-party affair thereafter, however. Politicians in both houses of Congress yearned for some way to increase the power over the citizenry of the federal government, power which they could use to enhance their own power through their offices. They strained against the harsh limitations on federal action mandated by the Constitution, earnestly desiring the federal government to take whatever steps politicians dreamed up purportedly to promote the national economy – even if only purportedly to increase our security from invasion by European powers.

And, of course, like people seeking political power in all places at all times, individual, self-promoting politicians wanted to be able to be publicly identified as promoting DOING SOMETHING supposedly in the national interest – and using taxpayers' money to pay for their self-promotion.

In this regard, it was obvious that, particularly after the Louisiana Purchase, this is a very large nation, with a compelling national, commercial interest in facilitating the transportation of goods and people throughout its territory.

The history of, and the Constitutional and political debates concerning, the question of "internal improvements" financed by the federal government is discussed above in Chapter 11.

As anyone with any understanding of what happens when the state/government gets involved in "assisting" or "funding" any private commercial activities, for the reasons discussed in Chapter 4 above, its mere presence in all attendant transactions spreads corruption, incompetence and, inevitably, business disasters at some point. All these occurred in connection with all the "internal improvements" and, most notoriously, in the building of railroads throughout the United States – and in the corrupt cronyism which federal funding of the railroads injected into the economy for the first time.

## The Very Beginnings of Our Modern Political Parties

By the 1850s, the Democrat party had cemented its role primarily as the only party explicitly supporting continued slavery in the South. Otherwise, it had nothing else we would recognize as a real animating ideology. Outside the South, It operated primarily as a local-government patronage machine, a role it has never relinquished. In that regard, wherever it had the political clout to do so, it unabashedly employed the "spoils system" – as all American parties similarly did to the extent they could, during and after the presidency of Andrew Jackson who formally initiated that practice.

Briefly, the "spoils system" consisted of making sure all appointed government positions, at all levels of government, were used as patronage booty, staffed exclusively by loyal party members – and unashamedly removing any such officials whose loyalty to the controlling political party following any election was less than complete. Although celebrated by partisans (such as Arthur Schlesinger Jr.) as a vehicle for ensuring "efficient operation" of government bureaucracy, it was also – if not primarily – a corrupt use of political power and public assets to foster party loyalty – and, to the extent possible, to use state (violence) power against "enemies."

This system of institutionalized venality was happily followed by the Whig party, and, later, the Republican Party, which emerged in the 1850s. The Whig party had a brief life, beginning in the 1830s, including politicians with a wide variety of views – including Abraham Lincoln. Its only unifying principle was opposition to Andrew Jackson in all respects, a principle whose utility obviously became less and less relevant after the Jackson presidency ended.

All American political parties promoted "internal improvements" – with the corrupt patronage opportunities they presented for their own partisans – throughout the 19th century, with the notable, individual exceptions of the three Democrat-Republican presidents Madison, Monroe and Jackson. Although substantial sums were indeed spent on the building of roads and bridges and canals in that regard, Monroe's prohibition on any other Federal involvement (ownership, management or direction) in such programs beyond such funding alone was, in fact, adhered to – until 1887.

In the 1850s, however, the Republican Party emerged with an animating ideological vision — opposition to any spread of slavery in the Republic. Once it was successful not only in that initial, limited opposition to slavery, but in ending it for all time in the Republic through its President Lincoln in the Civil War, it too took up the cause of patronage/corruption to fund its activities and fueled the power – and, yes, the personal finances – of its politicians in a manner functionally indistinguishable from the patronage corruption of the Democrat party and, indeed, it arguably brought federal political cronyism/corruption to new heights, initially through the involvement of its politicians in the crony capitalism/socialism of the federal-funding of the railroad business, which began in 1862 – yes, while the Civil War raged all around it.

## The Railroads

Everyone recognized almost immediately after the invention became known that the railroad was so transformative and revolutionary an invention that it literally changed the nature of life in America by untold orders of magnitude: it provided the first and, at the time, only means safely to transport people, raw materials and finished products rapidly and over distances throughout the Republic at a cost and with capability previously inconceivable. Its power to move troops and the tools of war – cannons etc. – could transform the Union's prosecution of the Civil War itself.

That was the immediate rationale of Pres. Lincoln and the Congress for providing funding for the particular private businesses that were involved in building the railroads. Lincoln viewed completing railroads throughout the nation as a multi-faceted, strategic boon – including projecting railroads into prospective Civil War battlefields, and connecting California with New York, and so thereby make the vast size of the nation an asset, instead of a threatening obstacle to its political and economic progress, as it had been before. Thus, building out the tracks on which the railroads run as rapidly as possible – literally racing to do so – became a national imperative, which only the private businesses could accomplish.

Destroying the railroads the Confederacy had built, for similar military-strategic reasons, in the South was also a major, and successfully-completed, strategic objective of the Union Army during the Civil War. Continued Union promises to rebuild them after the end of the Civil War were never honored. Although space here does not permit a full and fair discussion of Reconstruction, that failure by the nation was a continuing source of animosity after the War, and a major reason for the continuing poverty in much of the South long after the War was over.

Lincoln had never been a small government politician in the mold of Jefferson and Madison. Prior to joining the Republican party at its founding, he had been a Whig – and an outspoken advocate of using federal funds for "internal improve-ments." Prior to the building of the railroads, the nature of those "improvements" – roads, bridges and canals owned and operated primarily by local governments – and never by the federal government, consistent with Monroe's position – arguably always served a genuine public benefit, with minimal risk of creating private windfalls.

Nevertheless, as Madison, Monroe and Jackson explicitly recognized, federal in-volvement in funding alone presented enormous risks of corruption.

The funding the federal government provided the railroad construction com-panies during and after the Civil War consisted of two elements over time – loans and, more importantly, grants of literally miles of federal-owned land on all sides of all finished track they laid down. The presence of the railroad track itself multiplied the value of the land many times, since proximity to the railroad and its stations was of critical importance to the cities and towns which grew up around it.

It is apparent that these methods of funding the railroad construction by the federal government could easily be rationalized by the politicians who approved them based on a multitude of practical and legal considerations. From a legal/Constitutional point of view, this funding was in all respects consistent with the views expressed by Pres. Monroe in 1822: specifically, the federal government provided nothing but purely-financial support for the railroad construction and took no ownership interest, nor any control, over the railroads themselves, which were exclusively owned and operated by private businesses. And mere, previously-useless land, and not money (except for loans) was given out.

From a practical point of view, in the 1860s and 1870s when this construction was proceeding, American capital markets were barely in their infancy compared to today and the only real source of financing for business was banks whose capitalization was minuscule compared to what became the norm later in our history. Aside from the current-operating cash provided to the railroad construction companies in the form of loans, the federal contribution of land – by far its most valuable contribution to the effort – principally provided collateral for additional funding which might otherwise have been difficult to obtain.

Rapid completion of the railroad track during the Civil War was viewed as a clear militarily-required imperative, justifiable for that reason alone. Once that process was set in motion during the War, no rationale was presented for terminating it after the War's successful completion, particularly in light of the virtually-endless amount of land the government owned which otherwise would be of little value without the railroad to link it to the nation, and in consideration of the mind-boggling benefits to the economy of the railroads once they were in operation.

It is no exaggeration to say that from the time when it was first introduced on the scene, the railroad became the nation's overwhelmingly-primary means of transporting everything. It replaced wooden carts drawn by horses and oxen – literally bringing transportation from 9th-century technology to that of the 19th century overnight. It made entire industries – such as the steel industry – and the mass production of products, possible for the first time ever. It made travel by citizens from coast-to-coast a safe, relatively inexpensive and rapid reality – instead of, as had been the case, traversing the vast country perilously using technology (wooden, ox or horse-drawn carts) unchanged since the Middle Ages.

Once all the transcontinental railroads were completed, the amount of land, previously owned by the federal government, acquired by the railroad owners was so enormous that it consisted of roughly 10% of the total land of today's United States.

Needless to say, with the enormous amounts of land they received in that manner, the railroad owners mostly (other than the notorious Credit Mobilier scandal) had no problem repaying the loans the federal government had extended to them initially to fund the railroads' construction, simply by selling tiny amounts of the land they acquired — from the government. Genuinely vast fortunes were acquired by the railroad owners in this manner, independent of the railroads' profitability and, since they did so because of well-known federal largess, their entire industry came into the crosshairs of politicians, and American Collectivists of all stripes, including the press and the self-identified "intelligentsia."

In the 1870s, journalists, including Mark Twain, wrote widely-circulated, devastating supposed "expositions" of the corruption of the railroad business and politicians it owned, including blaming that business for the lengthy quasi-depression/bust during that time, which in fact had many sources.

But simultaneously, the public benefited from the railroads' services enormously – services which prior to its construction <u>simply did not exist.</u> Traveling from the east to the West Coast not only had become possible, it was relatively easy – compared to the incredible hazards citizens attempting to travel into the Louisiana Purchase lands, and lands acquired after the end of the Mexican war in 1848, had previously had to endure. Previously, such travel was genuinely life-threatening; with the railroads constructed, danger was largely eliminated (except for the very rare train robberies), and actual luxury was available for those who could afford it incident to the railroad travel.

But the very visible success of the railroad industry, made possible both by the acumen of its owners in constructing, and successfully operating, the railroads and the extraordinary ease they had in obtaining their financing from the federal government, ended up producing enormously wealthy industrialists whose government-funding made them easy to smear by journalists as supposedly uniquely corrupt. And that fueled national cynicism about them and their ability – which was genuine – to purchase influence and power in Washington from politicians they funded and corrupted, both personally and politically – making possible highly publicized caricatures of such business cronies mirroring the caricatures of all businessmen of antibusiness/anti-property Marxists so prevalent among all the political battles in Europe, especially after the 1840s, and among the intelligentsia and journalists in America, who overwhelmingly became enamored with the ideas of Karl Marx, as discussed below.

There were also notorious railroad bankruptcies and scandals (e.g. Credit Mobiler) particularly during the Grant administration. And, as always, wealthy businessman were the invariable targets of Marxist cartoonists memorably caricaturing them – and vilifying them (with the invariable picture of fat bodies in tuxedos wearing spats smoking cigars with money bags for heads).

It is an inherent fact of democracies and republics: the more important to the people a particular business, or entire business sector, becomes, the more politicians desire to claim power over it — if they are allowed to – to direct its pricing, its employment policies, and even the details of its particular operations. By the 1870s, legislation was proposed in several states, though not yet in Congress, to establish "regulatory" agencies to do precisely that with the railroad industry – exactly as was being done with all the businesses in Europe, as had been the case with all businesses in France since the time of Louis XIV. In the 1870s these clearly-unconstitutional state-level efforts were voted down.

But by 1887, the entire Democratic Party, which was the only party in elected offices in the South after the end of Reconstruction — the same South where resentment for Reconstruction itself and the continued failure of the nation to rebuild the railroads destroyed in the Civil War remained open wounds — avidly pushed for such "regulation." And there simply no longer was any genuine opposition to it – anywhere, from any political party, nor even (at least in public) from the businesses to be regulated; and the process began in the pattern that was to become familiar – and identical – in every business to be so targeted for federal "regulation" by politicians again.

First, a few words about the passivity of the businesses to be regulated – in this case the railroads – and their apparent willingness for the process to continue: Once the "regulatory" process is initiated against them by politicians, businesses who are its intended targets have to decide whether it is worth the risks to oppose the process, or to permit it to happen and try to take advantage of the fact that the regulation inevitably creates impassable barriers for new would-be competitors to surmount.

In short, the presence of "regulation" over a business sector guarantees that the only businesses left in that market sector will be incumbents, large enough to absorb the costs and difficulties of coexisting with the regulation, who will inevitably become a monopoly/oligopoly, also because of the presence of that regulation.

In the case of the railroads in the 19th century, their owners had already made so much money that they were confident they could control the politicians and bureaucrats who intended to take command over them. And that was indeed the case. Unfortunately, their maneuvering to deal with the situation – by paying tribute to the politicians to purchase them – was a virtually open secret, so that the image of corruption in the entire industry increased, rather than decreased, after regulation commenced.

The regulations themselves, as always, failed to achieve any of the promises to the public which were trumpeted for them by the politicians at their outset.

In short, no one really benefited from the entire process — other than the politicians and bureaucrats, and the lawyers whose services became critical as intermediaries between the railroads and the bureaucrats. Most of the politicians involved in the corruption of the railroads, and other businesses, were Republicans, and extracting tribute from businesses, while pretending to benefit them, was the particular brand of corruption the Republican Party specialized in for the rest of the 19th century, just as the Democratic Party specialized in corruptly enlisting the loyalty of gangs and poor immigrants, and eventually the unions, in America's large cities who, along with the Ku Klux Klan in the South and the Midwest, became the Democrats' foot soldiers in their quasi-criminal and real criminal political machines in those cities.

As always, the politicians began the "regulatory" process by claiming – with the noisy incitement and/or approval of journalists, including Karl Marx himself and Mark Twain, coupled, in the case of the railroads, with a "populist" movement drummed up by Marxist agitators among agricultural constituencies claiming they were being priced unfairly by the railroads relative to other customers – that the targeted business sector – the entire railroad industry – had experienced a "market failure" absolutely requiring the federal government to impose itself.

Politicians claimed, as always, that they could "solve" the "problem" and "rationalize" the supposedly-faulty market, and would do so by setting up a government agency to "regulate" the business sector involved, manned by "experts" who would operate in a wholly "nonpartisan" and "scientific" manner.

Of course none of what they promised was true – or even possible. Or Constitutional – an issue that was not even discussed in connection with the regulation of railroads in 1887, even though all Americans were well aware that it was the clear unconstitutionality of that federal action which had prevented politicians from imposing it ever previously on any other business.

Federal involvement guaranteed ongoing, continuing political manipulation since the "regulators" had their own interests which they would follow, and they had no choice but to answer to the politicians in order to keep their jobs – to say nothing of minimizing the risk of devastating humiliation from any "error" they were guaranteed to commit, and, after World War II, being publicly vilified on TV in congressional hearings. And there are no "experts".

Over a period of nearly 100 years, literally hundreds of thousands of government employees – all paid by the taxpayers – were involved in one ICC bureaucratic regulatory scheme after another to manipulate the prices of the railroads, none of which resulted in prices coming down for anyone, indeed none of which provided any benefit to anyone other than the parasites – there is no other word for them.

The interstate Commerce Commission which Congress created – the first of all the federal alphabet regulatory agencies – literally did nothing but ruin the railroad industry for 100 years to the point that even Jimmy Carter realized the disaster that had been created and proposed legislation which was eventually enacted in 1995 substantially to eliminate the regulations – although not federal involvement in the railroad industry, the entire passenger portion of which had been utterly ruined by the federal involvement, which survives to this day in the form of the taxpayer-funded boondoggle known as Amtrak.

The federal "regulatory" process necessarily takes the business away from its customers and owners, deliberately destroying its actual market, and turns it over to the politicians and bureaucrats and other parasites. That is not a a bug, but rather a feature of the process – its intended results.

Typically the politicians and regulators proposing federal takeover promise particular customers that they will enjoy some special benefit from all this – a benefit which never, in fact, materializes, but which is the political pretext for the government take-over of the entire industry in the first place.

This is precisely what has occurred most recently in connection with the Obama administration forcing the hands of the Federal Communication Commission to impose regulatory power over the Internet, power virtually identical – and, indeed, based on the Interstate Commerce Act which created the ICC – to what the railroads were subjected to – until Jimmy Carter! A recent book – *American Railroads*, By Robert E. Gallamore and John R.Meyer catalogs 100 years of regulatory disaster for the railroad industry caused by the federal government's destructive "regulation" of it.

Once the federal regulatory power is instituted, the following is guaranteed: No new competitors can or will enter the now-regulated business, and all innovation in its product and/or service will come to an end. The incumbent businesses who dominate prior to regulation effectively become state-directed "utilities" – businesses that do what they are told and provide employment for the armies of "regulators" for whom employment is created, lawyers and lobbyists who become essential representatives of the owner to intercede with the "regulators." Real economic growth incident to the entire industry – which growth usually was huge prior to its "regulation" because of the dynamism of the industry the government seeks to seize power over – comes to a screeching halt.

The very importance of the seized business to the public – which attracted the interest of the politicians and journalists in the first place – guarantees that it cannot be allowed by the politicians and "regulators" to wholly cease to exist. But all progress in that business – and any contemplated price reductions become impossible. The business cannot die – and it also cannot prosper or improve or permit new competitors.

A business cannot be only partly "regulated" by the state. Doing so to any extent is guaranteed to ruin its entire market for everyone who actually should matter – its customers, present owners, and (now-precluded) future competitors. And all of the costs for salaries etc. for all of the utterly-nonproductive functionaries inevitably, ultimately must be borne by the customers – who must inevitably pay more than they had prior to all the "regulation" in the first place, for a product or service whose quality inevitably stagnates or declines because of the increased built-in costs of regulatory compliance, none of which can possibly add to the value of what the purchaser gets.

Expecting any outcome from all this process other than the disaster that always occurs is itself a form of madness. And yet, because of the political pressures that guarantee that all this will occur precisely as just described, the only way to prevent it is to outlaw politicians from doing this at all.

Which is precisely what our founders thought they were doing in the Constitution by precluding any federal power over citizens or their businesses other than to prevent interference with them by the states. Additionally, as I have also shown above, any claim that the "regulation" of the business is not the theft of the ultimate management of that business is facially nonsensical. And the stealing of that business' management and direction from its owners is a direct violation of the commandment "thou shalt not steal." And, of course, the theft is always facilitated by "false witness" fraudulent claims of the benefits that will follow the "regulation", and demagogic incitements of the forbidden emotion envy from the politicians and parasites demanding the "regulation."

# BOOK PART FOUR:

## THE AMERICAN COUNTERREVOLUTION

# CHAPTER 13

## The Second American Civil War — an Overview

America has endured not one, but rather <u>two each</u> of revolutions and civil wars.

The first of each revolution and Civil War were armed, military conflicts, with Americans fighting other Americans (plus, primarily, British and Hessian soldiers in the Revolution) on both sides. Each such conflict ended in the complete victory of one, ideologically-driven side— and the clear defeat of the other.

In the following pages I describe the true nature of, and the main events in the progress of our second Civil War – the phenomenon which I have characterized as our Counterrevolution.

Although the formal, legal institutionalization of that Counterrevolution has produced enormous, radical changes in the laws of the nation which, in turn, have required political forces, and individual political actors, in all three branches of the federal government, to be effected, our Counterrevolution has strongly resembled its direct, lineal ancestor, the French Revolution, in that it has never been simply a political/legal event, but rather has progressed by permeating multiple aspects and elements of American society.

Indeed, all its legal conquests have depended for their success on victories first achieved elsewhere in society, which victories have won over, by various means, various constituencies within society which constituencies have, in turn, often without realizing it, advanced the Counterrevolution's agenda politically – and with legal effect.

The Counterrevolution has achieved its victories because it has always had a clear policy and strategy behind it – and has never faced any genuine, organized strategic opposition.

Moreover, since 1912 at the latest, the Counterrevolution has been actively promoted by a major American political party – the Democrat party – and its multitude of members/supporters populating all three branches of government, including particularly the multiple federal "regulatory" agencies created as essential components of, and foot soldiers in, the Counterrevolution. And no major political party, including the Republican Party, has ever seriously opposed it with more than lip service.

The Counterrevolution's policy can be simply stated: to <u>completely transform</u> America, its business environment (which has always been America's heart and soul and, together with belief in God and morality, the source of all the nation's truly-exceptional growth, energy and promise, and its peoples' strength), and Americans' minds themselves, from a nation in which equal justice and the rule of Good Law, individual liberty, achievement and merit are prized above all else, and property rights are recognized as the most fundamental right of all, into a mirror-image of all major, continental European nations, including France since Louis XIV. It has been an effort, quite simply, to impose the French Revolution and its Bad Law on us, and completely to undo and upend our own profoundly-different revolution – and the Constitution itself – without even straightforwardly proposing any Constitutional amendment to legitimize its policies under the exclusive provisions for amendment in its Article V.

Like all collectivist revolutions, as described above, our Counterrevolution has viewed genuine belief in God, all Western religion, and all private property rights with contempt, whereas the American Revolution recognizes, and is based on, understanding their paramount importance to all individual liberty, with preservation and protection of individual liberty, including property/contract rights, being the American Revolution's single, paramount goal.

The reason for this is simple to state: our founders clearly understood that the strength and substantiality of all rights depends both on that belief in God and the strength of property rights. No one can be free without possessing inviolable property. Having no property of his own is the fundamental feature of a serf or slave.

And if the property rights of <u>any</u> citizen – or his business – are less than sacrosanct, <u>all</u> property rights of <u>all</u> citizens are necessarily harmed and under assault by the state whose paramount purpose should be to protect them.

Consequently, property rights are, in the10 Commandments themselves, as shown above in chapter 2, designated by God Himself to be sacred, and ordered therein to be protected from loss or abridgment for any free citizen except, under Good Law, as the result of his actual, harmful misconduct, adjudicated in a fair court, administering genuinely-blind justice, to have been a violation of the Common-Law (Good Law).

Anything short of those strong property rights for everyone turns a previously-free nation whose government is subservient to the people <u>into its very opposite</u>: a nation whose people are ruled by their government — and its individual officeholders — with precisely the kind of absolute control over all aspects of its subjects' lives – initially, all details of the conduct of businesses with their customers and employees, and eventually everything – which is exactly what has prevailed throughout continental Europe under all political regimes there since the time of Louis XIV in France. And that abomination is <u>precisely</u> what our Counterrevolution and its supporters have strived mightily to impose on us since the late 19th century.

Under the regime the Counterrevolutionaries have sought to impose here, literally turning our own original Revolution on its head, property rights are weak, and virtually nonexistent, subject to politicians' directives and whims: nobody owns anything, except at the sufferance of the state – and its functionaries; everyone and all his assets are reduced to abject subjects of the state and its functionaries, instead of being citizens whom the state is required to serve, as our founders intended for America.

And the influence, and even the mere presence, of the state and its officeholders of all kinds, with the implicit power of violence they always wield, corrupt and poison and weaken all aspects of the nation and its society they choose to "regulate." Moreover, the nature of all the "regulatory" agencies created is that they never recognize any limit on their power and jurisdiction — except to the extent that they are physically stopped and forced to do so by other, countervailing political (violence) power.

And those under its thumb are powerless to even explain their true plight to the rest of society without fear of destruction at the hands of their "regulatory" masters. Yes, it's that pernicious. Freedom of speech for them? Nonexistent.

American politicians, since early in the 19th century, well-aware – and jealous – of the power, and opportunities for using their offices to further empower and enrich themselves which they well knew was wielded by their European counterparts, have strived mightily to duplicate that state power which they could use to their own advantage – all the while proclaiming themselves dedicated public servants with nothing but the good of the Republic in mind.

They have brazenly wielded the most dangerous – and Constitutionally-forbidden, as shown above – political power, pretending to be providing "benefits" or "services" to citizens, and always blaming the "regulated" businesses for all (the inevitable) failures, followed by demanding more state power over them.

Our Constitution, which resulted directly from our victory in our real Revolution, unambiguously established, in legally-binding writing, Good Law (as discussed in chapter 5), legally precluding impermissible expansions of power by the state and any taking by it of any private property (or any rights incident to such ownership) except pursuant to due process of law, and with fair compensation to the owner for any property taken.

Judicially-adjudicated legal misconduct by a property's owner, was the <u>only</u> permissible, legal basis for taking that property in this nation – the first time in world history any nation had provided such property-protection in a written constitution – and that Constitution contained clear, explicit substantive and procedural limitations on the federal government it created <u>and on its officeholders</u> designed to preclude enactment of Bad Law (also as described in chapter 5) anywhere in the nation, including in any of the states.

Our first Civil War, together with the 3 Constitutional amendments enacted after its completion, extended the Good Law guarantees of the Constitution *de jure* (although they were violated de facto throughout the nation for many decades, based on a number of corrupt Supreme Court rulings) to the few remaining Americans to whom such Good Law had previously been denied – the black former slaves emancipated by that war.

The armed, military portion of that first Civil War lasted less than five years and began nearly 80 years after the first Revolution ended. The active military portion of the first Revolution took longer, but was less than 8 years, by any date picked for when it began.

The second American Revolution and Civil War (together, the "Counterrevolution") have, unlike the first ones, occurred <u>simultaneously with each other</u>, with no military engagement whatsoever, and no material political opposition prior to each "victory" which <u>one side – the Counterrevolutionaries – alone</u> has, so far, notched along the way – but nevertheless <u>remain ongoing and far from resolved</u> politically/ideologically today.

Specifically, the Counterrevolution has consisted of ongoing efforts to impose Bad Law, in clear violation of the Constitution, on one market after another in America. It has literally been a war waged throughout all of our institutions culturally and, legally/politically, on paper and in briefcases, contained in numerous pieces of federal legislation or, in some cases, mere presidential orders, each which enactment had the identical effect of first unconstitutionally creating, then expanding, often dramatically, the police power of the federal government over the citizenry.

Each and every one of such legislative enactments remain highly-vulnerable and subject to repeal — or judicial elimination as unconstitutional — at any time. Although each of these federal power expansions have their own, often very narrow and publicly-secretive, constituencies continuing to support them, actual, popular support for the edifice as a whole remains far from certain and, indeed, highly doubtful.

Moreover, only one single legal creation of the entire Counterrevolution has achieved genuine legitimacy under a constitutional amendment permitting it – the federal income tax.The rest is all completely unconstitutional, as shown above in chapters 8 and 11.

Although all three branches of the federal government have been pretending that the rest of that Counterrevolutionary edifice complies with the Constitution, as shown above in chapter 6, all their arguments for such claim would have been recognized as patently frivolous nonsense for the first 100 years of the Republic.

<u>Nothing</u> in the Constitution permits its amendment unless its mandatory procedures in its Article V thereof for doing so have been followed – as has only been the case concerning the federal income tax – and <u>none</u> of the rest of the Counterrevolution's enactments (since the amendments creating, and then repealing, alcohol Prohibition – whose creation was another product of the Counterrevolution) have any Constitutional legitimacy whatsoever. The courts, American lawyers and all other "experts"supporting it and pretending otherwise have literally been "Big Liars."

The ongoing second American Revolution/Civil War have/had numerous other significant differences from their predecessor events, including the following:

(1)  Our second Revolution/Civil War, that is, our <u>Counterrevolution</u>, has been a transplant to America of the radical-egalitarian Collectivist revolution which has been ongoing in France since it began there in the early 1790s, waged (often unconscious of its true ideological dimensions and pedigree – and implications – by its American proponents) against the very ideological and legal victory for citizens' individual liberty against central state power (always a zero-sum struggle) achieved <u>in our first Revolution</u>, and its institutional, legal embodiment in our Constitution.

(2)  Unlike its predecessors, the Counterrevolution has been proceeding very gradually and incrementally — and, indeed, stealthily, its true ideological nature and direction consistently masked, and its patent unconstitutionality cavalierly disregarded by its proponents – since the mid-19th century.

(3)  The Counterrevolution's major, active revolutionaries/proponents have consisted of all three, Constitutionally-created-and-limited branches of the federal government <u>and their individual officeholders</u> who, in their Counterrevolution, joined together as a de facto "faction", precisely as feared by Madison in Federalist No.47, to expand their power (and wealth) at the expense of all the citizens' freedoms, in multiple, direct assaults on the property rights, rights on which, as our Founders knew, <u>all</u> other rights depend- of the American people.

(4)  This Counterrevolution has, all along, been proceeding with virtually no material opposition from any organized political party, notwithstanding its multiple violations of the Constitution, and the invariably harmful effects on both freedom and economic growth of each "victory" it has notched – and, when properly understood, its inherently anti-American Revolutionary nature. Politicians promoting each of its "advances" along the way have drawn on often massive, propagandistic, and purportedly-"intellectual", assistance and backing from other, non-state quarters of society – the so-called "professions" who, as shown in the next chapter, had huge, self-interested, institutional reasons to promote collectivism. By "professions," I'm referring to the worlds of journalism, mass media and entertainment, universities and other educational institutions, all organized political parties, labor unions,

and even the most prominent organized religions in America, and even businesses (by choice or coercion) affected directly by each such "advance." All those "professions'" power, prestige and wealth have grown with each such expansion – exactly as in absolutist France under both the Bourbons and Napoleon — at the (largely hidden) expense of all citizens..

(5) Each incremental development in the course of the Counterrevolution has, at the time of its legal enactment, by various means, managed to command significant, if not always overwhelming, popular support – often obtained in large part by what amounts to trickery, by finessing its unconstitutionality, both in Congress and the federal courts, and by masking, if not actively concealing, the overall direction and underlying ideology of the Counterrevolution, and the strategic role played by each such enactment in actively advancing it.

(6) The American people themselves have never been given the chance directly and explicitly to express their approval or disapproval of the Counterrevolution itself; its ultimate, logical effect, if it continues unopposed, and until repealed, increasingly imprisons Americans in a Napoleonic-type (its actual original model), absolute state dictatorship.

In fact, I am confident that once, for the first time ever, the Counterrevolution is clearly, simply and massively exposed in its entirety for the unconstitutional destroyer of the true rule of Good Law, all individual liberties, economic growth and prosperity and, indeed, national solvency which it is, the American people almost certainly would overwhelmingly disapprove it in its entirety if given an up or down voting opportunity regarding the entire, Counterrevolutionary edifice that has been built.

Each of its incremental governmental "victories," again, arose with no material opposition, based on a combination of corrupt arrangements among politicians and various purportedly non-political actors supporting each such development. Such support, in turn, arose either out of genuine, ideological agreement with the Counterrevolution's overall collectivist goals and their supposed virtues generally, or some corrupt, private benefits anticipated by them out of the particular proposed enactment they supported – invariably at other citizens' expense – or, as has also often been the case, out of fear of retribution or other adverse consequences if they refused to go along with the particular proposed enactment – and with ostensibly "popular", political support almost always based on completely fraudulent representations to the public of what was being built, its unconstitutionality – and why.

The Counterrevolution has been a collectivist one, and the Collective's methods for winning over Americans have followed the same pattern as elsewhere. With one big difference: in America, where the nation is both overwhelmingly Christian, and was founded on a set of beliefs diametrically antithetical to those of the European Collectivists, although American Collectivists – particularly their leaders – are constantly engaged in attempting to promote the Cause, they have rarely been overt in promoting clearly political issues forthrightly.

Woodrow Wilson, while still an academic, before his presidency, wrote extensively on his desire to undo the Constitution to permit the federal government to completely take over all American businesses through the use of law and bureaucracy, and so force them to conduct all their activities only with the approval and permission of "expert" government functionaries who would be answerable only to politicians.However, he was virtually alone among American collectivist major party politicians in honestly disclosing those intentions publicly.

And, like all Collectivists, Wilson did not debate these points; he simply described — in the 1880's — what he wanted to do – no discussion necessary. But he was truly unique among American Collectivist politicians in the honesty and forthrightness of those "academic" writings – an honesty which did not continue in his national political life when running for, and winning, the presidency.

The most common approach adopted by American Collectivists to promote the Cause has been to promote so-called "movements" of various kinds, each of which purport to promote one or more particular issues – often with the claims that there is nothing political about the Movement, and that it is simply intent on securing a supposedly-unquestionable, morally-compelling "good." There have been numerous such Movements since the beginning of the 20th century, the most important of which are discussed in detail in chapters 14, 16 and 17.

The following few paragraphs provides a thumbnail sketch of several of them:

Some claim to be "civil rights"-type movements – especially after all public and private racial discrimination was declared illegal in federal legislation in the mid-1960s – supposedly promoting the "liberation" of one "victimized" group or another (such groups have included supposedly "pro-woman" groups promoting the "right" of women to terminate the life of any fetus they are carrying, up through the moment of birth – and even thereafter, if they attempt to abort it and it survives); some claim to promote "peace" – almost invariably in the form of promoting unilateral American disarmament, surrender or retreat against an enemy, never demanding any similar disarmament or retreat from any American enemy, including the former USSR when it existed; more recently, many have claimed to promote the "environment," or "consumers."

These movements are always based on the fraudulent (usually unspoken) presumptions that America is uniquely evil and unjust to its own people, and uniquely bellicose and enslaving, through its military, outside the nation. Many such Movements have been intent on providing justification for confiscating property owned by others – either federal control of corporations or simply of the use of land, to prevent its serving as a productive source of oil and gas and/ or minerals, forests, etc.

All such antibusiness movements – of the "consumer" and "environment" sorts – have had, as their clear objective, compelling the federal government to take over complete control of significant parts of the economy and land to prevent people from buying or selling goods and or services others want from them.

Thus, in the name of "helping" consumers, advocates of this nature demand that consumers be <u>forbidden</u> from buying various goods and services – and that the companies that provide them be forced to eliminate those they provide, or do so only according to specifications – specifications which often are remarkably detailed – provided by such Movement advocates/radicals to the federal government's "regulatory" agencies and their controlling bureaucrats for them to enact into "law" and use the power of the government violence and its criminal laws to enforce.

## <u>The History of Collectivism in America – its Proselytizing/ Evangelizing Efforts Over the Years</u>

Since its beginnings in revolutionary France, Collectivism, in all its various versions, in every country in which it has materialized, has operated in all respects like an organized religion – a quasi-church, if you will – complete with a passionately-devoted body of followers/true believers, a quasi-priesthood of leaders/ preachers, a quasi-catechism of core beliefs, a number of its own version of virtually-sacrosanct quasi-virtues/principles, events and institutions, and its own brand of what could be called outreach/evangelizing/conversion efforts.

It simultaneously, also invariably differs from any normal religion in many ways —

(1) the particular emotions it always seeks to incite (hatred, envy and resentment by groups of citizens against other groups, guilt for believing in the importance and value of individual accomplishment — instead of love)

(2) the fact that God- and individual soul-denying atheism/anti-Christianity is one of its also-invariable core beliefs; and

(3) in always seeing itself as an embattled nation, experiencing itself always as facing determined, existentially-powerful enemies both from within and without whatever spheres (geographical or otherwise) it otherwise controls – enemies who the Collective is determined to silence and/or even extinguish, both terrified of its own vulnerability if it fails to do so, and also seeking to extend its influence and control transnationally, beyond any borders.

Although each self-identified Collective (whether it be a controlling group within a single nation, as in the case of revolutionary France, a labor union, or a combination of multiple nations, like the expansion of the French Revolution throughout continental Europe under Napoleon, or the former USSR) always sees itself as a political presence and force, its efforts to convert "non-believers" to the Cause almost never involve what could be called issue advocacy – that is, attempts to raise and discuss issues for public debate for purposes of intellectually proving the merits of its position on issues — at least not the issues the collective truly cares about.

Instead, Collectivists invariably simply announce their positions on particular issues and demand agreement from all, always insisting that any disagreement with them is, and all who disagree with them are, morally reprehensible and beyond the pale. A consistent feature of all revolutionary Collectives and Collectivists is that they invariably presume and act as if their views on all subjects are in fact universally held – without regard to whether that is the case. When multiple media voices – or even mere mobs – echo and amplify the Collectives' positions, the Collective is able to project the image of such universal acceptance, which can be profoundly intimidating to all who are not believers in the Cause.

The existence of the Collective and the sense of "community" and unanimity it strives to present provides a centripetal force exerted on those who come within its orbit and influence. Similarly, the sense of unanimity and the emotional attractiveness for its members of feeling that they belong to the revolutionary Cause which Collectives invariably are able to project provide a centrifugal force as well. Eric Hoffer described this phenomenon brilliantly in his discussions of what he called Mass Movements.

Collectivists do not debate (except on purely tactical matters, and do so exclusively within the collective itself)– and have no interest whatsoever in doing so. To the extent that they even try, through argument, to convince others, they make whatever claims they deem necessary (which, because of the absolute imperative of bringing all others into the Collective, can literally include anything, including outright lies, fraud and threats) to excite agreement/acquiescence, together with some emotional response – guilt, anger, envy/resentment – from whomever they are attempting to convince.

If, after those efforts, anyone continues to disagree with them, the Collective has zero tolerance for that disagreement, and uses whatever methods are available to silence, utterly discredit, and destroy the lives of those who disagree.

The Collective's conquest and continuing, emotional hold over its members derives from a multitude of paradoxes: on the one hand, it explicitly denies the importance of any individual relative to the group. Collective members flatter themselves with the notion that that preference for the group over the individual is virtuous – what they flatter themselves by calling "compassion" or "altruism" – the virtues which, incidentally, they invariably claim to prize above all others.

On the other hand, the Collective only exists to the extent it can win over the loyalty of actual people — i.e., individuals – a loyalty it achieves by preying on their needs, both material and emotional (including their need to expiate guilt). Because the individual is always vulnerable.

The Collective's members are exceptional primarily in their simultaneous solipsism and their guilt regarding what they call – particularly in others they observe – "selfishness": they are individuals who deny the existence of God, rejoice in the superiority they feel arising from that denial, are invariably overwhelmed with self-absorption who, nevertheless, feel guilty about that fact (which they are aware of, but pretend not to notice), and who experience the Collective's undeniable valuing of the community over the individual as a kind of virtuous redemption from the guilt they experience about their own self-absorption.

They are blind, or utterly indifferent, to the zero-sum nature of the Collective's preference for itself over any individual – the fact, that is, that that preference repudiates any real value that each of them, as an individual, possesses, except as a drone/slave functionary serving the Collective's directives.

## The French Revolution and Our Counterrevolution

Since the beginning of its takeover by the Jacobins in the original (the French themselves count six national reinventions of it so far) French Revolution, the inherently transnational, radical-egalitarian, collectivist revolution it and its eventual champion, Napoleon Bonaparte, originally spawned, has been metastasizing, in various forms in different nations, through its various communities of supporters in each such nation, <u>wherever it is not actively and consciously opposed</u>.

All along, absolutely integral to the French Revolution's promise and appeal, it has been promising "liberty" – along with equality and fraternity.

But its definition of "liberty" as a concept, as discussed above, bears <u>no</u> resemblance to the individual liberty from state power fought for and secured in the American Revolution. Indeed, it makes no sense as a concept of "liberty" at all except within the upside-down world dictated by the angrily anti-Christian, radical-egalitarian collectivism preached by Rousseau – in which absolute, total obedience to the collective's/state's directives and, as importantly, its underlying belief system, is demanded – of all citizens, who are all necessarily true believers in the Cause, and not just by the state's rulers – and <u>individual</u> liberty from state control is necessarily smothered and precluded – and an always-angry, atheistic <u>anti-</u>religion is followed fanatically.

Again, if you doubt any of this, simply read Rousseau; or save yourself the trouble and review the explanation of this paradoxical notion of "liberty" in the quote from Robespierre In chapter 6 above in which he eloquently articulated the essential spirit of his revolution.

That the regime established by the Jacobins in France, and all who sought to imitate them in other countries, including in the United States, was indeed totalitarian by any rational standard is proven by both the total control over all actions of all citizens, and their businesses, which its bureaucratic enforcers exerted, and by its absolute insistence on total loyalty of everyone to the collective Cause of the revolution: "thought crime," as brilliantly described by Orwell in *1984*, has always been the most serious crime of all in such regimes, invariably punishable by the most extreme means available.

Again, if you doubt this, you will see it spelled out in no uncertain terms in that quote from Robespierre – and in the intolerance invariably exhibited by Collectivists everywhere, including in America.

To remind you of what is explained above in my chapter 6: that such a regime could even pretend to be providing "liberty" and/or "liberation", and such be believed by anyone, may seem like sheer madness of all involved. But as we have seen, for example, throughout the 20th century, the most rigid, murderous Communists, in their invariable doublespeak, typically call themselves "National Liberation Fronts."

But their claims of providing "liberty" for the citizenry always rest on their foundational claim, absolutely accepted by its true believers, that all their bureaucratic directives are based exclusively on the requirements of pure "reason" (as opposed to the Bronze Age, foolish religious superstition they supposedly supplant) and, because the virtue and claimed "compassion" of their collectivist regime is invariably presumed/demanded by them to be considered literally beyond question. Indeed, the (presumed by all attentive to the regime and its propagandists) universal loyalty to the Cause, including the cold-blooded enforcement of such rule of "reason," ostensibly provides an environment for the citizenry in which all obey/conform because all (who remain alive) supposedly agree — and are apparently genuinely happy to do so.

And it is that environment of total conformity to such supposed "reason" and "virtue" which supposedly provides all the "liberty" the citizenry could ever desire.

That is their invariable logic. I'm simply describing exactly what J.J. Rousseau and Robespierre – and Marx, Lenin, Trotsky and Mao later – unambiguously revealed when they were honest about it — honesty being their rarest trait.

Again, the overwhelming power of the state to enforce its will over everything, including each citizen, is itself always seen by the collectivist true believers as a virtue and not a defect at all – a feature, not a bug. It is as if the idea that this total, absolute control could be too radical and genuinely-destructive of actual liberty simply never crossed their mind and, if it did, was immediately rejected out of hand. And that is true for all collectivist revolutions, beginning with the French one, and including our Counterrevolution – at least for its own true believers.

And if you are wondering why I am spending so much time here, and above, on this, I have 2 reasons: (1) although the Collectivism which began with the French Revolution acquired additional features (which themselves never commanded more than minority support in France) a few decades after its beginning, in the writings of Karl Marx, and in the self-described Communist revolutions which, in turn, institutionalized his "teachings," beginning with the Bolshevik revolution in Russia, and which themselves each added their own additional features to the mix, all such additions also retained the features I have been discussing in the original French Revolution as well and, (2), of particular importance in America, often without understanding what they were doing in this regard, this <u>very same</u> Collectivist, totalitarian anti-religion, first institutionalized in the French Revolution, is precisely what American counterrevolutionaries have been working tirelessly to promote, institutionally-establish and, ultimately, force universal compliance with in America, the history of which efforts, and their multiple successes, are described below.

To further explain:

The spreading of that cancer spawned by the French Revolution to America has manifested itself in our second Civil War and Counterrevolution.

In its original, French version, as just indicated, although the French Revolution was not a struggle to impose centrally-directed Bad Law on a people who, as here, <u>otherwise enjoyed individual liberty</u> (the French were already under Bad Law under the Bourbons), in its American manifestation, that is <u>precisely</u> what it has been attempting to do: by attempting to impose the anti-Individual liberty concept of Rousseau and the Jacobins on an American people whose Revolution sought <u>precisely the opposite</u>, it is literally an attempt to <u>undo the victory</u> achieved in the American Revolution, which was a struggle for individual liberty against the tyrannies of a British monarchy which tyrannies were, in fact, trivial impositions compared to those the French have endured under all their tyrannical regimes – before and after their Revolution.

This is why understanding the difference between Bad Law and Good Law is critical to understanding all these revolutionary and counterrevolutionary processes in both France and America: in the French Revolution, the Bourbon Bad Law simply continued with minor modifications, eventually simply renamed the Napoleonic Code. None of those (truly minor) modifications had the effect of increasing individual liberty for any Frenchman.

In the American Revolution, the Good Law which the British in their Common Law and in their series of previous revolutionary upheavals, beginning with the Magna Carta, both had, and were in the process of creating, was both <u>re</u>-enforced, to the extent that the British monarchy was violating it regarding its American colonists in the mid-18th century, and expanded and strengthened, with all the anti-Bad Law protections built in substantively and procedurally in our Constitution which, unlike the British one, was actually written out in a single, simple, easy-to-read document.

<u>A Brief History of America's Collectivist Counterrevolution</u>

Unlike the original French model it seeks to replicate here, which completely took over the entire state and civil society in France virtually overnight, openly and extravagantly flaunting its most radical features for all to see, as graphically shown above in the Chapter 6 Robespierre quote, our American Counterrevolution has proceeded like Carl Sandburg's famous fog "on little cat feet," invariably masking and concealing its presence, strategy and true, ideological nature.

This is not surprising because, as mentioned above also, for the first 100 years of our Republic, no one in American public life seriously contested the genuine fact that our Constitution was utterly inimical to every element needed to legislate any portion of that Collectivist Counterrevolution – notably, each Bad Law element of the ultimately massive expansion of central, federal power needed to replicate it here.

And individual liberty, including particularly property rights— precisely what the Counterrevolution seeks to crush — and the world-unprecedented prosperity which that liberty alone fosters and permits, are what the overwhelming majority of Americans have always prized above all else – and what the immigrants from throughout the world who have been coming here in droves since the nation's founding have sought to find here.

The Counterrevolution's growth in America began in earnest in the 1840s. Perhaps its proponents recognized the hopelessness of the necessity, for it to achieve its collectivist objectives of both (1) eviscerating the clear, well-known meaning of the Constitution, and (2) damaging/eradicating the uniquely-American individualistic spirit. In any event, its proponents did not begin by trying to alter federal law at all – yet. Instead, the Counterrevolution first manifested itself primarily in other, purportedly non-political quarters (an approach to American transformation its collective has continued, even after also expanding into politics and the law) of civil society.

Specifically, it began as an elitist enthusiasm (which, even after it gathered "proletarian" support, it has always remained, notwithstanding its perennial pretense of promoting the "little guy" against supposedly-evil business moguls) among America's self-proclaimed "intellectuals"/*bien pensants* populating American universities, and among certain journalists and others who, for a variety of reasons, felt a kinship with the so-called, continuing, in continental Europe, Enlightenment or "Age of Reason", as it pretentiously proclaimed itself (which had spawned the French Revolution), and its religion-hostile, supposedly-"scientific" and "rational" continental European "intellectual" enthusiasts.

Additionally, as discussed in chapter 14, those particular American Collectivist "Professional" enthusiasts, while pretending to be animated by deep public-spiritedness, have in fact always had significant self-interested reasons for their support of the Counterrevolutionary cause – reasons which grew enormously as the 19th century, with its globally-unprecedented (and unseen in Europe – ever) growth in America of private business wealth and innovation progressed.

The 1840s were themselves, like the rest of the 19th century, a time both of enormous economic growth in America, and a time of enormous revolutionary upheaval in Europe – events well-known in America; and Karl Marx published "The Communist Manifesto" in 1848.

As discussed above, the essence of, and animating force behind, Marx and his writings is their virulent hatred, and unqualified moral (while noisily proclaiming the nonexistence of any God other than the claimed force of History) condemnation of America itself, all private property rights, all private business and, in particular, all businessmen, who he characterized as monstrous thieves profiting solely from raping their customers and employees. During his lifetime, and ever after, he has enjoyed great popularity among America's self-proclaimed "intellectuals," on university faculties and elsewhere, journalists and other writers, as he has similarly those of continental Europe.

His list of revolutionary demands is quoted in Chapter 6 above, and his American acolytes immediately began militating to achieve those of his proposals they considered most possible – particularly his proposal for universal public schools. Thomas Jefferson had expressly written that the federal government <u>could not</u> be involved in any aspect of education without amending the Constitution to permit such, as was well-known. Thus, the Counterrevolutionaries strove to get each of the states to create those public schools.

I do not question the sincerity of America's "intellectual"/Europhile Collectivists in genuinely believing themselves, and those particular aspects of European "civilization," superior to ours. In particular, they have consistently viewed the American Revolution as inherently inferior to the French Revolution.

In part because of the guarantee of free speech they enjoyed in America under our Constitution, they were completely unconcerned by the thought of the state imposing what I call Bad Law constraints on them, or even on "the means of production" – businesses, in particular – perhaps because they themselves have not been in business and so <u>themselves would be unaffected</u> by any such constraints and, indeed, they no doubt have genuinely believed they and the citizens at large – and especially supposed "victim" groups they identified and have purported to advocate for in the proposals they have supported – of the nation would benefit from such constraints on businesses – constraints which have ultimately resulted in businesses' absolute control by the state, just like in France, before and after its Revolution.

Indeed, our Counterrevolutionaries have always explicitly viewed the freedom enjoyed by American businesses in the 19th century as a kind of crude, deficient provincialism, which simply had no place in a civilized nation. The fact that it produced truly amazing benefits for the entire nation somehow never factored into their thoughts. To summarize what that growth consisted of, referring only to post-Civil War, post-slavery, years:

From 1869 to 1879, the US economy grew at an annual rate of 6.8% for NNP (GDP minus capital depreciation) and 4.5% for NNP per capita. The economy repeated this period of growth in the 1880s, in which the wealth of the nation grew at an annual rate of 3.8%, while the GDP was also doubled. Real wages also increased greatly during the 1880s. By the beginning of the 20th century, per capita income and industrial production in the United States led the world, with per capita incomes double that of Germany or France, and 50% higher than Britain.

Our Counterrevolutionaries have similarly been indifferent to the undeniable fact that economies and businesses throughout continental Europe, invariably subjected to government control substantially identical to what they have been tirelessly promoting in America, have consistently been stagnant, corrupt and dependent on innovations produced by American and British businesses for what little growth they have ever achieved, growth which has never come close to that of Britain and America in the 19th century.

That is the reason growth in Britain and America far surpassed that of Germany and France during the 19th century, as described in the previous paragraph, with America's growth exceeding that of Britain since its economy was the freest of all of those three. But it was the tyrannies of Germany and France which the Counterrevolutionaries in America admired and sought to replicate here.

The benefits produced by British and American businesses in the 19th century were financial, technological, and personal, created at a rate of speed never seen anywhere elsewhere on the planet, Including in Britain and America after 1900, benefits enjoyed by all Americans and Brits, improving the lives of everyone by many orders of magnitude and, indeed, as just mentioned, producing improvements which, when copied by Europeans, were the sole engine for any economic growth in Europe whatsoever.

The Counterrevolutionaries have literally been blind to two crucial facts, facts which are the very opposite of Marx's nonsensical, insistent claims – (1) that American employees have always been attracted to work for businesses for numerous reasons, that all such work was purely <u>voluntary</u> (no one forced them to accept employment from anyone), and (2) that the success enjoyed by American businesses in the 19th century, as always, resulted not from harming customers, but rather from providing goods and services that their customers were eager to purchase.

And it was, precisely as claimed by Adam Smith, the profit realized from sales to customers by American businesses that increased the wealth of the nation as a whole, rather than being some monstrous evil economic rape, as claimed, without evidence, by Marx who, along with his followers, have invariably claimed that the rich get rich solely by stealing (what?) From the poor who have nothing, never noting that if the poor have nothing <u>they have nothing to steal</u>. As discussed in Chapter 4 above, Marxists simply have no concept of where wealth actually comes from because they are blind to the difference between market power and the (wealth-destroying, not producing) power of violence, and derive all their nonsensical claims from that confusion/blindness..

247

American 19th century businesses indeed enjoyed great power in accumulating wealth – but, at least before they needed to purchase political power to protect themselves from political onslaughts, <u>that power was market power alone</u> (their ability simply to provide things others desired, as discussed in detail in Chapter 4 above) which produced their wealth and success. No one forced their customers to buy from them or their employees to work for them; and without the customers, where would their wealth and their business' success have come from? As shown in Chapter 4, the very nature of market power is that it only denotes the ability to provide benefits to others, without any possibility of harming anyone.

The entire "logic" of Marxism depends on complete denial of the existence of God, individual human dignity and ingenuity (which is why it cheerfully and explicitly repudiates — as quoted in Chapter 6 — <u>all</u> private property rights of individuals and businesses) and, above all else, the denial of such a thing as market power: it pretends that the only power in society is the power of violence, and demands that it be imposed on all individuals and businesses.

Marxism in all its forms is filled with hatred (there is no other word for it), as its fundamental driving force — hatred for America, all businesses and private property itself. This is because it nonsensically pretends that hatred, resentment, envy and violence are the sole drivers of all human action. It utterly rejects the notion that any contract for goods or services of any kind is ever entered into voluntarily – including any business contracting with any customer or employee, which business, Marxists invariably claim, uses solely the force of violence to compel the other party to agree to any terms.

Marxism's claimed "scientific" analysis of all human actions – its entire approach to, and analysis of, all psychology, sociology, history, and economics – derives from its absolute certainty that all humans can be intelligently studied and analyzed as virtual automatons, precisely as one would study the behavior of insects, rats, and other animals, which animal species invariably act based primarily, if not solely, on instinct, without ever having done a single inventive or creative thing – ever. Marx himself freely admitted this fact – calling it "materialism," pretending it provided a genuine, valid, scientific basis for observing humans.

In fact, all Marxist analysis is radically reductionist, and gratuitously presumes — based on no evidence whatsoever — that humans are nothing but mindless drones responsive solely to external directives and forces at all times – precisely what Marxism requires, in real life, of all societies subjected to its monstrous tyranny.

Consistent with their Marxist analysis of America – including radical contempt for the nation and its Constitution – 19th Century American Counterrevolutionaries had two goals, initially, both consistent with the spirit of the French Revolution: (1) to eliminate the previously-dominant religious nature of American universities and transform them instead into centers of purely secular study, particularly of both the natural sciences and the so-called social "sciences," and (2) to follow

Marx's *Communist Manifesto* demand and promote the establishment of mandatory, state-operated-and-controlled schools (what came to be called public schools) with compulsory attendance, to give the state, rather than families and churches, control over the nation's children's upbringing and training – and to propagandize their students, as an institutionally captive audience subject to being graded by the schools, into belief in collectivism and disbelief in God.

Only beginning in the 1960s, after public school teachers were unionized – and so protected from firing by union contracts with, and corrupt funding of, politicians, and by virtual lifetime employment guaranteed by "tenure" — did they openly attempt that last, explicit, propagandizing Marxist endeavor.

As in the case of all other victories it has notched along the way, after achieving them, the Counterrevolution has never abandoned its consuming interest in completely controlling all American educational institutions and, after it secured complete victories in the just-described two educational goals, it has continued to expand its control over all American educational institutions – and magnify their importance in American society in every way it can (remember: its first hard-core group of loyalists were themselves American university professors).

Indeed, the history of the Counterrevolution in America has involved a sequence of victories for the Counterrevolutionary "cause" in which, as discussed in the next chapter, one by one, numerous self-proclaimed "learned" professions have been won over by it, often based on the genuinely-enormous political victories it has also notched along the way – and their own power-enhancement from its successes.

Although Rousseau's notion of a gestalt consciousness for a nation, which he termed the General Will, is a fanciful, romantic notion with no basis in reality, it does have a certain tautological energy <u>which engulfs those who themselves become true believers in the radical-egalitarian Collectivist cause</u>: specifically, without ever needing to actually communicate with each other in a manner that would be called a conspiracy, there is a certain group-think aspect to such true believers: whether specifically directed to do so or not (as, for example, Political Correctness mandates to their present-day true believers) they end up genuinely acting in unison – and thinking that way especially.

It must be emphasized that even as multiple professions succumbed to the Counterrevolution and were won over by all or part of its ideological imperatives of radical egalitarianism and hostility and resentment directed towards our Constitution, all businesses and, particularly, successful businessman, who were given various pejorative appellations such as "robber barons," and even as legislation and even Constitutional amendments were enacted instituting increasingly massive amounts of Bad Law, the American public has never actually been won over to the Cause and, even through the depths of the Depression and the triumphs of FDR and the New Dealers (many of whom were barely-disguised Marxists) have remained overwhelmingly Christian and, accordingly, fundamentally anti-Marxist, passively enduring the Counterrevolution's multiple victories and largely lulled into accepting them based on misrepresentations regarding what they really were.

The sequence of victories for the Counterrevolutionary cause beginning in the 1840s can be summarized as follows:

Initially, as indicated above, American self-identified "intellectuals," journalists and university professors were overwhelmingly won over. They then undertook great efforts to have what we now call public schools institutionalized so that the state governments would ultimately be in charge of supervising the lives and education/indoctrination of America's young – well-aware, as stated by Jefferson, that the Constitution precluded any federal government role in that activity, but wanting government at some level to take charge. By the 1870s, public schools were indeed instituted throughout most of the states.

Major political victories began to be added to the Counterrevolution's conquests/cooptions of particular professions beginning in 1870 with the creation of the Or-wellian-named federal Justice Department, initially formed to enforce the new-ly-created, multiple federal criminal laws imposed on the defeated South incident to Reconstruction, followed by federal regulation of the railroads in 1887, the Sherman Antitrust Act of 1890, and accelerating by many orders of magnitude after the assassination of William McKinley and Theodore Roosevelt's resulting ascension to the presidency.

It was Roosevelt himself who began the genuinely-revolutionary, radical, federal domination of American business, publicly announcing his devotion to Progres-sivism/Marxism, and explicitly stating his refusal to be bound by the Constitution (characterizing it as a no-longer-relevant oddity from an earlier time, although he did promote formal amendment to it regarding the income tax). He promoted both the institutionalization of a graduated income tax and an estate tax, both central planks in Karl Marx' Communist Manifesto of 1848, for the express socialist purpose of confiscating wealth from the nouveau riche (as he snobbishly viewed successful businessmen of his day – himself a kind of American Brahmin claiming to be above such mundane matters as earning a living and building a business).

Proclaiming himself a devotee of the central elements of the French Revolution (without explicitly referring to it), he advocated these measures, along with an agency, ultimately instituted as the FTC, to engage in perennial, ongoing, gra-tuitous investigations into the affairs of all businesses, among other clearly-un-constitutional federal tyrannies, all supposedly to prevent radical inequality of income and the development of a new noble class (a straw problem which, in fact, could not happen legally since it was expressly precluded under the Consti-tution itself).

Additionally, in his second term as president, after actually being elected in 1904, he began to take increasingly radical collectivist/socialist acts – nationalizing vast tracts of land supposedly to preserve it from the depredations it would suffer if left in private hands, and promoting legislation, explicitly based on a fraudulent novel by the Communist Upton Sinclair, supposedly to promote public health with it's enactment, in 1906, of the legislation which ultimately led to the creation of today's FDA, which exerts an iron-like grip over what citizens are allowed to manufacture, and to buy and sell, when it comes to food, drugs and any devices with any medical benefits – with absolutely no constitutional basis for doing so.

And, as described in Chapter 3, the FDA has never had any genuine, provable benefit to anyone's health ever, and has caused catastrophic destruction to individual lives, liberty, and choice, with the fabulous expense of obtaining government approval for any drug ultimately inevitably being borne by drug customers, increasing the price of all pharmaceuticals astronomically – simply to limit citizens' health care options and to drastically increase the power of the state.

Additionally, Theodore Roosevelt happily promoted the institutionalization of the Federal Reserve Bank, promoting a precursor to it in 1907. He did so after the panic of 1906, which he had himself caused by the terror he deliberately created within the business community of threatened, massive federal takeovers, antitrust prosecutions, and other tyrannies.

He fanatically abused American business corporations of all types (he made no secret of his utter loathing of businessmen in general, just like Karl Marx) through the prosecution of frivolous antitrust claims, caused the panic of 1906, as just mentioned, which in no small measure contributed to the public's ultimate acceptance of the nationalization of the currency by the Federal Reserve Bank, established in 1913, the federal income tax, the federal estate tax – all of which had been accomplished in 1913 and, most significantly, split the Republican Party in 1912 and facilitated the election of the even more-radical Marxist anti-constitutionalist Woodrow Wilson in 1912 who continued the process begun by Roosevelt in earnest of creating as much of a radical regulatory federal control of all aspects of the economy – Bad Law – as he could get away with, with no effective political opposition, in an unabashed effort to duplicate here what the totalitarian German Kaisers had imposed on the German people in the 19th century.

# CHAPTER 14

## Major Extra-Political Features of the Counterrevolution

<u>The Counterrevolution's 19th Century Capture of the Professions — An Overview</u>

As described in greater detail below, although the Counterrevolution scored some major political/legal victories (against Americans and our true Revolution), particularly beginning after the Civil War, its most far-reaching and significant conquests during the 19th century consisted of its capture of all American educational institutions, and of overwhelming portions of members of a number of other vocations and, even more importantly, enormous, and increasingly-controlling, power over entire vocations <u>as collective groups</u>.

Every externally-identifiable, and potentially-internally-coherent, group of any kind – professional, racial, sexual, you name it – is, to collectivists of all types, a potential, separate collective whose conquest is sought and desired by them and their Cause; and no one understands the political dynamics of an actual or potential collective better than collectivists themselves – including the very members of any such group targeted for such conquest by the Counterrevolution.

Once they are themselves won over to the Cause, new collectivists work tirelessly to capture the minds of as many of their group colleagues and, when possible, the particular collective group, as a whole, to which they belong. Once the group as a whole is captured, the collectivists within it who have engineered that victory, inevitably seek to weaponize the group as a whole to effect further conquests within society, including against the Cause's targets/enemies.

That ability — to create the appearance at least of capturing the loyalty of <u>entire self-identified groups</u> within society and, from that position of apparent dominance, to exercise power and influence over the group's individual members— has always been one of the most extraordinary attributes of all collectivist movements. The nature of such conquests is that, although the identifiable group (lawyers, journalists, teachers) so captured, as a group, may appear overwhelmingly supportive of the particular collectivist cause, many, if not most, of its individual members may actually feel very differently about it.

Each such group has its own internal, political dynamics, and the collectivists within it invariably find their way to the group's levers of power to maneuver the group <u>as a collective force</u> to favor the Cause, without regard to the actual wishes of its members. If any vote at all is actually taken, it occurs only when the collectivists who have taken charge already can be certain of their power to determine its outcome.

Thus, the strategically-minded collectivist leaders first capture the group as a whole, and then use that position of power to influence the loyalty of its individual members. Once that capture is complete, the collectivists are able to make loyalty to the Cause a professional requirement for continued membership in the group – with group members loyal to the Cause favored for advancement, and with any "disloyal" previous members disfavored, and even deprived of professional legitimacy in some manner.

As discussed below, this appearance of virtual-unanimity among America's "best and brightest" – particularly their Counterrevolutionary attacks on American business, and invariable demands for increased federal government power – was exponentially amplified in the 20th century by the enormous, influential power of broadcast media, whose similar, unanimous echoing of those themes was overseen by the FCC's existential control over them.

The particular vocations first so captured by the American Counterrevolution in the 19th century (ignoring, for the time being, blue-collar "workers" eventually targeted for union membership) liked to think of themselves, and have invariably characterized themselves, as the "learned professions," including, in the order in which they became Counterrevolutionary enthusiasts (in many cases unknowingly), university professors, journalists, various middlebrow and highbrow writers styling themselves as "public intellectuals," followed eventually by lawyers, law professors, and judges, and eventually many members of the clergy of all organized religions.

Each of these professional conquests were profoundly important, both with respect to the won-over professionals themselves, and the inevitable influence they have held over the rest of society, including its wealthier and better-educated members, who read books and articles by, and even often were students of, those personally-impressive Counterrevolutionaries.

In the 19th century the won-over, Counterrevolutionary professions successfully advocated for the creation of state-run public schools in America and the secularization of America's previously-religious universities. They also were enthusiastic supporters of the principal legal/political successes of the Counterrevolution in the 19th century – the enactment of the 1890 Sherman Antitrust Act and the 1887 Interstate Commerce Act.

As explained below, there were profoundly-important and powerful structural reasons why university professors and journalists, in particular, were drawn to the anti-business ideas of Karl Marx as soon as they began to appear in print in the 1840s, ideas which, when promoted by them in their particular professional published work, actually provided professional and financial advantages to them personally.

This does not mean that everything they wrote was a form of propaganda. Many things came into play. For example, within a profession, those with power like to promote those who agree with them and, in the case of each of these professions, those in charge found advantage for themselves in promoting the Collectivist Cause.

## The Professions' Extraordinary, And Largely-Invisible, Spreading of the Collectivist Mindset

As described in Chapter 6 above, in addition to their remarkable unanimity in their various political and quasi-religious ideas, devotees of each collectivist movement/Cause each display similar unanimity in their own, particular, psychological mindset. The most basic and constant feature of that mindset — common to members of all collectivist movements — is its attitude regarding assessing/judging all people — including themselves.

On the one hand, collectivists invariably consider judging anyone or anything taboo – because of their devotion to moral relativism – to the point that the very term "discrimination" – of any kind – is considered deeply offensive, something they strive to "rise above." In real life, we are all constantly involved in making judgments about everything, resulting in our choosing – or "discriminating" – something or someone over something or someone else. When we pick our friends, or our spouse, or even which restaurant to go to, we are "discriminating" against all other options. And yet, for collectivists, accusing others of "discriminating" in any manner is among their greatest — and most frequent —insults.

Nevertheless, because judging others and the world around us is a basic aspect of human nature, they do it all the time — just like everyone else. But to accommodate their anti-judging, relativistic taboo, they do so in a particular manner. Specifically, collectivists' invariable mindset refuses to view anyone, and to judge him, purely as an individual – as is, in fact, required by the very Christianity they consider themselves to have "transcended" and, in turn, by the English Common Law, itself derived from that same Christianity.

Instead, their mindset insists on viewing and judging people primarily, and often solely, on the basis of their purported membership in one, always-superficially-observable, group or another. Marx's writings, incidentally, added a particular energy/hysteria to this mindset. Specifically, his self-trumpeted, "economic/historical" writings insisted both on viewing everyone who was employed by someone else solely as a "worker," and claiming that all (inherently-evil) business and other property owners were the collective "bourgeoisie" who, he claimed, preyed on everyone else, particularly their own customers and "workers," for whose sake he demanded the "salvation" he claimed would be provided them by communism/socialism.

The equally-important, specifically-anti-American, portions of Marx's writings uniformly emphasized race as the supposedly-defining paramount, group-identifying feature of all Americans (19th century Europeans were almost exclusively white). This is because he (correctly) recognized that the American Revolution's central, moral/political feature was its absolute devotion to promoting individual liberty; the then-existing, primarily-Southern, black slavery was obviously utterly antithetical to that American moral purpose, and so provided a ready basis for criticizing as hypocritical the American Revolution whose simultaneous, genuine promotion of individual liberty was always a direct threat, ideologically, to collectivism of all sorts, including particularly socialism/communism.

In real life, Marxist ideology demands the complete subjugation of all individual liberty (for everyone other than its dictators) – and invariably produces entire nations of imprisoned slaves to the state. Thus, Marxists' anti-American accusation regarding slavery is itself utterly hypocritical – a classic Freudian projection.

But Marxism's absolute opposition to, and contempt for, the very notions of God and the human soul, and so to America's imperative for individual liberty and dignity, always demanded some argument for Marxist revolutionaries/devotees to raise against the American Revolution as their cause's inherent antithesis – any claim to assert about America to foment endless, rage-filled hatred, something to allege to be America's unforgivable sin. The African slavery which still existed in 1848 was, quite simply, the only thing Marx could come up with – and he and his followers have endlessly milked it for that purpose ever since, insisting on its, and America's, utter, eternal depravity — and continued doing so since 1865 based on that thereafter no-longer-true fact.

Indeed, Marx (and all his followers to this day) insisted, nonsensically, that black slavery so permeated America as to be no mere hypocrisy/inconsistency with, but rather was itself the central, supposedly-unique, and defining feature of, the American Revolution — and this from the propagandist/promoter of an ideology devoted to stealing all property from, and enslaving, everyone, not simply a tiny minority, in a world which had never previously lacked the institution of slavery in virtually any nation. In fact, during his own lifetime, Marx witnessed the genuinely-historically-unique action by America (and Britain which he similarly detested) in freeing all its slaves.

Because American slavery itself, prior to 1865, was indeed a racial phenomenon, unlike in earlier times when white people also had been legally-enslaved as indentured servants, Marx's collectivist mindset and arguments insisted on declaring the eternal guilt of all Americans other than the slaves themselves, without regard to any actual participation by them in slavery at all. His collectivist mindset permitted him to smear the entire nation and everything about it, for all time, without regard to any slave-liberation it indeed effected, in that manner – because America, like all nations, always was viewed and judged by Marx — and all his followers — purely as a soulless collective, and never as an assemblage of individuals, each deserving judgment based solely on their own actions.

Marx's American followers – calling themselves Progressives, either because they fancied their antibusiness/anti-property collectivist views different from his, or simply because of Americans' well-known loathing of Marxism/socialism – have particularly, and only, since the 1960's, after the enactment those years' civil rights laws continued this particular, identical smear against the entire nation and, in particular, against all its whites, endlessly, long after slavery had been legally ended. Following Marx's approach, American Progressives, endlessly-seeking, as propaganda, alleged "victims" of America's supposed malignancy, have similarly so identified women (because they originally couldn't vote) after slavery ended, and have ever after looked for – and invariably found – new "victim" groups to pretend to champion, which championship, in their minds, provided them moral superiority.

Their invariable demand for loyalty from all of the "victimized" groups they purport to "champion," typically by demanding special legal and/or financial priv- ileges for them, has primarily been based on the hatred and envy they invariably profess against those collective groups they claim have been the "victimizers" – typically again, only, since the 1960's, white Christians, particularly males.

The point I am emphasizing here is that it takes a particular mindset – a mindset which, itself, can exist apart from any particular political beliefs – to insist on seeing people exclusively as non-individuals, and purely as members of col- lective groups, always for purposes of either damning or claiming to champion each such group. And that inherently anti-Christian, anti-individual mindset must exist in order for anyone to find credible the group-smears or group claims of victimization invariably advanced by collectivists.

As each of the various vocations/professions discussed in this chapter were won over by the collectivist cause, they "bought into" that collectivist mindset them- selves – and propagated it throughout society. The effect of that mindset-prop- agation by them was to provide a kind of received-wisdom credibility among non-collectivists in the nation for those collectivists' group-smear arguments, arguments which they otherwise would have found reprehensible, as clear as- saults both on the very idea of individuality on which America was founded, and on any notion of true justice, under both biblical and Common-Law principles. That genuine justice is always to be applied separately to each individual based exclusively on his own conduct — and never to groups.

Spreading this collectivist mindset among the population at large both rendering it susceptible to believing, or at least finding non-reprehensible, collectivist pro- paganda from all sources of media, and "softening-up" those who bought into that mindset for purposes of eventually capturing them as true, collectivist Counterrevolutionary devotees.

It is a virtual certainty that the overwhelming majority of American professionals who participated in promoting this collectivist mindset subliminally to the public had no idea that that was what they were doing, but rather were simply themselves captured by collectivism and its mindset so that it made sense for them to be doing what they were doing without any consideration of its underlying, radical collectivist nature. They were simply interested in being good citizens and advancing within their profession, a profession which had been truly captured by collectivism, with only the very few strategic promoters of that result even aware that that was what was going on.

## American Marxists'/Progressives' Collectivist Racism

Without attempting, or purporting, to provide a comprehensive history of the phenomenon, since I have noted Marxists' ongoing collectivist-smearing condemnation of America and all Americans collectively for all time, based on the undeniable fact that African slavery existed here until 1865, and legally-enforced and compelled discrimination against American black citizens (Jim Crow laws, e.g.) continued thereafter until the mid-1960s, nothing would be more erroneous than to believe that American Marxists/Progressives have ever themselves treated American Blacks like equals, devoid of race-consciousness. Consistent with their collectivist attitude towards all superficially-identifiable "groups" they have always been literally obsessed with race-consciousness, and have consistently shown particular contempt for blacks.

As discussed in earlier chapters, the Democrat party, which dedicated itself to the Progressive cause, beginning no later than the 1880s, had been the party of slavery until its abolition in 1865, and thereafter, except during Reconstruction, itself unilaterally ruled the entire South for over 100 years, authoring and imposing the Jim Crow laws, with the Ku Klux Klan effectively serving as its armed militia in the Midwest and South until the mid-20th century. It has never ceased to treat American Blacks purely as a collective group; it has changed its policies regarding them beginning with the Lyndon Johnson presidency, promoting legislation and policies designed to ghettoize Blacks, disempower them, and lead them to believe themselves dependent on the welfare state and the Democrat party as its principal pillar, bringing to a screeching halt the enormous economic and social progress American Blacks had been making, particularly in northern cities, prior to the imposition of those policies.

Progressives have shown nothing but race-conscious contempt for Blacks throughout their historical existence in America. Their early champion, Woodrow Wilson, was a virulent racist who unilaterally ordered the segregation of races throughout the federal government, including the military, immediately after taking office, a federal government and military which had previously been completely racially-integrated since the 1870s and had been one of the few places in the country where educated Blacks could obtain employment and have real careers. Wilson brutally ended that. Like many Progressives, he openly advocated for eugenics — with blacks viewed as an inferior race. Margaret Sanger, an ardent Progressive, the founder of Planned Parenthood, promoted abortion specifically as a means to reducing, or eventually eliminating, the population of American Blacks.

Modern Progressives remain obsessed with the race, sex and gender of anyone they describe or encounter and invariably insist on treating Blacks as a separate, collective group – pretending to act on their behalf in vilifying all their own political opponents as supposed "racists" and "bigots," and in promoting policies whose undeniable result for decades has been to legally promote out-of-wedlock births and destroy the American Black family, predictably resulting in keeping large numbers of Blacks in poorly- educated poverty, while spending massive amounts of taxpayer money to maintain the system which has had those monumentally-destructive effects on real life American black citizens.

### Collectivism's Benefits For the Captured Professions

Collectivism provided a major, synergistic financial and professional advantage for journalists and academics. University professors relished being considered "experts" supposedly qualified to pontificate on various subjects, and journalists found in them supposed "experts" they could refer to in that capacity as authorities on topics of interest in the articles they wrote. That very belief in "experts" was itself a major, central component of the Collectivist cause – with "experts," in their view, comprising a virtual nobility authorized by their "expertise" to rule over others.

You will note that neither of those professions were actively involved in business – that is, the creation of actual products and/or services which the public was interested in buying – other than the written articles and education which the journalists and educators provided.

Counterrevolutionaries and Marxists (who, in America, unlike Europe, typically refuse that label, preferring euphemisms such as "Progressives", or even more misleadingly "pragmatists," and eventually "liberals" when FDR adopted that term for himself based on his eventual opposition to the particular Progressive cause of alcohol prohibition) eventually have become so ubiquitous among America's "intelligentsia" that, at some point, many Americans who never heard of Rousseau, and read neither him nor Marx, came to feel, just like actual collective members, that the positions of the Counterrevolution on many, if not all, subjects were simply "what all right-thinking people" believed – and that any who disagreed were automatically discredited by virtue of that disagreement itself.

Additionally, and simultaneously with their growing enthusiasm for the Counterrevolution, as discussed below, multiple vocations, insisting that they should be characterized as "professions," strove mightily in the 19th century, and ever after, to "upgrade" their status – and power – in society, which upgrading took a variety of forms and produced significant effects, effects which have continued to grow.

To take the example of universities and their faculties in this "upgrading" context: early in the 19th century, universities had very limited importance in American society – primarily as institutions to train clergyman. And, until relatively recently, university professors were commonly viewed as purely-academic, studious, book-worm eccentrics – an image epitomized by the stereotypical "absent-minded professor" – utterly disconnected from the real world of real people.

However, as the various, upwardly-mobile professions (which previously had been mere vocations) "professionalized" their own membership in a variety of ways, including by establishing educational-prerequisites to membership, those professions — and universities in particular — managed to upgrade their status in society as a whole, and effectively became de facto "credentialing" institutions for virtually all white-collar professionals of all kinds – thereby gaining the power to inculcate their own values further into all the power centers of society, including the very businesses they typically disdained or resented.

That universal white-collar accrediting power, coupled with their power over students' grades, which they gained vastly increased their power to influence the ideas and thought processes of their students and admirers, ideas which, at their insistence, became increasingly required for students whose accreditation they had the power to prevent, or to hold up, in order to obtain that accreditation – ideas invariably of the Counterrevolution, and even of Karl Marx – even though those ideas were often presented as mere enthusiasm for the welfare administrative state. Even that political commentary was absent from most humanities departments until the mid-20th century, when enthusiasm in those departments for the Marxist ideas of Paul de Man, Michel Foucault and other so-called deconstructionists overwhelmed all other approaches to their subjects.

Thus, university professors and universities were won over by collectivism, and even Marxism, and acquired the power during the course of the 19th century, which power increased drastically during the 20th century, to inculcate those ideologies into America's intelligentsia of all kinds and in all professions – because getting good grades from them became a prerequisite to being credentialed to serve in all white collar professions in America, and their control over that credentialing process gave them a power they had never had before, further enhancing their affection for the Counterrevolution.

The Counterrevolution's conquest of the legal profession, discussed in detail below, solidified in the mid-1930s, and resulted in that profession, with its unique, purportedly-expert relationship with all laws, effectively giving its supposedly-professional, "expert" blessing to the legal and Constitutional legitimacy of the truly-radical, crassly-political, 1930's rulings by the Supreme Court, purportedly based on the Commerce clause, which literally undid all of the Constitutional safeguards from tyranny fought for by our founders in our Revolution, as clearly shown in previous chapters.

Additionally — and profoundly destructive to the rule of law in the nation under traditional, individual-applying Common-Law principles— as the collectivist mindset, discussed above, was absorbed by America's legal system and courts, in addition to the legal profession, the courts increasingly accepted as legitimate the idea of (purely-collectivist) group remedies, and group victimhood claims (class actions) of various kinds – that is, court-imposed legal mandates based solely on non-individual criteria, directly contravening the previous, Christian and Common Law absolute requirement for individual justice alone.

These group remedies are utterly reprehensible under biblical and Common-Law notions of justice, and have included things such as forced busing of school-children to bring about "racial balance" in schools – a notion which ipso facto required viewing people purely as members of a race, rather than as individuals – and permitting and even mandating racial quotas, euphemized as"affirmative action," in which members of certain, supposedly-always-victimized groups, Identified solely by race and/or sex, have been given extraordinary advantages in competing against others for limited space in schools, employment, etc., and marginal whites, particularly men, have been consequently disadvantaged, simply because of their race.

Completely ignoring the actual attributes of any individual member of each such so legally-privileged or disadvantaged race or sex is inherent to that process, since the actual beneficiaries of such treatment necessarily never were themselves slaves, and may have suffered no more at society's hands than anyone else (they could even be rich and benefit, for example) and the marginal whites rejected in favor of the favored racial-group members, may themselves have suffered more growing up than those who actually benefited from their being rejected, and may actually have championed the victimized groups in their own lives.

The contempt for religion, property rights (of all), opposing viewpoints, our Revolution itself, and even human dignity and life itself, inherent in all forms of collectivism, has typically escaped the attention of its American enthusiasts of all kinds. They have listened to the siren-song happy talk promises of utopia and "free benefits" for all of collectivism and Marxism, exposed as sheer, impossible nonsense in chapters above.

## The FCC and the Professions

As mentioned above, in the 20th century, when broadcast media entered the scene, under the absolute rule of the FCC, the power and (by-then virtually-unanimously-held) point of view of these Counterrevolutionaries within broadcast journalism – as the voice of "the news," as opposed to mere "news," which all Americans heard and, when TV came to be, saw – was greatly amplified by several factors.

First of all, the FCC deliberately limited the total number of private television broadcast networks to three. Because of its (and Washington politicians') absolute, existential stranglehold over those networks, and the fact that journalists had been completely won over by the Counterrevolution by the mid-19th century anyway, those networks' news programs all delivered virtually identical "information" concerning world and national events – "information" invariably consisting of a video or radio summary of the front page of the New York Times – according to the wishes of the Marxist-populated (anti-business, pro-big government) bureaucrats at the FCC, with no dissenting or alternative points of view permitted by them on the broadcast media they controlled in America.

Thus, the Counterrevolution was able to control — through the power of the FCC — all "news" content, presenting itself to the public, through multiple broadcast networks, as <u>the only legitimate voice for all information</u> about what was happening in the world. It was as if events they chose not to report simply didn't happen.

And the events reported were always assumed by the effectively-captive audiences of those substantively-identical networks – practically all citizens – to have happened according to the way they reported it, with the purported "journalists" – who, in reality, were (wittingly or not) Counterrevolutionary operatives – pretending to their audience that they were merely delivering "objective""news" – as if there is such a thing as an "objective" description of any event (think of the multiple, highly different, descriptions of a single litigated event by different actual witnesses to it at trials), let alone complex world events involving multiple governments, politicians, spoken and hidden agendas etc..

The ability of those broadcast networks – under the direction of the FCC – substantially to control citizens' understanding of all events in the nation and the world was further amplified by the fact that the <u>substance</u> of what all of them report to the public about everything has always been <u>virtually identical</u>. This <u>unanimous</u> description of events by such purportedly objective and authoritative "journalists" – always purporting to include "all the news" – itself had the effect of promoting the public's illusion of legitimate certitude about all these matters, so that anyone purporting to know additional, or even contrary, versions of events or facts, or holding any other views – including the value of individual liberty and property rights – automatically could be marginalized as presenting an inherently-unbelievable, minority fringe point of view.

Moreover, by selecting those particular three networks as the only permitted ones, the FCC gave them a certain official imprimatur (from the government of the country all decent Americans truly loved, with unquestionable loyalty) – without in any way suggesting that they were effectively propagandists for a particular political/social point of view —which, in fact, they have always been — if only because they have had no choice, due to their need to answer to government masters holding existential control over them.

Indeed, their propaganda has always been all the more effective because it had the appearance – and pretension – of being nothing of the kind. That fact too has continued to this day in what is widely characterized as "mainstream media."

The New York Times, which always was a deeply-committed organ of the Counterrevolution, while literally claiming to be the authoritative source of "all the news [sic]" for all decent, educated Americans, has been able to present itself, for example, as a middle-of-the-road, purely-objective source of information to the public — and its front page typically was since early in the 20th century, and has remained, the actual source of, and echoed in, all the "news" stories reported by most other American newspapers and virtually all broadcast media "news" outlets.

Regarding this self-proclaimed virtuous and objective professionalism of the New York Times, as but a single example among many which could be specifically pointed out: in the 1930s, the New York Times ran a series of articles authored by its then-star Moscow reporter, Walter Duranty, purporting to describe Stalinist Russia, and painting it as a virtual paradise, replete with numerous absolutely-fraudulent representations, and no mention whatsoever of the mass murder (of tens of millions) and concentration camps that it was responsible for. The New York Times and Duranty won a Pulitzer Prize for those absolutely-fraudulent articles, a prize which it retains to this day proudly (the Times has since admitted the articles were "some of the worst reporting…" – a monumental understatement — while never disavowing their lies or its Pulitzer).

Thus it is no exaggeration to say that the New York Times has always been a mouthpiece and propaganda machine for viciously-anti-American, radical-collectivist positions – all while masquerading as an authoritative, patriotic and objective source of "the news."

All those attributes of the FCC-governed networks and the New York Times have remained true to this very day.

The following is a more detailed description of the essential features of the Counterrevolution, including its underlying ideology, and a more-detailed description of its capture of all our so-called "learned" professions:

The Self-Interested Motives Behind American "Intellectuals'" And Journalists' Support For The Collectivist Counterrevolution.

As described in Chapter 6, Karl Marx's principal "contributions" to the Collectivist pseudo-religious Cause were:

(1) his demand that business owners/employers, America, Britain (and, yes, his fellow Jews, who he described in Nazi-like language) all be considered utterly evil, and so be the eternal objects of endless, Revolutionary, quasi-religious, venomous hatred;

(2) his claim that the virtually-divine force of History was driving ineluctably forward to completely eradicate all (supposedly immoral) individual, private-decision-making over any aspect of the economy (what he sneeringly called Capitalism), and its replacement by supposedly-dutiful, "scientific/expert" government officials acting as representatives of the "workers";

(3) his claim that all societies, Including Constitutionally-classless America, were divided into multiple, self-conscious economic "classes", which were so at-odds as to be literally "at war" with each other; and

(4) the prolific, journalistic propaganda, and supposedly-"scientific" books and pamphlets he wrote in support of these propositions – and attacking what he proclaimed to be the absolute evils of America, its Revolution, and particularly its Constitution, which he recognized, correctly, as the antithesis of everything – absolute, centralized state control, no private property allowed, over all citizens' actions – he was advocating for.

### Collectivists' Eternal Anti-American Smear

With respect to Marx's viciously anti-American writings: the particular criticisms ("racist", "enslaving") he offered have remained the endlessly-repeated staples of all anti-American collectivists ever since — none of whom, by the way, have ever noticed any problems with the real-life Marxist revolutions and states which have mass-murdered and poisoned the lives of literally billions, and enslaved and imprisoned their entire populations. I have accurately exposed and deconstructed the monstrous evil, fraud and literal insanity of Marxism in Chapter 6 above.

Again, the particular Marxist criticism, which has been invariably repeated, after American blacks' disempowerment legally ended in the 1960's, by all Collectivists, of America has been that, because African slavery existed in America at the time of the Constitution, and continued until it was ended during the Civil War, that fact constituted an eternally unforgivable sin on the parts of America and all (non-progressive) white Americans collectively forever, regardless how completely unconnected to any aspect of harm to black people any of them might be.

That mass, collectivist, specifically-non-individual "indictment" is what I have exposed above as a standard, collectivist smear – accusing a mass of superficially-identifiable people (by race, sex, etc.), with no evidence against any of them individually.

As but one example: to a Marxist collectivist, all rich people can be condemned as evil simply because they are rich since, to him, the path they each, individually, took to acquire their wealth is irrelevant: they are each a member of a collective group singled out by collectivists for hatred simply, and solely, by virtue of their unavoidable membership in that group. If their wealth can be successfully taken/ stolen from them, collectivists/Marxists rejoice in so doing, calling it virtuous "social justice" – obviously the complete opposite of actual justice.

Nothing is more fundamental to collectivism in all its forms than its utter contempt for, and indifference to, all individuals <u>as individuals,</u> including any individual's actual guilt, innocence, responsibility – or achievement. That is what permits their complete indifference to individual lives and any individual's property rights, and his right to be judged solely for his own actions – and to be worthy of the fruits of achievements earned through his own efforts.

According to all American collectivists at all times, the mere fact that America's <u>long-ago- ended</u> African slavery ever existed supposedly forever renders all America's claims of, and institutions for, promoting individual liberty a complete nullity.

In this context it is worth noting again that, invariably, and in real life, under Marxist societies, <u>everyone</u> who is not part of the Revolutionary governing elite is a slave to the state who, in most cases, is subject to the death penalty if he attempts to leave the country or otherwise resists his enslavement. Accordingly, this eternal Marxist anti-American "indictment" (the bloody shirt it forever waives) – continuing today – is a classic example of soulless projection.

Never once have Marxist critics of America made note of their own hypocrisy in this regard in their criticism – nor have they ever acknowledged that America indeed long ago legally ended African slavery, and has provided better lives for all the former slaves and their descendants than any communist country has provided to any of its people – ever. Moreover, the former slaves were free to move to Africa; very few chose to do so – and wisely so.

### Collectivists And American Politics – An Overview

Note: never have more than a tiny minority of Americans either actually read any of Marx's drivel nor agreed with anything he had to say. Rest assured: if there were ever actual, American popular support for his ideas, Constitutional amendments authorizing the socialism and communism he advocated would have been put before the public and ratified long ago by his genuine supporters in America. Not only has that never happened, explicitly-socialist candidates for president in America (and there have been several) have never won more than a minuscule share of the popular vote.

And, while actually promoting plainly-socialist policies since 1900, the Democrat party has always noisily <u>disavowed</u> any characterization of it as at all socialist – and has always used every means available to it to silence anyone who points out the origin of its policy-preferences in the writings of Karl Marx. Compare the self-Identified Socialist party 1929 platform with the policies promoted by the Democrat Party throughout the 20th century and see if you can find a single difference. And the Republican party has often itself promoted socialist policies (Theodore Roosevelt and Nixon most egregiously), and has never offered any real resistance to them.

## The 19th Century Social-Climbing and Self-Promotion As "Learned Professions" Of Various Vocations – And Their Increasing Collectivism

As mentioned above, America's "intellectuals," particularly those who populate university faculties, and journalists (who invariably aspire to be considered among the intellectuals, typically recognize their middle-or lowbrow status in that regard, and follow the lead of their intellectual "betters"), have been huge fans of Marx ever since his incendiary writings first appeared in the 1840's. Their enthusiasm for his views has arisen from factors similar to those inspiring a similar enthusiasm among European "intellectuals," both on university faculties and otherwise; indeed, the American "intellectuals,'" and their journalist imitators', desire to <u>emulate</u> the European "intellectuals" was itself an additional incentive for their continuing enthusiasm for Marx.

Indeed, their desire to self-identify as a europhile, intellectually-superior elite virtual-nobility in an officially-classless America, whose great unwashed masses, as they have snobbishly always viewed the rest of Americans — who invariably have opposed Marx's ideas — may have itself been a further spur to American "intellectuals'" Marxist enthusiasm.

European "intellectuals'" enthusiasm for Marx has been so overwhelming that since the middle of the 19th century, never more than a tiny minority of university professors throughout continental Europe have not been in complete, or at least partial, agreement with Marx's views on all subjects, though not necessarily on his demands for violent revolution to achieve them (the Nazi professors on German universities beginning in the 1930s in most cases simply continued their enthusiastic Marxism, with only a slight increase in their vocal anti-Semitism necessary to maintain their — mandatory — Nazi loyalty).

## America's Self-Proclaimed Elites' Class Aspirations

European nations historically had genuine, juridical classes, each of which had actual, different, legally-recognized rights, privileges or, in the case of serfs, unpleasant duties of various kinds. The American Constitution absolutely forbids any such juridical classes, specifically forbidding any titles of nobility whatsoever. Accordingly, America was founded (again, with the exception of African slavery until 1865) as a self-consciously legally-classless society.

Unfortunately, that fact has not stopped a number of self-identified groups from insisting that they qualified as a kind of nobility or elite among us.

Those insisting on so interjecting a hierarchy into American society, with each of them claiming to be deservedly at its apogee, of course, have consisted of people pursuing particular vocations – university faculties and other self-proclaimed "public intellectuals," lawyers, journalists and, beginning in the 20th century, thanks to the above-mentioned, FCC-controlled technological inventions which vastly increased their societal impact (radio, sound recordings, movies, television), Hollywood and other media "stars" (including TV news readers), popular musicians and, eventually, as a direct result of the federal government's massive power accumulation, even politicians in certain, particularly-powerful offices.

A major societal development during the 19th century was the fact that members of certain of these vocations – lawyers, journalists, university professors, and eventually public accountants – decided to "upgrade" their status by proclaiming themselves to be "professions," supposedly providing indispensable, "expert" services to society, insisting that their membership should be restricted to "qualified" (by them) entrants only, pursuant to rules, educational attainments/degrees, and other requirements imposed by them.

In both insisting on their extraordinary value to society and on themselves alone policing their membership, these self-upgraded vocations were behaving like medieval Guilds. As part of this "professionalism" process, the vocations developed their own processes for members to advance their careers within them — or to be shunned.

Thus, by the end of the 19th century, the first law schools and journalism departments were created at universities and, increasingly, university professorships were restricted to those possessing so-called Doctorate degrees. In other words, those professions decided they knew how to educate their members – what to inculcate in them and what to require of them for professional legitimacy – and insisted on doing so – further enhancing the power and prestige of those "profession" members who succeeded in climbing politically within the power structures of those professions.

Marxism – as a thought process, and mindset (i.e. contempt, and even hatred, for businessmen and America itself), though not necessarily explicitly as a political philosophy – increasingly became demanded for membership among journalists and "intellectuals" engaged in the so-called "social sciences," though not the literature departments – yet. As an explicitly-atheistic ideology, imposing its own reductionist stick-figure template on all human behavior, Marxism claimed to provide an ever-ready explanation for everything humans do. Marxism claimed to have improved on the foolish superstitions of the past – that is, all religions believing in God – based on its claimed devotion to reason and "science" – claims which were enormously seductive to America's educated, self-proclaimed "elites," and which have remained so ever since.

And if you begin all social analyses by ignoring the possibility of individual merit/culpability or responsibility, and of the human soul, and view society abstractly/theoretically in a completely mechanical, materialistic manner, Marxism can offer a certain seductive, theoretical appeal, an appeal that proved irresistible to those academic groups, and to those with political power in every country that has applied its principles in real life, with the enormity of the real life evil and monstrousness from such application in direct proportion to the extent to which it exists – the more Marxism, the more poverty, death and tyranny. That fact is simply not rationally debatable after the 20th century.

One obvious feature of all these professions, facilitating their Marxist-inspired hatred of businesses, beginning in the 19th century, is that <u>none of them</u> were themselves engaged in businesses (the ones particularly detested by Marxists) which businesses, through the goods and services they invented/manufactured or otherwise provided, alone created America's then-rapidly-growing wealth (mineral/oil extraction, providing electricity, shipbuilding and seafaring commerce, railroad creation and operation, finance, inventing and mass production manufacturing, e.g.).

That fact, together with certain structural features of each of these professions discussed below, resulted in all of them eventually having genuine, self-interested reasons for enthusiastically promoting Marxist ideas and thinking (i.e., that all businesses are evil, that exposing their evil is good, and that the government can do no wrong) – even when, in many cases, they were unaware they were doing so.

To the extent that anyone analyzes public events presuming as automatic facts the non-existence of God and the foolishness of all religions, the evil of businessmen and the virtues of government officials, knowingly or not, he is advancing a Marxist agenda, since those notions, along with America-hatred, are the very heart of Marx's thought.

Paradoxically, Americans' ubiquitous patriotism made them particularly susceptible to automatically believing in the virtues of their government – because it was <u>our</u> government — and everyone assumed that the Constitution completely protected us from any tyrannical harm. The problem was, that it only did so so long as those in power did not violate it or, if one branch did so, another branch would intervene to prevent the Constitutional misconduct.

True, massive Constitutional breaches became possible when, increasingly in the 20th century, multiple federal branches were populated by people <u>politically-aligned with each other</u> who subscribed to all or most of the Marxist views described above, and who together facilitated collusively the unconstitutional actions – in many cases based on belief in the credibility of the legal profession's blessing as legitimate and Constitutional monstrously unconstitutional actions by both the political branches of the federal government and the courts themselves rubber-stamping that misconduct..

The Marxist/Collectivist Exaltation Of "Experts"

I have clearly shown in Chapter 1 that there are no real "experts," and that anyone claiming to be one is a pretender/fraud for that reason alone.

Two major reasons for Marxist enthusiasm among all these professions – particularly Marx's demand that all industrial businesses be confiscated by the state and be operated by "experts" supposedly for the good of all — is the fact, alluded to above, that none of these self-proclaimed "elite""professions" would themselves be targeted for that confiscation — and the additional fact that they themselves could benefit from the seizures of others' property by claiming to be the very "experts" available to succeed to the management and control of those confiscated businesses.

Indeed, in their desire to consider themselves superior to those they considered their inferiors, intellectually and otherwise – particularly mere manufacturing businessman whose wealth they resented and envied – they were snobbishly and arrogantly certain that they <u>deserved to be richer</u> than those perennial targets of Marxism.

Thus, <u>they had much to gain, and absolutely nothing to lose, from such Marxist-demanded property/ccontrol confiscations</u> since <u>they</u> would not themselves be targeted for such – and would become beneficiaries of those takings by being the new masters. And, in their fantasies, all those goods and services they loved supposedly would, in their magical Marxist view, be cheaper and the businesses better run by them as the ruling philosopher-king "experts" who weren't, like the businessmen whose businesses they wanted taken, also in their Marxist view, simply out to cheat their employees and customers to obtain (evil) profits.

The very core of Marxism is its radically-simplified reductionist analysis of all human behavior – its claims that violence is the <u>only</u> power (and that market power, discussed at length in Chapter 4, <u>simply does not exist</u>), that no person acts as an individual, but rather exclusively as a soulless member of his "class" engaged in a death match with all other "classes," with genuine wealth-creation impossible, and "fair" redistribution of the existing goods a moral (without God) imperative. When believed and applied as a supposedly-valid analytical tool, this reductionism lends itself to providing an analytical structure — however nonsensical — for events which otherwise are difficult to explain.

Additionally, as discussed below, the particular, well-trodden <u>paths to achieving personal success</u> in each of those professions have always created enormous incentives for their members to promote <u>particular kinds of improbable, or even fundamentally-fraudulent, "narratives"</u> in their published work – and it is their published work which has always been the primary basis for any of them achieving professional success in each of their respective professions.

"Intellectuals" have had an additional reason to find absolutely irresistible the appeal of Marxism and its American variants sporting different names – Liberalism, Progressivism, whatever.

Specifically, they have had a religiously-held belief that genuine <u>"expertise" in fact exists,</u> that experts' judgment should not be questioned by anyone else and, of greatest interest to American "intellectuals" is the notion that the greatest repository of such "expertise" is contained in America's academic communities – since they are the ones who can be festooned with academic degrees and who study particular areas of inquiry supposedly with greater intellect and depth – which in turn provides them with their tautologically-claimed "expertise."

Accordingly, this notion of the exalted brilliance and superiority of academics as "experts," which Marxism in all its American variants both proclaimed and have invariably insisted should become institutionally empowered by the brute force of law, fed the egos, career ambitions, and bank accounts of academics who either believed such nonsense about their actual superiority, or simply cynically sought to personally-benefit from the public buying into such. This has been particularly true among academics in fields calling themselves the "social sciences" – economics, anthropology, archaeology, sociology, psychology, political "science," and even, according to some, history (correctly recognized by the Greeks as an art form with its own muse Clio).

There is nothing scientific about anything practitioners of those fields do, and their claims to the contrary are, quite simply, utter fraud. Their motives for insisting on such claim is a naked power and wealth grab by them – demanding others pay homage to their "studies," which never stand up to any actual, scientific analysis – since there is nothing genuinely scientific or objective about them.

In short, multitudes of "intellectuals" who insist on their "expertise," particularly in the so-called social "sciences," and who, in their dreams, wish that the great unwashed should be legally-forced to follow their guidance, have been engaged in a purely self-benefiting behavior pattern to acquire wealth and power for themselves, at the expense of others, and particularly at the expense of those who they have professionally found utterly unbearable – the businessmen who, unlike those academics, acquire great wealth from their businesses, wealth resulting directly from the genuine attractiveness of what they produce to their customers, without which genuine value their wealth-production could not exist – wealth which those "intellectuals," following Marxist ideology, invariably characterize as corrupt ill-gotten gains, regardless of the enormity of their contributions of goods and services to the nation's wealth, and the amount of parasitic political and bureaucratic control and rent-seeking such businessmen are forced by politicians to deal with.

Collectivism, and the Counterrevolution it has animated, has enormously benefited all those "intellectuals" in pursuing those self-interested aims.

A particular feature, hinted at above, common to both journalism and university/academic life has created an additional, enormous personal-financial and professional reason for members of both those professions to be personally-drawn to Marxism as an ideology – and to seek, in the bogus "narratives" their vocations/professions promote, to promote their claimed superiority as consistent with its various ideological claims – including its criticisms of free markets, all business owners, etc.

### Journalists Rewarded for Anti-Business And Improbable Stories

To take the simpler case first: journalists, including political activists/ ideologues purporting to be "objective" journalists, above all need to be both believable and exciting in what they write – so that their readers look forward eagerly to whatever they write – next.

Since the beginning of the Republic, the most exciting things to report about – aside from crimes of violence and military events during wartime – have involved business activities of various kinds – especially beginning in the mid-19th century when truly-free (subject to market forces and common law rules alone) business enterprises, run by imaginative, energetic, ambitious men, were busily creating truly-revolutionary new products and services which the public benefited from enormously (literally creating entire new markets), along with their wealth creation, at what can only be described a breakneck speed.

Collectivists of all stripes eventually succeeded in smearing and slandering all these businessmen as "robber barons" – branding them with the nonsensical, explicitly-Marxist accusation of relying on robbery (armed, violent theft) alone for their wealth-acquisition. This, of course, amounted to classic projection: who is the true thief/robber – the man who earns his wealth by pleasing customers who buy his goods, and his employees motivated to make them at his direction, or the bureaucrat or intellectual who takes it from him under state-enforced and dictated threat of violence?

Clearly, the presence of these previously-unimaginable, virtually-magic new products and services (railroads, diesel engines and the ships they powered, electric power transmission, and others) excited powerful emotions from the public, including genuine delight and, unfortunately, anger or jealousy aimed at someone else's vastly-enhanced market power resulting in enormous wealth, jealously regarded by some as inherently-criminal, or at best mere "good fortune."

This combination of truly amazing public benefit resulting from such inventions and their implementation for public availability by American entrepreneurs, resulting in private market power and wealth for some and jealousy from many, guaranteed the popularity of "news" stories which involved fabulously-and newly wealthy businessman who, in the case of railroads, had obtained at least some of their wealth arguably as windfall benefits at public expense, purportedly harming less-wealthy people (employees, customers) in some manner – even if only allegedly "overcharging" for the genuinely revolutionary benefits they were in fact able to provide others.

The image promoted by such stories – of predatory capitalists supposedly despoiling/consuming their customers, employees and/or any other innocent bystanders – is literally the very essence of the "teachings" of Karl Marx, which, as shown above is:

> "all businessmen are thieves and scoundrels, with monopoly power at all times over both their customers and employees, subject to <u>no</u> constraints whatsoever until all their property is confiscated by, or put completely under the control of, the state and its "experts," who

will far more efficiently and "fairly" manage it, on behalf of their "workers."

It is no exaggeration to say that throughout American history, and increasingly so since the mid-19th century, numerous journalists have spent considerable efforts seeking out precisely those kind of major, or even minor, business scandals to report on — or fabricate — which, in a country as vast and industrious as this one often are available – even if they were one-offs, or had to be manufactured or distorted and turned into something even more sensational, and even "shocking."

Of particular, prurient interest were stories suggesting immensely wealthy businessman, whose wealth could be depicted as having been acquired primarily from publicly-funded windfalls, exercising practically-controlling power over public officials. Indeed, journalists targeted public officials typically only when they could depict them as corrupted by businessmen, with politicians' own scandals usually minimized.

That was precisely the ongoing theme of numerous stories concerning the multiple railroad owners in the country – particularly those who owned railroads crisscrossing the wild West – beginning in the 1870s. Cartoonists began depicting the railroad magnates – and other successful businessman – in the well-known caricature (straight out of the Karl Marx coloring book) in which their heads are money bags, and their bodies are enormously fat, dressed in tuxedos smoking enormous cigars.

Quite simply, journalists need/want to be able to tell a story their readers will find both personally interesting and emotion-exciting, a story that, like all good stories, needs one or more villains and, ideally, the possibility of a hero who can ride in and save the day with some magic solution. People living normal, happy, productive lives, including honest businessmen producing goods and services without adverse incident, obviously provide no "news stories" at all.

## Journalists' Career Advancement

There are in fact multiple reasons why individual journalists, themselves reporting to editors, who in turn reported to owners, all had multiple effectively built-in motives for a bias favoring what could be called Marxist anti-business "narratives" suggesting, or based on, the implicit collectivist assumption of, the inherent desirability of the federal government ultimately getting involved as Savior in one manner or another, supposedly to "correct" whatever "shocking," or at least ostensibly-harmful, outcomes one or more business might be able to be accused of having created.

## Journalists Assault The Railroad Industry

The entire situation in the nation which arose, beginning in the 1870s, after the extraordinary funding provided by the federal government in various manners to facilitate the extremely rapid implementation and creation of various railroad lines, created the paradigm of these type of antibusiness narratives which numerous journalists – including Mark Twain, among others – used as a cookie-cutter against numerous businesses thereafter, once the railroad business was subjected to the first federal business-"regulatory" agency ever created, in the first federal legislation enacted to impose the federal government on any business – The 1887 Interstate Commerce Act, which created the Interstate Commerce Commission.

As it happened, depicting the excesses enjoyed by the railroad industry prior to 1887 was pregnant with genuinely-interesting, journalistic scandal-exposure opportunities. And of course journalists never depict their own industry in a negative light: their multiple articles which served their purpose of turning the entire railroad industry into an object of anger and envy by large segments of the public all constituted vicious accusations against persons OTHER THAN THE JOURNALISTS THEMSELVES.

And, of course, it was always the (blameless) politicians, who happily provided the financial windfalls to the railroads, beginning in the 1860s, initially to encourage their rapid construction and development and who then, beginning in the 1870s, expressed outrage at the railroads' windfalls those politicians had themselves funded, and then, following noisy journalistic "exposure" of the excesses, were eager to have the federal government intrude on the railroad business, proclaiming themselves to be the rescuing heroes of the public by such intrusions, and that those intrusions would fix everything – which they never, ever did in fact.

By the 1880s, the railroad owners, responding to the two major motivating factors of all businessmen – fear and greed – had come up with their own solution to accommodate what they viewed as the likely inevitable federal intrusion into their business. And their solution was one which the politicians were happy about – because it turned the railroad industry and its wealthy owners effectively into "clients" of the politicians permanently in need of paying those politicians to minimize the injury to themselves personally from such federal intrusion, and as the only means available to the regulated businessman to influence the "regulators" themselves.

All these interrelationships between the regulated businessmen, the politicians and the regulators had the effect of benefiting the then-incumbent businessmen by virtually precluding new market entrants from competing with them, since any new market entrants would have to immediately reach a similar accommodation with the controlling politicians and regulators before they could function without the threat of existential disaster at all times – a threat which clearly would at least throw very cold water on any interest they had of investing in the railroad business – as opposed to the multiple other business opportunities which still remained open at that time in America.

Railroad "Regulation"

Indeed, the history of the entire railroad industry in America after the enactment of the Interstate Commerce Act can be summarized as follows:

> the few incumbent, dominant railroads that existed at the time of its enactment achieved complete, dominant control of the industry which no new entrant competitor could challenge – until permitted to do so marginally decades later; although the major complaint against the railroads was their perfectly-rational and legal price dis- crimination among customers (offering better rates to huge ones than for small ones), nobody's rates were ever reduced once regu- lation came into place, as they had been falling for everyone prior thereto.

Over the decades since 1887, literally hundreds of thousands of government bureaucrats, lawyers and lobbyists received vast amounts of money, ultimately funded by the railroads' customers, in connection with "regulating" every minute detail of the industry and acting as intermediaries between the railroads and the government, design and technological innovation barely occurred at all, although it had been occurring at a rapid pace before "regulation," politicians received vast amounts of money both legally and illegally from the railroads as "protection money," bribes and/or campaign contributions – take your pick – and the entire industry experienced multiple bankruptcies and financial disasters and safety problems for over 100 years, with multiple "legislative fixes" by Congress along the way, none of which did anything other than add to the bureaucratic complexity for railroads and all who dealt with them, until the industry was sub- stantially deregulated in 1995.

it took over 100 years for the government to admit that all its efforts at railroad "regulation" were disastrous and achieved nothing other than additional expense for the public, and funding of parasites living off the regulation in one way or another. To this day, that industry has not recovered, and substantial parts of the country receive railroad passenger service operated by the federal government itself at vast cost to taxpayers, with the usual utterly incompetent management one would expect from government operations of any kind – terrible accidents, grotesque costs of everything, corrupt unions, you name it.

The journalists' "stories" regarding businesses singled out for this type of attack, beginning with the railroad industry, of course never included com- pensating descriptions of the remarkably innovative benefits to the business' customers which the attacked business was providing before regulation – benefits which, invariably, had previously been unavailable at any price to anyone – and the benefits to the business' employees who both obtained employment and, if the business were free to grow and develop consistent with market demands regarding it, unconstrained by political/"regulatory" impositions, would have the opportunity either to grow with it or, based on what they learned by working for it, actively compete with it if they thought they could do it better.

Specifically, the story of what would happen to everyone affected by the business if the federal government never got involved in its affairs never could be told – since it had not yet happened and was effectively precluded from happening by that very federal intervention. No one – other than Adam Smith, who had already written his books on the subject – showed the benefits of the free market continuing constrained only by the common law.

And, of course, under the common law in effect in every state, if any business had truly harmed anyone it had any interaction with in any capacity, and the harm was due to <u>actual fault </u>by the business, multiple claims under business tort law could be made against it legitimately by any individual actually so harmed.

But a central pillar of collectivists in America has always been to pretend away the very existence of the common-law protections of actual individuals, and to claim that the federal government must exercise control <u>prior to</u> any actual injury to any actual person, purportedly to preclude any injury from ever even occurring to anyone, a promise that can never be fulfilled in real life.

This is another reason journalists were drawn to collectivism – and were themselves subjected to it in the kind of group-think mentality it invariably imposes and demands of all who succumb to it: the writings of Karl Marx after the 1840s showed them how to go about attacking businesses and their owners and managers – as a collective target – while proclaiming themselves the protectors of other collective groups of persons – employees, taxpayers as a group (who had provided financing for the railroads' development during the 1860s) and, of course, railroad employees who supposedly, according to Marx, were being "exploited" by the railroads simply by working for it.

Another reason for this collective bias towards Marxism (usually, but not always, unconscious) by journalist in the 19th century was its popularity among the intellectuals who the journalists often looked up to – and who they often aspired to become peers to and be accepted by.

And American University faculty members, and other self-identified public intellectuals, similarly found promoting Marxism through Marxist-inspired "narratives" irresistibly attractive for multiple, additional, self-interested reasons as well, while invariably proclaiming themselves personally-and-academically-disinterested observers of society, earnestly seeking the greatest good and the greatest truth above all else. In other words, they each invariably have proclaimed themselves an "expert," demanding to be followed by the great unwashed to whom they deign to provide guidance.

<u>To Summarize The Reasons for the Marxist Predilection Of Many Professions:</u>

(1) Marxism purported to present a simplified, supposedly "scientific" explanation for <u>virtually all human history</u>. European and American journalists and more-exalted intellectuals – whose own lives were completely divorced from producing anything tangible in the real market – overwhelmingly were convinced of its truth, in no small measure because many of them shared, snobbishly, in the hatred and resentment for actual businessmen which was at its heart, and the multiple financial and career benefits they derived both from following its precepts, and actively promoting it – with no personal downside to them since they and their property were never its targets.

(2) "Intellectuals," particularly so-called "social scientists" such as economists, sociologists, political "scientists" etc., tended to favor Marxism as a guiding, reductionist political philosophy in conducting their research, "studies" and in the ostensibly "scholarly" papers they published based on such, both because of its very nonsensical nature which is at its core (everything it says about people defies common sense and actual experience of normal people interacting with others), and the general respect "studies" purporting to "prove" such "remarkable" ideas would therefore command among other "intellectuals."

The particular value of the nonsense Marxism promotes for career-advancing purposes of intellectuals in all fields is that if somebody writes a paper proving something which is obvious or what common sense would predict, it obviously has nothing remarkable about it. However, if someone can design a "study," or otherwise provide some supposedly-impressive "proof" for a proposition which is inherently nonsensical and <u>defies</u> common sense, that is always deemed a true "accomplishment" for its academic or journalistic author.

Since there actually is nothing genuinely scientific about "social science," anyone with some native intelligence and imagination, intent on "proving" virtually any proposition – no matter how preposterous it may be – can devise a "study" which can produce results which he can at least argue "prove" the nonsense he is propagating.

If the proposition he is advancing is appealing to politicians – and other academics – that will virtually guarantee further accolades for it. And this is without regard to the unscrupulous "social scientists" who simply lie and make up their claimed "experimental" results. It is a notorious fact that many highly-celebrated social "scientists," including the "anthropologist" Margaret Mead, among others, have done precisely that.

Thus, for example, a "study" which claims to "prove", contrary to common sense and the laws of economics, that an increase in the politically-mandated "minimum wage" results not in a decline in employment, but an <u>increase</u> in such, is guaranteed to be applauded both within the Marxist segment of the economics profession, and among politicians intent on convincing constituents of the virtues of minimum-wage legislation which, as any idiot knows, simply has the effect of rendering it illegal to hire people for less than the mandated minimum wage —

precisely if they want to be so hired, forcing them into involuntary, legally-mandated unemployment.

Similarly, Keynsian economics "studies" and papers, invariably based exclusively on tautoligically-presumed notions that such spending <u>automatically</u> produces growth by some nonsensical "multiplier," often accompanied by elaborate ostensibly-mathematical formulations, which "prove" the benefits of politicians spending taxpayer money, instead of saving it, are guaranteed to be popular among such politicians who are ever-eager to find some claimed intellectual/"-expert" support for policies they would favor anyway.

So promoting Marxist "narratives" – by any means – and stirring up public anger and jealousy directed at businessmen as a result of their articles and other writings, and so supposedly "educating" the public about the evils of those businessmen, proved to be a professionally and personally-emotionally (and financially) gratifying enterprise for journalists, university professors and other "intellectuals" virtually from the time they first read Marx's drivel beginning in the 1840s.

Indeed the fact that <u>Marx himself</u> was arguing for an even more extreme collectivist state let them congratulate themselves as comparative "moderates."

And the inevitable political control of Marxism – including, ultimately, thought-control – which had been a proven disaster as an economic growth-promoting political arrangement everywhere it had been tried already throughout continental Europe, was a detail they had no interest in themselves – and no interest whatsoever in writing about.

Indeed, they have always – to this day – pretended otherwise, worshiping the supposed idealism and even the "liberating" effect of all prior Marxists and, whenever confronted with their mass murder and/or undeniable practical failure, pretend their own brilliance lets them improve on the original, claiming that those earlier Marxists simply didn't know how to do it right – and that once Marxism is done right — by them — its value will be undeniable.

Having been drawn into the religion of collectivism, as "developed" by Marxism, they may truly believe their own nonsense in this regard: loyalty to the "Cause", once one is drawn into collectivism, is invariably enforced internally and by the rest of the collectivist true believers – and no one is allowed to leave the fold alive. Whittaker Chambers and David Horowitz are literally the genuinely-brilliant and moral exceptions that prove this rule.

All these features of journalists and "intellectuals" began to be institutionalized by the late 19th-century, with them also claiming to have themselves "matured" their trades into "professions" worthy of particular societal regard and respect. In part because of the increasingly-hierarchical nature of those two professions, and the benefits – financial and otherwise – to each individual member of those professions of continuing to share in an underlying ideology of anti-business/pro-government collectivism, especially as focused by Marxism.

In both such professions, senior members of the profession – and, interestingly, not the non-Marxist public they have supposedly served – have increasingly had control of the advancement by more junior members, a control which ultimately became institutionalized at universities in the 20th century once the notion of "tenure" for university professors became an established, economic fact for them: once they obtained that designation, they had professional sinecures for life and, of course, professional recognition for having attained that status.

Similarly, journalists succeed based on the popularity of their writings both with the public and with their superiors in the journalistic publications employing them. As shown in Chapter 6 above, one of the remarkable features of collectivism, once it is absorbed by its adherents, is its group-think consequence, so that those won over by the collectivist ideology do not have to be instructed, and do not have to conspire: because of their shared religiously-believed, reductionist ideology, through the lens of which they view everything they see, with all contradictory viewpoints or information automatically rejected or ignored, if not hidden from view by the mechanisms of the collective itself: all collectivist true believers invariably reach identical opinions about any particular circumstance or issue – without even needing to be told to do so.

## The Counterrevolutionary Capture of the Legal Profession

In the 19th century, where virtually all scientific research was conducted either by talented "amateurs" trying to invent new products, or on university campuses, the only other profession with any claim to be "learned" was the legal profession, consisting of lawyers and judges (there were no law schools until late in the 19th century) – and it too produced nothing in the way of new products or services (the legal advocacy services provided in court were obviously valuable, but by no means a new phenomenon, as was, for example, the railroad). Although many involved in the founding of the Republic were lawyers – e.g. Jefferson, Madison and Hamilton – none of them limited their professional lives to practicing law, and none of them ever contemplated that lawyers would have a particular, supervisory/dictatorial power over the laws and institutions of the republic.

Nevertheless, early in the history of the republic, the legal profession began to sense that the importance of the rule of law – initially Good Law only, until 1887 – created opportunities for their profession to grow and prosper, and achieve a degree of importance it never had had in England or here before our independence – in marked contrast to the enormous importance of the legal profession under the tyrannical "regulatory" governments of continental Europe.

Quite simply, in a country ruled exclusively by Good Law, the only real things for lawyers to do in the economy are conducting litigation in the courts on behalf of clients, and advising clients on real estate, contract matters and estate planning – i.e., drafting legal instruments. Business planning, under a regime of Good Law, only principally involves business, and not legal decisions – with no need to waste time currying favors with regulatory agencies, which do not exist.

The first major opportunity lawyers saw occurred in early Supreme Court decision when the Supreme Court announced that it had the power – unique among all government institutions – to declare what the Constitution and other laws say. This was a radical position for the Supreme Court to take, plainly violative of Article V of the Constitution to the extent it was claiming the power to change the Constitution's meaning, and it is likely that few took it seriously at the time – including John Marshall, the author of the legal opinion which announced that "rule" – *Marbury v. Madison* (that opinion, ruling against Marshall's own Federalist party position, and thereby precluding complaints by the prevailing party therein, has some genuinely-nonsensical features which would have been apparent to his contemporaries, discussion of which is beyond the scope of this book).

Lawyers saw their profession's power-grabbing opportunity developing in the 1870s, with increasing journalistic anger, energies and propaganda aimed at the railroad business; and they were well aware of the enormous power possessed by members of their profession in Europe because all businesses there were indeed "regulated" by the state – and had been for centuries. That power was a direct result of the destructive potential over every industry by the government's "regulation" of it: everyone wanted the industry to produce its product and/or service, but the state wanted to control it, so that the only practicable way for the industry to operate was to pay, as a business expense of operation, for lawyers/lobbyists who would act as essential intermediaries on its behalf in dealing with the "regulators".

Thus, the presence of that state bureaucratic power over the businesses itself generated the particular need for lawyers' assistance of clients in circumstances where no such need had existed previously – and, because the (existential, violence) power the regulatory agency exercised over the client was so massive, the lawyers could charge accordingly for rescuing the client from the clutches of that agency.

Thus, the legal profession had an enormous interest in approving and promoting the growth of federal regulatory agencies empowered by Bad Law over more and more businesses, even though the inevitable (see chapters 4 and 5 above) effect of such agencies was to stifle all innovation and growth in those businesses — the lawyers' own clients!

These circumstances powerfully drew the legal profession itself increasingly into being captured by the Collectivist cause. The end result of over 100 years of these processes is that law firms today are literally 10 times the size they were a mere few decades ago (for example, today, large law firms have thousands of partners and associates; as late as the mid-1970s, the largest law firms in the country had no more than 200).

The presence of multiple regulatory agencies in the nation results in fewer and fewer businesses in each area of business, with each such remaining business necessarily large enough that it can deal with the regulatory costs of competing in that business – and complying with the directives of the agency. Since most large businesses today are subject to the tyrannical direction of multiple such federal agencies, any law firm representing them necessarily requires expertise – and political clout – in dealing with multiple such agencies.

Thus, each law firm client gets bigger, as their total number is reduced (since fewer and fewer businesses can compete in each market, which becomes a virtual oligopoly under the thumb of the regulatory agencies controlling it), and only the very largest law firms can fully service such massive clients. Smaller law firms can only survive if they offer boutique-type services for discrete portions of client needs — or old-fashioned simple legal services and/or litigation expertise.

Because the federal regulatory agencies are centered in Washington, this entire situation ultimately results in the need for all large law firms to have an office in Washington, and for Washington to be the center of power in the nation – both private and public – since no law firm or business can succeed without the approval of the agencies which have existential control over every business in the nation – and all its people.

And the lawyers and their firms, in order to ingratiate themselves with the politicians and regulatory agencies they have no choice but to deal with, similarly have no choice but to voice their approval and promotion of the entire Counterrevolutionary "regulatory" administrative state. That is how corporate lawyers become collectivists – even if only to serve and please the masters they have no choice but to answer to.

Towards the end of the 19th century, for the first time, law schools were created and lawyers were "schooled" by them. Faculty at law schools were influenced by the same perverse, career-enhancing motives as other academics, as described above —and by the increasingly-Marxist faculty of the rest of the universities the law schools were part of.

Specifically, law school faculty members, like other university professors, won recognition among their fellow legal academicians by writing law review articles promoting novel, expansionary legal arguments, including particularly arguments why the Bad Law should be promoted, and extended to — and so imposed on— various circumstances previously free of its force, supposedly to advance civilization. As shown above, Bad Law always destroys individual liberty and serves no one but parasites – including the lawyers, politicians and bureaucrats who benefit from its presence.

Again, as other academics found, the more preposterous and counter-intuitive the legal theories law professors chose to write about and advocate for were, the more impressive their fellow academics have found them – and the more career benefits the legal academics have earned for themselves, benefits and accolades similarly bestowed on judges and legislators who adopted the most preposterous and counter-intuitive legal theories so advanced as actual legal directives.

Thus, in a nation founded on principles demanding the tightest restriction of government and law, respected academics in the legal profession have found it to their advantage to push law beyond those boundaries of constitutional constraints and to advance theories on why the Constitution should be disregarded, or "interpreted" in a manner directly contrary to that which common sense, and its own text, demanded, and judges and other politicians were acclaimed and received career advancement when they turned those academic absurdities into real law affecting real people.

## The American Collectivist Mindset And Mental State

I have attempted in chapter 6 above, with great care, accurately to describe both the basic beliefs common to individual collectivists of all stripes (including self-identified liberals, progressives, French Revolutionary/Jacobin/Rousseau-enthusiasts and Marxists of all types) and the major, intellectual sources which originated them.

I have personally known many collectivists of all different stripes, and have observed many others, resulting in the following observations about a number of mental traits they tend to have in common, traits which seem to make them particularly susceptible to being won-over to the arguments of other collectivists who initially convince them to join the Cause, and which result in their ongoing, intense loyalty to the Cause – and deeply-emotional opposition to, and loathing of, all its opponents, real or imagined.

That loyalty is such that, even while invariably thinking of themselves as open-minded, independent, radical or even revolutionary freethinkers, they view any disloyalty to the Cause as monstrous treason, and so invariably ignore, belittle, and otherwise hermetically seal themselves off from arguments – and any arguers – of any kind, in any way critical of the Cause.

In addition to all of the particular beliefs and other psychological characteristics of collectivists discussed below, an essential feature of all of them, as discussed in Chapter 6 above, is their, consistent ontological attitude regarding other people, and sometimes themselves as well, as having little or no individual moral value, viewing humans invariably as simply interchangeable, soulless members of always superficially-identifiable groups, groups typically described according to racial, sexual, economic status (what Marxists call "class").

This attitude has the effect of dehumanizing individuals so characterized, a dehumanization ultimately necessary for collectivists to find moral justification for disregarding the value of those people individually.

Radical collectivists – Stalinists, e.g. – find in this dehumanization the basis for legitimizing the mass murder undeniably committed by Communists everywhere they have obtained power sufficient to do that. Less drastically, viewing people that way justifies Marxist arguments in favor of dividing entire populations of individuals according to those individually-irrelevant criteria, to turn them against each other – literally manufacturing Marxist class warfare – to facilitate their conquest and defeat.

Additionally, the mindset involved in viewing people in that collectivist manner makes individual collectivists susceptible to collectivist-type arguments – favoring certain groups because of those humanly-irrelevant criteria, and similarly disfavoring others, creating "narratives" of collective victimization by identifying particular such groups as "victims" and others as "oppressors." This permits those buying into this mindset to buy into notions of supposed racial guilt spanning multiple generations and centuries – smears – resulting in demands, for example, for all white people in 20th-century America, simply because of their race, to owe a permanent debt to contemporaneous Blacks who have themselves never been slaves, as but a significant, and often repeated, bloody-shirt example.

Many collectivists in all age groups view the Cause as "hip" or "liberating," for a variety of reasons, including its typical opposition to (ostensibly personally-restricting) religion and morality of any kind and, particularly since the 1960s, the fact that it is invariably championed by most show business personalities – rock musicians, Hollywood, celebrity artists and fashionistas. This pretense to "hipness" was introduced and initiated as a recruiting tool by the avant garde of the New Left (themselves actually confirmed Stalinists determined to put a prettified face on that abomination), as discussed in Chapter 17.

Even the fact that collectivism invariably favors actual, or virtual (through "regulations") federal take-over of the very businesses which produce all the products and services we enjoy, including all aspects of the petroleum business, without which our modern, incredibly-comfortable, lifestyles would be utterly impossible and we would be forced to live at the bare subsistence level (no cars, appliances of any kind, heat and air-conditioning, toilets, literally no power) which virtually all people lived under – including the very wealthiest – until American entrepreneurs both invented virtually all those remarkable products and devised and executed the means for delivering them to their customers – with nothing but interference, if not outright opposition, from the federal government after 1890, which government itself neither invented nor produced anything but business and growth impediments.

Obviously, these attitudes about the Cause – including collectivists' absolute loathing of its opponents – are based on ignorance or indifference to that Cause's actual exclusively-destructive effects on individual liberty and, indeed, on the very nature of the Bad Law it promotes. Nevertheless, these (mistaken) beliefs about the Cause by its collective members greatly enhance the enthusiasm of their support for it – an enthusiasm similar to that of "fanatic" sports fans for their favorite team.

I have observed several clearly-identifiable intellectual and emotional threads (I don't know what else to call them), in virtually all collectivist enthusiasts, including both those particularly determined, brimming with narcissism, solipsism, and ambition, to become leaders of the Cause – in the always-elitist avant garde proclaimed by Lenin and Stalin – and those willing to be mere followers. These threads invariably themselves interweave in the minds and hearts of those collectivists synergistically, binding them to the Cause, in a deeply personal manner, beyond mere ideology, with a pseudo-religious (even though they rarely stray from atheism) fervor.

Most, but not all, collectivists either actively despise all religions (at least those they are aware of), and even the very notion of God Himself, or are deeply-ambivalent about God and/or religion, even if they consider themselves members of a religion. Aside from a majority of highly-secularized American Jews and Protestants, the principal exception to this are the many Catholics who buy into the notions that Christ was a quasi-socialist and/or that welfare is a genuine form of charity – notions typically based on teachings to that effect from Catholic clergy including, most recently and prominently, Pope Francis, but also many American bishops and priests, following official (although not purporting to be infallible) church teachings in support of the administrative welfare state since 1871.

I have shown in Chapter 2 that these post-1870 teachings of the Catholic Church have no basis whatsoever in Scripture.

As I have pointed out repeatedly, all continental European countries – many of which at least used to have large Catholic populations – have never known any citizen-policing laws since the 17th century other than Bad Law, as described above, including the full-blown welfare administrative state by the mid-19th century. Query: was the 1871 Catholic embrace of the welfare administrative state a politically-conscious attempt to please continental European governments and church members who were already plainly committed to that course of action? The Catholic church embrace of collectivism is all the more astonishing otherwise in light of the virulent anti-Catholic nature of collectivist revolutions of all kinds, as discussed above.

These intellectual and emotional threads in collectivists include (1) overwhelmingly-powerful negative emotions (anger, envy, resentment, terror, pain, guilt) which, when coupled with each collectivist's pre-existing beliefs, both precede their commitment to the Cause, and are invariably magnified and fanned incident to that commitment, and the influence of the remaining two threads, (2) profound intellectual and emotional support for one or more of the various Movements, briefly discussed below, championed by the Cause and deployed by it strategically to recruit new members and intensify the loyalty of all members, and (3) a deeply-felt loathing/condemnation of some particular aspect of America in particular, focused on intently, and even obsessively, by the collectivist, as an always-unforgivable sin requiring unending restitution – like Lady Macbeth's "spot" – of some kind, particularly from those Americans seen as (immorally) willing to forgive that sin.

Committed Collectivists invariably are passionate people, devoted to feeling (that is the precise word for what they seek) that they are indeed "compassionate" and "doing the right thing," typically deeply-doubting that they are doing so, and so feeling guilt-ridden, or otherwise deeply dissatisfied, <u>before</u> finding the Cause and its collective group.They typically experience themselves as magnetically-drawn to, and finding a kind of personal, quasi-religious salvation in, the Cause, and any particular collectivist Movements they are drawn to, and in feeling themselves an integral part of its always-welcoming collective group.

As mentioned, they are driven by powerful emotions both before and after finding the Cause – pain, fear, anger, guilt, envy, resentment and/or various combinations of those emotions, emotions directed both at perceived, external evils they desire to defeat, and/or at themselves. They see and experience the Cause, and some or all of its Movements, discussed below, in a very personal manner– a salvationary antidote to the suffering and emptiness they, in their souls' godlessness, otherwise experience.

<u>Collectivist Movements — in General</u>

Apart from committed, Marxist ideologues, who often are sociopaths drawn to that ideology because of its promise of limitless power over others – at least to its hard-core leaders – most American collectivists are drawn in by one or more of its so-called Movements, which they find morally, as well as ideologically-compelling. That is, of course, many such Movements' true purpose – to <u>create the appearance of</u> an ostensibly-morally-compelling, apparently-non-political, Trojan-horse-like magnet for the Cause.

Indeed, although obtaining absolute political power over the citizenry has always been the Counterrevolution's goal, it has invariably promoted that Cause indirectly and tangentially (well-aware as it has always been of the unpopularity of its true Marxist political intentions) – through such "movements" of various sorts, many of which pretend to have no political dimension whatsoever. Indeed, that "non-political" pretense is typically the disarming hook they use to gain favor from many who would be horrified if they understood what truly was afoot.

There have been many such Movements. As discussed above, in the 19th century, the Counterrevolution first gathered its deeply-entrenched strength among influential professions. It then drew on those constituencies and their influence over the rest of society to create Bad Law Counterrevolutionary legislation (first, the Interstate Commerce Act and the Sherman Antitrust Act). Those professions' influence by the late 1880s was so great that those truly-radical European-type laws passed with virtually no opposition – notwithstanding their clear unconstitutionality.

All those constituencies captured in the 19th century for the Counterrevolution have remained integral parts of it ever since. With that strength already existing in support of its radical program, the Counterrevolution has particularly relied on its various Movements since the 19th century to establish what might be called extra-democratic support.

Collectivism's Unnamed, All-Permeating, Radical Nihilist Movement

Throughout the remainder of this chapter, and in Chapter 17, I discuss most of the very-visible Collectivist Movements, each of which have adopted particular "popular" names for themselves, which names I use in my discussion. However, underlying and permeating all these Movements is an additional one which has assigned no name to itself, but which is profoundly important in all other collectivist movements – and even constantly invents new ones.

I have presumed to name this additional Movement the All-Permeating, Radical Nihilist Movement. It manifests itself when the Cause promotes multiple emotion-laden "ideas," each of which would have been considered utterly insane and preposterous until very recently, under traditional Western Judeo-Christian moral and legal concepts. Each of these ideas so promoted is genuinely revolutionary and profoundly societally-disruptive — as its central purpose,

Each such concept is also calculated to divide us angrily and hurtfully against each other, against all Western religions (Christianity in all its forms and Judaism), against our own American history and traditions, and to destroy all of the most fundamental institutional aspects of the Western civilization and civil society whose origins were in Jerusalem and Athens — the civilization which used to be the central focus of a university liberal arts education, and which has become the object of angry, constant denunciation and ridicule at those same universities.

The "intellectual" and/or theoretical origins of this Movement can be recognized in the writings of Friedrich Nietzsche, after he had lost his mind, those of Martin Heidegger, the Nazi academic philosopher whose nihilistic views continue to completely dominate university philosophy departments, the writings of Herbert Marcuse, R.D. Laing, and Michel Foucault and all the other promoters, including Paul de Man and Jacques Derrida, of the nihilist academic movements referred to variously as Post-Modernism and Deconstructionism.

This Movement, whose theme, as I mentioned, permeates all other collectivist Movements, effectively asserts that everything any rational, non-Marxist, Christian, highly-educated or not, Westerner would have thought around, say, 1900, is itself utter nonsense, and literally insane, and that, in fact, the opposite of everything such a person would have thought is the actual truth, absolutely certain belief in which is required to not be insane and/or evil. This Movement literally tries to convince everyone that our world is like the Bizarro world in Superman comics – everything is backwards, reason is unreason, insanity is sanity, convicted criminals are innocent victims, while the police are interested only in preying on the innocent, particularly members of any minority group – Blacks, Muslims, you name it.

This Movement is the principal driver behind the transgender rights movement, for example, which literally takes a formerly-clinically-judged form of insanity – gender confusion – and not only promotes it as a legitimate, perfectly rational choice, but actively promotes it throughout society to the point that multiple states are now using criminal law to enforce its logic against their own citizenry, no more than a minuscule portion of whom actually buy into this.

Another recent, blatant example of this Movement is the so-called Black Lives Matter movement which pretends that a minuscule handful of what are almost always, in fact, clean shots fired by policeman against criminals threatening those policemen and others, which criminals happen to be black, are "proof" that all policeman are out to kill and execute <u>all</u> young black men, and that racist policemen are in fact responsible for most black deaths – a facially nonsensical proposition (as proven by the very very few number of cop-shooting-black youth incidents that even arise in a country as large as this).

Each such cop-shooting incident is (deliberately) misrepresented by the Movement as both an unjustified police execution of an innocent young black man, and as frequently-occurring. All of these underlying "facts," which the Movement exploits as its sole justification for existence, are sheer nonsense, to the point of being blatant lies every time they are repeated.

Nevertheless, an entire movement has arisen out of this anti-police, race-themed Movement, a movement which has been able to succeed as much as it has largely because of the open respect it has received from Obama, who has literally lent all the prestige of his office to support the validity of this obviously nihilistic Movement — and its underlying lies.

The Black Lives Matter and Transgender Rights movements are the most current and blatant examples of this underlying nihilistic Movement asserting itself, but its nihilism is present throughout all the other collectivist Movements.

As but one additional example of that, modern collectivists invariably pretend that they are ardent proponents of science, and that anyone who disagrees with their "scientific" beliefs is "anti-science," an assertion they make repeatedly. This arises in the modern Environmentalism movement in which already-undeniably-falsified computer models (all predictions made under the logic of those models have been proven to be nonsense when applied to known facts from the past) predicting doom for the entire planet are claimed to be unassailable, scientifically-proven facts.

Under any actual notion of science those models are, in fact, scientifically-proven nonsensical garbage. Nevertheless, totalitarian collectivists insisting on their claimed-undeniable correctness demand that all Western economies be destroyed, by abandoning all the irreplaceable energy sources they depend on, literally, for everything, all in service to preventing the already-falsified "predictions" from those models from coming true and supposedly destroying the planet.

Thus, in both these Movements, actual science is claimed to be fiction, while nonsense is claimed to be "science." This is typical of the nihilism of collectivism – and its radicalism. Proponents of this particular example of nihilism are presently actively attempting to make it a thought crime to disagree with them. For example,

United States Senators have attempted to enlist the Justice Department to criminally prosecute those who disagree with the predictions from those models – as if computer models predicting the future are scientific "proof," let alone mere evidence of, anything, particularly when those models have been falsified already. And as if the First Amendment does not exist.

Collectivism's Capture of the Civil rights Movement —
After it Achieved all its Legislative Victories

One of the most prominent movements in the 20th century was the mid-century Civil Rights Movement, a movement with many supporters including, most prominently, Rev. Martin Luther King who insisted particularly on its religious, moral underpinnings, in attacking specific state laws, primarily throughout the South – the so-called Jim Crow laws – which had institutionalized "separate but equal" provision of all services, in a manifestly-racist manner, as specifically authorized and blessed by the monstrous 19th-century Supreme Court in *Plessy v. Ferguson*, discussed in Chapter 11.

That movement was actually not a collectivist movement at all until <u>after</u> Martin Luther King's assassination, <u>after</u> the enactment of various civil rights laws by Congress in the mid-1960s, after which, to a great extent, genuine radical collectivists – Jesse Jackson and, later, Al Sharpton and assorted card-carrying Communists (e.g. H.P. O'Dell) who took over King's SCLC even before his death – effectively pushed their way into control of that no-longer-necessary (after all racially-discriminating laws and actions were legally outlawed) Movement. Its sole purpose thereafter became following the long-standing Marxist script of inciting continuing racial division and, particularly, resentment and the mentality of victimhood among Blacks, and demanding racial spoils and white racial punishment on a purely-racist, and collectivist, basis, utterly without regard to <u>actual individual responsibility or injury</u> on the part of both the "victims" and those against whom retribution was sought.

The most radical, collectivist aspect of the modern civil rights movement has been its insistence on that racially-conscious spoils system – so-called "affirmative action," supposedly based on "diversity" (a "goal" suddenly discovered in the 1970s solely because a concurring opinion in a Supreme Court case — *Bakke* — suddenly discovered its supposed importance and asserted that "diversity" as the only conceivable legitimizing rationale for any racial discrimination, for it to overcome its facial violation of the 14th amendment, when any state action is implicated therein).

Overwhelming pressure from federal regulatory agencies with existential power to inflict grave harm has now imposed that spoils system poisonously throughout society, including in corporate hirings, university admissions, etc. The manifestly collectivist nature of this is revealed in the fact that all harms and "benefits" inflicted and provided by it are based <u>solely on the race of all the favored, and the</u>

rejected, people, with no consideration whatsoever for actual justice to anyone in any case.

Again, quite simply, there is no other word for affirmative action except as anti-individual collectivism in action: It imposes purely race-determined punishments and supposed rewards – "benefits" to its "beneficiaries," and losses of opportunities to those who pay its price – all without regard to anyone's actual personal guilt or innocence. It is utterly destructive of racial relations, in its actual effects on its supposed "beneficiaries," and on the marginal whites who it gratuitously harms and, in its exclusive focus on racial criteria without regard to individual merit or culpability, is utterly destructive of Good Law and justice in society.

## Pacifist-Type Movements

A major purpose of many collectivist Movements is to gather popular support for a proposition whose true purpose is to provide a supposedly-indisputable, overwhelming moral imperative demanding the setting aside of all other legal considerations – particularly America's national security needs, and all private property rights – always for the principal purpose of inflicting damage to America (always the collectivist Cause's opponent) in particular, while purporting to simply be a supposedly-benign, and superficially-morally-commendable, position.

Typical of this anti-American type of Movement are the various pacifist and quasi-pacifist Movements, vigorously promoted throughout the 20th century by various Stalinist-backed Front groups (as proven beyond any doubt in the Venona Papers), and later popularized by the so-called New Left (as discussed in chapter 17), such as the so-called Antiwar, Anti-Nuclear, Nuclear Freeze, and other similar Movements, all devoted to obtaining virtual-or complete unilateral disarmament and disempowerment of all our American military's capabilities and/or military surrender by the United States – and only the United States (our nominal, military allies in NATO gutted their militaries long ago and unilaterally disarmed, counting on American protection, always pretending to moral superiority in so doing, no Movement necessary).

The deep anti-Americanism of these Movements is proven by the fact that never once have any of them demanded similar disarmament or surrender, nor any other action they demand from America, by any hostile-to-America nation, including the USSR and modern Putinist Russia, Revolutionary Iran, Islamist terrorists Hamas, ISIS, al Quaeda and Hezbollah, and Communist China, Cuba, North Korea, Vietnam, and even 1970's genocidal Cambodia.

The Pacifist Movement's greatest influence has been radically to restrict the actions by the American military during every war America has fought since World War II— vastly increasing the duration and lack of real victory, and the number of U.S. casualties, in each of those wars.

288

Specifically, those pacifist and quasi-pacifist movements have had enough of an influence that politicians of all parties have felt the need to try to conduct our wars and our intelligence operations with our troops and intelligence officers subject to elaborate, legal restrictions on their actions ("Rules of Engagement") which have made progress in such wars, especially ideologically-driven counter-insurgencies, extremely difficult, resulting in such wars – Korea, Vietnam, Iraq, anti-Terrorism, etc. – lasting inordinately long, with indecisive endings, instead of us obtaining the rapid, overwhelming victory we could have if all our true powers of violence and intelligence were unleashed on the enemy in a ruthless manner calculated to break its will, as was last permitted in World War II, and as has always been necessary to defeat any enemy throughout all history.

Environmentalism

One of the most radical collectivist Movements, which has had some of the most far-reaching, destructive effects, has been the so-called Environmental Movement, with all its various elements. Although it could be the sole topic of a lengthy book addressing its history and content, I include here just a few words about it in the present context – understanding what makes collectivists tick, and what draws them into the fold.

When Environmentalism was first introduced in its post-conservationist incarnation in 1970, there were indeed numerous chemical and other poisons in the air of many American cities – particularly Los Angeles – and in numerous American waterways. The word "pollution" originally referred to those actual poisons alone, and most Americans were indeed in favor of eliminating them. It is apparent that nothing in the Constitution permits the federal government itself to be involved in such activity at all. However, Pres. Nixon gratuitously and unilaterally — with no underlying legislation at all then!— purely by executive order, created the EPA, supposedly to oversee cleaning up those poisons. All those actual poisons were substantially eliminated by the end of the 1970s.

But by then multiple, unconstitutional federal regulatory agencies – the Departments of Transportation, Energy, the EPA, federal energy regulatory commission, to name only the most prominent – had been created and, as always with such agencies, their quest for agency-empowerment was only at its beginning once there was no longer any even-arguable, practical purpose for their continued existence.

They, like all such federal agencies, were and are all literally unconstitutional federal citizen-policing agency "solutions" ever in search of a problem. And, because of their existential claims regarding "environmentalism" and so-called "pollution" (as if any substance in the air or water is truly alien to the planet, rather than an earth-created substance that is simply located somewhere busy-body government regulators don't think it should be), they have constantly sought to expand their jurisdiction and impose their power wherever they could – and wherever the politicians and courts let them – in complete disregard for all private property rights and the Common Law itself, and the Constitution.

Without exaggeration, "Environmentalism" in all its forms has presented itself as an inherently-limitless justification for limitless Bad Law, whose purpose and effect is the absolute control over and destruction of all individual liberties and productive capabilities possessed by citizens, landowners and businesses it is able to confront and, through limitless Bad Law, trump. It and its bureaucrats recognizes no limiting principle whatsoever anywhere it is able to claim itself applicable – which happens to be anywhere in the "environment," meaning the air, the Earth, all rivers, lakes and other waterways. It effectively demands and claims the moral (without regard to God) right to an absolute governmental permission-requirement and veto over all human activities it claims might interfere with the supposed "purity" of the "environment."

Since "the environment" exists everywhere, this "imperative" effectively trumps every consideration, including all law concerning all citizens' use of their own property everywhere. Again, nothing whatsoever in the Constitution permits any of this to be done by the federal government.

Environmentalism invariably presents itself as a supposedly-moral imperative which, as just mentioned, trumps all other concerns. You will note that nowhere in the 10 Commandments is there any such moral imperative —to "subordinate the prosperity and other interests of men to the interests of preserving the planet in a pristine condition forever" — whatsoever.

Indeed, God's actual, Biblical commandment regarding man, all animals and the earth itself after the banishment from Eden was <u>precisely the opposite</u>:

> "And God blessed them, and God said unto them, Be fruitful, and multiply, and replenish the earth, <u>and subdue it: and have do-</u><u>minion</u> over the fish of the sea, and over the fowl of the air, and <u>over</u> <u>every living thing that moveth upon the earth</u> [emphases added]<u>."</u>

> — King James Bible, Genesis 1:28

The "moral" imperatives whose fulfillment is demanded by environmentalists are to do <u>exactly the opposite</u> of that Biblical mandate – to restrict and constrict all economic activity and growth of as many people as possible, and subordinate all human interests to the entirely-mythical, supposed needs supposedly required for the planet to remain in its supposedly-pristine state, with nothing whatsoever on it allowed to change, <u>forever</u>.

In other words, rather than "subdue [the earth]… and have dominion over every living thing…" "Environmentalists" proclaim that man should have <u>no power</u> <u>whatsoever</u> to rearrange or dominate the earth and its creatures in any manner and, instead, is required to <u>subordinate all his interests</u> (other than the personal interests of the "environmentalists") to theirs.

290

In America, massive amounts of Bad Law have been created since the 1960s in service to these truly anti-Biblical, anti-human, truly-radical, and literally insane mandates of the most radical environmentalists.

As but one example: the Endangered Species Act was enacted as "law" – without a single, even arguable, authorizing provision for such in the Constitution, and in direct violation of numerous actual Constitutional provisions – forcibly requiring the preservation of <u>every single then-existing species</u> in America, utterly without regard to the nature of any such species, its value to man, the cost of preserving it endlessly to the nation or to any individual, or to anyone's property, affected thereby.

That law has been routinely used by the most radical environmentalists to force landowners into being unable to use their own property in any manner, without first going to the prohibitive expense and humiliation of obtaining literally endless permissions from multiple government agencies and from the "environmentalists" themselves, through the license that Congress and the federal courts – flouting all the Constitution's protections for property rights and the Constitutional requirement for an actual "case" for federal court jurisdiction – have granted them endlessly to sue real people.

And that dictatorial power – threatening massive fines, financial ruin, and/or imprisonment for the slightest not-specifically-permitted-in advance action by the landowner with respect to his own property – is gratuitously wielded over such landowners without ever paying them a dime as compensation for their obvious loss of use of, and management rights over, their now-only-nominally-owned property. The endless litigation, bureaucratic processes and paperwork they are forced to comply with itself is a punishment – imposed simply because they own the land and want to use it.

Again, this monstrous outcome has been facilitated by the courts' adopting as "law" numerous legal fictions, including that all this obvious "taking" of people's property is not a "taking" within the meaning of the Constitution's Fifth Amendment — which explicitly requires paying them full compensation, <u>after</u> due process of law, for such. No credible historical or other basis for that just-mentioned "interpretation"/nullification of that explicit Constitutional clause has ever been plausibly presented by anyone, including any court adopting it.

The radical pretension of Environmentalism is that man effectively is a purely-destructive, evil enemy of the entire physical planet, and all its animals, in all his works and, to the extent that if any citizen, without first obtaining literally endless permissions from multiple government agencies and from the radical Marxist "environmentalists" themselves, "puts things into" anywhere in the environment, such constitutes "pollution," even though nothing can be put into any portion of any aspect of the environment by man <u>that does not come from the earth originally</u> anyway, and even though the earth is constantly changing — and evolving

— with all its animal and plant populations always coming and going. Charles Darwin anyone?

Environmentalism, or rather, its self-proclaimed champions, demand that literally everything, and every creature, on the Earth remain precisely as it was at some (unidentifiable, mythic) Edenic moment in time which the environmentalists in and out of the Government bureaucracies claim (based on no evidence whatsoever) was the perfect moment whose preservation supposedly constitutes such an overwhelming moral imperative, that it demands all the violent force of limitless federal power in its service, without regard to the moral, Constitutional, human and financial costs necessary — and without ever identifying any textual or other basis for this "moral" claim. There is none, except arising from the Bad Laws enabling their tyranny.

As anyone who applies any common sense at all to the preposterous, chicken little "the sky is falling" claims of post-1980's environmentalists realizes, those claims, particularly the particularly radical ones involving so-called "global warming" or "climate change," or whatever name is currently being applied to that unproven and unprovable nonsense, are nothing short of an abominable "big lie" supported by multiple useful idiots, government functionaries seeking power through it, "scientists" and other self-proclaimed luminaries whose livelihoods have come to depend on advancing the nonsense. And on no actual scientific proof, nor unspoliated, experimentally-shown evidence.

Briefly, all that "climate" nonsense involves predictions about the claimed future of the planet based solely on computer models – and not on actual scientific evidence. Those very computer models have, moreover already been proven to be utter garbage, since actual, known events from the past can be used to test the validity of their "predictions;" and doing so has invariably proven those models to be utterly worthless, consistently-incorrect "predictors" — so that all their predictions have, in fact, been scientifically-falsified and so proven to be absolute nonsense.

In real life, computer models whose predictions have been falsified in this manner are tossed in the garbage, and anyone who publicly announced "predictions" based on them would be fired — or tarred and feathered and run out of town.

It is of course indisputable that the climate is certain to change in the future – as it has always done, without regard to human activity, since the planet was formed.

The specific claim being radically promoted by the Movement with respect to the climate is the claim that our — particularly America's — increasing the $CO_2$ content above its tiny percentage in the atmosphere will inevitably increase planetary temperatures in a manner which, the radical alarmists insist, will be catastrophic to the planet and all humans on it. There is, in fact, no cause-and-effect evidence whatsoever that increases in $CO_2$ — which would undeniably be highly-beneficial to all vegetation on the planet, vegetation which uses it as its food — would in fact increase the temperature at all; and there also, similarly, is absolutely no evidence, let alone proof, that a several-degree increase in temperature would be anything less than enormously beneficial.

It happens that climate scientists – real ones – have calculated the percentage amounts of $CO_2$ in the atmosphere at various times in the past – time-periods spanning millions of years of actual Earth history, and not simply the brief period, beginning in the 19th century, for which there are actual, recorded temperatures – and have compared those data to the climates at those times and have proven that <u>there is no co-relation between the two whatsoever</u>: the Earth's climate has been both higher-temperature and lower- temperature throughout its history without regard to the $CO_2$ content of the atmosphere, which also has risen and fallen with no identifiable co-relation to planet temperatures.

In addition, it is well-known that there were times in the past when the planet's temperature was significantly higher than it has been for the past several hundred years – times for example, when Greenland <u>actually was green</u> and habitable by people with no heating technology more sophisticated than burning wood. Even the tough-as nails Vikings later had to abandon Greenland as a home when its temperature dropped to its present state.

In other words, it is readily-apparent to anyone with the tiniest amount of common sense, let alone any understanding of the scientific method, that neither (at least 6-8 degrees) higher planetary temperatures, nor $CO_2$, have any actual, overall adverse effect on the atmosphere whatsoever, with any actual climate problems for man and/or the planet perfectly capable of being addressed by a wealthy civilization's technological innovations – wealth and technological power which would both be drastically reduced, if not destroyed, by all of the climate alarmists' political demands.

The real reason its attackers have gone after $CO_2$ is their Marxist utter loathing of all American civilization and its still-nominally-free economy, which depend 100% on the only actual and reliable sources of energy – oil, gas and coal (and nuclear energy, which they also oppose). It is that eternal, fanatical, Marxist anti-American hatred driving the environmentalists' hatred of America's energy uses: all forms of energy consumed by man, other than nuclear energy, which have any genuine benefit to industrial society – coal, oil and gas in all their forms – produce $CO_2$. Thus, obviously, if one wanted to impose world socialism and/or terminate civilized, humane American civilization as we know it, legally ending the production of $CO_2$ from our energy sources would be an excellent way to do so.

And, of course, the only way any such insanity can be effected is by government seizing power over the American people and every aspect of our economy in a manner heretofore unknown except in communist dictatorships. The utter insanity of so doing has been proven by the Obama administration's energy policies which are self-admitted to be completely destructive of the entire present power plant industry in the nation, requiring the closure of hundreds of coal-fired energy plants, and will produce no identifiable CO2 reduction, nor any other benefit whatsoever — even in the administration's magical fantasies.

Specifically, the Obama administration itself <u>admits</u> that if its energy policies are followed <u>to the letter</u> for many decades, necessarily impoverishing and dis-empowering the nation and precluding it from having energy other than from sources that have yet to be invented, such policies will have an insignificant effect on the predicted temperatures on the planet (less than.015° – even assuming an amount that small is actually measurable, or predictable), and even assuming that any increase in temperatures would even do any actual harm (there is zero evidence for that proposition, and enormous, genuinely-substantial historical evidence against it), and further assuming – again, with no evidence whatsoever – that coal burning in America would have any effect on the climate whatsoever.

The self-admitted, utter practical-ineffectual reality of the massively-destructive "environmental" regulations pushed by the Obama administration proves by itself that actually improving the environment and the prospects for future citizens are matters of complete indifference to that (Marxist) administration, and that imposing dictatorial power over, and massively harming, the nation in all respects are the only, actual underlying purposes of all those "regulations."

Central to this particular radical "environmentalist" climate movement is its Marxist utter loathing of the United States as, its accusers invariably claim, the principal evildoer who has doomed the planet and now requires retribution. As bizarre as it may seem, that hatred of America, combined with the messianic vision inherent in the Movement itself – and the virtually-religious salvation promised by the Collective to those who promote it – and the intense emotions which promoting such a messianic cause excites in its true-believer adherents, together greatly animate existing and new adherents to the Counterrevolutionary collective in America. Note the interweaving of the three threads described above in these people in that regard.

<u>Multiculturalism</u>

Together with Environmentalism, Multiculturalism is a Marxist/collectivist Movement formulated and spawned primarily in the 1960s – an outgrowth of the so-called (Marxist) New Left. Both those Movements are so ambitiously expansive in their intended transnational societal and political reach, and so multifaceted and chameleon-like in their potential applications, as to totally dwarf the power, ambition, and reach of all other collectivist movements from earlier generations.

Although, like all such movements, they both misleadingly present themselves as purportedly benign, feel-good, happy-face, decency-and-civilization-promoting propositions, pretending to have no particular political dimension, they are anything but. Like all collectivist movements, everything about them is fraudulent.

Multiculturalism particularly pretends to promote liberty, domestic tranquility, and even human dignity. In real life, it does precisely the opposite.

Its greatest fraud, which is also its most fundamental and all-pervasive feature, is its pretense that in supposedly promoting all cultures, peoples and nations, it is neutral with respect to any one of them. In fact, it is anything but: its entire purpose is to be a frontal assault on America (and additionally, in Europe, on both all Western civilization, and Christianity especially, and on the very idea of nationhood) and its individual-liberty revolution, a revolution which is absolutely unique on the planet.

As discussed in Chapter 6, anti-Americanism hatred has always been one of the two ever-present features of, and is itself the driving force behind, Marxism, ever since Marx first enunciated it, arising out of his absolutely correct judgment that America's individual-liberty revolution is the diametrical opposite of his demanded communist one.

Multiculturalism, like all potent Marxist front movements, arises out of an intellectually-corrupt mixture of truth and falsehood, with the falsehood overwhelming its truthful aspects. The truthful concept was actually expressed uniquely in our Declaration of Independence – that all men are individuals who are created equal. But that is the last thing that Multiculturalism is really all about.

The fraud that is at its heart is its collectivist claim that actual individuals are utterly unimportant, and of no value, and all that matters are "groups"of various origins and races, and there is no moral difference whatsoever between any cultural or political ideas or ideals and any others, so that, for example, according to it, the ideas of Karl Marx have equal (or greater, actually) validity with those of the American founders. It doesn't matter how much human suffering and mass murder – the invariable, eventual consequences of Marxism everywhere it has been imposed.

That radical complete moral equivalence of all groups everywhere on the planet is the magical claim always insisted on by multiculturalists, as justification for their invariable assault on every aspect of America.

The central proposition of Multiculturalism is the idea of absolute ideological, cultural and political moral relativism. Although it has also been widely promoted in other countries around the world, particularly in Europe (where anti-Americanism is a perennial presence), Multiculturalism explicitly, and particularly, rejects any notion of "American exceptionalism," and the unique value of America and its culture in the world — and the consequent value of its historic "melting pot" feature requiring the assimilation into American culture of all immigrants.

It explicitly repudiates any notion that the extraordinary institutionalization of individual liberty against government power in the American founding documents has any extraordinary moral value whatsoever.

Multiculturalism instead purports to proclaim that the moral and political value and worth of every single country and culture anywhere on the planet today, or which has ever existed anywhere, is invariably-substantially identical, so that it is "morally"-repugnant and bigoted for anyone to claim any particular country — particularly America — or culture is "better" in any way than any other – or even to question the absolute value-equivalence of all cultures and countries.

In fact, even Multiculturalism's self-proclaimed claim to champion the notion, based on its radical notion of moral and cultural relativism, that all cultures should be considered absolutely equal in all respects, is itself a fraud: under Multiculturalism, as in all Marxist propositions, some nations and cultures are decidedly "more equal" than others. Specifically, in reality, it radically promotes the proposition that all cultures, other than those of the West, particularly that of America, are equal, and that Western and American cultures uniquely "deserve" to be reviled as, according to it, uniquely monstrous abominations on the planet.

It purports to represent an ecumenical, "moral" judgment that all judgments about moral value are morally impermissible. "Who are we to judge?" declares the true-believer Multiculturalist. But it does in fact judge — "morally" condemning the West, particularly America.

Multiculturalism's moral equivalence is extended to even the most vile and re-pulsive societies – e.g.,Muslim societies under Sharia law, which routinely engage in genital mutilation of virtually all female infants, enslavement of non-Muslim women, stoning and burying alive of former-Muslim "apostates," and of non-Muslims claimed to be proselytizing Muslims, and numerous other abominations no Western country would permit. It pretends, for example, that people living under communist governments and all other dictatorships are doing so volun-tarily, so that any Western effort to liberate them is deemed "cultural imperialism," and so reprehensible. It demands Israel surrender all defenses to "Palestinians" who unconditionally demand Israel be extinguished, happily sacrifice their children as suicide bombers and who cause, and commit, multiple terrorist acts against Israelis – supposedly in support of a "peace process."

And these are but a few examples where moral value judgment is forbidden by multiculturalism, except on its own quasi-moral terms – since any judgment based on actual Western morality would necessarily require condemnation of these just-mentioned, morally-reprehensible societies.

Multiculturalism is in some ways the purest expression in recent times of the Marxist thread discussed above focused particularly on absolute mortal hatred of the American Revolution and our founding documents. Behind its façade of "non-judgmentalism" and ecumenical love, Multiculturalism bristles with its own anti-morality (lacking any genuine religiously-authoritative textual basis) de-manding unquestioning "acceptance," no moral judgment permitted, of all ac-tions by all non-American people if they simply claim to be following their own traditions and culture. Once they assert that claim, anyone claiming any moral shortcoming on their behalf violates all multicultural cannons of decency and "morality" and must be condemned as a "racist," usually.

As shown above, America is absolutely unique in world history in that it is the only country which, in its founding documents, legally requires all law in the nation to be Good Law, as described in Chapter 5, with multiple substantive and procedural rules in the Constitution precluding enactment of Bad Law. That is what makes America truly exceptional. That, and not any racial, national or ethnic nature of our people is what has made us both exceptional and, when those laws were followed, the wealthiest, most powerful and most extraordinarily-productive nation ever – and the most generous.

And that is precisely what Multiculturalism directly attacks, claiming even the most monstrous governments are to be considered morally equivalent with us – and that it is even an imposition by us to seek to liberate their people from that monstrousness.

As mentioned above, all collectivism-and-Marxism promoting Movements have significant, anti-American dimensions. In the case of Environmentalism, for example, America and our (originally) free-market economy are singled out for particular blame as the supposed most-egregious culprit in supposed planetary destruction, requiring massive economic self-destruction, with a view, for example, to complete elimination, of all our present fossil-fuel energy sources at all levels, including preventing, wherever politically-possible, extraction of their raw products (oil, natural gas, coal primarily) and their processing, through power plants, pipelines, etc. into actual end-user energy.

To say that those fossil fuels are what our entire economy – and our lives – run on would be an understatement. Proposing their use-reduction, let alone their elimination, with no actual alternative fuel source to replace them – as no one denies is the case who has the slightest information about the subject – is tantamount to a doctor demanding his patient figure out a way to get rid of having blood in his veins.

It is a fact that America has been unique in the magnitude of its fossil-fuel consumption, a fact which has in turn led to our economy being vastly wealthier and more productive than that of any other country on the planet – throughout all history. Environmentalists claim that that energy use is an unforgivable moral violation (no authoritative basis for such claim given in any actual, known moral text), for which America uniquely must provide retribution both to the planet and to the other nations of the world – providing massive wealth transfers particularly to the most under-developed portions of the world whose underdevelopment has been reflected in their modest energy usage (although their actual atmospheric poison-generation is vastly in excess of that of the United States).

That is the primary, particular anti-American feature of Environmentalism. Multiculturalism is unique among Marxist movements in its anti-Americanism: frontally-attacking America's founders and our Constitution is actually what it is all about.

To fully appreciate the nature and purpose of Multiculturalism, it is necessary to fully appreciate the role of anti-Americanism in Marxism, uniquely among all collectivist movements. Specifically, the French Revolution never had any anti-American dimension, notwithstanding the enormous differences between those two revolutions, as discussed in Chapter 6. Marxism was altogether different in that respect, as well as many others.

Marxism can be seen as having two primary dimensions – (1) its (quasi-intellectual) idea-focused features (i.e., its purely-substantive views on God, religion, history, "classes," the economy etc.), and (2) its action-generating animating spirit which drives the fanatical enthusiasm for, and loyalty to, the revolutionary cause of its adherents, and infectiously draws in new adherents.

That animating spirit, in turn, has two dimensions – (1) endless desire for the (never-realized) utopia Marxism promises and which its adherents find singularly appealing, and (2) absolute hatred and resentment for — coupled with burning desire for total victory over — all people and ideologies perceived as opposing it or otherwise standing in its way, particularly America as founded, whose exceptionalism is described above.

These two profoundly-powerful, and ever-expanding, emotional drivers provide all the energy promoting Marxism's adherents focused devotion of their minds and willpower toward relentless support for the Cause.

All deeply-felt religions, ideologies, and quasi-religions similarly are driven by powerful emotions. It is the particular nature of those emotions, and who or what they are directed at, which define the very character of each religion, ideology etc.

As one example, few would disagree that the single emotion driving Christianity is love – for God and for all men ("your neighbor"), and that the particular desires at its heart are the desire for one's immortal soul's salvation and for justice, as prescribed by the Bible. The American Revolution was unmistakably an attempt to institutionalize precisely those Christian desires and precepts in this nation, in a manner markedly different from what any other nation which purported to be Christian had ever done, as shown in Chapter 2.

Marxism has always been precisely the opposite of the American Revolution in every respect – as Marx himself was keenly aware. He also recognized how completely antithetical to everything he advocated belief in God and the individual's immortal soul, and everything about the Bible was. His writings are literally filled with endless hatred of God, religion, the Bible and the United States and its Revolution (and Jews).

And as a quasi-religion, unlike the love which energizes Christianity, Marx and everything he advocated have invariably been emotionally-driven by those combined, and interrelated, hatreds, and attendant emotions (envy, resentment, terror – of potentially losing to any of those objects of its hatred).

As I said, those multiple hatreds – and angry hatred itself – have always formed the animating spirit of Marxism from its very start.

Multiculturalism – and the moral relativism it embodies – have served the purpose of initiating and stoking that Marxist hatred of America, its Revolution, God, religion and morality itself, all of which are animated by the belief that moral judgments must be made and adhered to. And, as shown in Chapter 2 above, the moral basis for the American Revolution and our founding documents, plainly derived from morally-compelling divine commandments in, and throughout, the Bible itself, is literally what America as founded is all about.

Multiculturalism has also served the purpose of promoting the various anti-American pacifist movements devoted to disarming America and preventing it from opposing manifest, ideological enemies in the ruthless manner they require, thereby aiding and abetting terrorist enemies engaged in counterinsurgency wars against us – because who are we to say they are not entitled to their anti-American ideology? That insanity is the precise attitude required by multiculturalism.

Moreover, by insisting, as Multiculturalism does, that immigrants to America who bring with them the cultures they came from (horrible, oppressive cultures which they came here to escape!) continue to hold on to those separate cultures and not assimilate into the general American culture, it compels a Balkanization of American society. This attacks the very heart of America in multiple ways, including creating additional criteria for dividing the population against itself – always a goal of Marxists seeking to conquer our nation.

Additionally, that Balkanization inherently weakens the nation since national unity and patriotism are vilified by the very notion of the claimed validity of multiculturalism. Again, like all such Movements, its advocates never demand that enemies of America give up their own nationalism/unifying forces and turn against themselves – as multiculturalism demands of Americans. And the moral relativism it bristles with inherently opposes the deeply-felt moral love of the American Revolution and its proponents for the institutionalism of individual liberty – with no recognition of any value for any collectivist notion whatsoever – which has always been our life force.

In practice, multiculturalism has been relied on by "reformers" of education at all levels in America to promote the teaching of American history as a purely-national-derogatory exposition, and to promote Marxist notions of race, gender and class as bases for division and "deconstruction" of the received wisdom in all the "great books" and to vilify all Western culture, claiming it has done nothing but rape and pillage.

All these negative accusations of America and Western civilization promoted under the aegis of moral relativism and multiculturalism are actually utter nonsense, with no actual historical basis in fact (no country in history has more selflessly aided other peoples and countries to secure their liberty and prosperity than the United States which, for example, selflessly rescued Europe twice during the 20th century from its self-destructiveness).

It is no exaggeration to say that most American educational institutions, at all levels, have, since the 1960s, been fixated on all these above-described Marxist/collectivist Movements – pacifism, racial spoils (affirmative action and purely-racial "diversity"), environmentalism and multiculturalism.

American universities in particular, as much as any educational institutions in the country, have literally become obsessed with these Movements to the point that promoting them has become their most-energetic activity at both the faculty and administration level. "Political correctness" is the Maoist enforcement mechanism for these Movements imposed both at these institutions and even throughout the rest of American society.

It is likely that no more than a tiny minority of the nation actually agree with the substance of what that "political correctness" demands. However, those who demand it are a brutal mob — with many populating and directing unconstitutional federal bureaucracies — intent on causing massive harm to any who disagree with them openly – and thereby commit thought crime.

Those Movements and their "political correctness" societal and government bureaucracy enforcement mechanisms – together with unions, life tenure for faculty, and total control of faculty and administration in most such institutions by radical Marxists – have poisoned all those educational institutions and turned them into pure Marxist anti-American propaganda-generating institutions.

And, because of universities' continuing power to provide credentials for those who are employed by businesses throughout the nation, that poisoning has in turn poisoned those businesses as well, so that multiculturalism's poisonous reach now extends to all American society, weakening every American institution profoundly, from the inside out – as is its purpose.

# Chapter 15

## The Counterrevolution's Efforts to Create "Classes" in America

<u>American Collectivists And Our Constitution</u>

A basic feature of America, enshrined in the Constitution, is that it is absolutely forbidden for any "nobility" – the historically-used term for a legally-privileged class of citizens – to emerge, or even exist, in the nation.

There was a deviation from this standard at the Republic's beginning, in the form of African slavery, followed by Jim Crow laws after its abolition. All those laws have been completely eradicated for over 50 years now and, accordingly, can no longer be pointed to as existing at all – except as a fraudulent, never-ending collectivist smear tactic against the nation. Constant invocation of this long ago feature of America has remained a continuing favorite tactic of radical collectivists since Karl Marx loudly railed against that then-fact of American life, deploying it as his only, factually-based criticism of America, invariably aiming it against the entire nation.

What is fascinating is that whereas Marx loudly and constantly complained — as have his followers including, most visibly today, Marxist race hustlers such as Al Sharpton — that America enslaved <u>some</u> of its citizens, countries that follow Marx's prescription enslave <u>everyone</u>.

Throughout history, virtually all other nations have indeed had actual, juridical (i.e. legally-consequential) class structures, in which particular citizens — nobles — did indeed have particular privileges relative to other citizens – privileges enforceable as a matter of law. Nothing of that kind is permitted legally in America. The Constitution absolutely and explicitly forbids it.

Nevertheless, since soon after this Republic's 1789 founding, numerous Americans have felt that they should be specially privileged over the rest of us in some manner, typically based on their inflated view of the importance of their education and/or their vocation. Numerous professions have sought – and, over time, have obtained – special, exclusive privileges regarding their "professional" status, affording members of their profession the right to determine who could belong to it, often involving state licensing of one sort or another. Obtaining that legally-enforceable virtual-Guild status for themselves has afforded numerous professions special legal rights – the equivalence of class superiority.

A particular pernicious example of this, as shown below, has been that federal (and many state and city) employees have effectively – and juridically – been granted special, legally-privileged status – a kind of virtual nobility – over all other citizens through multiple actions taken by politicians; to the extent that that is the case, the Constitution has been violated, no matter how many times that violation has occurred and how deeply-ingrained accepting it may have become nationally.

This is because, as discussed in Chapter 8, pursuant to its Article V, the Constitution can only be amended if its precisely-described procedures for doing so are followed to the letter; and mere "precedent" does not and cannot amend the Constitution, no matter how many times it is repeated. Violating the Constitution is a violation every time it occurs – and a crime against the nation each such time as well. Otherwise, the Constitution would have no force at all as the nation's fundamental law since the mere <u>violation</u> of its express terms WOULD ITSELF VALIDATE the violation – a facially preposterous notion.

Again, that notion is preposterous – and it is monstrous that such now requires any explanation – because it would not merely render the Constitution a legal nullity, but rather would <u>actually encourage</u> such violations since their mere occurrence itself would be their own reward, rather than an inherently-reversible and punishable act of grotesque misconduct against the fundamental law of the nation.

Leaving aside the issue of government employees acquiring special status over the rest of us improperly, the direct consequence of the Constitutionally-guaranteed preclusion of any legally-privileged class in the nation, as a political and social matter, has been that any purported discussion of "classes" in America is inherently obfuscatory, and without any factual legal foundation: since america has no actual "classes," any claim to the contrary is literally nothing but collectivist/Marxist-inspired nonsense.

The constant, fraudulent accusation by Marxists that there are indeed multiple, different "classes" in America is intended by them (to the extent they have any awareness of their own words) to serve multiple, critical functions on behalf of their "Cause."

First of all, Marxism as a purported political analysis/criticism of its targets completely depends on the assumption that the accused nation, supposedly like all others, is indeed divided into classes of all different types, each with varying degrees of privileges, power and legal rights, classes which are, it claims, literally at war with each other, a war in which, according to Marx, it is historically (and morally) mandated that the state intervene to crush the evil "exploiting" classes, and so rescue the cause of the claimed "exploited" or victimized classes.

Those concepts, together with the absolute, hate-filled characterization of all businessmen as being the single most monstrous "class" of supposedly always thieving (to Marxists, all profit is evil and stolen from its true owners) exploiters, is literally the very essence of Marxism in a nutshell.

Secondly, as in all versions of collectivism, whose acknowledged purpose is the complete conquest and subjugation of the entire population under the General Will, forcing all citizens into various, superficially-identifiable "groups" – which are either to be specially protected/favored or vilified/crushed – and simultaneously denying every individual's moral/spiritual value, is the single most powerful means for achieving that totalitarian purpose. This is more than simply a strategy of divide and conquer – although it is that.

Insisting on perceiving all people as simply drones, or soulless parts of one or another collective group, is a means both of devaluing and denying all their individual humanity – a denial absolutely essential to collectivist ideology – and a forensic technique for convincing followers of the supposed virtue of the collective's mission, and thereby promoting the desired, intense, ongoing emotional response from hoped-for followers: nothing is more important to all collectivist movements, including of the Marxist variety, and to their ideological/emotional appeal, than promoting the collective's members' constant hatred, envy and resentment towards <u>other</u> particular groups targeted by the Collective for defenestration, typically based on their alleged victimization of favored collective groups.

Generating that constant, ever-escalating emotional climate of hatred and resentment by members of favored/victimized groups directed at other, targeted groups, is also critical for making sure that collective members are invariably completely deaf to any substantive arguments from any source opposed to the Collective. Particularly if any such arguments emanate from anyone automatically-disqualified due to membership in any reviled group, it is critical that those making such arguments be perceived as absolutely beyond the pale, and inherently morally reprehensible, so that nothing they say can even be considered due to the vilification of the source.

Silencing, by whatever means necessary, anyone who deviates in any manner from thinking or arguing in accord with the dictates of the Collective, is viewed by it and its members as virtuous – a necessity. Free speech is only to be demanded for favored groups; all others are to be silenced by any means available.

Thus, quite simply, in a nation such as America uniquely is, where there simply are no actual classes except in the imagination of the deluded observer, Marxism is even more ludicrous than elsewhere: how can there be "class warfare" if there are no real classes?

But nothing has been more basic to the task of American Marxists seeking to undo the original American Revolution than to convince everyone here of what can only be called a "big lie" – that there are indeed exploiting classes in America

– e.g. businesses of all sorts – which are monstrous and must be subjugated and crushed by the federal government, since it is the only instrument capable of doing so.

A major problem for them has been the fact that everyone in America knows that it is private business <u>alone</u> which produces the wealth of the nation, and all goods and services which the citizenry needs and enjoys, including employment and career opportunities, which have always been the magnet for immigrants coming here from all the genuinely-oppressing nations around the world. If things are so terrible here, why do all those people want to come here? Somehow the Marxists never have an answer to that question.

Accordingly, the difficulty of convincing Americans of the validity of all the arguments they insist on is the reason why American Marxists have always gone to such pains to insist that, contrary to reality, America is a uniquely (the worst ever, according to them) evil/enslaving/exploitative nation in which there are indeed multiple, supposedly-victimized, or "exploited" groups, and other, targeted-for-hate supposedly-evil "exploiting" groups in America.

They invariably, and gratuitously, proclaim themselves the champions of the "exploited" groups/collectives (never individuals), determined to secure such groups' "right" to absolute equality of results and <u>outcomes</u> — never of opportunity, as the rule of Good Law enforces — of life with all other "groups" in all respects – including income, housing etc.

The Marxists proclaim the existence of such "classes" or "collective groups" of particular victims as excuses to demand special legal privileges for such groups – necessarily at the expense of actual individuals, as supposed members of other, supposedly-victimizing "groups" or collectives – all to be provided by granting the federal government special powers to enforce such privileges. They have been particularly obsessed about any variation in outcomes for groups identified by their race, sex and, in recent years, their "gender."

The racism inherent in much of this nonsense is such that Marxists in the 21st century, over 150 years since there have been any slaves in America whatsoever, still insist that American black people, simply by virtue of their color, have been inherently victimized by all today's whites – a collectivist racial smear against each individual white person (who is so judged and condemned without regard to any of his own individual actions), and a racial insult against each American black (who the Marxists implicitly proclaim is inherently incompetent, simply because of his color, in the absence of government interceding on his behalf) it purportedly champions.

Again, all this Collectivist/Marxist thinking/social criticism/propaganda depends, in order to be believed even by members of the Collective, on an internalized absolute acceptance of the notion that no individual has a soul, and that no individual is responsible solely for his own actions, so that it is appropriate to characterize people never as individuals, but rather as members of collective groups who are either to be considered favored or disfavored under the law.

Needless to say, nothing in the Constitution permits any of this nonsense – which is why Karl Marx and his followers have always hated the American Constitution above all else. Since they first appeared on the scene in the 19th century, self-identified American "progressives" (who usually claim not to be Marxists, though they share a common loathing for all private businesses and businessmen and their property, and demand the imposition on all businesses of completely-controlling federal "regulation"), including Wilson and Theodore Roosevelt, similarly expressed their contempt and disdain for the American Constitution – accurately identified by collectivists of all stripes as the antithesis of what they want as a foundation for their promised — and never realized — utopia.

Obviously some people always, everywhere, have more money than other people; but to call the rich citizens in America at any particular moment (income and wealth mobility and variability has always been, until its increasing, relatively-recent stagnation under the weight of federal regulations, enormous in America, with no one guaranteed anything) anything resembling an "upper class" is to render that concept meaningless: in Europe, unlike America, persons with titles of nobility genuinely had legally-enforcible privileges that others simply did not have, and this remained a disturbing and divisive problem in countries, such as England, even after it had largely abolished virtually all of those juridical privileges by the 19th century, where centuries of class deference arguably created a habit of self- perceived inferiority among those who lacked various indicia of belonging to the upper class, which indicia, in Britain, were extremely visible and have remained so, as dramatized by the Fabian socialist George Bernard Shaw in his famous play "Pygmalion."

Specifically, people of different social classes in England had, and continue to have, spoken "accents" which vary enormously, and are readily recognizable – literally as soon as someone opens their mouth – as are their clothes etc. In America, even that limited, spoken-accent indicator of class simply does not exist and never has; and yet, here in America, there are and have been those who genuinely consider themselves superior and, accordingly, resent the fact that they are entitled to no special benefits or deference legally, financially, or otherwise; they simply believe that they have successfully elevated themselves above all others, and so should indeed be treated as an upper-class of sorts.

That is a fair description of America's self-identified "intelligentsia" since the beginning of the Republic, including university professors, purported "public intellectuals" and journalists and, increasingly, the so-called learned professions. That is a prime reason why all those supposedly superior American intellectuals have been insisting since the mid-19th century that they are in fact "experts" in various matters – and that in a well-ordered nation, "experts" – like them – should run everything and tell everyone else how to live their lives.

In fact, as I have proven above in chapter 1, the whole claim that anyone is an "expert" is inherently fraudulent, for the simple fact that no human being has comprehensive knowledge of everything and, since a single changed fact added or subtracted from those "facts" believed to be understood can completely alter one's judgment – or so-called "expert opinion" – about any matter. Since no one ever has such comprehensive knowledge, and no one ever knows what facts he does not know, nor even what "facts" he thinks he knows which are in fact not true, genuine human "expertise" is inherently impossible.

There are indeed individuals who have more information about certain subjects than others. But that does not make them actual experts in anything. Moreover, it is a rare subject on which multiple self-identified "experts" even agree; the very fact of their disagreement itself proves that none of them are "experts" who should be thereby empowered to direct other citizens in their lives and choices regarding their own property.

Nevertheless, a supposedly-utopian rule over the masses by "experts" – like the supposed rule by "philosopher Kings" famously satirized by Plato in his *The Republic*, and similarly by Aristophanes in his then-contemporaneous play, *Ecclesiazusae*, itself clearly consciously mirrored by Plato in *the Republic* – is precisely what American Progressives have been promoting since the end of the 19th century – a position argued for at great length, and with absolute clarity, by Woodrow Wilson in the 1880's and, incidentally, actively promoted by the Republican president Theodore Roosevelt, whose contempt for Americans' ability or right to run their own lives was boundless, as shown in his own words: "I don't know what the people think, I only know what they should think," he said. The "ability to fight well and breed well [and] subordinate the interests of the individual to the interests of the community [is] crucial to true national greatness."

Thus, if anyone had any doubts about it, his own words prove Theodore Roosevelt's devotion to the Collectivist Counterrevolution – as did his multiple actions promoting it.

As mentioned above, the Counterrevolution began in America in the first half of the 19th century as an extra-political "movement," for lack of a better word. Its Europhile American devotees – that is what they were – may well have had political ambitions as well, but they no doubt were well-aware of the absolute impossibility, at that time of continuing patriotic enthusiasm for the American Revolution and the Constitution, of enacting any (collectivist/secularist) political program they favored – at least at the federal level.

Instead, the earliest American Counterrevolution's proponents directed their energies and efforts principally at moving, by whatever means were at hand, American public opinion to favor a European-type, militantly-secular administrative state, supplanting the individual liberty established in our Constitution and, specifically, promoting the establishment of what we now call public schools throughout the nation, exactly as demanded by Karl Marx in *The Com-*

*munist Manifesto*, to effect the forced institutionalization of all American children for extended periods of time, claiming to "educate" them, in a deliberately secular, as opposed to a religious, manner, to inculcate in them skills which they could use as, in the dehumanizing, invariable, Marxist terminology, "workers."

Religious instruction had previously always been a central feature of formal education of children; the American Counterrevolutionaries were determined to eliminate any such religious content. Interestingly, although they claimed such schools would would also have the civic virtue of greatly improving the literacy level of Americans, it is a fact that Americans were, indeed, highly literate as a people prior to the existence of the public schools; and, indeed, there is scant evidence that those schools have ever, in fact improved the nation's literacy overall.

The Counterrevolution's connection to public school education has remained a central feature of its program, a feature which was greatly magnified beginning in the 1960s with the advent of teachers unions – an inherently corrupt lobbying group lobbying for public funds, always falsely claiming to act in the interest of students when, in fact, the interests of the unions themselves and the politicians they choose to favor (invariably those politicians who use public money to benefit their public employee unions) have always been paramount to the unions.

The other major efforts of the early American Counterrevolution consisted of promoting the secularization of American universities, all of which had primarily, and institutionally, been religion-focused centers of training, primarily for clergyman, whose academic focus was mostly on the subjects of theology, philology (deep understanding of language and its role in structuring human thought, including mastery of Latin, Greek and other languages) and what we would call today the Great Books. Secularizing universities was seen as critical to the Counterrevolution's deeply anti-clerical "movement" because it's self-identified "intelligentsia" proponents derived their own claims to special intellectual status from having acquired "credentials" from having been degreed by the universities – and it was critical for them, as true-believing Europhile Collectivists, to transform those institutions away from their religious foundations.

Because hatred for religion, particularly Christianity, has always been a central feature of all Collectivist revolutions and movements. Unlike Europeans, whose general dislike for Christianity mushroomed beginning in the late 18th century and has never ceased, Americans have always been overwhelmingly a deeply religious, Christian people.

Changing — destroying, actually — that Christian feature of America has always been a central part of the program of all American Collectivist adherents who recognized, accurately, that without obliterating that feature of America – which they have still yet to accomplish – they cannot ultimately succeed in their Counterrevolution.

The Counterrevolution has succeeded in all its efforts at changing American educational institutions. Indeed, ever since instituting the public schools, and secularizing American universities, in the 19th century, the Collectivist Counter-revolutionary cause has preserved those victories and used them to build on its influence, particularly since the 1960s. Those secularized universities – self-consciously modeled after those in Germany under the Kaiser –have bestowed degrees on their graduates, with such degrees purportedly designating "expertise" on their recipients who, festooned with such tokens of brilliance, claim superiority over ordinary American citizens sufficient to tell them how to live their lives. And journalists breathlessly report remarkable findings from "studies" from such "experts" as purported news stories. And, of course, journalists and all prominent government employees are themselves all graduates, similarly festooned with degrees, from those same universities.

And, of course, the Collectivist Counterrevolutionary cause has also expanded its influence throughout the entertainment industry, modern mass media and, of course, the government itself.

Given all those remarkable victories over opinion-influencing institutions throughout the nation, it is all the more remarkable that the Counterrevolution has never won over the American people themselves – not by a long shot, as consistent polling proves. The Counterrevolutionaries are only too well aware of that fact: they know that all their victories are built on a house of cards in this nation which, notwithstanding their efforts, remains a democratic republic whose laws can be changed in an instant, repealing every last one of their victories.

As described above in chapter 6, an enormous source of energy and political direction entered the Collectivists "movement" in the 1840s with the writings of Karl Marx which added several new features to the Counterrevolutionary stew: as mentioned above, claims of multiple victimized/exploited "classes" in need of rescue by the virtuous from the victimizing/exploiting "classes," resulting in Marxism's essence – profound, virulent, unqualified hatred and resentment (and envy) of businesses and all businessmen and, closely related to that, similar hatred and resentment for Britain, Jews and, yes, the United States, all of which were the unique objects of hatred of Karl Marx, who accurately recognized each of these objects of hatred as utterly incompatible with his own utopian totalitarian vision, each for a different reason, interestingly, though the reasons were inter-tangled with his loathing of business and businessman (a detestation made particularly deep by virtue of the fact that he was well aware that all products and services people actually rely on in real life for their survival are made exclusively by – businesses).

# CHAPTER 16

## The Counterrevolution Before and during the Wilson Presidency

As mentioned above, 19th Century American politicians' understanding of both the plain meaning of the Constitution's implicit prohibition of any federal policing laws — other than the very few specified therein — and the then-well-known intentions of the founders, alone prevented them from attempting any significant federal government intrusions on the American economy until the last part of that century – apart from simply providing <u>funding</u> to build roads, bridges, canals and, beginning in the Civil War, railroads, all of which provided genuine, national, benefits, as Pres. Monroe insisted the General Welfare clause on its face requires for all spending. As shown above, President Monroe had reluctantly conceded such funding was permitted, as the <u>sole</u> Constitutional action which the federal government could take (other than regulating would-be state, indian tribe and foreign economic <u>regulators</u> – the sole, actual power granted to it in the Commerce clause).

As described in Chapter 12, because of the enormous value of lands the federal government had acquired by the 1850's (primarily in the Louisiana Purchase and in the conclusion of the Mexican War) and not yet sold or given away, during the Civil War, the federal government was able to provide, without spending actual money, enormous financial incentives (loans and lucrative land grants) to railroad companies to hasten their building of railroads.

Politicians, of course, with a view to using their political offices for their own, personal financial and career advantage, always had enormous incentives for wanting to maximize federal involvement in economic matters: they could use it to enhance their personal political visibility and stature with the electorate (gratuitously promising public benefits from the spending of others' money they promoted), by claiming personal credit for all (taxpayer) money they used their offices to be spent, and (corruptly) demanding tribute and patronage of various kinds from whatever people or businesses received the individual benefit of such spending.

And, as noted above, once politicians are <u>allowed</u> to spend money, anyone seeking to oppose it is easily ridiculed by his opponents — the spenders — as a cold-hearted, niggardly opponent, supposedly of the public "good" itself.

That is why the only way to prevent politicians from using public money for spending projects calculated to enhance their own, personal power and provide corrupt financial benefits for themselves, as well as for the supposed beneficiaries of the taxpayer-funded largesse, is constitutionally to absolutely prohibit all such spending – and enforce the constitutional prohibition both legally and through public opprobrium by making such waste of taxpayer money absolutely taboo.

Monroe was very specific that it is never permitted for federal funds to be spent for any private benefit, nor even for the benefit of simply some, as opposed to all, citizens: a truly general benefit, he insisted, is what is genuinely required for each payment, not simply some larger program the payment is claimed to further. He ultimately differed with his own earlier, and Madison's, views, and believed spending for major transportation infrastructure, supposedly benefiting the entire nation, had a sufficient, Constitutionally-permissible, general benefit equivalent to that of funding the national defense in wartime.

In Monroe's time, federal spending for subsidies of any kind to private businesses, or poor-relief measures (such as today's welfare, food stamps, job training etc.) was never even contemplated. Because all such programs inevitably involve private benefits, always extracted from other taxpayers, they could not meet the Constitutional requirement he insisted on.

During the Civil War, the federal government assumed a multitude of wartime powers over all aspects of the nation which may well have, to some extent at least, "softened-up" the public to accepting federal intrusions above and beyond the mere spending of taxpayer money – even massive ones – into their lives. After its defeat in that War, the entire South was treated like a conquered enemy, and subjected to extreme, forceful repression completely under the thumb of the federal government (like the peoples of all continental European nations have been since the 17th century under the tyranny of Bad Law intended precisely to turn them into virtual serfs of the ruler) during Reconstruction for decades after the Civil War.

And, far from incidentally, after the capitulation by Monroe in accepting the Constitutionality of federal spending on whatever general-welfare-claimed-benefit Congress desired, there was literally no longer any political party in America – as the Democrat-Republicans had been under Jefferson and Madison and, previously, Monroe – officially and ideologically standing absolutely in the way of any expansion of federal power.

Indeed, since that time, there has never been <u>any</u> major American political party seriously and fervently opposing any federal expansion whatsoever. And, today, no American politician, let alone any political party, has seriously proposed the dismantlement of any federal agencies or federal operations – no matter how unconstitutional, how destructive of prosperity and liberty, and how corrupting, the existence of such agencies and operations has been – and even after elections in which the politicians who had created such agencies were publicly rejected and replaced by new politicians.

Considering the personal benefits available for politicians for advocating expansions of federal power (which claimed justifications can always be colorably argued for, once any expansion is accepted as constitutionally permissible) – promised (though never delivered in fact) benefits which have only increased as the federal government itself has – and the fact that the damage incurred from such federal actions is much more complicated to understand, and is always incurred after the spending, and after the politicians have reaped the political and/ or financial benefits from legislating the federal actions – it is far from surprising that no national political party has seen any advantage for itself in opposing federal expansions.

And no political party has ever proposed repealing any federal encroachments on citizens, even long after their utter worthlessness was proven beyond doubt (except, finally, for the 1995 repeal of the Interstate Commerce Commission, after its more than 100 years of parasite-empowering, massively-expensive destruction of competition and all innovation in the railroad business, and a few other relatively minor programs).

Nevertheless, throughout the 19th century (and later), Americans were well aware of the Constitution's limitations on federal power, of the fact that the American Revolution was fought precisely to prevent central government power from intruding on, or policing in any manner, actions by citizens (virtually all policing of whom was explicitly Constitutionally-required, and well-understood, to be a function solely of state government), citizens' business activities in particular, and all private property.

Quite simply, the universal understanding of these basic facts concerning the founding of the nation and its Constitution prevented politicians from otherwise even attempting to intrude on the American economy until well into the second half of the 19th century.

From 1870 through 1890, the first three major legal/political victories of the Counterrevolution were enacted and institutionalized in the nation. Together, these three legal/political creations vastly increased the power of the federal government – and of federal politicians and bureaucrats – over the citizenry and all American businesses, and constituted the first American instances of Bad Law – coupled with, in the case of the Justice Department, a threat of unprecedented (in America), and virtually unlimited, discretionary, potentially politically-motivated, criminal prosecution – and, together, they initiated an element of genuine terror throughout America.

And, truth be told, their doing so was intentional by all who participated in their creation: the whole point of such Bad Law and its (naked threat of violence against persons and property) enforcement mechanisms is to replace Common-Law-and-market-participant choice rules otherwise governing the market and citizenry subject to it, with precisely that threat of discretionary, political control — its bullying threat of existential destruction for any noncompliance inherent in them

– the very centralized, tyrannical, controlling mechanism which the English Parliament and its revolutionary supporters had defeated in the 1640-1660 episode of the periodically-occurring English revolution, tyrannical laws which all continental Europe have been subject to under absolutist rulers of all kinds (kings, Jacobin revolutionaries, and "social" democrats alike) since the 17th century.

These American 19th-century Counterrevolutionary legal/political developments were as follows:

(1)  the creation of the federal Department of Justice in 1870, whose sole, original purpose was selectively to prosecute crimes newly-created under federal Reconstruction law, imposed on the defeated South – federal law which imposed dictatorial control over all the formerly-Confederate states and all their citizens as a form of collective punishment/management. This had the effect of <u>criminalizing previously-innocent activity</u> – since the states were previously alone empowered to prosecute all common-law crimes, and all federal criminal jurisdiction had been extremely limited to the few crimes specified in the Constitution itself. The Justice Department became used to wielding enormous, discretionary prosecutorial power during Reconstruction, and has continued as a potential political weapon ever since – long after Reconstruction ended — throughout the country. As federal crimes have multiplied since 1906 under "legislation" – i.e. regulations, which are indistinguishable substantively from laws – created by federal alphabet agencies, the Justice Department's discretionary and arbitrary political power has increased exponentially.

(2)  enactment of the Interstate Commerce Act In 1887, creating the Interstate Commerce Commission for purposes of "regulating" – that is, federal dictation to its former owners of all activities, including, eventually, pricing etc. – the railroad business, and

(3)  enactment in 1890 of the federal Sherman Antitrust Laws which, because of their massive, criminal penalties, and inherently vague and ambiguous nature, resulting in its arbitrary application against particular politically-selected targets, were truly terrifying to businesses. To this day, the Antitrust laws' assumption that a monopoly can actually arise and continue in a free economy, subject to regulation only by the common law, in the absence of the government itself forcing it on the market, remains a completely unproven social "scientist"-invented theory/fantasy. That private businesses could, however, be penalized under those very laws simply for becoming dominant in an industry which, as shown in Chapter 4, in a free market, occurs only by virtue of actual, customer preferences (in a free market no one forces the customers to buy anything), has always been particularly frightening.

In fact, and in real life – independent of the fantasy world of political "scientists" — it is invariably the government itself which alone actually creates monopolies and oligopolies: there is literally no known instance in history in which any actual, privately-held monopoly both arose and lasted more than an insignificant amount of time in any market that was not dominated by the government.

§1 of the Sherman Antitrust Act made criminal any action which, in the purely-discretionary judgment of federal officials, constituted a "restraint of trade"– an inherently-vague, and therefore gratuitous in application, legal construct, particularly since state tort laws had already long-provided for civil liability against any actual business misconduct, including fraud, theft, abuse of fiduciary power, negligence, interference with other persons' contractual relations, etc., if claimed by anyone genuinely injured thereby.

This grant of such massive, ambiguous, discretionary power to federal function-aries – making newly-illegal or, even more ominously, potentially-illegal, vast amounts of commercially-reasonable conduct which had been perfectly legal previously – was a massive increase of arbitrary federal power, all threatening the actual providers of the nation's real goods and services – and ultimately their customers as well. It was terribly destructive to all markets in America and fright-ening to any businessman —particularly those who did not have political clout sufficient to feel insulated from existential harm, with a sword of Damocles of that nature hanging over their heads.

The sole mitigating factor regarding the Antitrust Act was that the 19th Century Supreme Court initially severely restricted its potential application shortly after it was enacted – limiting it to restricting union activities as improper combinations in restraint of trade — which they clearly were – protecting businesses, which had been its legislative targets, at least for the time being. Until Theodore Roos-evelt noisily threatened prosecutions under it in 1906 knowingly in violation of the Constitution – causing a massive financial panic that year.

Each of these three, enormous Counterrevolutionary 19th century legal devel-opments were all the more remarkable in hindsight in that they occurred <u>with virtually no opposition</u> – including from the very businesses targeted in all such laws (all businesses in the case of the Antitrust laws and the Justice Department, and the railroad business alone in the case of the Interstate Commerce Act).

However, when one considers the political power that both gave rise to such legal developments and the force and existentially-threatening violence such laws empowered unelected bureaucrats with over such businesses and their owners, their apparently-silent acquiescence to these developments is perfectly under-standable: above all else, like all private citizens, they prized their own survival in the face of such existentially-threatening, unconstitutional legal developments.

Because the only power wielded by the businesses and their owners was simple market power; and yet, in the 1880s, there they were, faced with the existential threat of the federal bully – a threat which was all the more catastrophically frightening since its intrusion on their lives and businesses was a newly-created, lawless act itself, known by all to be forbidden by the Constitution.

And, with the well-known constraints of the Constitution breached, there simply was no other limit on the destruction that could be visited on businesses thereby, with the totality of such circumstances forcing businesses to curry what favor, from whatever source otherwise available, they could with the bully – before the actual imposition of the bully's boot on their neck.

Thus it is simple to understand their silence: how does any rational person deal with someone known to be a cold-blooded lawbreaker pointing a gun at his head? Preventing the citizenry from the threat of such tyranny was precisely one of the many purposes of the Constitution.

And, by the mid-1880s, the railroads knew some kind of federal intrusion on their business was probably politically-unavoidable for them – notwith-standing the damage that was sure to follow for them, the entire public and the nation. The motive behind the demand from the press, the public (or at least certain very-vocal members of it) and politicians for creating such is easy to summarize: envy – the very emotion uniquely forbidden in the 10 Com-mandments.

Specifically, the railroads, and their owners, had acquired spectacular wealth and enormous, virtually-unprecedented in the rapidity with which it was acquired, market power simply by virtue of the enormous value of the revolutionary ben-efits they were providing the entire nation, including both their own actual cus-tomers and, in the case of the businesses whose raw and finished products they transported, the customers of their customers – and their customers as well. And much of their wealth had, of course, come in the form of the vast amounts of valuable land they had received – perfectly legally – from the federal government in the course of creating their railroads.

Indeed, those lands' value was itself enhanced exponentially synergistically by the very success and utility of the railroads themselves: simple proximity to the railroad – and the towns and cities that grew up precisely because of its presence and, especially, the presence of its stations – by itself created value. And railroad customers were only too happy to pay to obtain a previously-unimaginable service.

But envy – truly bitter, European-style envy – arose from many quarters, be-ginning in the 1870s – cheered on and enhanced by politicians, journalists and "intellectuals," all of whom wanted what they viewed as "their fair share" of the bounty from the railroads – property rights, and the future value of the railroad business itself, be damned.

Of course, none of those who, prior to its enactment, were demanding to be in the position of European-type tyrannical state-control over the railroads ac-knowledged the vicious, predatory, self-serving nature of their own such de-mands. A so-called "populist"/mob Movement – named the Grange Movement by its various promoters, including particularly politicians and journalists – developed among some farmers in the Midwest who were agitated into becoming envious of rates obtained from the railroads by other customers thereof. The very value of the service offered by the railroads fueled their envy – both of the railroads and of those other customers.

Their particular goal in seeking legal mandates on the railroads was to obtain federally-compelled price controls uniquely favoring themselves. In effect, their hostility to the railroads derived directly from the very extraordinary benefit those railroads provided them: they just wanted it to be cheaper for themselves, and for the government to force the railroads to provide them what the market alone had been, in fact, providing – but cheaper.

The Grange movement, which arose in the 1870s within a brief period after the railroads began national operations, initially pressed state legislatures to impose price and other controls on the railroads – since everyone knew the federal government was forbidden to do any such thing. But the Constitution similarly prevented states from doing so – in its Contract clause.

But the noisy clamor for such controls over the railroad business – and the sophistication of the railroad owners who were well aware of similar controls burdening their European counterparts – made those owners fear they would be facing a similar fate sooner or later – without regard to the Constitution. No national political party was opposed to that imposition. And, as always, the courts were populated by politicians as well.

The railroad owners were also well aware – again, well-knowing the crushing effects of such centuries-old laws on European businesses – that such "regulation" of inherently-valuable businesses had the practical effect of precluding new competitors from entering the market and, simultaneously, resulting in a guaranteed, if reduced, profit stream for their businesses since the politicians demanding that federal control would themselves be politically punished if that invaluable business were ever completely choked out of existence.

Thus, whether they did so happily, corruptly and voluntarily, or were simply making a virtue of what they perceived to be unalterable political necessity, over the decade ending in 1887, the railroad owners had come to accept the virtual inevitability of federal control over their businesses, and so actually participated, through their lawyers, in the legislation-drafting and creation of the Interstate Commerce Act, and the "regulatory" Commission created under it – with no political party actively opposed, notwithstanding its obvious unconstitutionality — and its inevitable damage to their businesses.

At first, although that Commission was legislatively granted plenary power to investigate every aspect of the railroads, with virtually no limit on its power to do so, it had no actual power to dictate rates (which rate-setting power, ironically, had been the sole goal of the Grange Movement). But within decades its powers were expanded to include that rate-setting power, which itself exponentially increased the power of everyone (other than any customers) connected with the Commission – including its own bureaucrats, the politicians who demanded tribute from the business owners, supposedly to police it – lawyers and lobbyists galore, and the very businesses subject to it, oddly enough, because of the political power over the politicians controlling it which their very oligopoly-protected wealth made possible.

There can be no doubt of the enormity of the victory for the Counterrevolution which the enactment of the Interstate Commerce Act in 1887 constituted. It was a truly seminal event in the history of this Republic: it was the first, actual creation of (Constitutionally-forbidden) Bad Law here, and it was imposed on a highly-visible and immensely valuable – to everyone – market and businesses subjected to it.

However, like all victories of the Counterrevolution, in real life, it achieved absolutely none of its (price-reduction) benefits to the public that its proponents had claimed it would achieve. In fact, it had the directly-contrary (and predictable), corrupt effect of <u>enhancing</u> the pre-existing market power of the railroads, by shutting out any new competitors, and forced them to <u>increase</u> their prices to carry the cost load of complying with the demands of the ICC, and provided them additional, political power over the politicians who were supposed to enforce controls over them – but who they were wealthy enough to buy favors from.

And all those circumstances together increased bitterness among the various "learned professional", journalist and other Counterrevolutionaries over the fact that their own "victory" over the "robber barons," as they sneeringly characterized the railroad owners, had proven so hollow from their perspective. Specifically, in demanding the "regulatory" legislation, they had been seeking power <u>for themselves</u> over the railroads and politicians. That complete failure, in turn, itself gave rise to additional demands from them for additional federal law, both to further constrict the power of successful, powerful businesses and, specifically, to reduce business' influence with politicians – the first Collectivist, mob-inspired attempt at what is today characterized as "campaign finance laws" – the real purpose for the 1890 Sherman Antitrust Act.

It too, like the Interstate Commerce Act, was enacted with the full approval of both national political parties, with virtually no public opposition whatsoever, notwithstanding the extraordinary, unconstitutional, arbitrary, discretionary power it provided unelected federal bureaucrats over private businesses. As shown in multiple previous chapters, nothing in the Constitution permits that policing legislation over any American businesses. And everyone knew that at the time.

Indeed, that complete lack of any real political opposition for such radical enactments has been true for every single political/legal victory the Counterrevolution has notched.

Federal "Regulatory" Agencies And Laws
Institutionally Explained/ Deconstructed

All three off these Counterrevolutionary political/legal "achievements" must be fully understood to appreciate the cancer and corruption surrounding us today in our still-blessed Republic. That cancer and corruption, including the over-whelming capture by the Collectivist Counterrevolution of all of the so-called "learned" professions, and the institutions they dominate and control, together create the illusion that that Counterrevolution has become so all-pervasive in our nation, and so deeply-rooted, that it will continue to metastasize endlessly, so that we are now forever doomed to be suffocated by it, even against the majority will of the nation, with no recourse.

In fact, nothing could be further from the truth: every single one of the "achieve-ments"/victories of the Counterrevolution can and should be completely undone – an achievement which simply awaits the political will of the true majority of Americans – who have never voted for <u>any</u> of the Counterrevolution's laws and bureaucracy, and who would, by a wide margin, vote, if given the chance, to repeal them.

That's the real reason Americans in polls invariably say the country is going in the "wrong direction" by margins of 3 or 4 to 1, and that the federal government is both incompetent and doing "too much." It's also why they invariably say they detest Congress by margins of 4 or 5 or more to 1: they have come to hate Wash-ington's usurpation and destruction and that's who they identify as the cause; pollsters never ask them what they think of the welfare/administrative state – because neither political party wants to know the answer, which is that, even though recipients of federal checks and empowerment for themselves love those benefits at their fellow citizens' expense, the public as a whole loathes it and its increasingly obvious empowerment of the federal government and its function-aries at the expense of the economy's strength and opportunities for citizens of all kinds, including employment.

The "learned professions" and the politicians and bureaucrats empowered by the Counterrevolutionary "achievements" have been the sole, actual beneficiaries of the Counterrevolution's "achievements" – benefits they have realized at the ex-pense of the lives, fortunes and freedom of the Republic's overwhelming majority of people, the economy – and the liberty, solvency and integrity of the nation.

It is way past time for the entire Counterrevolution to be overturned and the indi-vidual liberty of the citizenry, which that Counterrevolution has worked so hard to subvert, to be reinstated and rectified.

All three of the above-described 19th century Counterrevolutionary "achieve-ments" constitute monstrous examples of Bad Law. As discussed above, Bad Law is inherently corrupting and destructive of Good Law – and therefore of the rule of law itself. Bad Law always grants existential power, exercisable on a purely discretionary basis by the government functionaries vested with it, in the "regulatory" agencies, literally turning those agencies and whatever politicians have control over them into the equivalent of organized criminal enterprises, with the ability to engage in a "protection racket" victimizing all actual market participants – including all employees and customers – involved with every business, and the market and/or markets in which it operates, which they are granted the power to "regulate" – or rather, more accurately, exercise tyrannical, dictatorial control over.

This is no exaggeration. Consider: The nature of the power of the Mafia Don is his ability to reward or punish whoever he wants, in his absolute, lawless discretion – with no procedural or legal restraint on his power (other than the criminal law itself, which is not a problem for the government bureaucrats' protection racket).

The difference between the power of a mafia don and a legitimate government is that a legitimate government is supposed to be subject to the rule of genuine law and procedures governed by the constitutional requirement of "due process" before it can impose "justice" – in the form of orders, or extracting money judgments – on citizens. Bad Law turns all those legal and procedural constraints on government functionaries completely on its head: those functionaries are empowered by the Bad Law to exercise purely discretionary powers over the citizens subjected to their jurisdiction – directing their activities, and imposing fines and other punishments, including the threat of complete financial destruction, if they fail to follow those directives – just like a mafia don, and completely unlike the legal procedures contemplated for this nation by our founders and in the Constitution.

To understand this with crystal clarity, consider the circumstances under which actual, due process permits the state – through its courts – to impose orders or judgments on citizens who are summoned before them and subjected to their jurisdiction: no such orders or judgments can be entered against those citizens until after they have been found – adjudicated by a jury, for example – to have violated some actual Good Law requirement, and only after the careful requirements of "due process" have all been satisfied.

The agencies empowered by Bad Law – and by the federal courts which have cheerfully been rubber-stamping and enforcing it since the mid-1930s – are specifically empowered under that law to create their own, even more detailed, laws ("regulations"), and even to determine the extent of their own jurisdiction (which, not surprisingly, is constantly expanding to cover new subjects – and targets), and to impose orders, directives and even money judgments and fines on the citizenry – no prior adjudication of misconduct, nor any other due process, required, nor even permitted.

To further put this in its legal and historical context, this discretionary, Bad Law power exercised by each of these "regulatory" agencies is precisely the kind of extra-judicial kangaroo court-type power that the Stuart kings, claiming the right to be absolute monarchs over the nation, used in England before the English Civil War/ Revolution of 1640-1660, in what was known as their court of Star Chamber

– a court operating outside the normal judicial system, which permitted no juries, which followed nothing but the purely-discretionary political directives of the crown. In a major victory by the English people for their individual liberty over the tyrannical, absolutist pretensions of the Stuart kings, Star Chamber was <u>specifically outlawed</u> as a result of the English Revolution of 1640-1660 <u>precisely</u> because of the tyrannical dictatorial power exercised against the people in it.

And yet the tyranny of Star Chamber is precisely the kind of absolute, discretionary power, unconstitutionally combining all three types of government power (legislative, executive and judicial) exercised by <u>every single one</u> of the federal alphabet "regulatory" agencies. Without regard to all their other violations of the Constitution, that fact alone proves their utter unconstitutionality – as was well recognized by everyone in America until 1887.

Our Founders, the American revolutionaries, continuing the English revolutionary tradition, had no intention whatsoever of granting the federal government power of that nature – in effect, <u>reinstating</u> Star Chamber – which even the English crown they rebelled against as a tyranny had been forbidden to exercise over the citizenry ever since that 17th century English Revolution/Civil War – the liberating effect of which our Revolution was intended to <u>build on</u>, and not to <u>reverse</u>.

Yet that reversal of all individual liberties obtained in our Revolution is precisely what the American Counterrevolution has presumed to "achieve" with its creation of multiple such "regulatory"/Star Chamber agencies which now govern all lands, energy creation and transmission, all aspects of employment, indeed every single aspect of American businesses – and even micromanage the design of virtually all products American citizens desire to purchase (e.g., automobiles, gasoline, pharmaceuticals, washing machines and all other appliances, toys, lightbulbs – virtually everything). And not a single one of those areas of federal regulatory control is mentioned in Article I section 8 of the Constitution as a permissible subject to federal legislation at all.

The Interstate Commerce Act was the first American legislation of its kind, i.e. legislation directing the discretionary, federal bureaucratic micromanagement of an entire industry. It was followed, unfortunately, beginning in 1906, by virtual cookie-cutter copies of every aspect of its control-confiscation (without compensation) from all the businesses affected by it, eventually affecting every aspect of American business – and all our personal lives as well.

Without exception, each Bad Law legislation of this type, and all the "regulatory" agencies created thereunder, constituted monstrous Counterrevolutionary virtually-criminal tyrannies, indistinguishable from the tyrannical laws which have been suffocating, and utterly corrupting (as anyone who has ever done business there can attest) all continental Europe since the time of Louis XIV.

Again, every abominable aspect of that original un-American Counterrevolutionary legislation has been copied on multiple occasions by American politicians. In so doing, they have aimed each such legislative abomination at one highly-prized (by the citizenry) industry/market after another. Indeed, the more highly-prized each such business was to the public, the more likely it was to find itself in the crosshairs of such legislation – and the "federal regulatory" agency created and empowered thereunder.

Each of these legislative abominations unconstitutionally injected into every aspect of each business so targeted (again, beginning with the railroad business in that 1887 legislation) the federal government's monopoly power of existential violence, wielded by politicians and government functionaries, to destroy – there is no other word for it – the market power of all participants in the affected business, by subordinating their market power to the existential power of violence of the federal government – in that first case, every aspect of the railroad business. By "every aspect" of the business, I am specifically referring to not only all competition, including price and quality competition, among actual or prospective competitors in it, but also all technological innovation in any aspect of it – any conceivable improvement which would otherwise have been created through competition.

This destruction of the market power of everyone involved in the affected business had devastating effects also on all its customers – notwithstanding the fact that the pretext for imposing federal power on the industry in the first place – invariably trumpeted by the politicians, the journalists and members of the "learned professions" who together loudly advocated/propagandized for the creation of the "new" "regulatory" agency – was supposedly to "help" at least some of the customers by supposedly using federal force to "empower" those customers to the disadvantage of the railroad and/or other customers, or both, supposedly to effect a reduction in prices the customers supposedly so favored would be charged by the railroad.

In other words, the government-control racket is always sold to the public as a price control scheme; its actual result is always to <u>raise</u> prices for everyone, to bring all competition and technological innovation among providers to a halt, and to provide corrupt enrichment to an entire class of parasites who contribute nothing of value to the business itself, but who became essential to the operation of the "regulated" business as intermediaries between the business operators and the government functionaries who they were now forced to answer to about every detail of their business. Who pays for all that extra work which produces no additional value to railroad or any other service or product? Who do you think – the customers, in whose name this entire abomination is always created.

In fact, there has never been <u>a single instance</u> of any customer in any business so "regulated" by the federal government in this manner <u>saving a dime</u>. Never. "Protecting" customers – often coupled with the ludicrous claim of "protecting the integrity of, and competition in, the market" – is always the pretext for the federal government and its functionaries being empowered to "regulate" any business and the market in which it operates,.

In fact, as anyone with the slightest understanding of market power, and the completely-different power of violence wielded by the state – which is the only attribute the state has – as discussed and explained in Chapter 4 above, would understand, the inevitable, actual consequence of this federal "regulation" is the elimination of all healthy operations of the market so "regulated," including the normal operation of Good Law governing it, as the actual, inevitable consequence of such federal intrusion in it. That market destruction is a feature, not a bug of federal regulation.

This market destruction resulting from the federal takeover/"regulation" of each highly-prized market and all the businesses operating within it has had the inevitable effect of creating federally-imposed monopolies or oligopolies within each such "regulated" business in which no new market participants can compete, and has done incalculable harm to the public served by such businesses and the employees of such businesses (whose employment opportunities are necessarily damaged by the harm to the businesses themselves), with the only actual beneficiaries of such violence to the Constitution, the market and the public being the lawyers and other members of "learned professions" who become necessary intermediaries once such legislation is enacted, and the federal officeholders/functionaries seeking to use their supposedly "public service" offices to gain highly-compensated employment, or otherwise enrich and/or empower themselves, at the expense of everyone involved in any capacity in the targeted business (all businesses involved in any manner in the business, their employees, and all customers wanting to purchase from them).

Without exception, every market in which the federal government has so interposed itself was, prior to such interposition, so highly-valued by the public that the federal government and its political officeholders simply couldn't keep their unconstitutional hands off of it.

It is impossible to know the enormity of the benefits which would have flowed to the public, and which federal "regulatory" interposition and tyranny have deprived us of, had the politicians been able to restrain themselves from imposing each federal "regulatory" agency they have created, strangling each market affected thereby.

That it has been enormous cannot be doubted. Simply comparing the pre-1900 incredible growth rate of the economy in America with that of then-contemporaneous continental Europe – whose growth rate was less than half that of America during the period – subjected to "regulatory" laws indistinguishable from those which the Counterrevolution has been imposing on us, gives at least an inkling. That "regulation" is also the reason America has never duplicated that growth rate ever since then – even in periods of relative "boom" – and has suffered numerous serious panics and depressions far worse than any ever experienced prior to 1890, even following Pres. Jackson's catastrophic edict eliminating all paper money for a time..

The easiest way to understand the violence these agencies as a whole have inflicted on our economy is simply to look at where it is today, including where any innovation is occurring in it: the only places still alive in that manner are those few places in the economy which are not subject to federal "regulation" – specifically, the entertainment and sports businesses, where participants simply keep getting better and better all the time, even if the profits don't necessarily go up, and, until the Obama administration decided to impose regulations identical to those previously imposed on the railroad industry, on the Internet, and all businesses associated in any manner with it – i.e. the so-called tech industry, the world of apps, and all aspects of the communication business.

Ever wonder why only three American or quasi-American companies even make automobiles anymore, why cars have become so expensive (10 to 20 times what they were barely 40 years ago), and why all automobiles look the same in 2015? It's because federal regulations emanating from multiple agencies essentially dictate the entire design of all cars so that engineers have to spend most of their effort complying with those regulations, with any innovation on design available only marginally – and with most of the cost-consuming efforts of the manufacturing company spent complying with worthless federal "regulations" drafted by dictatorial functionaries who have their own interests in mind – and not the interest of the public nor of the automobile industry.

The most notorious and obvious example of mindlessly-destructive regulation, in an effort to subject a major American business to the state control its European analogs have long been subjected to, is the almost boundless regulation, emanating from multiple federal agencies, which has been imposed on every aspect of the financial services industry, beginning with the creation of the Federal Reserve in 1913.

Consider: the Federal Reserve was created for two reasons: (1) to preserve the value of the dollar, and (2) to prevent cyclical busts or panics in the economy. Prior to its creation, the most recent such panic occurred in 1906 – the direct result of Theodore Roosevelt, the president, radically threatening all successful American businesses with purely-discretionary federal destruction under the new various federal agencies he wanted to create to investigate them, and thereby subject them to endless procedural nightmares, and his threat of prosecuting them – and potentially destroying them – under the bizarre and ambiguous discretionary destructive power of the Sherman Antitrust Act.

Again, the Federal Reserve was formed in 1913 in the first year of the Woodrow Wilson administration for two purposes: (1) to prevent erosion of the value of the dollar and (2) to minimize or prevent the risk of panics in financial markets and the cyclical busts they produce. Consider: the dollar today is worth 1/23 of what it was in 1913, and since the creation of the Federal Reserve (with endless additional regulations imposed on the hapless financial service industry thereafter on top of it) the financial panics which have occurred thereafter – including the Great Depression, the crash of 1987 and the financial panic of 2008, among others – have been vastly more extreme than any panic experienced by the nation prior thereto, with each such event proven to have been caused largely by actions of the Federal Reserve Board and the multiple agencies regulating the financial services industries.

After every single one of these financial catastrophes, government functionaries have complained that the problem was private greed and insufficient regulation of the financial services industry – which has been, since 1913, the most heavily-regulated industry, from multiple federal agencies, not simply one, of every business in the economy. If that does not prove the utter worthlessness of all such federal regulation what does? And what value can it possibly have any claim of having produced?

Federal "regulators" claim that they are performing services for the public in their regulation of each industry under their thumb. In fact, they have no qualification whatsoever to perform any service for anyone. Since the time of Wilson, their claim has been based on their insisting that they are "experts," with virtually omniscient ability to micromanage the business under their control – and to do so better than its owners, owners who have every incentive to maximize their own profits and preserve the business. All these claims of "expertise" and performing "services" by the federal agencies are nothing but lies – as they have been proven to be time and time again.

## American Political Parties and the Counterrevolution

Quite simply, although the Counterrevolution has had multiple supporters on many different fronts, including the active support of prominent members of both major political parties and, indeed, consistent, powerful and highly-effective support from the Democrat party, particularly since the election of President Wilson in 1912, there has never been any American party actively opposed to the Counterrevolution strategically: so America has had explicitly Marxist and Progressive/Liberal political parties and, in the case of the Democratic Party for most of the 20th century and all of the 21st, a Radical Secularist/Corporatist/Collectivist party masking its true nature.

But never in American history has there been an explicitly anti-Marxist/anti-Collectivist political party (although virtually all American politicians at least claimed to be anti-Communist during the Cold War).

Although the Republican Party, since 1908, has generally claimed to represent free markets, low taxes and small government, the few victories of that nature it has actively fought for and achieved (income tax cuts during several Republican presidencies are pretty much the only such victories) overall amounted to no more than speed bumps for the Counterrevolution's progress.

Indeed, the truth is that some of the most radical and far-reaching victories notched by the Counterrevolution since its beginning as a political force in the late 19th century have been achieved not simply with the quiet acceptance/acquiescence to the inevitable of the Republican party: prominent leaders of that party have actually been major forces in achieving, and even forcing, those various Counterrevolutionary victories.

Indeed, no such Counterrevolutionary victories were more profound than those notched by Theodore Roosevelt, both during his presidency and thereafter. It is fair to say that without his actions, it is doubtful the Counterrevolution could ever have achieved any of its post-1900 extraordinary victories – all of which were achieved as a result of politicians' claims that, in enacting such measures, they were "fixing" supposedly-huge problems, problems which, to whatever extent they even actually existed, in fact, resulted directly from victories earlier notched by the Counterrevolution.

Theodore Roosevelt – The Counterrevolution's
Single Most Consequential Champion

Central to the "teachings" of Karl Marx is his claim that there is no God, but that History itself constitutes a quasi-Providence which is ever-present, and forces its will, and its own quasi-morality (effectively the opposite of the biblical one) on all men and nations. The career of Theodore Roosevelt may well be the closest thing to a "proof" of those otherwise-nonsensical claims.

Specifically, but for a series of completely bizarre, and unpredictable, events, Theodore Roosevelt would never have been promoted to high, national office by his own, Republican Party – and the extraordinary victories he obtained for the Counterrevolution.

Those victories resulted directly from his willingness simply brazenly to seize power for the federal government lawlessly and unconstitutionally, based on his own publicly-proclaimed contempt for the Constitution, seizures made possible by Congress' supine unwillingness to oppose them, and from a combination of his own personal charisma and the power he obtained as president, all coupled with his own, simultaneously-held Marxist/collectivist political opinions and, oddly enough, both his genuine American patriotism and his profound psychological pathology (his infantile emotions observed by all intelligent advisors surrounding him, his probable bipolarity, his obvious, profoundly-narcissistic self-aggrandizement and contempt for all those he viewed as his opponents). All these factors combined to result in an extraordinary stew which, further coupled with his vast energy and raw intelligence, simply could not normally have taken place – at least in the manner in which they did – absent a truly extraordinary sequence of improbable events.

Although the Republican Party had no real ideological core once slavery was abolished, actively opposing, and certainly not supporting, Marxism and its associated ideas was simply never on its policy agenda at all – until Teddy Roosevelt forced those ideas on the nation, particularly after he was actually elected president for the first time in 1904. And, amazingly enough, it wasn't as a party ideologically opposed to Marxism that that monstrous ideology came on the Republican Party's radar: under the presidential leadership of Teddy Roosevelt, the party initially actually became an ardent supporter of the economic and social views of Karl Marx.

Roosevelt's first term as president resulted solely from his having been vice president to William McKinley, who was assassinated a mere six months after his inauguration for his own second term in office, in 1901.

Roosevelt was the vice president at that time solely because of a fluke — the grotesque miscalculation of leaders of the national Republican Party and its New York chapter, who had conspired to put him on the ticket as vice president simply to "kick him upstairs" and remove him from office as governor of New York where he was intent on accomplishing crazy, radical Marxist things, which no one else in the party wanted to have anything to do with.

In short, Roosevelt had been recognized as a truly dangerous radical. He did not deny that fact, as a friend and fan of Herbert Croley, a supposed "public intellectual" and the publisher of "the New Republic," who was himself a barely-disguised Marxist, with Roosevelt admittedly differing from orthodox proponents of that ideology solely with respect to the militant methods they invariably advocated at that time, and by his loving, and not utterly detesting, America – although he had nothing but contempt for our Constitution. His fellow New York Republicans had known all this, and were determined to remove him from any position of power. Hence their desire to get him out of his governorship in New York and put him in the vice presidency – an office with no power whatsoever, except...

And McKinley was indeed assassinated – by an otherwise ineffectual anarchist revolutionary — an anarchist who, against all odds, completely changed American history by that murder.

When he was simply finishing out McKinley's term in office, Roosevelt held back, for the most part, his radical Collectivist/Marxist proclivities, respecting the fact that McKinley had been elected without promoting any such policies (McKinley was an old-fashioned, corrupt Republican politician interested only in promoting American businesses through tariffs on foreign competition, with no interest whatsoever in Marxism, nor in imposing European-style Bad Law regulation on them).

Roosevelt did, however, early on, rattle the sword of the antitrust law – a powerful, antibusiness law (its original purpose for enactment) which, as mentioned above, had, initially, been largely defanged by the courts prior to Roosevelt, after its 1890 enactment, for a variety of reasons – including its known probable unconstitutionality – except for its use as a vehicle for suppressing labor unions, which clearly were forbidden by its very terms (they were indeed combinations in purposeful restraint of trade, potentially actionable under existing state tort law).

Roosevelt, a man of inherited wealth who never held a non-political job in his life, snobbishly looked down on "mere businessmen" whose self-created wealth vastly exceeded his and who lacked his Harvard education. He happily used the platform provided by the presidency to play the part of a noisy, existentially-dangerous bully, and demanded multiple federal attacks on businesses. including the creation of a whole new federal agency (which later became the FTC) to subject them to constant, politically-instigated, harassing "investigations," and use the antitrust law to punish them – as the thieves he, in his Marxist view, viewed them always to be anyway.

Roosevelt was an extremely charismatic man who had been lavishly promoting himself in a variety of ways well prior to his election as governor of New York – including his highly-publicized activities with the Rough Riders during the Spanish American War. I make the observation: it is far from unusual for sociopaths (pathological narcissists) to be extremely charming on a personal level, however cold-blooded and nasty they might really be.

In that regard, you should know that Theodore Roosevelt unabashedly announced his complete agreement with the Radical Collectivist revolution, including its utter contempt for the citizens as individuals and their liberty – and for the Constitution itself: "I don't know what the people think, I only know what they should think," he said. The "ability to fight well and breed well [and] subordinate the interests of the individual to the interests of the community [is] crucial to true national greatness[emphases added]."

Roosevelt viewed all commercial deals as, in his own words, "mean and sordid" — just like Karl Marx.

As mentioned, he created a whole new agency whose sole purpose was to investigate and bully corporations, and he proposed radical regulatory legislation specifically modeled on that of Germany under the Kaisers – virtually identical to legislation later passed during his cousin, FDR's New Deal – the National Recovery Act, which even the 1930s Supreme Court ruled unconstitutional.

Arguably the most significant Counterrevolutionary "achievements" of Roosevelt during his presidency were his promotion of the enactment of legislation which ultimately resulted in the creation of the second (after the Interstate Commerce Commission resulting from its 1887 enabling legislation) federal "regulatory" agency, whose purpose was to legally control, and thereby confiscate existential, controlling power over, all businesses operating within it, without any compensation to any such businesses for such "taking" – the FDA.

He also demanded and accomplished massive nationalizations of large amounts of real estate by the federal government – supposedly in the name of its "preservation" – as if that land would be destroyed if it were held by private persons, who might actually have an incentive to keep its forests from burning, and to preserve for everyone, including themselves and their families, its extraordinary physical beauty.

Roosevelt's promotion of the agency which ultimately became the crushing-ly-monstrous and deadly FDA (discussed in Chapter 3) was itself highly instructive of the kind of fraud and power-grabbing involved in creating all such federal "regulatory" agencies.

The politically-proclaimed purpose for creating such an agency – and enacting the clearly-unconstitutional legislation enabling it – was to prevent supposed catastrophic behavior by businesses then involved in modernizing all aspects of providing the public with food – vastly increasing its availability and quality, at significantly lower prices for everyone, literally freeing the nation of the need to work on farms to obtain food at modest prices – and innovation in the development of medicines of various kinds (a then-novel business with unlimited potential for human betterment).

His claims that such businesses – particularly the meatpacking business, which was revolutionizing the availability of inexpensive, quality meat throughout the nation – were committing evil monstrous acts against their own employees and customers were promoted in a patently fraudulent (well-known to be such), 1906 novel by the self-identified Marxist Upton Sinclair entitled "The Jungle". Theodore Roosevelt, while president, well aware of the fraudulence of that novel specifically based his demands to regulate – that is have the federal government become dictator to – the entire food and drug industry on the very claims in that novel.

Of particular importance to the progress of the Counterrevolution was the fact that a nominally-Republican president proposed the creation of such a radical, and clearly-unconstitutional, government agency. The FDA was specifically authorized and intended to exercise what has always been known to be tyrannical, combined, effectively unlimited, Bad Law powers – executive, legislative (it was authorized to write its own rules – or laws) and judicial (regulating such businesses involved by dictating – or ordering – what they could and could not do, just like a court, except without any due process preceding such orders, and destroying them or their customers with fines and/or jail if they failed to get pure-ly-discretionary approval from its bureaucrats — for everything) over all aspects of the businesses to be regulated.

Arguably, the Republican Party has never recovered from the split it experienced at its convention in 1912 in which Theodore Roosevelt refused to accept his defeat – as an explicitly radical progressive candidate – for the Republican presidential nomination, and angrily and energetically formed a new third political party – the Progressive or Bull Moose party – which, because of his personal charisma and following in the Republican Party, split the Republican vote, resulting in both Taft and Roosevelt losing to the very radical progressive Woodrow Wilson, whose "scholarly" articles prior to his presidency detailed his intentions, and those of America's other radical Progressives, completely to undo the Constitution, effectively disregard its limitations completely, and impose a Bismarckian/Napoleonic administrative-dictatorial bureaucratic state on the American people and all their sources of wealth and market power – on all American businesses, that is.

Specifically, in his writings before becoming president, writings which led to his becoming president of Princeton, before becoming governor of New Jersey, Woodrow Wilson unabashedly spelled out in detail the ideology of Progressive (i.e. American-pseudo-Marxist) bureaucratic "expertise" and the super-superiority of "intellectuals" who should be placed in charge of that as rulers of society – whether or not the great unwashed clamored for such, with all opposition intended to be silenced in the face of the authority of such "expertise."

Wilson literally made no bones about any of this his fundamentally anti-American, fascist arrogance (he was also a vicious racist and eugenicist who despised blacks – he alone ordered the racial segregation of the federal government, including military, which had been fully-integrated racially since the Civil War – and Jews, although he had permitted some to gain professorships at Princeton).

Had Teddy Roosevelt not insisted on competing as a third-party presidential candidate in 1912, it is inconceivable that Wilson – an unabashed racist, who detested the American Constitution (he explicitly acknowledged in his writings, unashamedly, that implementing his program required eliminating the Constitution which facially precluded it), openly admired the totalitarian fascist rule of the Kaisers in Germany (until he was forced to go to war against the Germans politically), and earnestly sought to imitate its laws and program into American law – could ever have been elected president. Thank you Teddy Roosevelt.

In fact, Wilson as president – though indeed very radical and clear about his intention to effect absolute control over the economy in administrative agencies run by the executive branch, superseding previous state common-law jurisdiction over such matters and aggressively increasing the power of the presidency over all other branches and over all American citizens – was actually no more radical than Theodore Roosevelt had been in the second term of his presidency.

Indeed, Wilson's most radical progressive accomplishments consisted of completing processes actually begun by actions and/or proposals of Theodore Roosevelt: he achieved legislatively the establishment of the Federal Reserve Bank and its fascist system, which, for the first time, like all the Napoleonic European tyrannies, nationalized the currency, in 1913 (which Roosevelt had proposed in infant form), with its continuing pretense of being an apolitical body neutrally supervising the nation's money, supposedly to prevent monopolistic private oligarchs' control of it; he established the Federal Trade Commission, continuing Roosevelt's policy of harassing businesses with federal power – and threats of its arbitrary deployment with virtually no measurable standards governing federal action, in the event private businesses chose to take actions undesired by the politicians in Washington; and, of course, Wilson effected the first, constitutionally-sanctioned federal income tax in 1913, for which Roosevelt had also fought, after the adoption of the 16th amendment.

# CHAPTER 17

## The Counterrevolution After Wilson

Even a relatively-perfunctory account of the seemingly-endless, massive, polit-ical-legal victories scored by the Counterrevolution since the watershed year of 1913 would take many volumes – and be both mind-numbingly boring and in-credibly depressing to anyone who still believes America remains a free nation with anything resembling a free market economy, or at least a political process permitting its reinstatement after the Counterrevolution's unopposed onslaught since 1887.

Since 1913, virtually every product and service sold in America, all private-ly-held land, and every business have become legally-subjected to the juris-diction and tyranny of at least one – and often multiple – federal agencies, each which agency's power – and that of all its unelected bureaucrats – is plainly tyrannical because it is purely discretionary and, in real life, gratuitous and arbitrary. All those nameless bureaucrats are themselves virtually immune from being fired, and are often highly-politicized, and subject to virtually no actual review nor, as a practical matter, any limiting principle of any kind, all as described in Chapters 3-5.

Counterrevolutionary legislative/"regulatory" "achievements" proliferated and mushroomed during the presidency of Woodrow Wilson, beginning in 1913: (1) the creation of the Federal Reserve, which, for the first time, subjected the United States currency to government/political control (while politicians have always noisily claimed otherwise), (2) the enactment, pursuant to the Constitution's 16th amendment which expressly permitted it, of the undeniably Marxist (one of the 10 central demands in Marx's *Communist Manifesto*) graduated federal income tax and, (3) the proliferation of more and more federal agencies supervising/dic-tating to more and more segments of American life – often referred to as the economy, though the effects permeated all American life. After a brief pause during several Republican presidencies in the 1920s (none of which presidents attempted to repeal any of the Collectivist legislation which preceded their pres-idencies), the Counterrevolution accelerated enormously during the FDR presi-dency, and, indeed, throughout the rest of the 20th century.

By the end of the 20th century there literally was not a single area of the American economy – other than the Internet – nor indeed, because of that very fact, any portion of Americans' private lives, that was not subject to massive — usually deceptively hidden or obfuscated— discretionary, crushing, unconstitutional, bureaucratic federal control. Virtually all businesses, including all with more than a handful of employees, have to answer to multiple federal agencies staffed by bureaucrats, issuing often conflicting directives, with respect to every single one of such businesses' contractual relationships with everyone – employees, customers, other businesses, you name it.

All such agencies have invariably exercised existential control over everyone and every business subjected to their tyrannical, virtually omnipotent jurisdiction.

The direct result of all this federal, bureaucratic control was massive destruction to all previously-private markets, and the rule of Good Law itself, inevitably resulting in massive politicized corruption and incalculable harm to the economy, prosperity, and citizens' vocational and employment prospects. Because of the overwhelming conquest, described in Chapter 14, by the Counterrevolution and its collectivist ideology over all the "learned professions" and the mass media, whenever undeniable economic misfortunes arose – unemployment, bank failures, panics, you name it – all blame was falsely laid at the feet of private businesses and their owners, who themselves were already under the thumb of massive federal "regulation," followed invariably by calls for additional federal control over them.

Again, the power of each such federal agency and its bureaucrats over all Americans subjected to them can fairly be characterized as tyrannical. As both a legal and practical matter, the actions of such agencies and their bureaucrats have been subject to no real judicial (or other) supervision whatsoever: specifically, the federal courts have ruled that all such "regulatory" actions by the bureaucrats and their agencies – including the actual, unconstitutional enactment by them of laws (euphemistically called "mere regulations") all enforceable by, yes, actual criminal penalties in the form of jail time and massive fines – is perfectly legal and permissible unless, in the view of federal judges, any such bureaucratic action is proven (by "clear and convincing evidence"), to the satisfaction of a federal judge (no jury permitted) to be an "abuse of discretion"– significantly more than just "erroneous" – by anyone daring to oppose the bureaucrats' actions.

Any citizen daring to challenge – always at his own enormous expense – any such bureaucracy does so knowing he remains subject to that bureaucracy's continuing arbitrary control – a plainly chilling fact on his desire to run the risk of challenging his bureaucratic masters in any manner.

Because these agencies enact their own laws ("regulations"), and enforce them directly against citizens by imposing their edicts, they effectively combine executive, legislative and judicial powers – the very definition of tyranny, according to James Madison, citing Montesquieu for this precise point, in Federalist number

47, which our Constitution was specifically designed to preclude by dividing those three types of power into three separate government branches. This very feature of the Constitution – its absolute preclusion of such multi-power bureaucracies – was the explicit promise made by the founders in that *Federalist* number 47 in promoting its ratification.

Legislation establishing and enabling each of these administrative agencies and cabinet departments has been enacted by both Democrat and Republican presidents and congresses, with certain noteworthy historical inflection points when such legislation was particularly abundant – e.g., throughout the Wilson presidency, throughout the 1930s, the 1960s, the 1970s, and during Obama's first two years.

Prior to the mid-1930s, on the rare occasions when actions by any of the by-then proliferating federal administrative agencies were contested as unconstitutional, the Supreme Court generally (consistency has never been its virtue) did indeed uphold the Constitution's requirements and ruled unconstitutional such litigated agencies and/or their particular actions challenged in the case before it.

However, as described in multiple chapters above, in the mid-1930s the Supreme Court turned the Constitution on its head, pretending that its Commerce clause authorized those agencies and their actions – a blatantly-political move by the Court lampooned thereafter as the "switch in time that saved nine." As Constitutionally-baseless, political and gratuitous as that radical change by the Court was, such has nevertheless been that Court's invariable position ever since then in the multiple cases that have thereafter come before it.

Virtually none of that legislation, nor the "regulations" created by federal agencies, has ever been repealed or repudiated by the elected branches of government – even by new administrations winning office against opponents in the opposite party. For example, the Republican Eisenhower administration made no effort whatsoever to repeal any of the New Deal legislation, programs or bureaucracies, left over from the FDR administration. Similarly, neither the Reagan nor the George W. Bush administrations made any effort to repeal any New Deal or LBJ-era Great Society legislation – nor even any of the monstrous regulations created by the bureaucracies that legislation created and empowered.

But those bursts of such legislation are actually only the most-visible part – the tip of the iceberg – of the Counterrevolution's massive legal conquests.

Based on the legal empowerment provided by that legislation, and the effective refusal of federal courts, or any other branch of government, to exercise any actual review of either that legislation or, more importantly, the actions of federal "regulatory" agencies and their unelected bureaucrats, the real Counterrevolutionary action has primarily occurred clandestinely and out of public view within those agencies, following their legal creation, as they churn out endless — hundreds of thousands of pages of — criminally-enforceable "regulations," and unilaterally and arbitrarily's enforce them against citizens and their businesses.

This action within those agencies and, in many cases, lobbying to create and shape them, has been massively facilitated and energized by Counterrevolutionary radicals promoting various "movements," as described in Chapter 14, each which "movement" animated multiple such "regulatory" agencies. All such actions with respect to those agencies have invariably taken place as far out of the public's view as the activists – and the politicians promoting their activism – involved have been able to manage. Stealth, obfuscation and outright fraud have been the Counterrevolution's most potent weapons – against the nation that has never actually agreed with or to any of its revolutionary principles – with no organized opposition at any time to any of the Counterrevolution's assaults.

Two such "movements," not previously discussed here above in Chapter 14, arose, beginning after the Kennedy assassination (Query: did that assassination and its aftermath contribute to the rise of those "movements?"), which Movements provided particular energy to the Counterrevolution, including its Cause of promoting the proliferation of such federal agencies, the content of their "regulations" and their breathtaking claims to be promoting moral imperatives of such overwhelming importance that all other public policies and individual rights have increasingly been legally-forced to yield to them – with no provision in the Constitution permitting such subordination of individual rights and, indeed, the entire Constitution written precisely to promote those rights' absolute primacy over any claimed federal or state power.

These two additional "movements," discussed below, similarly provided synergistic energy to each other, to various leftist-driven "social" causes designed to weaken traditional institutions of civil society (e.g., marriage, nuclear families, Christian morality, including the sanctity of life itself), to further entrench radical leftism in the multiple institutions the left had already captured in America (universities and schools at all levels, unions, journalism, the courts and the legal profession, and even many churches), and to all the movements discussed in Chapter 14 as similar, supposed moral imperatives.

These two "movements" were, in their own self-descriptions, The New Left, and the Lawfare and Consumer movement, the latter driven, in its multiple campaigns, by Ralph Nader and the various radical, activist groups he spawned.

First a brief word about the interrelationship between these two movements.

All the leaders of each such movement were deeply-committed orthodox Marxists, steeped in Marxist ideology and, accordingly, filled with fanatical loathing for the American Revolution and its exultation of individual liberty, and for all private businesses – that is, productive enterprises driven by the profit motive and subject both to the constraints of market forces and of the common-law, neither of which such Marxists recognized as having any legitimacy or substance, to the extent they had any concept of their existence at all.

All the leaders of both such movements were fanatically-committed to achieving a Marxist-Leninist revolutionary dictatorship in America (literally turning the country into what it would have looked like had the USSR defeated it in war), using whatever methods, without regard to scruples, ethics or morality, they believed could work. Their fanatical devotion to their Cause provided, in their minds, an absolute moral imperative for that Cause's complete defeat of America as founded – the American Revolution – justifying absolutely any action to achieve that end – so long as it could do so.

Specifically, they wanted the federal government to be able to dictate the terms of virtually every private business contract, to dictate what products could and could not be sold or purchased, who would be allowed to borrow or lend money – and even who banks would be forced to lend to – all employment decisions, and all other matters related to commerce of any kind – without even bothering with an actual, visible revolution to achieve these clearly-revolutionary, and unconstitutional results.

The principal difference between these two movements was in the particular American institutions they each, separately, focused on and sought to transform, and the different methods they each used for doing so.

Regarding such movements' disparate methods:

The New Left romantically fantasized about presenting itself as a genuinely-charismatic phenomenon which they dreamed would galvanize public support for an old-fashioned communist revolution in America, beginning with enlisting support on American university campuses and, by presenting itself as "hip" in a manner supposedly appealing to young people, acquiring sufficient support for a Marxist take-over of the government and all other American institutions.

Its methods were always confrontational, beginning with various forms of civil disobedience on American campuses, graduating to mass demonstrations as public opposition to the increasingly-stalemated Vietnam War – and fear of the military draft – increased in the early 1970s, and eventually spawning various genuinely-militant terrorist groups, including the Weather Underground beginning in 1969, whose revolutionary exploits — kidnappings, bank robbery, bombings, etc. — its members romantically dreamed would charismatically attract new revolutionaries.

The Ralph Nader-led movements, though similarly dedicated to the complete, revolutionary Marxist transformation of America, took an approach that was the virtual opposite of that of the New Left. Specifically, rather than assaulting American institutions from the outside confrontationally, it sought to use law and various legal institutions to ensnare and assault American businesses both substantively and procedurally, promoting their subjugation by endless, multiple federal bureaucratic agencies, and by promoting "developments" in the law itself as administered by courts to similar effect – and recruiting an army of lawyers and bureaucrats to wage and institutionalize that war against all American businesses from such multiple fronts.

The Naderites' purpose was both to create additional, new federal agencies with power indistinguishable substantively from the power exercised in the Soviet Union by its various bureaucracies – and to populate all the federal agencies with fanatically-committed Marxists from within its own ranks.

Ideologically, each of these two movements' strategically-focused leaders were identical in their total commitment and fanatical belief in all the features of Marxism described in Chapter 6. Nevertheless, they each pursued completely different paths in their quest to impose that ideology, and its practical, governing effects, on America. In the following few paragraphs, I outline the overall differences between these two, different, strategic approaches to imposing Marxism here, and their differing analyses of the then-state of the Counterrevolution in mid-20th century America, which analyses undoubtedly informed their differing strategies which resulted.

The New Left overtly and noisily announced itself as a revolutionary movement in the mode of the French Revolution – with its own music, "lifestyle choices", contempt for all religion and morality, etc. – seeking to attract new converts to the cause by stressing the romantic, utopian, revolutionary aspects of itself – at least initially. Its new approach to "marketing" the actually-enslaving Marxist Leninist program it, like the Stalinists of earlier generations, was intent on imposing, was largely to gloss over its substance completely and to emphasize superficial, non-political features of the various poses – all intended by them to suggest "coolness" and "hipness" – which its members adopted, constantly criticizing America as it was, but very rarely describing what they actually had in mind – which was simply good old-fashioned communism – once they had secured America's defeat, a defeat which was always their goal.

The overtly-radical revolutionary pose they invariably adopted strongly suggests that their assessment of the previous "accomplishments" of the Counterrevolution which, as shown above, had been ongoing since 1887, was to view them as not amounting to much.

It is, indeed, perhaps their enormously-different assessments of the extent of the prior success – or lack thereof – in imposing Marxism on America of the Counterrevolution, which primarily informed the resulting strategic differences between the New Left and Ralph Nader.

Nader was a sophisticated, Harvard-educated lawyer who began with the (accurate, as shown above) view that the most important, strategic, extra-constitutional legal victories necessary to impose Soviet-style institutional Marxism on the nation had, by the 1960's, already been achieved, so that no additional legal revolution was necessary — just the full implementation of that "achievement."

On the other hand, the New Left at least professed the view that the entire revolution they desired had yet to begin before they arrived on the scene. Nader viewed his efforts as simply building on those earlier very-real (if always Constitutionally and politically fragile and undoable) Counterrevolutionary legal/political victories – particularly those of the Theodore Roosevelt and Wilson administrations, which had unilaterally created federal agencies as intrusive as any in continental Europe, completely indifferent to their unconstitutionality, and the 1930's Supreme Court's complete shredding of any Constitutional limitation on the federal power to police private citizens and businesses (a police power which is, in fact, precluded under the actual Constitution, as shown in previous chapters).

Nader's absolutely-correct insight was that Americans had already shown a willingness to accept, or at least tolerate, blatantly unconstitutional, Marxist dictatorial control over businesses and the purchasing decisions of individuals, and the Supreme Court had announced its corrupt total acceptance of the complete constitutionality of all such, so that the law required no further, underlying transformations for any additional such control to be imposed over the areas of the economy and individual choice not previously subject to such federal "regulation."

## History of the New Left

Briefly, the New Left was a movement initiated by old-line, deeply-committed Marxist-Leninists in an effort to promote and popularize their revolutionary ideology, particularly among the post-World War II baby boomers and, beginning in 1968, to take the Democrat party, which major party collectivists of various stripes had already firmly controlled ideologically since the end of the 19th century, much further to the left than it had ever been before.

The Cause of Collectivism in America, including its outreach and recruiting efforts, has had many different communities supporting it in different ways and a long and varied history. As discussed, above, throughout the 19th century, its principal supporters were journalists and university professors, and other self-proclaimed bien-pensant enthusiasts of the French Revolution – continuing to fancy the delusion of that revolution as a "liberating" phenomenon. As also discussed above, among their principal, 19th century political achievements was their successfully promoting the institutionalization of mandatory public schools, just as demanded in Marx's *Communist Manifesto*, throughout the nation – no small achievement that, which has, in turn, proven to be an enormously-valuable captured institution for the Cause.

Also as mentioned above, the Cause also achieved several revolutionary political accomplishments. The most revolutionary (in America) of these consisted of the 1887 subjugation of the entire railroad industry under the first federal agency of its type – the Interstate Commerce Commission – pursuant to the first federal legislation authorizing such – the Interstate Commerce Act – and the enactment of the Sherman antitrust laws in 1890.

The next significant political/legal achievements of that nature by the Cause had to await the presidency of Theodore Roosevelt. Theodore Roosevelt, a Republican, succeeded to the presidency as vice president to William McKinley who was assassinated. Roosevelt explicitly characterized himself as a Progressive – the euphemistic name American Collectivists adopted for themselves well aware that the American public had no appetite for Marxism/socialism, let alone for explicitly undoing the American Revolution.

American Progressivism, which flourished beginning in the last decades of the 19th century, had a number of causes it promoted, including women's suffrage, alcohol prohibition, a federal income tax and estate tax. Roosevelt had a particular, brahmin-snobbish loathing of businessmen, but differed from doctrinaire Marxists in America and Europe in his genuine American patriotism (doctrinaire Marxists invariably have detested America as the mortal enemy of their ideology), and in his opposition to even mentioning the idea of outright nationalizing any private assets.

Nevertheless, Theodore Roosevelt promoted the creation, through legislation that eventually established it, of the second (after the Interstate Commerce Commission) federal agency which assumed radical "regulatory" control over a major sector of the private economy – the agency that eventually became known as the FDA, formally instituted during the presidency of his cousin, FDR, which has exerted literally dictatorial control over the inspection and permission-requiring of all drugs, medical devices, and even the inspection of food in the nation. Roosevelt also engaged in so-called "trust-busting," consisting of brutally, and gratuitously, threatening entire industries with prosecution under the draconian and ambiguous federal Antitrust Act.

His hostility to business also resulted in his creating a government agency, eventually named the FTC, whose sole, initial purpose was gratuitously to investigate all the activities of businesses – effectively a permanent fishing expedition designed to intimidate them into knuckling under to the demands of politicians.

The result of all his antibusiness policies — actual and threatened — likely was the Panic of 1906, in which J.P. Morgan personally intervened and performed a famous rescue operation of the American financial system. That Panic in turn served as a claimed excuse for the creation of the Federal Reserve a few years later, an institution which had the effect of nationalizing the currency and subjecting it to political control (while fraudulently pretending otherwise).

Additional Counterrevolutionary actions by Roosevelt was the creation, for the first time, of national parks in which vast amounts of land were nationalized, with such nationalization supposedly necessary to "save" such lands from destruction.

American Collectivism, although always extremely (privately) respectful of the ideas of Karl Marx, has almost never publicly admitted to his influence – except in the always-unpopular American versions of the Communist and Socialist parties, and the various other parties and front groups that have served as their surreptitious surrogates – a secretiveness itself arising from, and motivated by, the continuing, well-known unpopularity of socialism/communism among Americans.

Like their European counterparts, American collectivists have held a fairly wide range of views among themselves, from the most radical revolutionary communists at one extreme, all the way to advocates primarily focused on various individual liberties and, at one time, even fairly doctrinaire anti-Communists at the other extreme.

Within mainstream political parties, collectivists of a fairly wide range of views have been present in both the Republican and Democrat party throughout the 20th century, with both such parties at least pretending to be anti-communists after World War II – at least in international affairs – and with both such parties, or members thereof, both initiating and joining, however reluctantly, in promoting legislation and otherwise institutionalizing government agencies dedicated to major assaults on citizens, their businesses and the Constitution and its principles of individual liberty and property rights.

The approach to politics of the most radical, self-admitted American Marxist-Leninist partisans, like those who eventually created the New Left, has gone through several, clearly-identifiable transformations since the beginning of the 20th century.

Prior to World War I – and the Russian revolution in 1917 – a multitude of revolutionary Marxist and anarchist groups proliferated in America, one of whose number – an anarchist – profoundly affected American history by assassinating William McKinley, and thereby bringing about the presidency of Theodore Roosevelt. Some of those groups actually dreamed of a violent communist revolution in America – however improbable that may seem.

Indeed, Theodore Roosevelt, while openly acknowledging that he, snobbishly, considered all businessmen to be thieves, and so favored precisely the kind of radical state control over the citizenry and the entire economy demanded by Karl Marx, explicitly differentiated himself from purer Marxists both by disavowing any desire to use military or other force to impose a Marxist military dictatorship on America, and by his patriotism. While acknowledging that the Constitution precluded a government of that nature, he considered that at most a minor inconvenience – and knowingly, and deliberately, massively-violated it during his presidency in promoting, among other things, the establishment of what eventually became the FDA and the FTC, and nationalizing huge tracts of land supposedly to protect them – as national parks or national preserves – from the supposed depredations of private citizens, beginning in 1906.

After the Bolsheviks took over in Russia in 1917, however, those American Collectivists who considered themselves Communists very self-consciously became a kind of fifth column here, respecting Russia as the center of the Communist revolution and desiring and anticipating its eventual expansion to America – an outcome they both desired and believed inevitable. They very definitely saw themselves as a subversive force within the United States, and their many now-indisputable acts of treason and espionage were all calculated to assist Communist Russia in any way they could – often under direct control by Soviet communist handlers.

They were loyal Stalinists when Stalin ruled Russia. Although they were delighted to cultivate additional. new communists in America, they viewed the (inevitable in Marxist terms under the directive of History) ultimate communist takeover of America as something to promote in every way – but not at the ballot box, and never in a direct manner. They were a minuscule minority in America – although one that was very active, at least secretly, within the Democratic Party and in other venues, including inside federal bureaucracies, particularly the departments of State (Alger Hiss, most famously), and Treasury, where they thought they could lend particular assistance to their Stalinist cause.

However, there was nothing appealing about them from the point of view of American popular culture, and they made little if any effort to change that fact – until the 1960s.

In the mid-1960s, only a few months after the self-admitted Communist Lee Harvey Oswald assassinated JFK, American Communists – and, yes, that is what they were – came up with an entirely new approach to selling their very old, by then, and unappealing, totalitarian product – serfdom-imposing communism, in which nobody owns anything other than the state, which owns everything, and every one is nothing but a functionary drone/serf subject to party/state control in all his actions.

Their new idea both began, and began its implementation, at what had become Marxism's most-longstanding, true American institutional home as of then – the American university. Chapter 14 explains the multiple, self-interested reasons why university professors – and other so-called "learned professions" – were drawn to Marxism beginning in the mid-19th century.

Like all communist initiatives, it had both a public and a secretive, largely-hidden, dimension. Its public (false) face/mask – initially, the self-named Berkeley Free Speech movement – presented itself as a supposedly student-led "movement" supposedly striving to promote students' freedom from the allegedly stifling anti-intellectual environment resulting from post World War II "suburban culture" and the Eisenhower administration – four years after that administration had ceased to exist.

They claimed their free speech was being stifled, requiring them to engage in acts of civil disobedience to assert their free-speech rights – as if free speech for anyone other than Communists was what they ever actually wanted. And as if such claim of free-speech denial was even true — it wasn't.

The movement in fact was largely driven by out-of-view hard leftist faculty members at UC Berkeley who acted as its strategists, leading the students like puppeteers, many of which students were actually their graduate students dependent on their approval for their careers, in the protest activities they engaged in. All those truly active at a strategic level in the movement also had an academic agenda in mind – the complete, Marxist takeover of all aspects of the University. That way Marxists could have complete control over deciding the credentials of all American white-collar job-holders, and who qualified as a university-credentialed "expert" in a society which, under Marxist principles, was thenceforth to be dictatorially led by "experts."

This new "movement" had the good luck of arising at a time when America was experiencing enormous cultural turmoil, turmoil from which the American Communists sought advantage for themselves and their Cause – what soon was called the sexual revolution and, soon after, the arrival on the American scene of hippies, illegal drug use and the promotion of psychedelics (LSD, peyote and mescaline primarily) used and promoted by, among others, then-Harvard Professor Timothy Leary.

These various developments, combined with apparently-idealistic ideas, such as various forms of pacifism and so-called anti-establishment rhetoric, soon became known as the New Left. The self-consciously-promoted purpose of its promoters was to present the old wine (communism) in supposedly new bottles, pretending to be "humanistic," liberty-promoting, and exciting in a way that old-fashioned Stalinism could never pretend to be. Its promoters pretended to be "hip" by using jargon previously used by jazz musicians, and by talking about things like "lifestyle," "free love," etc.

It was, in reality nothing but a marketing concept by good old-fashioned communists, who had never previously enjoyed more than the minuscule support – probably no more than 6% of the population – one would expect for their viciously anti-American-and-liberty, totalitarian ideology: The self-described New Left was their creation.

Thus the New Left proclaimed itself interested in individual liberty – at least when it came to its own speech, drug use and other "lifestyle" issues, such as "free love", meaning sex outside of marriage, the unrestricted right to abortion – all of which, they claimed, were matters of "personal liberation" inconsistent with what they claimed was the dominant, "conservative" Ozzie and Harriet-type culture of America. The fact that that older, "conservative" culture had actually generally favored individual liberty, was not something the New Left was interested in talking about – and, luckily for it, in the strange world of the 1960s, no one else was either.

Additionally, the movement took advantage of the increasing unpopularity of the Vietnam War, an unpopularity which grew with the sense that it was a bloody quagmire (as it was, because Kennedy had permitted the infiltration of South Vietnam by the North Vietnamese guerrilla army, known as the Vietcong, by refusing to militarily-destroy the Ho Chi Minh Trail in Laos and Cambodia, a catastrophic strategic mistake made even worse by the operational constraints imposed on the military by the LBJ administration) and on the fact that various, faddish intoxicants – primarily marijuana and LSD – were subject to legal prohibition by both the federal and state governments.

The New Left was able to take advantage of that drug prohibition — opposing it — in much the same way that FDR had been able to take advantage of alcohol prohibition: by not-incorrectly presenting their opposition to the prohibition as consistent with individual liberty battling tyranny. Unmentioned by the New Left was the fact that all federal drug laws – and the FDA itself – like the repealed alcohol prohibition, were creations of Progressives of the Counterrevolution, with nothing in the Constitution, after alcohol prohibition's repeal, even permitting their enactment by Congress.

The military draft, to which all young men were subject at the time, made the unpopularity of the Vietnam War a fertile source of opposition to the existing American government which was conducting it – particularly among young men fearful of being drafted, and their girlfriends and wives. The New Left tirelessly attempted to turn opposition to the draft, and to the Vietnam War, into its own rallying cry, often claiming to be opposed to the war on grounds of pacifism when, in fact, they, as committed Communists, were actually simply in favor of America losing the war to the Communist enemy they strongly supported.

Over the years between 1968 and 1972 the New Left successfully took over virtually all American universities, with faculty approval, with those universities even establishing entire departments — Black and Women's Studies, e.g. — dedicated solely to stoking Marxist resentment against America as a supposedly racist, sexist, and otherwise utterly monstrous place. It also largely took over the Democratic Party, and some of the more radical elements of it committed multiple acts of terrorism – bombings, bank robberies, shooting of police officers etc.

However, by the late 1970s, most of the most radical members of the New Left realized that violent revolution was not in the cards for America and so they turned their efforts to more long-term projects – further institutionalizing Marxist ideology and notions throughout the curriculum and administration of American universities, and creating and instituting entire approaches, required of all education department students, to the training of the teachers for primary and secondary schools, to inculcate Marxism in those teachers and encourage and train them, in turn, to use the controlling nature of mandatory public school to propagandize and indoctrinate their captive students.

All those activities resulted in enormous "success" for the New Left to the point that by the 1990s at the latest, primary and secondary schools in America had become fabulously-expensive, taxpayer-funded virtual Marxist indoctrination centers with education in substantive matters at best a secondary focus of the curriculum in most public schools (exactly as demanded in Marx's *Communist Manifesto*). Textbooks written by Marxists – such as Howard Zinn's supposed American "People's history" book (a fraudulent, Anti-American, slanderous tract devoid of accuracy and most real American history) – increasingly were selected by Marxism-inculcated teachers, to the extent they had the power to do so.

The unionization of teachers, which began in the 1960s, contributed enormously to these developments. The teachers unions invariably have been led by fanatical Marxists intent both on imposing strict discipline on union members to support their causes and on solidifying the power of the Marxist teachers unions within the state governments themselves, facilitating the unions' ability to extract tax-payer money from politicians beholden to them both to pay the union members and to use as bribes/contributions to politicians — almost always Democrats — of their choice to further their control over them.

## The Ralph Nader-Led Law-fare Revolution And "Consumer" Movement

Ralph Nader, though far from unknown, is rarely, as he deserves to be, recognized as perhaps the single most extraordinarily-successful behind-the-scenes American Marxist activist of all time. Throughout his politically-active adult life, Nader has tirelessly and energetically pursued power for the Marxist Cause — and not for himself personally — in America, in a truly remarkable, single-minded, multi-pronged approach, with a Machiavellian genius, and a highly-sophisticated understanding of both the power of Bad Law to impose Marxist dictatorship, and of the American civilization he was engaged in assaulting throughout that time.

Like all American Marxists, Nader was sensitive to the fact that explicitly pro-claiming himself to be such would diminish his ability to influence others to join his cause. Such evangelizing to recruit the army of troops needed to achieve endless Bad Law bureaucratic-smothering of all businesses and products, and to institutionalize such to ensure its permanence, was always central to his mission. But, though rarely explicitly calling himself a Marxist, Nader never hid the sub-stance of his radical views, leaving it to those familiar with Marxist ideology to understand that such was indeed what he was promoting. Specifically, Nader always made plain that he fervently believed each of the following:

(!) All private business — necessarily engaged in profit-seeking — is inherently predatory and evil and requires overwhelmingly-intrusive, federal Bad Law (not a term he ever used) intervention to dictatorially supervise every step in the production, sale and purchasing of all goods and services (as discussed in Chapter 3, this has always been both the core American Marxist belief and the mandatory, invariable, subliminal message required of all FCC-regulated electronic media);

(2) Alternatively stated: All those who actually produce all "consumed" [sic] goods and services – i.e., those who provide all of us with everything without which our lives would be impoverished ("nasty, brutal and short," in the words of Thomas Hobbes), like those of all but a relative handful of humans since the dawn of time, and who require the profit motive to engage in their businesses — must be micromanaged by state-empowered "experts." (Nader always considered what he and all Marxists characterize as mere "economic rights" – that is, contract rights and rights to and over one's private property – unworthy of any legal protection and rightfully the target of unlimited state power, inevitably exercised by politicians and bureaucrats.)

(3) Selflessly promoting, evangelizing and proselytizing for these beliefs constituted a personal moral imperative for Nader – an imperative he energetically sought highly-educated followers similarly to subscribe to and, once recruited, to promote in every way they could through the creation -- through the courts and federal bureaucracies, always as secretly as possible, with little or no congressional involvement – of Bad Law.

It is no exaggeration to say that Nader and the various movements and organizations he created, and the activist ideologues he personally recruited, for the Cause, without his ever actually winning and obtaining any political office, have together shaped and contributed as much to the massive increase in federal, and even state-law, judicial and bureaucratic power over all aspects of the American economy since the mid-1960s as anyone else who has lived during that period.

And it is precisely that dictatorial, bureaucratic Bad Law, federal control over all aspects of the (previously) private American economy that has been the goal of all American Marxists since the 1880's.

Additionally, that complete control by the federal government, armed with the practical power to destroy and terrorize any business, and any individual involved in any such business, it claimed jurisdiction over, meant that the bureaucrats who administered such control were empowered to dictate everything about those businesses, including the products they could sell, how they could sell them, all their hiring and employment practices – everything. And their control over employees and executives of those businesses arose from the fact that they, as individuals, are always vulnerable, so that those individuals have had no choice but to conduct all their activities in a manner pleasing to such bureaucrats – if only to preserve their own careers.

And the whole point of Nader's efforts was not only massively to increase the sheer amount of federal Bad Law controlling all American businesses, but to populate the bureaucracies with fanatically-committed Marxists.

Based on Marx's own writings and fundamental principles, the underlying rationale for such is overwhelming: to again restate and reiterate those Marxist principles/ideological tenets: (1) all businesses and their owners and executives are vile thieves, amassing profits exclusively through the theft and abuse of their employees, customers and the nation at large; and (2) the central government – invariably operating selflessly and "expertly," without regard to (evil) private profit-seeking motives is, at least compared to those businesses, a "better and fairer" steward and operator of all the nation's "means of production" (i.e., all property, including businesses) – must seize all such "means of production," or at least operational control over them.

Dictatorial bureaucratic control over them guarantees that complete operational control – without any need explicitly to nationalize them, or claim technical legal title to them, as the cruder Marxists in the Soviet Union, Cuba and North Korea, for example, did. The use of dictatorial, terrorizing bureaucracy to govern businesses and the people involved in them in lieu of seizing them provides the fig leaf pretense that the Marxists presiding over all that are not the radical socialists they actually are.

And Nader perfectly understood the proposition that, as between the federal government and private individuals and businesses, power is a zero-sum game: the one's power increases in direct proportion to the diminution of the other's.

No one who understands the legal-bureaucratic transformations American society has undergone, particularly since the 1960s, can fail to recognize both the fact of the metastasizing growth of the federal bureaucracy, and the inevitable consequence of that growth – the increasingly-dramatic decline in the number of sectors of the economy exhibiting robust entrepreneurism and growth, the centralization and consolidation, under massive federal bureaucratic control, of all aspects of American enterprise – manufacturing, finance, you name it – and the increase in the roles of lawyers, lobbyists and politicians, particularly the president, throughout the economy, all of which have mushroomed during that period.

Ralph Nader personally recruited a huge portion of the personnel who have populated the federal bureaucracies and the courts imposing that massive control over all private business concerns — and on their customers' choices. Those Nader-recruited bureaucrats have never required orders to use their bureaucratic power to impose the harshest, terrorizing control possible over the corporations and people they rule over. Indeed one of Nader's most extraordinary "accomplishments" has been to vilify the very word "corporation."

Like other, equally-dedicated, and ultimately influential, 20th-century American Marxists (Saul Alinsky, members of the Weather Underground after, beginning in the 1970s, they understood the hopelessness of their original, romantic aspirations for popular, violent revolution here) Nader understood, along with Karl Marx, the Cause's needs both to conquer America and its Revolution as its eternal, existential enemy, and — his insight — to do so solely by using the very openness of American society itself as a gaping doorway to entering all America's existing institutions, so as to hollow them out and destroy them from the inside out, rather than in an attempted frontal assault.

Nader understood and appreciated the fact that federal bureaucratic control over corporations alone would guarantee absolute control over them, their "culture" and even their personnel, who each would necessarily be forced to follow the Marxist dictates of the bureaucrats who controlled them – or else. Thus, America's largest corporations increasingly, since the 1970's, became populated almost-exclusively by Marxism-infused, "politically correct" products of America's increasingly-Marxist universities, who alone have been acceptable to the federal bureaucrats who hold ultimate control over all such corporations through multiple agencies, each of which agencies have the power to destroy any corporation, and any of its employees, who fail to follow, and mentally-conform to, bureaucratic dictates – and who even dare to complain about them publicly, or in the courts.

To those who question why chief executives of large corporations now, and increasingly, command such lofty compensation packages, the answer is that the universe of people who can both actually manage the actual business of a corporation and deal with the bureaucratic demands it has no choice but to follow is very tiny, and the few who are able to do that must be paid a premium to do so.

But the effect of corporations and their executives having to spend such a huge portion of their time and energy pleasing bureaucrats, and conforming to their dictates, both drastically reduces the real productivity of those corporations, and effectively forces them to constantly further increase their corrupt involvement with politicians and bureaucrats, in order fully to exploit the non-market, competitive advantage that cronyism provides them simply to survive, and to have any ability to compete against market competitors who are certain to compete as much for that political edge as for actual customer satisfaction. Quite simply, the existential power of the violence-powered bureaucracy over them forces them, who alone have only market power, into such corruption, regardless of their actual preferences.

Nader began with the proposition, which previous generations of self-styled Progressives – Wilson in his Princeton-days' writings and, to varying degrees, virtually all American presidents, of both political parties, after the McKinley assassination – had proven, i.e., that a collectivist revolution in America requires no military dictatorship, but rather can be accomplished purely by radical, elitist lawyers armed only with laws, briefcases and paper, legally-empowered by radical courts and/ or legislation authorizing the creation of bureaucracies, each with its own open-ended jurisdiction, further empowered by those judge- and/or legislation-made laws to create laws of their own, laws enforceable by criminal sanctions, and the threat of personal and financial ruin.

Nader took that proven proposition, like taking a bull by the horns, to multiple new frontiers – wherever law can exercise power – constantly promoting multiple uses of law, and seeking and recruiting the legally-trained (and intellectually brilliant and driven) army of troops necessary to effectuate his multi-pronged attack on all of America's institutions, particularly its large, corporate businesses. The nature of his lawfare (i.e., warfare through law) revolution required such an army:

no one man, not even Ralph Nader, could pull off the complex, multi-pronged, multi-front, successful legal assaults he, his Marxist ambition, and his ideas engineered.

Central to his strategy was the idea of creating legal assaults on businesses and other institutions from multiple directions – multiple bureaucracies, litigation, and even simply endless compliance burdens – to literally create a seemingly-endless assault against them, enmeshing them in the sheer, multi-front complexity of having to deal with all that. Thus, having his troops assist private litigation in numerous ways – including by generating "laws" in the courts, Congress and the bureaucracies to strengthen the cases of private litigants against businesses – and, of course, by staffing and running bureaucracies and writing the laws they themselves would enforce – necessarily required thousands of such troops which his proselytizing on American campuses served to recruit.

The enormity and complexity of the legal transformations and expansions effected by Nader-inspired lawyers and judges literally makes it too vast and legally-technical to discuss in any detail here. I have described the general process through which bureaucratic Bad Law was created, with Congress passing unconstitutional laws empowering anti-business litigants and creating bureaucracies which in turn created their own even more unconstitutional laws euphemistically known as "regulations."

The additional, anti-business Nader-inspired process for generating transformations of the Common Law itself, both substantively and procedurally, was more complex. To summarize the overall process involved in that remarkable Marxist "achievement": Marxist law professors would write "scholarly" law review articles arguing for new forms of legal liability (strict tort liability, for example), sometimes explicitly admitting in those articles that the purpose for doing so was simply to socialize the costs of compensating victims – victims who had typically failed to properly use often very-popular products which injured them, and/or who had failed to acquire insurance which would cover the damages they suffered.

The more honest of the law professors arguing for radical, unprecedented tort liability expansion admitted that they expected businesses simply to build in the additional cost of anticipated liability for such prospective victims in their pricing of their products – significantly increasing prices of course – effectively spreading and socializing those costs among all their purchasers whose prices for the products necessarily included an added, invisible, implicit insurance premium, which was all the more expensive since it necessarily insured against idiots' misuse of the product.

Additionally, similarly-Marxist professors argued for the expansion of legal procedures to permit "class actions" predicated on the very idea that some persons might each be harmed in certain circumstances in a manner <u>so insignificant</u> that they simply could not afford to bring a lawsuit themselves, so that the "class" would consist of such persons, each with such insignificant injuries exclusively.

Thus each such "class" was to be legally-manufactured solely to extract payments from the putative source of those multiple insignificant injuries – but actually primarily benefiting the lawyers who claimed to act on their behalf, without being hired by them – and causing massive financial harm to businesses, businesses which had, in fact, caused no more than insignificant damage, at most, <u>by definition</u>, to any putative plaintiff.

As courts accepted the permissibility of, and adopted, all such radical changes in the law, including both such class actions and lawsuits against defendants who had not even committed any active negligence, let alone any intentional damage, massive new litigation opportunities against American businesses were manufactured out of thin air. Ralph Nader-inspired lawyers were involved in all phases of these legal developments, including as judges on courts approving such.

That Nader has always been a committed Marxist, though rarely himself using that term explicitly when on camera or being recorded, has always been apparent to anyone watching his actions, including his recruitment activities. He has dedicated his entire life since the 1960s to using the federal bureaucracy of the administrative state to achieve Karl Marx's dream of the complete takeover of absolute control over every detail of all American businesses of any size – replicating the power over all America's means of production achieved by the Soviet bureaucracy over its own fully-nationalized former businesses – no visible, military revolution necessary.

In addition to the complete dictatorial control over all American businesses exercised by the multiple administrative agencies, those agencies also literally manufactured new causes of action – all based on the unconstitutional statutes which created them – against private businesses, causes of action which clearly would have been precluded under the common law. These causes of action include claims of "sexual harassment," the thought crime of "discrimination" allegedly based on racism, sexism, etc., often based on frivolous, purely-statistical "evidence," such as mere "failure" to hire "enough" members of various superficially-identifiable groups according to their distribution in the population – even though the law purported to preclude "mandatory quotas" of any kind. The very existence of these causes of action was designed to promote Marxism and thought-conformity ("political correctness") in the population and in businesses – all in grotesque violation of the Constitution.

And, of course, the actual, anticipated costs of complying with all this bureaucracy and legal liability also had to be built into the costs of all products and services, so that ultimately the public paid the full compliance price for all this Marxist control over business activities – all imposed in the name of "protecting" the public and multiple purported "victims" within its ranks, with those victims and the public actually bearing all the true, hidden costs of all this — with no actual value added to any product whose price was so inflated.

Beginning in the early 1960s, Nader traveled America's campuses – particularly its most supposedly-elite institutions – explaining the nature of the Marxist regulatory/legal revolution he had devised and seeking students to man the legal barricades on behalf of that revolution. I personally attended a rally/speech he gave at my undergraduate college – Cornell University – in the early 1970s, in which he both vilified America and all private business in the most doctrinaire Marxist terms, and openly explained his approach to defeating the American Revolution through the use – and endless expansion – of American law and the federal government.

He made plain he was seeking troops to man the sophisticated, complex and labor-intensive revolution he described, that he, like a penitent priest, had given up his own quest for money and power, and was asking us Cornellians to follow his example and do the same – in support of the same clearly-Marxist cause. He was a passionate, charismatic evangelists for that cause – as I myself personally witnessed.

A complete description of all the multiple activities Nader and his followers have engaged in would take thousands of pages – and that is no exaggeration. I will simply attempt here to outline some of his most notable achievements:

Quite simply, even though he has never held any public office, Ralph Nader, and the Army of activists and self-proclaimed "public interest" organizations he personally inspired and led, directly or indirectly, literally has been responsible for as rapid and massive growth of federal bureaucracies exercising existential power over virtually the entire nation as any other individual in American history, elected or otherwise.

To understand the enormity of his achievement in that regard, it is necessary first to understand that, prior to his efforts, which began in the 1960s, all the most significant expansions and rapid creating of such bureaucracies were essentially top-down efforts, promoted and effected by presidents, typically with the active assistance of both houses of Congress. As described above, although expansion of the federal bureaucracy has been a bipartisan, ongoing, never-ending government activity since the assassination of William McKinley, the presidencies of Theodore Roosevelt, Woodrow Wilson, FDR, LBJ, Nixon, and Obama have all been times of particularly rapid federal growth – invariably at the expense of liberty and prosperity for individuals and the nation at large.

Nader did exactly the opposite: without holding any federal office, and with no grassroots or other public demand that he or the government do so, he, as a private citizen, presided over, and essentially originated, multiple, interrelated, and mutually-supporting, processes which resulted in growth of federal bureaucracies over the private economy and citizens as extraordinary as that overseen by any elected big-government politician. Specifically, he did each of the following:

1. He pioneered new means — and purported rationales/pretexts — to pro-liferate, and expand, government bureaucracies exercising virtually-endless jurisdiction over multiple, new areas of the economy: he evangelized and recruited an army of highly-educated "Nader's Raiders" who, while pretend-ing to be disinterested scholars and "experts" in various areas of the economy (purported "consumer" issues, such as auto and other product "safety," "envi-ronmentalism," etc.), lobbied Congress to create new, and expand existing, government agencies to micromanage all land and water, and all business-es and their products, provided staff and executives, including top admin-istrators, for those agencies, with his army's personnel, all of whom were radically-committed to maximizing government power over all areas of the economy, and lobbied all those same agencies, providing claimed-"expert" recommendations, for purposes of creating administrative records purport-edly "supporting" the most radical expansions of their bureaucratic power.

2. He created multiple, new pretexts – most notably, "consumerism" (the con-cept of "the consumer" as a virtually-moronic eternal victim of vicious, preda-tory capitalists, who supposedly requires massive federal protection in all his purchases) – and assisted others in promoting others — "environmentalism" — for driving that bureaucratic expansion and proliferation from inside the agencies, from using aggressive litigation, and from lobbying by his various "public interest" nonprofit organizations before Congress – and before the very organizations whose creation he had facilitated, which themselves were staffed, and often run, by former employees of his multiple organizations.

3. He and his multiple "non-profit, public-interest" groups formed formal and informal alliances with government bureaucracies, multiple private law-yers and legal professional organizations, including law professors, and even entire law school faculties and "think tanks," particularly at the nation's most-prestigious law schools, for purposes of using the courts to "develop" expanding bases for liability (including "strict liability in tort," where previ-ously actual defendant negligence, at a minimum, had been required) to be imposed on businesses and private landowners, and impose multiple pro-cedural (including greatly expanded use of class actions) and substantive complications and adverse legal consequences on them, with all such efforts acting synergistically with each other.

To illustrate the nature and substance of these multiple achievements by Mr. Nader, consider just a portion of his affect just on automobiles, beginning with his book-length literary attack on a single car model – the Chevrolet Corvair – Unsafe at Any Speed – a book which appeared in 1965 and constituted a Puritanical Marxist attack on a particular car marketed by GM as a very-inexpensive car with the look and feel of a sports car, which had four seats, unlike most sports cars, and had numerous fea-tures making it appealing as a kind of adult toy. In that book, purporting to play the role of a self-appointed advocate, supposedly on behalf of potential purchasers of the car, Mr. Nader purported to show how that car was the most dangerous object that has ever been marketed by any company to anyone – a facially preposterous notion. And, after all, if what he was saying about the car were true, anyone who bought it thereafter would be doing so well aware of the risks.

Nevertheless, the hysteria Mr. Nader was able to generate – while assisting, or lending assistance, with his Raider "expert" personnel in numerous lawsuits alleging "product liability" again Chevrolet – eventually led to the creation of multiple federal agencies all dedicated to micromanaging every detail of the design of all American automobiles, supposedly for the benefit of "consumers," which has had the actual effect of drastically reducing choices available to consumers, and drastically increasing the prices of cars (prices are roughly 10 to 15 times, for equivalent cars, today what they were only 40 years ago).

Politicians, of course, loved the multiple excuses for "regulating" the automobile industry – the manufacturer of products as popular as any which have ever existed in America – resulting in those multiple agencies, and vast amounts of legislation and "regulation" of every detail of cars' design and manufacture.

That is simply one example of one product Mr. Nader targeted in his behind-the-scenes Marxist revolution intended to achieve the effect of completely subjugating all business sectors to political and bureaucratic control. In 1960, immediately before his private revolution began, most of the American economy was still free, although subject to confiscatory income taxes.

The "environmental" movement – which created and radically-promoted the notion that there was such a thing as the "environment" whose protection from all human activity was a moral imperative of such paramount importance that all rights and considerations were required to yield to it, even if the only one claiming that any particular activity would create problems for the environment was some activist organization – e.g. the Sierra Club, or some other environmental group – which could identify no actual, particular harm to itself which the activity could create, but which nevertheless were granted "standing" by courts to interfere with real private landowners' activities on what had been their own property.

That use of litigation to crush private activities for claimed reasons of purely-manufactured moral imperative was among the many activities promoted by Mr. Nader and his organizations.

## The Consumer Movement

As discussed in Chapter 3 above, the fraudulent novel *The Jungle* attacking the meatpacking industry by Upton Sinclair was cynically used as a pretext by Theodore Roosevelt to promote the establishment of what became the FDA. Sinclair actually initiated the idea of the "consumer" as a special "victim" category.

Nader took that concept and expanded it to demand federal micromanagement of all businesses that created any products purchased by anyone – effectively imposing the same micromanagement on the entire product-producing economy that the FDA had long been imposing on the food and drug industries. Nader and his followers did not neglect pursuing those industries already regulated by the FDA, by the way, with his personnel infiltrating the very highest offices in the FDA, as well as all of the other so-called "consumer" alphabet agencies, which are too numerous to even name here.

Like many Counterrevolutionary "movements," the self-described "consumer" movement rests on a number of myths – about how businesses actually interact with their customers, and even who those customers are. Specifically, its very term "consumer" actually means anyone who purchases, always voluntarily, some good or service from someone else.

The "consumer" movement has always been a Marxist revolutionary activist cause based on the notion that those purchasers – "consumers" – are always, necessarily, victimized by the other parties to the transaction – the sellers – and, accordingly, that federal intervention, supposedly on behalf of such purchasers, is called for to "protect" them from their own decisions. No proof of any actual injury to any one of them is ever claimed by such activists. Instead, they rely on the Marxist smear that all businesses are necessarily predatory, particularly in specifically-identified businesses, so that their customers must be treated by the federal government like children, and radical restraints must be imposed visibly on sellers – the "consumers'" contractual counter-parties.

What is always invisible in such constraints supposedly imposed only on the sellers is the radical constraints they actually also impose on buyers by simply precluding them from buying what they actually want, and limiting them to purchasing what the government does not forbid – with such government stipulation supported by the force of criminal law on both buyers and sellers, as if the products buyers want should be treated like contraband.

The actual effect of such regulatory control over those sellers consists of federal mandates precluding them from selling multiple products their would-be purchasers actually want – supposedly to "protect" those purchasers. In addition to drastically restricting those purchasers' choices, compliance with those federal "regulatory" bodies set up to administer all this drastically increases the cost of even those increasingly-few products those would-be purchasers are permitted to buy.

The actual effect of creating the mythological notion of a "consumer" is to provide a pretext for the imposition of Marxist controls over businesses who sell goods and services others actually want. The pretext for this state intervention is the claim that some separate victim class of people exist who can even be called "consumers." The nonsensical nature of this claim is apparent if one considers the fact that every single one of us is a consumer to the extent we buy things – which everyone does who is not completely self-sufficient with respect to everything.

## American Marxists' Shift to Conventional Politics
## After 1968 to Capture the Presidency

As discussed above, throughout the late 19th and the entire 20th centuries, the Democratic Party had, at the state and local level, tolerated extreme, "machine-politics" corruption within its ranks (i.e., systemic election fraud, ties to organized crime and corrupt unions) and had, to a greater or lesser extent, substantially committed itself to promoting the Counterrevolution; meanwhile, its only, genuine rival political party – the Republicans – practiced their own brand of corrupt extortion from "regulated" businesses, never provided any strategically-focused opposition to the Counterrevolution and, in many cases (Theodore Roosevelt, Herbert Hoover, Richard Nixon), actively participated in facilitating and even creating its legal institutionalization.

However, until 1968, the Democrat party never permitted genuine, committed Marxist ideologues to obtain nomination for high, national office under its banner and, when it seemed that one may have done so and, because of FDR's precarious health, could likely succeed him to the presidency – vice president Henry Wallace – he was purged from his position and replaced on the ticket by Harry Truman and, when he chose to run for president against Harry Truman and Thomas Dewey in 1948, Wallace did so as a third-party candidate, losing ignominiously.

Although many 20th century Democrats romantically sympathized strongly with the Soviet Union and could be fairly called anti-anti-communists, all its candidates for president, winners and losers alike, until 1972, at least posed as genuinely-committed cold warrior/anti-communists, a position the party as a whole at least claimed to support. Indeed, throughout that time, the corrupt local-government "bosses" who held the Democrat party's levers of power for selecting presidential nominees would have considered it absolutely taboo – and ultimately suicidal politically in a country whose citizens have always remained staunchly opposed to Marxism – to permit a Marxist entry into the corridors of power at that level.

All that changed with the 1968 Democratic convention in Chicago. In 1964, LBJ had won the presidency, as the successor to the then-virtually-sainted JFK, against a deeply-divided Republican Party, in a huge landslide victory, winning over 61% of the popular vote. He had overseen the enactment of the most extensive and radical domestic legislation – garnering significant Republican support – since the New Deal (civil rights acts, Medicare, the Great Society legislation) – all of which was enormously popular, particularly with Democrat voters. But, less than 4 years later, he had become so detested that, in March, 1968, he announced he would not run for reelection.

A revolution in the Democrat party literally took place, both inside and outside, at the party convention later that year. That revolution resulted directly from huge opposition to the Vietnam War, which LBJ had inherited from JFK, opposition particularly strong among draft-age college students and other anti-anti-Communist Democrats.

Specifically, while riots by students, led by long-time members of the New Left, were televised taking place dramatically on Chicago's streets outside the convention hall, the local-government "bosses" who had long controlled the Democratic Party and who could become its presidential nominee, literally were ousted from that control, prospectively, by massive changes in the party's nominee-selection rules, changes which would become effective for all future elections – changes intended to unify the party behind the candidacy of Hubert Humphrey by pacifying its most virulent anti-war constituencies.

Those rule changes literally "democratized" the nominee-selection process, greatly enhancing the importance of primary elections – thereby permitting, for the first time, anyone who could win enough such primaries to actually obtain the nomination. The party bosses were stripped of the veto power they previously had held which they had exercised primarily to keep the party and its nominees within the mainstream of American public sentiment – thereby preventing the nomination, or even the attempt to achieve such, of a genuine radical, let alone a Marxist true-believer. Those bosses had been primarily interested in preserving their own local-government power, and not permitting radicals at the national level from destroying them – and the party itself.

Moreover, it has always been obvious that no genuine Marxist could ever get elected president, unless he were a genuine sociopath – someone able both to charm the public and to be enough of a pathological liar that he could constantly wear an utterly-false mask, pretending to be a normal, patriotic American, interested in promoting the growth and prosperity of the nation, while actually, consistent with his ideology, despising America and seeking to harm it and revolutionize or "completely transform" it from the nation it was founded to be – a nation dedicated to preserving individual liberty and freedom from Bad Law control.

For the reasons discussed in Chapter 7 above, once any such sociopath is tolerated at all as a candidate by a major political party, and permitted by it to compete for office, it is inevitable that no non-sociopath would be able to compete with him, since there is no limit to what he is willing to do to win. Because of the multiple constituencies the Counterrevolution had already conquered long before 1968 – journalism, the legal profession, university professors and educators at all levels – and because the Democrat party had become a willing servant of the Counterrevolution long before then, with those 1968 rule changes, it indeed became possible for a genuine sociopath to become the Democrat nominee for president, and get away with it because of the support from all those quarters – particularly the mass electronic media – that he could count on.

Thus, the perhaps paradoxical effect of the democratization of the Democrat party presidential nomination process after 1968 was to virtually guarantee the eventual success of the most extreme sociopaths – including Marxist radicals –

in obtaining the party's presidential nomination. This was, indeed, precisely the result intended by the New Left radicals who were instrumental in obtaining the party rule changes in 1968.

In 1972, in the first presidential contest held thereafter, no sociopath contended for the nomination. George McGovern won it running as a radical anti-anti-communist demanding virtual-surrender by America in the Vietnam War (immediate, gratuitous, complete retreat of our military and complete abandonment of South Vietnam, our ally, which had been infiltrated by a guerrilla communist army since Pres. Kennedy had refused to take any action to prevent that), and a domestic program indistinguishable from European socialism.

Because of his personal integrity, and the American public's continuing revulsion at such policies when announced publicly, McGovern lost in a humiliating 49-state landslide against Richard Nixon, a Republican who himself governed like a Marxist dictator (a defeatist policy of appeasement and "negotiations" with China and the USSR and, in Vietnam, virtually inviting the eventual defeat of our anti-communist allies there by a complete, McGovern-like retreat/withdrawal of all American forces, creating the EPA and OSHA unilaterally, instituting economy-wide price controls on everything, including wages, unilaterally revoking what was left of the dollar's gold standard, as merely a few examples).

After 1968, the policies of George McGovern remained the ongoing policy platform of the Democratic Party. Jimmy Carter was able to win the presidency running on a slightly modified version of those policies, presenting himself as a purported conservative by emphasizing his own born-again Christianity and by benefiting from the virtual implosion of the Republican Party after the resignation of the generally-reviled Richard Nixon and his pardon by Gerald Ford, who Carter narrowly defeated.

But Americans hated the results from those policies – humiliation abroad and economic disaster at home – and Carter lost in a landslide against Reagan in 1980.

The truth is, only a sociopath would be able to sell the McGovern policies to an American public who detested them thereafter. Neither Walter Mondale nor Michael Dukakis who ran on those policies in 1984 and 1988 were such sociopaths – and both lost in landslides.

In 1992, the Democrats finally were blessed with just such a sociopath in Bill Clinton, a genuine, pathological liar who was able to win the Democratic nomination against a number of non-sociopaths who, because of that fact, never had a chance against him, for the reasons discussed in Chapter 7. In 1992, when he was elected, Clinton ran pretending to be "a different kind of Democrat," officially disclaiming the McGovern positions while running for office, and benefiting from a multitude of circumstances, including the third-party candidacy of Ross Perot, the ineptitude of Pres. George HW Bush who both refused to make the most potentially-devastating attacks against Clinton which were clearly available and, more self-destructively, failed to refute the nonsense arguments Clinton hurled at him (that the mild, cyclical recession, which had actually ended before the election, represented "the worst economy" ever – a facially ludicrous accusation).

Numerous aspects of Clinton's past (e.g., his previously-expressed "loathing" of the military, his notorious philandering, his thin resume) would have made him an easy opponent for any aggressive Republican candidate to defeat.

But both Clinton and President Bush set the templates for each of their respective parties' presidential candidates from that time forth: Bush pulled all his punches and failed energetically to unite his party behind himself, and Clinton brazenly lied about what his eventual presidency would look like, pretending he was anything but a radical collectivist. Once in office, for his first two years, until catastrophic Democrat congressional defeats in 1994, he governed like a true radical, even blessing a Democrat attempt to impose socialized medicine, oversight of which project he left to his wife, Hillary, who, unlike her husband, had long had deep ties to the New Left (among other connections, she had personally lionized and corresponded extensively with one of its icons, Saul Alinsky).

Whatever his own personal ideological views were, after the Democrats' enormous electoral losses in 1994, Clinton plainly was interested primarily in furthering his own political power and achieving reelection. To do so, he pragmatically altered course for the remainder of his presidency and ended up agreeing to legislation with the Republican Congress that both significantly reformed the welfare system (requiring work and cutting off benefits after a two-year period) and cut capital gains taxes dramatically. Although the economy had stalled during his first two years after his tax increase, once he took those later steps, economic growth was dramatic and, notwithstanding numerous personal scandals during his presidency, he left office relatively popular. He also benefited from the ability dramatically to cut military spending at a time when America was the sole superpower with no serious challenger on the horizon.

His vice president, Al Gore, won the popular vote in 2000 but lost the election narrowly in the electoral college, arguably because of the third-party candidacy of Ralph Nader.

### Nader Running for the Presidency

Ralph Nader never ran for any political office until 2000 when, for the first time, he ran for president as the candidate of the Green Party, a political party dedicated exclusively to promoting the cause of "environmentalism" for purposes of subjugating the entire private economy under its supposed moral imperative – as had been the case for the entire "environmentalist" movement since the first "Earth Day" in 1970. "Environmentalism" had become the single-minded focus of Mr. Nader by 2000, his various "consumer"-advocacy groups having so empowered themselves by then both inside and outside the government that they no longer required his constant attention to promote his overriding ambition of imposing Marxism – total political state control – over the entire economy. "Environmentalism" — because of the sheer limitlessness of its "moral" claims and demands for power -- was uniquely designed and intended to achieve precisely that result.

Query: what was Mr. Nader's strategy in running for president in 2000? How did doing so for the first time that particular year fit into his lifelong, single-minded quest for achieving his Marxist goals? Those goals can be simply stated, in a simple update of the agenda for Britain and the United States demanded by Karl Marx in *The Communist Manifesto*, quoted in Chapter 6, above:

(1) confiscatory estate taxes, and a steeply-graduated income tax both to facilitate the redistribution of income by the state, and to guarantee unlimited, discretionary state power to review all details of all citizens' finances; and

(2) complete state control over all electronic (the most powerful) means of communication, the currency and all financial institutions, all land (the purpose of "environmental" laws and "regulations"), and all other "means of production," including all goods and services produced by them – "them" meaning all American businesses – including, particularly, absolute state control over all aspects of the provision of any healthcare services or goods.

Nader's presidential campaign in 2000 arguably had the effect of defeating Al Gore and electing Republican George W. Bush to the presidency. This is because it is a fair assumption that at least some of the 2.74% of the vote he realized nationally would otherwise have gone to the other radical environmentalist in the race – Al Gore – and would have been more than sufficient to at least have gotten the few remaining votes Mr. Gore would have needed to win in Florida, a win which would have made him victorious. I believe it is quite possible that Nader had his own, long-game, strategic reasons to hope for precisely the outcome so achieved – the election of George W. Bush.

As a radical Marxist and a keen student of American politics and politicians, with a Machiavellian willingness to do absolutely anything to achieve his long-term strategic goals, it is likely that Nader viewed Mr. Bush, for a variety of reasons, as someone who, though nominally a conservative, would do untold damage to the American Revolution during his presidency and so further the cause of the Marxist counterrevolution – without himself intending anything of the kind.

Nader had already seen what Mr. Bush's father's presidency had been like, after the relative hiatus in the onward march of the Counterrevolution during the presidency of Ronald Reagan. The key fact about both of the Bushes was their complete failure to comprehend the very existence of the ongoing Counterrevolution – something they would clearly have opposed had they not been utterly blind to its existence, as all their actions proved throughout both presidencies – and their resulting belief that it was possible to appease and "compromise" with their political opponents, compromises and appeasement which invariably resulted in harm to the nation's prosperity and security — for which harm they always received all the blame. That blame, fanned by a hostile, Marxist mass media, and based on their own, undeniable actions, created splits and divisions within their own Republican supporters, and in turn paved the way for them to be succeeded by committed Counterrevolutionaries.

As a ruthlessly-committed Marxist ideologue, Nader viewed America exactly the way Louis XIV and Robespierre had viewed France – as an enemy to be subdued and shackled as completely as possible through the use of law, politics, spectacle and the threat of violence. He fully appreciated that such conquest would be facilitated by the enemy being both completely unaware of what it was facing – so that the element of surprise would be available against it – and as divided as possible within itself. Nader had already seen George HW Bush facilitate his own defeat against the obvious charlatan huckster Bill Clinton; and that was after Bush had achieved a military victory against Iraq which only one year prior to 1992 had pushed his approval rate above 90%.

Whether Nader intended or anticipated it, George W. Bush, as president indeed softened up the nation's receptivity to a radical Marxist successor by doing nothing himself to oppose the Counterrevolution, and by presiding over measures which paved the way for the financial panic of 2008 (whose immediate causes were panicked, grotesquely-inconsistent federal reactions to unusual financial circumstances, circumstances brought about by multiple, internally-inconsistent, directives to massively-regulated financial institutions from multiple different federal regulatory agencies), conducted the initially-popular and victorious war in Iraq in a manner which resulted in its unpleasant elongation, and deeply tarnished the entire conservative brand by refusing to oppose the constant barrage of Counterrevolutionary propaganda and smears he and conservatism were constantly subjected to by Democrats and the media throughout his presidency.

Bush did absolutely nothing to dismantle any of the existing, Counterrevolutionary federal administrative state — even when his party controlled both houses of Congress, and so had the power to repeal at least some, if not all, of the legislation which created and enabled it. He engaged in fruitless, pointless negotiations over nuclear weapons with the terrorist states – who he had correctly so identified – North Korea and Iran. He conducted war in Iraq self-defeatingly restricting the military under paralyzing rules of engagement – after an initial, strategic victory achieved in record time.

And he divided his own, conservative supporters with his constant, massive, Counterrevolutionary federal spending, his enormously increasing the already-oppressive — and unconstitutional — federal regulation of businesses, and his continual choices for office – always intended to appease his opponents as supposedly "bipartisan" selections – of people who were themselves proponents of counterrevolutionary causes, including multiple foolish treasury secretaries, none of whom showed any affection for free markets, and his selection of a radical Keynesian/Marxist Princeton academic Ben Bernanke to rule over the money supply and the banking system as chairman of the Federal Reserve.

Bush's last Treasury Secretary, Henry Paulson, ultimately caused genuine panic in the financial community by both completely misdiagnosing multiple, though then as-yet fixable, economic problems beginning at the end of 2007, and responding erratically and inconsistently to financial failures, first at Bear Stearns (bailed out), then at far-larger Lehman Brothers (bailout refused, causing real panic), all combining to facilitate the financial panic of 2008 which, together with the utter incompetence of John McCain as a candidate (he ruled out any criticism of any kind of his opponent, including simply highlighting his opponent's radical Marxist associations and proclivities – characteristics which would have normally disqualified Obama as a candidate in America), and the utter loathing of the public for George W. Bush at the end of his presidency, all contributed to the election of Barack Obama.

The election of Obama achieved the ultimate goal the New Left had been seeking ever since the time of its takeover of the Democratic Party in 1968 – the nomination and election of an undiluted, but masked, sociopathic-liar, Marxist-Leninist ideologue to the White House who would have the ability to use the enormous power of that office to effect massive damage to the public finances, economy and military of the nation, and effectively entrench the Marxist revolution in the administrative state even further than Nader had been able to do.

That Obama is indeed a cold-blooded Marxist-Leninist who despises everything about America as founded is manifest from his own testimony in his two autobiographies: specifically, he unambiguously identifies his only two mentors in those books – his anti-American Marxist racist minister for 20 years, the Rev. Wright, and Frank Marshall Davis who, to his dying day was a card-carrying Communist dedicated to Stalinism and the destruction of the American Revolution.

That Obama has governed absolutely consistent with such loathing of America and determination to harm its economy and military in every conceivable way – including accelerating the massive growth of the federal regulatory state, and promoting its political weaponization, "fighting" wars even more self-defeatingly than Bush, massively and pointlessly increasing the national debt, gratuitously releasing from captivity violent radical terrorist enemies captured by the military, facilitating the nuclear weaponization and enrichment of the self-declared enemy and terrorist state Iran, and undoing military victories previously won in both Iraq and Afghanistan – is not seriously disputable by anyone paying any attention.

### The Federal Bureaucracies Today

For multiple reasons, the federal bureaucracies in all the alphabet agencies today are staffed and directed almost-exclusively by dedicated Marxists who are utterly hostile to all American businesses, private landowners, and American citizens who do not share their radical views, views which they use all their powers

357

to impose on everyone they are able to subject to their jurisdiction, often in a brutal manner. This they do by both creating law ("regulations") and by administering/judging it against the citizenry. Enormous numbers of those bureaucrats were personally recruited for this very purpose by Ralph Nader. And enormous numbers of additional bureaucracies were created based on the efforts of Ralph Nader and his followers.

But mention should be made of a second event which occurred in the early 1960s which greatly magnified the influence of the federal Marxist bureaucrats. That event was the simple Executive Order issued by Jack Kennedy permitting federal employees for the first time to unionize, as had always previously been forbidden. The presence of those federal employee unions – there are a number of them, not simply one – each of which is run by dedicated Marxists, together with the unanimity of views of the Nader-recruited bureaucrats, has vastly facilitated the imposition of Marxist discipline against any bureaucrats who would otherwise resist it – if only to preserve their personal career opportunities within the bureaucracy that employs them.

It is the combination of all these factors, in addition to the inherent nature of Bad Law, which makes it absolutely mandatory, if the federally-institutionalized Counterrevolution resulting directly from Nader's efforts and Kennedy's executive order is to be undone, that it be <u>completely extinguished</u>, all at once, with no attempt simply to reform any of it.

The sheer vastness of the laws and bureaucracies that it has created in our midst, coupled with the multiple corrupt constituencies that feed off of it, and the consistent, Marxist/collectivist zeal of the bureaucrats who man it, guarantee that any effort to reform it will be subverted by them until every single lever of state power is removed from the bureaucrats forcefully, by the complete repeal of all legislation creating their bureaucracies. As long as they hold their offices, that is how they behave – regardless who has been elected to the political branches of government, including their ultimate superior, the president.

The only difference in the extent of their Marxist activism in office arises when a president who actively approves of their Marxist activities is in office – as has been the case with Obama. The highly publicized activities of Lois Lerner at the IRS, as a rare, publicly-visible example, provide the public an undeniable spectacle of merely one bureaucrat's zealously partisan actions in office, undoubtedly acting with the approval of all her supervisors, who selected her for her position precisely because her previous government job performance — as a partisan zealot at the FEC — guaranteed that that was how she would act in her IRS office.

This zealously-Marxist abuse of bureaucratic offices is all the more pernicious because it is always effected by bureaucrats who are supposedly "non-political career" persons — the invariable claim of those who know precisely what is really afoot with them — and clueless Republicans, like George W. Bush, who actually believe the claims of nonpartisanship — and are hopelessly blind to the Counter-revolution's existence.

The truth is, <u>everyone</u> in the government, at every level, is political – just like everyone else; except people in the government have the power to destroy others based on their political views. The only difference in the ruthlessness with which federal bureaucrats might seek to use/abuse their offices to harm those they view as their political opponents arises from whatever active supervision they are subject to – and only when such supervision is not subverted by the bureaucrats' cynical use of bureaucratic infighting methods, methods they learn to be expert in, including endless methods of hiding their actions.

As fanatically-loyal collectivists, they invariably use all the power over others they can extract from their offices always to promote their radical Cause and to harm in any way they can get away with everyone who disagrees with it who, based on their collectivist mob mentality, they invariably view as mortal enemies to be defeated and harmed and silenced in any way available to them. That is, quite simply, what all collectivist mobs have always done. That was Ralph Nader's explicit purpose in recruiting them for their federal bureaucratic jobs.

As long as they hold office as law-empowered federal bureaucrats, they, and the entire collectivist bureaucracy that employs them, will use their power – and freely abuse it as they see necessary – to harm anyone who seeks to unseat them and/or eliminate the agencies they work for. It is imperative that they not be given the opportunity to stage their own continuing counterrevolution against the constitutional branches of government – and the properly elected officials within them – prior to their complete defenestration. Nothing is more guaranteed to arouse their most injurious impulses than any publicly-ventilated threat to the existence of their agency and their own power – until that threat is realized and their agencies are all completely eliminated. As a master strategist observed, "If you set out to take Vienna, you better take Vienna."

# CHAPTER 18

## The Welfare/Administrative State's Beliefs

Other than the 10 Commandments, which a super-majority of Americans continue to believe were instructions from God, all laws policing citizens' behavior are made by mortals, intent on using the law – and the threat of personal harm resulting from its violation, a threat only law has the power legally to wield – to impose particular behavior directives based on particular value judgments regarding the government, society and the people, conformity to which is to be forced on all by that law.

By its very nature, every law constrains the liberty of the citizenry in some manner – all citizens if the law is evenhanded, even if, as a practical matter, only a few are likely to run afoul of it. That behavioral constraint is the precise purpose for the law. Punishment of some kind – prison, fines, possible personal destruction – is promised when the law is disobeyed.

Thus the real-life impact of any law, good, bad, constitutional or unconstitutional cannot be doubted – if it is actually enforced. If it is passed by its authors with the corrupt expectation that it will not or, worse, cannot, be enforced, either of those outcomes would have its own effects as well. Those effects would consist of damage and cynicism to any expectation of genuine justice by the citizenry – a terribly destructive outcome in a nation where respect for law and equality before the law are both fundamental governmental promises to the citizenry – as has always been the case uniquely in America.

It is a fundamental fact that the law's authors always have a particular agenda or motive driving them to create the law. That agenda or motive may be practical (AKA utilitarian), purportedly moral, or both. This motive, in turn, rests on one or more judgments, concerning both the law's proponents' assessment of how things are without the law, and about how things "should be" – again, practically and/or morally. The enactment of the law is supposed to achieve that specifically-desired goal.

Thus, the law can be seen as a "tactic" enacted to achieve a societal "victory" on behalf of a "policy" or strategy which, In turn, has various components: (1) the policy assumes both that the behavior which the law is intended to correct or forbid is both susceptible to such correction, and that the new law can actually accomplish that correction; and (2) a judgment, whether based on moral principle or purely pragmatic or other considerations, that the behavior "deserves" such correction and that the brute power of the state's threat of violence to the citizenry should be invoked as the necessary enforcement mechanism of the law and its underlying policy.

Accordingly, any judgment by any one or more citizens about whether the law is "good" or "bad", must rest, in turn, on multiple value judgments consisting of deciding on the legitimacy of (1) the policy motivating the law, (2) the law's likely efficacy in at least promoting, if not fully achieving, that policy and (3) whether the law may have additional, collateral, undesired consequences known of at the time of its enactment, and/or at a later time after it's real-life effects has been experienced, counseling for its repeal regardless of its efficacy, and the desirability, of achieving its underlying policy.

The Welfare/Administrative bureaucratic State, and each of its component parts, that has been erected in the United States since 1887 by politicians, and rubber-stamped by the judicial branch, rests on a foundation consisting of each and all of the following, ideological beliefs/presumptions, <u>none</u> of which have ever been seriously publicly debated; nor is it likely that a majority of Americans have ever agreed with any of them (that being the likely reason these have never been debated, since the last thing on earth those who want this abomination to continue want is actual debate).

Every single one of these propositions are sheer nonsense:

(1) the federal government has <u>both</u> the power, including the Constitutional power,<u> and the actual, practical ability</u>, to improve the functioning of any product or service or market which politicians desire to impose "regulation" on, in derogation of the property rights, and all other rights (privacy, choice, e.g.), of all participants in that market.

      (a) corollary: in the event the interventions by the federal regulatory agency do not result in the elimination of all supposed problems with the product, service and/or market it is regulating, the best solution invariably is for all the jurisdiction and powers of federal agencies assigned the task of effecting such regulation <u>to increase</u> the extent of their regulation as it or they see fit.

      (b) corollary 2: the Constitution grants Congress the authority, without limitation, to create administrative agencies in charge of "regulating" any economic matter or any business and to grant those agencies the power to write the laws pursuant to which they so "regulate", including criminal laws for purposes of enforcing those "regulations", and to create their own courts for adjudicating US citizens who such agency claims have violated any of its "regulations".

(c) corollary 3: the Constitution grants Congress the authority to delegate its legislative power to executive agencies and their employees, even though no such persons are employed by Congress nor are they elected pursuant to be very precise procedures contained in Article I of the Constitution.

(d) corollary 4: all decisions of any nature, including the drafting of laws, decisions by any administrative courts created by such agency and all other administrative actions by such agency and its employees affecting American citizens are <u>within the discretion</u> of the administrative agency and its officials, and can only be changed or undone <u>if</u> (1) a federal court agrees to review the action and (2) the court, without a jury, determines such action has been proven to be "clearly erroneous" and an actual abuse of the agency's otherwise unbridled discretion.

(2) the combination of competition between rival individual citizens and businesses and the policing power of tort law, as supplemented by the criminal law,<u> is incapable</u> of providing sufficient encouragement and incentive for American citizens and businesses to both prosper and treat their employees and customers morally and fairly, and <u>only the discretionary direction and "regulation"</u> and law created by a federal agency and its employees is capable of achieving that result.

(3) numerous people exist who are not only knowledgeable about any conceivable subject which can be studied, but indeed are genuine <u>experts</u> in each such subject, possessing <u>genuinely comprehensive and authoritative knowledge of such subject</u>, whose expertise is readily available to government agencies (whether they are employees of such agencies or otherwise) which the agency has discretion to rely on in any and all of its decisions of any nature, including the drafting of laws and administering them against citizens and businesses.

(4) "regulating" the activities of citizens, their business or land is substantially different from forcibly taking effective ownership of important rights over that citizen's business or land away from its actual owners, so that the citizens do not become serfs of the state as a result of such regulation being imposed on them, and they are entitled to<u> no</u> compensation by the state for being required to subject their business/property to the directions of federal employees, and <u>no</u> compensation for their compliance with directives from those federal employees.

(5) private ownership of land and operation of any productive or extractive operations or business thereon (such as mines, forestry, farming)<u> is inherently harmful</u> to that land and causes identifiable injuries to the public which the federal government must prevent by <u>either</u> (1) seizing ownership of the land and operating it itself or (2) directing and controlling all activities on supposedly "private" land for the protection of the public and/or the "environment."

(6) federal regulatory agencies and their employees are morally superior to business owners and their appointed managers, and are capable of acting without regard to any personal or political considerations, and with greater wisdom since they are guided by genuine experts – and can reasonably be expected to do so.

(7) all businessmen are thieves and scoundrels intent on, and capable of, stealing as much as they can from their customers and their employees, and/or otherwise harming them sadistically and/or gratuitously, unless they are forcefully stopped from doing so by having all their activities directed by federal employees and regulations they promulgate.

(8) all business owners are racists/bigots who will act out their bigotry, without regard to morality or market forces or public opprobrium, if not forbidden from doing so by federal regulators.

(9) the free market economy, left to its own devices and the policing mechanisms of the common law, is incapable of providing sufficient prosperity and economic growth to minimize poverty among the population to the point where private charity would be sufficient to take care of the needs of the poor.

(10) The free market economy, left to its own devices, including all private citizens, will always refuse to provide funding for private charities sufficient to take care of the needs of the poor, and only the federal government's forcing citizens to provide such funding is capable of doing such, and a better result is achieved for the poor by the federal government providing them the "right" to transfer payments sufficient to take care of their basic financial needs and to forcibly extract the funds for such transfer payments from those who the state determines can afford to fund such.

(11) citizens cannot be allowed to purchase whatever they want which might in any way affect their or their children's bodies, and any such goods or services must be first approved of by federal agencies and their employees, with citizens absolutely forbidden to purchase any such until it has been approved by such federal regulatory agencies, without regard to the costs of such approval process, or injury to citizens from being deprived of the ability to purchase what they want.

(12) all products of any nature which citizens might "consume" must to be and are absolutely banned and forbidden to be sold, manufactured or produced in any manner except to the extent approved of by at least one federal regulatory agency and, indeed, all such agencies which could arguably have jurisdiction over such matters.

(13) without regard to any property rights of any person, the "environment", including the land and everything above or below it, including any animals of any nature or vegetation as it exists RIGHT NOW, or as of the day it was

nationalized by the federal government, is public property and must be preserved in its pristine form without regard to any factor except to the extent permitted by the federal government, and such will result in the best preservation of the "environment", since human activity invariably harms it and must be prevented at all cost.

(14) federal regulatory agencies and their employees are immune to the forces which apply to individuals participating in markets, and will usually act wisely and selflessly and exclusively in the "public interest" (i.e., they will not restrict or ban activities or products for self-preservation purposes)

# CHAPTER 19

## How To Defeat The Counterrevolution

In this book, I have shown that the entire American administrative police state — i.e. all federal citizen-policing agencies and departments other than the IRS — agencies which the elected branches of the federal government have legislatively enacted and empowered, and whose Constitutionality the federal courts have rubber-stamped, first beginning in 1887, is each of the following:

(1) unspeakably immoral, as shown in chapter 2, based on the highest moral authorities recognized by all Christians and Jews – the 10 Commandments and the few, relevant, explicit commands of Jesus Christ, with no genuinely-authoritative, moral text providing otherwise;

(2) completely unconstitutional, as shown in chapters 5, 8 and 11, with the contrary arguments purely-politically-and corruptly adopted by the courts and the entire legal profession not only utterly without merit, but patently frivolous;

(3) devastatingly destructive to the freedom, prosperity, the very security of the nation and its citizens, and the rule of Law itself, as proven by the actual performance of every such federal agency with a long-enough, measurable track record, including the Interstate Commerce Commission which, after 100 years even the federal government admitted was nothing but a destructive, worthless abomination (its judgment, but not its actual words), and the Federal Reserve, under which the currency's value is now 1/23 what it was in 1913 at the time of the Fed's creation (after the then-previous century in which the dollar never lost any value whatsoever, and the nation financially and economically flourished as never since), and under which we have had numerous financial panics – all directly attributable to actions by the Federal Reserve and other financial regulatory agencies.

This monstrous destructiveness is true of every single such federal agency, and there is no actual evidence that any of them have ever been of any value whatsoever – to the causes, that is, of citizen freedom and prosperity, as opposed to amassing power for politicians and endless numbers of parasites in and out of the government.

I have described and explained the utterly-malignant ideologies and, historically, the nature of the multiple absolute dictatorships, which together are the true authors of all the legislation which has given rise to the abomination which is our administrative police state.

I have shown that it must be eradicated *in toto*, like the cancer it is, and that that must be done virtually overnight – in what could be called a bloodless revolution. Because to the extent it and its bureaucrat enforcers remain in existence and in power, knowing that they are under assault they, and all the numerous political, professional, and business constituencies they visibly provide corrupt power and financial benefits to, at the mostly-invisible cost of massively harming and stealing from most Americans, including the destruction of our liberty, security, and the entire nation's wealth — including even that of its seeming beneficiaries — all are certain to react viciously, and do massive damage and violence to all who oppose them.

Those federal agencies all recognize no limits to their jurisdiction and powers over the citizens and our businesses/work — until they are forcibly stopped, by legal repeal of all their power.

That is precisely why, among many reasons, all those federal citizen-policing agencies must be publicly-exposed and condemned for what they are, and be utterly eliminated and destroyed, so that all Americans can then personally experience the almost-unimaginably-rapid increase in our freedoms of every kind, in our wealth/economic growth, in our security from foreign and domestic menaces, and in the true rule of law, all of which benefits are certain to follow that complete destruction, and thereby ensure that the malignant monster so slain will remain dead and buried as long as the memory of our experience without it is preserved.

Whatever "services" any of those agencies perform which are of any true value can be performed by private businesses — if there is any actual demand for such services — businesses subject to the discipline of the Common-Law and of the market itself, both of which are unforgiving in punishing incompetence and harm to citizens. That is the very opposite of government's response to its own bureaucrats' consistent incompetence and harm to the citizens: it invariably demands to be rewarded particularly for each of those, with more power and more citizen money.

As Cato the Elder, a deeply-patriotic Roman, famously observed repeatedly against a similarly-existential, longstanding malignant threat, which kept returning as a menace even after the Roman then-republic militarily-defeated it twice, "*Carthago delenda est*" (or, more likely, "*Ceterum censeo Carthaginem esse delendam*,") both meaning "Carthage must be utterly and absolutely eradicated forever."

Rome did exactly that, defeating and not only leveling Carthage, but also sewing salt into its land so that nothing could ever grow there again. And Rome thereafter thrived, prospered and ruled a vast empire of many different nations who also mostly thrived under its rule and the peace it guaranteed them (if they did not rebel against it), for many hundreds of years.

So how exactly are we to accomplish this complete eradication of the entire administrative police state? That is the subject of this chapter.

## 1. Elect Enough Officials To At Least One Branch of the Federal Government, Or At Least One House of Congress, Who Are Committed To Accomplishing The Desired Result.

First, the simplest way this peaceful revolution/total administrative police state eradication could all be accomplished is by the Supreme Court Justices actually honoring their oaths of office to uphold the Constitution and reversing all that Court's rulings since 1870 upholding the Constitutionality of any of the federal administrative citizen-policing (as opposed to the perfectly legitimate federal-employee-policing) agencies and any of their actions. For multiple reasons, it is politically inconceivable that the Court would do so without an extraordinary transformation of its membership.

However, if Congress and the president desire, and have the political will, to effect the necessary change to the judiciary, the Constitution provides several different ways for them to accomplish that, since the Constitution ultimately grants them control over the membership of the federal judiciary at all levels, and over the jurisdiction of all federal courts below the Supreme Court.

Leaving those judicial branch possibilities aside, how many elected officials are actually necessary to both eliminate all the citizen-policing federal agencies and undo all their prior, destructive actions?

Obviously, if a political party is genuinely committed to doing so, and controls both houses of Congress and the presidency, that entire (revolutionary) undertaking could be accomplished in a fairly orderly manner by passing regular-order legislation explicitly announcing and describing the unconstitutionality of the creation of all those agencies, and the complete legal-nullity of all their citizen-policing actions, since each of their creation (this would include any quasi-judicial actions taken by any of them, as well as any administrative actions), the immediate repeal of all legislation enabling them, and precluding any federal courts from exercising any jurisdiction addressing the Constitutionality of that new legislation, or to adjudicate any then-pending action begun by any of the then-eliminated agencies, or to enforce any previous judicial action taken at their instigation (as just mentioned, Constitution Article III grants Congress plenary control over the jurisdiction of the lower federal courts).

Any non-government-employee citizen who has ever been convicted of any crime unconstitutionally "legislated" by any of those agencies would necessarily be declared exonerated, and every fine ever imposed by any of them would be declared null and void and, if paid, immediately refundable. That is, quite simply, what the Rule of Law requires. Adequate means minimally to address the most civilly-chaotic fallout from all that will need to be devised and legislated simultaneously, a topic beyond the scope of this brief strategic outline.

If Congress were forthrightly to address the entire issue in this manner, it would probably be appropriate for Congress to grant a partial amnesty to all employees of those agencies so that they could not become subject to so-called civil rights *Bivins* lawsuits by injured citizens, except for cases in which they would be liable thereunder in the absence of the Congressional revolutionary repeal, and in cases where their official misconduct to citizens was knowing or intentional.

However politically-frightening the massive upheavals from this revolution may appear before they occur, transitional legislation, other than as just described, to soften its revolutionary effects should be avoided at all costs: any such moderating "transitioning" would inevitably keep unconstitutional, terminated agencies and policies alive. That would be disastrously self-defeating; and the agencies and their bureaucrats cannot be allowed to retain any power, because they cannot be trusted not to inflict grave harm to innocents, as they have become accustomed to doing, and sabotaging the entire government transformation.

That this clearly-revolutionary process will result in substantial dislocations of all kinds, including at least short-term unemployment of many hundreds of thousands of persons both in and out of the government (the overwhelming majority of whom, not incidentally, will be much better able financially to endure that unemployment and make new careers for themselves than the tens of millions who have been unemployed due to the agencies' crushing of economic growth and employment opportunities by their valueless tyranny over the economy), and much near-term confusion and chaos.

However, the liberated economy and people will find solutions to all that rapidly — and the economy will grow at rates unimaginable since the 19th century, with entire, new, previously-precluded by government tyranny, business sectors opening instantaneously. Americans are certain to rise to the occasion and pursue the infinite new business opportunities.

Today's multiple federal welfare programs will rapidly become obsolete, readily able to shrink and be completely taken over by private charities, without depriving any deserving poor of anything they receive now – which continued benefits they must continue, as truly needed, to receive, even though it is unconstitutional, at least by permitting the states to administer such, since it is the federal harm to the economy that has forced most of them into needing such assistance.

The orderly liquidation/monetization of all federal ownership of land, except as explicitly permitted in the Constitution, should begin immediately, including the sale of all so-called national parks, forests monuments, etc., the beauty of which and pristine character of which, can all be preserved by simply having any transfers of them subject to scenic easements. Proceeds of sales and/or other means of obtaining liquidity from such land in an orderly manner (secured bond sales, etc.) would be available to retire the monstrously-large actual, and contingent, national indebtedness and, in the short run, minimize fiscal issues arising from the transition to Constitutional government. The federal cost of maintaining all those lands would end, ending their being monstrous, self-destructing liabilities (massive forest fires, etc.) whose genuine market utility is precluded at the discretion of unelected, inherently-incompetent bureaucrats.

This revolutionary process is analogous to a country changing from driving on the right side of the road to the left: the change cannot be effected gradually without producing even more accidents and disasters than a clean, total, overnight change would produce. We remain, despite the cancerous presence of the federal regulatory agencies, a wealthy nation which will be far better able to manage the dislocations inevitably attendant upon such revolutionary change than, say, communist Poland and the Czech Republic were to manage their post-Soviet transformation into free nations: neither of them ever even had had any actual experience of such freedom in their entire history, unlike the United States.

The fact that a particular political party was politically able to secure control of both the presidency and both houses of Congress electorally, while running on an explicit platform of total administrative state repeal and eradication, would mean that the public favored such action unambiguously. To date, no party has ever run on such a platform, needless to say, although the Republican Party, which has never offered any serious opposition to any of the Counterrevolution, and has never sought to repeal any of it even when its members have indeed had control of the presidency and both houses of Congress, continues to insist that it is in favor of "smaller" government and genuinely-free markets.

Free markets, under the rule of Common Law laws, are institutionally precluded by the very existence of each federal "regulatory" agency and, as shown in previous chapters, that preclusion is the very purpose for the existence of each such agency.

But regular order, legislative repeal, in the form of actual, explicit, total repeal legislation, as described above, is by no means the only method necessary to achieving this goal. As indicated in the heading of this part above, all that is actually necessary, at a minimum, is to elect enough members to control one house of Congress alone, or a new president — if they, and/or he, are/is genuinely committed to accomplishing this purpose.

Yes, amazingly enough, under our remarkable Constitution, the president alone, or a simple majority in a single house of Congress, is all that is needed – and would be sufficient – to completely eradicate the entire Administrative state and terminate all payments to its employees immediately. There are multiple reasons why this would be sufficient.

The Constitutional method/procedure which would be utilized to effect this in that case is what is known colloquially as "the power of the purse," contained in Article I section 9, which provides: "No Money shall be drawn from the Treasury, but in Consequence of Appropriations made by Law [which requires the consent of both houses of Congress and the president, as provided in Article I section 7]."

Accordingly, a simple majority of either house of Congress, or the president alone, can simply refuse to agree to authorize the expenditure of funds to pay for any actions by any of the federal administrative agencies, including payments to any of their employees. Even if he has worked and earned what he has been promised by politicians in the form of compensation, no federal employee has any right to be paid a single penny without the actual approval of both houses of Congress, at a minimum, to each such payment under Article I section 9. As a matter of basic Constitutional law – "the Supreme law" – that provision trumps any purported legal claim any federal employee might otherwise have.

As mentioned earlier in this book, the Constitution makes passing any law – necessary for any federal money to be spent or for the federal government to take any action whatsoever – quite difficult, requiring the consent of both houses of Congress and the president, or a two-thirds supermajority of both houses of Congress if the president refuses to agree. On the other hand – and this is no accident – the Constitution makes <u>undoing</u> any law relatively simple, because the power of the purse can always be used simply to preclude any federal activity by anyone by a single house of Congress (or the President alone, in most cases) simply refusing to fund that activity.

This is what can be called the Downward-Ratchet bias regarding the scope and power of the federal government built into the Constitution: quite simply, it is Constitutionally <u>hard</u> to make it bigger or more powerful, and relative child's play to shrink or undo any of it. And no Congress can ever be bound by the actions of any previous Congress – nor even by its own previous actions, which it is always free to undo. When their terms are over, they're over. No politician, including any supermajority of them, has any power to exert any dead-hand legal authority over any citizens when his term is over.

Obviously, in our Republic, this purse-power method of stripping federal power can only be used if enough elected officials are committed to taking the necessary action of insisting on refusing any funds for any administrative agency. As is well known, the Republican Party has always pretended to be in favor of smaller government.

However, even though it has had more than sufficient dominance of both houses of Congress since January, 2015, those Republicans have been unwilling to use the power of the purse <u>at all</u>, even to defund multiple federal actions most Republicans claim to find abhorrent (e.g. Obamacare and/or Planned Parenthood, especially after its blatant selling of baby body parts has been proven and exposed in multiple videos).

Indeed, the Republican Congress has refused to take any steps even to minimize the effect of multiple unconstitutional actions taken by Obama, including his selective non-enforcement of law – which he does constantly – in direct violation of his unambiguous, Constitutional duty to "take care" to enforce <u>all</u> federal laws. The selective non-enforcement of laws was the very constitutional violation by James II which permitted his removal in the Glorious Revolution of 1688 – that misconduct being the precise reason for the inclusion of the "take care" clause in the Constitution's Article II.

But ultimately, all elected officials must face the public. In the original Constitution, senators could be removed by their state legislatures, who alone elected them. Members of Congress run for office every two years, and any of them who refused to commit themselves to the action proposed here could be faced with an opponent sworn to take the action if elected – in a primary, for example. What is required, of course, is sufficient public desire for that outcome to insist on that action by the elected officials.

## A Less-Decisive Step Either House of Congress Could Take To Educate the Public, And Gather Support, Regarding Complete, Revolutionary Administrative State Elimination

I have come up with a procedure which either House, or both, of Congress could take Constitutionally which, at a minimum, would publicly-ventilate all of the overwhelming arguments compelling the elimination of the entire Administrative State, and so use the power available to Congress in so doing to promote that course to the public – and show that at least some elected officials are intent on following through with that course of action.

The strategy described herein is, were the Republicans in either congressional house to pursue it at any time — even right now! — politically-"risk-free," in the sense that it would require no action, which Sen. McConnell, for example, has publicly ruled out, on the part of the united Congress susceptible to mischaracterization by Democrats and the media as "shutting down" the government, as would inevitably be the case in any actual deployment of the power of the purse by them under a Democrat president; nor would it require the politically-impractical use of the impeachment power against federal judges and/or a collectivist president – although it would have the additional effect of laying a powerful groundwork for proceeding with either or both of those mechanisms at any time thereafter should the Congress choose to do so.

The underlying legal basis for following the procedure I'm about to describe here is the clear fact of the complete unconstitutionality of each and every one of those federal agencies *in toto*, which I have proven above.

The Congressional action I describe and propose here would have the effect, at a minimum, of making it an unacceptable risk for any individual — i.e., any government employee — to continue to perform any duties, or take any actions in connection with imposing the power claimed by any such administrative agency against any citizen. Even if some such bureaucrats disregarded this action by Congress, once Congress has done what I propose, the bureaucrats would be doing so at their own, personal peril – a terrifying idea to any bureaucrat, and a course any competent lawyer would advise any of them to eschew.

As shown in multiple chapters above, the Supremacy clause, coupled with the amendment provisions in Article V, have the effect of rendering a complete legal nullity of any unconstitutional act by any federal official, even if joined in by all three federal branches and ratified by them repeatedly – if the procedures of Article V for actually amending the Constitution are not conformed to. The Supreme Court has announced its agreement with this principle in multiple, long-standing, rulings.

Specifically, clear, unambiguous, long-standing judicial decisions – yes, the Supreme Court sometimes gets it right – preclude any individual or agency from acting in reliance on any unconstitutional, and thereby illegal, "laws," "laws" which, in my here-proposed action, Congress would be institutionally and officially announcing, exceed the government's <u>actual</u>, legal authority, by virtue of their unconstitutionality, so that all bureaucrats acting in reliance on their belief in the legitimacy of such "laws" would be at risk of grave criminal liability for any federal criminal statutes (and there are multitudes of them governing every aspect of federal employees' behavior) they believe themselves empowered to violate with impunity solely based on such (now declared illegal) enabling "laws." *Utah Power & Light Company v. U. S.*, 243 U. S. 389, 37 S. Ct. 387, 61 L. Ed. 79(1917); *Federal Crop Insurance Corporation v. Merrill et al.*, 332 U. S. 380, 68 S. Ct. 1, 92, L. Ed. 10 (1947), both discussed below.

Quite simply, under those clearly-correct, long-established Supreme Court rulings, even if administrative agency employees think, and genuinely believe, that what they are doing is legal, since it clearly is not – as I have proven – none of them can rely on that belief to exonerate them, and so to avoid criminal liability for their actions. *Utah Power & Light Company v. U. S.*, 243 U. S. 389, 37 S. Ct. 387, 61 L. Ed. 79(1917) ("the United States is neither bound nor estopped by acts of its officers or agents [i.e., federal officials who enacted unconstitutional "law" previously] in entering into an arrangement or agreement to do or cause to be done what the law does not sanction or permit. [*citations omitted*]", 243 U. S. 389, 409); *Federal Crop Insurance Corporation v. Merrill et al.*, 332 U. S. 380, 68 S. Ct. 1, 92, L. Ed. 10 (1947) ("Whatever the form in which the Government functions, anyone entering into an arrangement with the Government takes the risk of having accurately ascertained that he who purports to act for the Government stays within the bounds of his [actual Constitutional] authority. The scope of this authority may be explicitly defined by [the Constitution or even by] Congress or be limited by delegated legislation, properly exercised through the rule-making power. And this is so even though, as here, the agent himself may have been unaware of the [Constitutional] limitations upon his authority [*citations omitted*]", 330 2 U. S. 380, 384).

The effect of this doctrine applied in the just-cited and quoted two cases by the US Supreme Court, is to preclude anyone, including government officers at any level, from relying on extra-legal or illegal, let alone clearly-unconstitutional, misconduct by any agent or official, or body of the federal government, regardless of the detriment they may suffer based on what would otherwise be reasonable reliance by them if they were dealing with an ordinary person or entity. The effect of this legal principle is _automatically to preclude_ any agent of the federal government from acting beyond the scope of his _actual, legal_ authority. That authority cannot include actions barred as unconstitutional due to the Constitution's always-supreme authority.

This rule protects both individuals and the Republic itself. Under this rule, private citizens need not fear federal officials (including Supreme Court justices, congressmen and presidents) harming them illegally/unconstitutionally because it automatically gives the citizens recourse; similarly this rule prevents the federal government from being harmed by rogue agents who enter into agreements or extend federal benefits of some kind, or make unconstitutional laws, without the legal authority to do so: for example, if a federal employee gratuitously decides to waste federal money by sending you, without authority of any kind, a check for $100,000, if you cash it and keep it you and he are deemed to have stolen that money from the federal Treasury.

Quite simply, this rule grants the federal government complete authority to undo completely any illegal act of any of its agents, including any action by any entire federal agency, which itself is illegal by virtue of its unconstitutionality. It renders all those illegal acts legal nullities automatically.

And, not incidentally, the 9th and 10th Amendments, under which all powers not expressly delegated to the federal government remain powers of the states and the people, also require this principle, since any federal official purporting to exercise power the federal government is precluded from exercising Constitutionally is necessarily usurping power of the states and the citizens under those Amendments.

My proposal: Congress simply has to officially and formally announce that all federal administrative agencies — other than the IRS — are, and have always been, unconstitutional, and so illegal, and that no one interacting with those agencies, including all their federal official employees, can rely on their legitimacy for any purpose, that if any persons act based on the erroneous assumption of the legitimacy of those agencies and their enabling laws, they will be doing so erroneously, and any bureaucrats doing so will be committing crimes whose statutes of limitations are long — generally five or six years.

Congress, in its public statement to that effect, specifically should cite and declare its official reliance on the cases discussed above, as well as spelling out the entire argument I made in Chapters 5, 8 and 11 proving the unconstitutionality of each and every one of those administrative agencies.

No judicial action is necessary to achieve this end: the law and the Constitution are what they are without regard to any determination of a court, and it is clear that Congress, as a coequal branch of the federal government, has every right and power to formally declare what the law already is, without needing to pass such as legislation requiring a presidential signature. For this purpose, to the extent a court would otherwise be necessary, Congress itself legitimately constitutes such a court.

In its declaration, Congress would be announcing its verdict, based on clear legal and factual principles, of the unconstitutionality of each and all of those agencies, their underpinning enabling legislation, all "regulations" passed by those agencies, and all actions taken by any of those agencies against any citizen, and how the law — the Constitution — should apply, and is in fact required to apply, to those actions and to any persons attempting to rely on them.

Moreover, Congress is no small potatoes as a branch of government. Nothing in Article I of the Constitution bars Congress from issuing its own orders and/ or judgments announcing decisions by it regarding conduct whose legal consequences it wishes to announce under existing law – just as a court does, for example. Unlike a court, it requires no case with particular litigants before it to make its legal declaration.

It is worth noting in this regard that Congress does indeed sit as a court in numerous circumstances (impeachments and investigations, e.g.), usually by committees of one sort or another, although nothing precludes it from doing so as an entire, joint body. Institutionally, though primarily a legislative body, even its legislative pronouncements are derived from judgments of various kinds. The British Parliament, on which Congress was historically based, based on its Norman French origins, was actually originally a purely judicial body, and not a legislature at all. Even today, the House of Lords sits as a high court on various occasions; the French version of Parliament, prior to the French Revolution, retained its purely judicial character throughout its existence and never became a legislature under the Bourbon Old Regime at all.

Accordingly, once — as could be the case now — Republicans seriously committed to eradicating the administrative state cancer control both houses of Congress, either, or preferably both, such houses can each adopt a resolution, which they can call whatever they want – an order (addressed to the individuals affected), a judgment (similarly addressed), a Congressional Constitutional declaration.

Congress can name its official pronouncement whatever it likes, and make it as powerful as it likes, so long as its content makes clear that it is announcing its recognition of already-existing Constitutional law, and discusses the legal authorities, including those of the Supreme Court cited and quoted above, from which that law is derived, its description of the facts of elected officials' and judges' previous, unconstitutional misconduct, and all the agencies' utter lawlessness, also outlined above (though a more detailed legal analysis would be both appropriate and highly educational for the public), and its explicit warning to all federal employees, as outlined above, that they will in fact remain criminally liable for the multiple crimes they would necessarily commit in continued reliance on, and in attempting to effect, any further actions based on the presumed legitimacy of those agencies and their underpinning, unconstitutional laws.

This course of action, though based on both the institutional power of Congress itself, and legal pronouncements of the U.S. Supreme Court – as well as the overwhelming legal arguments described in earlier chapters proving the unconstitutionality of all those administrative agencies – would require no fiscal cliff maneuvering nor any other action, and would drive a stake through the heart of those agencies – with devastating consequences to them – and, of course, to the Counterrevolution.

Individuals, including all federal bureaucrats and other officials, would be unambiguously notified that they place themselves in potentially-catastrophic personal legal jeopardy if they continue to act as if those laws and agencies are Constitutionally valid. The public would be educated in a way it never has been previously regarding all these matters – and the gravity of the unconstitutional misconduct the entire federal government has been engaged in since 1887.

Although much chaos may ensue from this Congressional action, no such chaos would be any worse than for those agencies to continue to harm the nation in multiple ways, including by virtue of their very unconstitutional existence, all as shown above – and as experienced by all American citizens.

Chaos inevitably happens in revolutions, and this reinstatement of our true American Revolution, and utter defeat of the Counterrevolution, is indeed revolutionary, even though requiring no blood or military action – and actually far less chaos than has ever accompanied any previous revolution in history, including our own.

2. Follow the Procedures In Article V Of the Constitution To Convene A Convention of the States For the Sole Purpose Of Declaring the Unconstitutionality Of the Entire Administrative State (And Repealing The 16th Amendment).

The Constitution, in Its Article V, provides various procedures for its amendment, including the convening of a Constitutional convention which can propose amendments. There is no risk of that convention becoming a so-called "runaway" convention hijacking the entire Constitution because any amendments it proposes only become effective once adopted by three-fourths of the states' legislatures.

Popularizing the ideas promoted in this book to the point that a majority of Americans openly and specifically agree with my positions on the unconstitutionality, and necessity for complete eradication, of all those administrative agencies, will ultimately result in the defeat of the Counterrevolution – one way or another. The American people still retain the power to control our destiny even after politicians have attempted to completely hijack it.

That fact, preserved in our Constitution, along with the fact that 70%+ of Americans remain believing Christians, are what completely differentiate us and our prospects for liberty from continental Europeans, who have no Constitution preserving individual liberty, no Common Law, and no longer believe in God (except for the unassimilated Muslims among them) – whose only escape from the oppressive tyrannies they have lived under, particularly since the 18th century, has been immigrating to America.

CPSIA information can be obtained
at www.ICGtesting.com
Printed in the USA
FFOW02n0838081116
29087FF